# SONG OF SONGS

WISDOM COMMENTARY

Volume 25

# Song of Songs

F. Scott Spencer

Lauress Wilkins Lawrence
*Volume Editor*

Barbara E. Reid, OP
*General Editor*

A Michael Glazier Book

**LITURGICAL PRESS**
Collegeville, Minnesota

www.litpress.org

| 1 | 2 | 3 | 4 | 5 | 6 | 7 | 8 | 9 |
|---|---|---|---|---|---|---|---|---|

**Library of Congress Cataloging-in-Publication Data**

Names: Spencer, F. Scott (Franklin Scott), author.
Title: Song of Songs / F. Scott Spencer ; Lauress Wilkins Lawrence, volume
    editor ; Barbara E. Reid, OP, general editor.
Description: Collegeville, Minnesota : Liturgical Press, 2016. | Series:
    Wisdom commentary ; Volume 25 | "A Michael Glazier book." | Includes
    bibliographical references and index.
Identifiers: LCCN 2016026386 (print) | LCCN 2016035385 (ebook) | ISBN
    9780814681244 (hardcover : alk. paper) | ISBN 9780814681497 (e-book)
Subjects: LCSH: Bible. Song of Solomon—Commentaries.
Classification: LCC BS1485.53 .S69 2016 (print) | LCC BS1485.53 (ebook) |
    DDC 223/.907—dc23
LC record available at https://lccn.loc.gov/2016026386

*To Janet, my one and only dearest love*

# Contents

# *Abbreviations*

Throughout the commentary, the letters "W," "M," and "D" stand for the Woman/Female protagonist, Man/Male protagonist, and daughters of Jerusalem, respectively, and the flow of speech is represented by an arrow. Hence, [W → M] signals the principal woman (Songstress) speaking to her male lover.

| | |
|---|---|
| AB | Anchor Bible |
| *ABD* | *Anchor Bible Dictionary* |
| AnBib | Analecta Biblica |
| *BBR* | *Bulletin for Biblical Research* |
| *Bib* | *Biblica* |
| *BibInt* | *Biblical Interpretation* |
| BibInt | Biblical Interpretation Series |
| BLS | Bible and Literature Series |
| BZAW | Beiheft zur Zeitschrift für die alttestamentliche Wissenschaft |
| *CBQ* | *Catholic Biblical Quarterly* |
| CEB | Common English Bible |
| FCB | Feminist Companion to the Bible |
| *HTR* | *Harvard Theological Review* |

| | |
|---|---|
| IFT | Introductions in Feminist Theology |
| *Int* | *Interpretation* |
| IVP | Inter-Varsity Press |
| *JAAR* | *Journal of the American Academy of Religion* |
| *JBL* | *Journal of Biblical Literature* |
| *JFSR* | *Journal of Feminist Studies in Religion* |
| JPS | Jewish Publication Society |
| *JSOT* | *Journal for the Study of the Old Testament* |
| JSOTSup | Journal for the Study of the Old Testament Supplement Series |
| KJV | King James Version |
| LHBOTS | Library of Hebrew Bible/Old Testament Studies |
| LXX | The Septuagint |
| MT | Masoretic Text |
| NAB | New American Bible |
| NASB | New American Standard Bible |
| NETS | New English Translation of the Septuagint |
| *NIB* | *New Interpreter's Bible* |
| NICOT | New International Commentary on the Old Testament |
| NIV | New International Version |
| NJPS | New Jewish Publication Society (Tanakh) |
| NRSV | New Revised Standard Version |
| NWSA | National Women's Studies Association |
| OBT | Overtures to Biblical Theology |
| OTL | Old Testament Library |
| OTM | Oxford Theological Monographs |
| *RevExp* | *Review & Expositor* |
| *Rhet.* | Aristotle, *Rhetorica* |
| SBL | Society of Biblical Literature |
| *SEÅ* | *Svensk exegetisk årbosk* |
| *SR* | *Studies in Religion* |

| SymS | Symposium Series |
| TOTC | Tyndale Old Testament Commentaries |
| Vg. | Latin Vulgate |
| *VT* | *Vetus Testamentum* |
| WBC | Word Biblical Commentary |
| YJS | Yale Judaica Series |
| *ZAW* | *Zeitschrift für die alttestamentliche Wissenschaft* |

# Contributors

Debra Band is a Hebrew manuscript artist, resident in the Washington, DC, area. Her illuminated manuscripts of biblical texts are informed by her studies of classical rabbinic thought, Israeli archaeology, and modern biblical studies. Her website is www.dbandart.com.

Rev. Dr. Lindsay Andreolli-Comstock served four years as an anti-human-trafficking specialist in Southeast Asia and is currently the executive director of The Beatitudes Society. For more on her work and publications, see www.lacomstock.com.

Dr. Melissa A. Jackson is a Hebrew Bible scholar and teacher. She has published several pieces on comedy and feminist-critical reading of the Hebrew Bible.

Dr. Elaine James is assistant professor of theology at Saint Catherine University. She is interested in the poetry of the Hebrew Bible and is completing a manuscript on landscape in the Song of Songs (Oxford University Press).

Dr. Lauress Wilkins Lawrence is an African American Hebrew Bible scholar. Previously on the religious studies faculty at Regis College in Weston, MA, she now balances her scholarship with work in philanthropy in Maine.

Rev. Jerusha Moses is an ordained Baptist minister, focused on ministry to children and families. A native of Chennai, India, she currently teaches as adjunct faculty at Virginia Commonwealth University and is working toward a doctor of ministry degree.

Dr. Sarah Zhang is assistant professor of Old Testament at Garrett-Evangelical Theological Seminary. She has cultivated a long relationship with the Song of Songs, leading to a dissertation, several essays, and a co-edited volume on the Song of Songs. Her recent writings explore the emotional and ethical aspects of lyrical experience.

# Foreword

# "Tell It on the Mountain"—or, "And You Shall Tell Your Daughter [as Well]"

*Athalya Brenner-Idan*
*Universiteit van Amsterdam/Tel Aviv University*

What can Wisdom Commentary do to help, and for whom?
The commentary genre has always been privileged in biblical studies. Traditionally acclaimed commentary series, such as the International Critical Commentary, Old Testament and New Testament Library, Hermeneia, Anchor Bible, Eerdmans, and Word—to name but several—enjoy nearly automatic prestige; and the number of women authors who participate in those is relatively small by comparison to their growing number in the scholarly guild. There certainly are some volumes written by women in them, especially in recent decades. At this time, however, this does not reflect the situation on the ground. Further, size matters. In that sense, the sheer size of the Wisdom Commentary is essential. This also represents a considerable investment and the possibility of reaching a wider audience than those already "converted."

Expecting women scholars to deal especially or only with what is considered strictly "female" matters seems unwarranted. According to Audre Lorde, "The master's tools will never dismantle the master's house."[1] But this maxim is not relevant to our case. The point of this commentary is not to destroy but to attain greater participation in the interpretive dialogue about biblical texts. Women scholars may bring additional questions to the readerly agenda as well as fresh angles to existing issues. To assume that their questions are designed only to topple a certain male hegemony is not convincing.

At first I did ask myself: is this commentary series an addition to calm raw nerves, an embellishment to make upholding the old hierarchy palatable? Or is it indeed about becoming the Master? On second and third thoughts, however, I understood that becoming the Master is not what this is about. Knowledge is power. Since Foucault at the very least, this cannot be in dispute. Writing commentaries for biblical texts by women for women and for men, of confessional as well as non-confessional convictions, will sabotage (hopefully) the established hierarchy but will not topple it. This is about an attempt to integrate more fully, to introduce another viewpoint, to become. What excites me about the Wisdom Commentary is that it is not offered as just an alternative supplanting or substituting for the dominant discourse.

These commentaries on biblical books will retain nonauthoritative, pluralistic viewpoints. And yes, once again, the weight of a dedicated series, to distinguish from collections of stand-alone volumes, will prove weightier.

That such an approach is especially important in the case of the Hebrew Bible/Old Testament is beyond doubt. Women of Judaism, Christianity, and also Islam have struggled to make it their own for centuries, even more than they have fought for the New Testament and the Qur'an. Every Hebrew Bible/Old Testament volume in this project is evidence that the day has arrived: it is now possible to read *all* the Jewish canonical books as a collection, for a collection they are, with guidance conceived of with the needs of women readers (not only men) as an integral inspiration and part thereof.

In my Jewish tradition, the main motivation for reciting the Haggadah, the ritual text recited yearly on Passover, the festival of liberation from

---

1. Audre Lorde, "The Master's Tools Will Never Dismantle the Master's House," in *Sister Outsider: Essays and Speeches* (Berkeley, CA: Crossing Press, 1984, 2007), 110–14. First delivered in the Second Sex Conference in New York, 1979.

bondage, is given as "And you shall tell your son" (from Exod 13:8). The knowledge and experience of past generations is thus transferred to the next, for constructing the present and the future. The ancient maxim is, literally, limited to a male audience. This series remolds the maxim into a new inclusive shape, which is of the utmost consequence: "And you shall tell your son" is extended to "And you shall tell your daughter [as well as your son]." Or, if you want, "Tell it on the mountain," for all to hear.

This is what it's all about.

# Editor's Introduction to Wisdom Commentary

# "She Is a Breath of the Power of God" (Wis 7:25)

*Barbara E. Reid, OP*

*General Editor*

Wisdom Commentary is the first series to offer detailed feminist interpretation of every book of the Bible. The fruit of collaborative work by an ecumenical and interreligious team of scholars, the volumes provide serious, scholarly engagement with the whole biblical text, not only those texts that explicitly mention women. The series is intended for clergy, teachers, ministers, and all serious students of the Bible. Designed to be both accessible and informed by the various approaches of biblical scholarship, it pays particular attention to the world in front of the text, that is, how the text is heard and appropriated. At the same time, this series aims to be faithful to the ancient text and its earliest audiences; thus the volumes also explicate the worlds behind the text and within it. While issues of gender are primary in this project, the volumes also address the intersecting issues of power, authority, ethnicity, race, class, and religious belief and practice. The fifty-eight volumes include the books regarded as canonical by Jews (i.e., the Tanakh); Protestants (the "Hebrew Bible" and the New Testament); and Roman Catholic, Anglican, and Eastern

Orthodox Communions (i.e., Tobit, Judith, 1 and 2 Maccabees, Wisdom of Solomon, Sirach/Ecclesiasticus, Baruch, including the Letter of Jeremiah, the additions to Esther, and Susanna and Bel and the Dragon in Daniel).

## A Symphony of Diverse Voices

Included in the Wisdom Commentary series are voices from scholars of many different religious traditions, of diverse ages, differing sexual identities, and varying cultural, racial, ethnic, and social contexts. Some have been pioneers in feminist biblical interpretation; others are newer contributors from a younger generation. A further distinctive feature of this series is that each volume incorporates voices other than that of the lead author(s). These voices appear alongside the commentary of the lead author(s), in the grayscale inserts. At times, a contributor may offer an alternative interpretation or a critique of the position taken by the lead author(s). At other times, she or he may offer a complementary interpretation from a different cultural context or subject position. Occasionally, portions of previously published material bring in other views. The diverse voices are not intended to be contestants in a debate or a cacophony of discordant notes. The multiple voices reflect that there is no single definitive feminist interpretation of a text. In addition, they show the importance of subject position in the process of interpretation. In this regard, the Wisdom Commentary series takes inspiration from the Talmud and from *The Torah: A Women's Commentary* (ed. Tamara Cohn Eskenazi and Andrea L. Weiss; New York: Women of Reform Judaism, Federation of Temple Sisterhood, 2008), in which many voices, even conflicting ones, are included and not harmonized.

Contributors include biblical scholars, theologians, and readers of Scripture from outside the scholarly and religious guilds. At times, their comments pertain to a particular text. In some instances they address a theme or topic that arises from the text.

Another feature that highlights the collaborative nature of feminist biblical interpretation is that a number of the volumes have two lead authors who have worked in tandem from the inception of the project and whose voices interweave throughout the commentary.

## Woman Wisdom

The title, Wisdom Commentary, reflects both the importance to feminists of the figure of Woman Wisdom in the Scriptures and the distinct wisdom that feminist women and men bring to the interpretive process. In the Scriptures, Woman Wisdom appears as "a breath of the power of God, and a pure emanation of the glory of the Almighty" (Wis 7:25), who was present and active in fashioning all that exists (Prov 8:22-31; Wis 8:6). She is a spirit who pervades and penetrates all things (Wis 7:22-23), and she provides guidance and nourishment at her all-inclusive table (Prov 9:1-5). In both postexilic biblical and nonbiblical Jewish sources, Woman Wisdom is often equated with Torah, e.g., Sir 24:23-34; Bar 3:9–4:4; 38:2; 46:4-5; 2 Bar 48:33, 36; 4 Ezra 5:9-10; 13:55; 14:40; 1 Enoch 42.

The New Testament frequently portrays Jesus as Wisdom incarnate. He invites his followers, "take my yoke upon you and learn from me" (Matt 11:29), just as Ben Sira advises, "put your neck under her [Wisdom's] yoke and let your souls receive instruction" (Sir 51:26). Just as Wisdom experiences rejection (Prov 1:23-25; Sir 15:7-8; Wis 10:3; Bar 3:12), so too does Jesus (Mark 8:31; John 1:10-11). Only some accept his invitation to his all-inclusive banquet (Matt 22:1-14; Luke 14:15-24; compare Prov 1:20-21; 9:3-5). Yet, "wisdom is vindicated by her deeds" (Matt 11:19, speaking of Jesus and John the Baptist; in the Lucan parallel at 7:35 they are called "wisdom's children"). There are numerous parallels between what is said of Wisdom and of the *Logos* in the Prologue of the Fourth Gospel (John 1:1-18). These are only a few of many examples. This female embodiment of divine presence and power is an apt image to guide the work of this series.

## Feminism

There are many different understandings of the term "feminism." The various meanings, aims, and methods have developed exponentially in recent decades. Feminism is a perspective and a movement that springs from a recognition of inequities toward women, and it advocates for changes in whatever structures prevent full human flourishing. Three waves of feminism in the United States are commonly recognized. The first, arising in the mid-nineteenth century and lasting into the early twentieth, was sparked by women's efforts to be involved in the public sphere and to win the right to vote. In the 1960s and 1970s, the second wave focused on civil rights and equality for women. With the third wave, from the 1980s forward, came global feminism and the emphasis on the contextual nature of interpretation. Now a fourth wave may be emerging, with a stronger emphasis on the intersectionality of women's concerns with those of other marginalized groups and the increased use of the internet as a platform for discussion and activism.[1] As feminism has matured, it has recognized that inequities based on gender are interwoven with power imbalances based on race, class, ethnicity, religion, sexual identity, physical ability, and a host of other social markers.

## Feminist Women and Men

Men who choose to identify with and partner with feminist women in the work of deconstructing systems of domination and building structures of equality are rightly regarded as feminists. Some men readily identify with experiences of women who are discriminated against on the basis of sex/gender, having themselves had comparable experiences; others who may not have faced direct discrimination or stereotyping recognize that inequity and problematic characterization still occur, and they seek correction. This series is pleased to include feminist men both as lead authors and as contributing voices.

## Feminist Biblical Interpretation

Women interpreting the Bible from the lenses of their own experience is nothing new. Throughout the ages women have recounted the biblical stories, teaching them to their children and others, all the while interpreting them afresh for their time and circumstances.[2] Following is a very brief sketch of select foremothers who laid the groundwork for contemporary feminist biblical interpretation.

One of the earliest known Christian women who challenged patriarchal interpretations of Scripture was a consecrated virgin named Helie, who lived in the second century CE. When she refused to marry, her

1. See Martha Rampton, "Four Waves of Feminism" (October 25, 2015), at http:// www.pacificu.edu/about-us/news-events/four-waves-feminism; and Ealasaid Munro, "Feminism: A Fourth Wave?," https://www.psa.ac.uk/insight-plus/feminism -fourth-wave.

2. For fuller treatments of this history, see chap. 7, "One Thousand Years of Feminist Bible Criticism," in Gerda Lerner, *Creation of Feminist Consciousness: From the Middle Ages to Eighteen-Seventy* (New York: Oxford University Press, 1993), 138–66; Susanne Scholz, "From the 'Woman's Bible' to the 'Women's Bible,' The History of Feminist Approaches to the Hebrew Bible," in *Introducing the Women's Hebrew Bible*, IFT 13 (New York: T & T Clark, 2007), 12–32; Marion Ann Taylor and Agnes Choi, eds., *Handbook of Women Biblical Interpreters: A Historical and Biographical Guide* (Grand Rapids, MI: Baker Academic, 2012).

parents brought her before a judge, who quoted to her Paul's admonition, "It is better to marry than to be aflame with passion" (1 Cor 7:9). In response, Helie first acknowledges that this is what Scripture says, but then she retorts, "but not for everyone, that is, not for holy virgins."[3] She is one of the first to question the notion that a text has one meaning that is applicable in all situations.

A Jewish woman who also lived in the second century CE, Beruriah, is said to have had "profound knowledge of biblical exegesis and outstanding intelligence."[4] One story preserved in the Talmud (b. Berakot 10a) tells of how she challenged her husband, Rabbi Meir, when he prayed for the destruction of a sinner. Proffering an alternate interpretation, she argued that Psalm 104:35 advocated praying for the destruction of sin, not the sinner.

In medieval times the first written commentaries on Scripture from a critical feminist point of view emerge. While others may have been produced and passed on orally, they are for the most part lost to us now. Among the earliest preserved feminist writings are those of Hildegard of Bingen (1098–1179), German writer, mystic, and abbess of a Benedictine monastery. She reinterpreted the Genesis narratives in a way that presented women and men as complementary and interdependent. She frequently wrote about feminine aspects of the Divine.[5] Along with other women mystics of the time, such as Julian of Norwich (1342–ca. 1416), she spoke authoritatively from her personal experiences of God's revelation in prayer.

In this era, women were also among the scribes who copied biblical manuscripts. Notable among them is Paula Dei Mansi of Verona, from a distinguished family of Jewish scribes. In 1288, she translated from Hebrew into Italian a collection of Bible commentaries written by her father and added her own explanations.[6]

Another pioneer, Christine de Pizan (1365–ca. 1430), was a French court writer and prolific poet. She used allegory and common sense

---

3. Madrid, Escorial MS, a II 9, f. 90 v., as cited in Lerner, *Feminist Consciousness*, 140.

4. See Judith R. Baskin, "Women and Post-Biblical Commentary," in *The Torah: A Women's Commentary*, ed. Tamara Cohn Eskenazi and Andrea L. Weiss (New York: Women of Reform Judaism, Federation of Temple Sisterhood, 2008), xlix–lv, at lii.

5. Hildegard of Bingen, *De Operatione Dei*, 1.4.100; PL 197:885bc, as cited in Lerner, *Feminist Consciousness*, 142–43. See also Barbara Newman, *Sister of Wisdom: St. Hildegard's Theology of the Feminine* (Berkeley: University of California Press, 1987).

6. Emily Taitz, Sondra Henry, Cheryl Tallan, eds., *JPS Guide to Jewish Women 600 B.C.E.–1900 C.E.* (Philadelphia: JPS, 2003), 110–11.

to subvert misogynist readings of Scripture and celebrated the accomplishments of female biblical figures to argue for women's active roles in building society.[7]

By the seventeenth century, there were women who asserted that the biblical text needs to be understood and interpreted in its historical context. For example, Rachel Speght (1597–ca. 1630), a Calvinist English poet, elaborates on the historical situation in first-century Corinth that prompted Paul to say, "It is well for a man not to touch a woman" (1 Cor 7:1). Her aim was to show that the biblical texts should not be applied in a literal fashion to all times and circumstances. Similarly, Margaret Fell (1614–1702), one of the founders of the Religious Society of Friends (Quakers) in Britain, addressed the Pauline prohibitions against women speaking in church by insisting that they do not have universal validity. Rather, they need to be understood in their historical context, as addressed to a local church in particular time-bound circumstances.[8]

Along with analyzing the historical context of the biblical writings, women in the eighteenth and nineteenth centuries began to attend to misogynistic interpretations based on faulty translations. One of the first to do so was British feminist Mary Astell (1666–1731).[9] In the United States, the Grimké sisters, Sarah (1792–1873) and Angelina (1805–1879), Quaker women from a slaveholding family in South Carolina, learned biblical Greek and Hebrew so that they could interpret the Bible for themselves. They were prompted to do so after men sought to silence them from speaking out against slavery and for women's rights by claiming that the Bible (e.g., 1 Cor 14:34) prevented women from speaking in public.[10] Another prominent abolitionist, Sojourner Truth (ca. 1797–1883), a former slave, quoted the Bible liberally in her speeches[11] and in so doing challenged cultural assumptions and biblical interpretations that undergird gender inequities.

---

7. See further Taylor and Choi, *Handbook of Women Biblical Interpreters*, 127–32.

8. Her major work, *Women's Speaking Justified, Proved and Allowed by the Scriptures*, published in London in 1667, gave a systematic feminist reading of all biblical texts pertaining to women.

9. Mary Astell, *Some Reflections upon Marriage* (New York: Source Book Press, 1970, reprint of the 1730 edition; earliest edition of this work is 1700), 103–4.

10. See further Sarah Grimké, *Letters on the Equality of the Sexes and the Condition of Woman* (Boston: Isaac Knapp, 1838).

11. See, for example, her most famous speech, "Ain't I a Woman?," delivered in 1851 at the Ohio Women's Rights Convention in Akron, OH; http://www.fordham .edu/halsall/mod/sojtruth-woman.asp.

Another monumental work that emerged in nineteenth-century England was that of Jewish theologian Grace Aguilar (1816–1847), *The Women of Israel*,[12] published in 1845. Aguilar's approach was to make connections between the biblical women and contemporary Jewish women's concerns. She aimed to counter the widespread notion that women were degraded in Jewish law and that only in Christianity were women's dignity and value upheld. Her intent was to help Jewish women find strength and encouragement by seeing the evidence of God's compassionate love in the history of every woman in the Bible. While not a full commentary on the Bible, Aguilar's work stands out for its comprehensive treatment of every female biblical character, including even the most obscure references.[13]

The first person to produce a full-blown feminist commentary on the Bible was Elizabeth Cady Stanton (1815–1902). A leading proponent in the United States for women's right to vote, she found that whenever women tried to make inroads into politics, education, or the work world, the Bible was quoted against them. Along with a team of like-minded women, she produced her own commentary on every text of the Bible that concerned women. Her pioneering two-volume project, *The Woman's Bible*, published in 1895 and 1898, urges women to recognize that texts that degrade women come from the men who wrote the texts, not from God, and to use their common sense to rethink what has been presented to them as sacred.

Nearly a century later, *The Women's Bible Commentary*, edited by Sharon Ringe and Carol Newsom (Westminster John Knox Press, 1992), appeared. This one-volume commentary features North American feminist scholarship on each book of the Protestant canon. Like Cady Stanton's commentary, it does not contain comments on every section of the biblical text but only on those passages deemed relevant to women. It was revised and expanded in 1998 to include the Apocrypha/Deuterocanonical books, and the contributors to this new volume reflect the global face of contemporary feminist scholarship. The revisions made in the third edition, which appeared in 2012, represent the profound advances in feminist biblical scholarship and include newer voices. In both the second and third editions, *The* has been dropped from the title.

---

12. The full title is *The Women of Israel or Characters and Sketches from the Holy Scriptures and Jewish History Illustrative of the Past History, Present Duty, and Future Destiny of the Hebrew Females, as Based on the Word of God.*

13. See further Eskenazi and Weiss, *The Torah: A Women's Commentary*, xxxviii; Taylor and Choi, *Handbook of Women Biblical Interpreters*, 31–37.

Also appearing at the centennial of Cady Stanton's *The Woman's Bible* were two volumes edited by Elisabeth Schüssler Fiorenza with the assistance of Shelly Matthews. The first, *Searching the Scriptures: A Feminist Introduction* (New York: Crossroad, 1993), charts a comprehensive approach to feminist interpretation from ecumenical, interreligious, and multicultural perspectives. The second volume, published in 1994, provides critical feminist commentary on each book of the New Testament as well as on three books of Jewish Pseudepigrapha and eleven other early Christian writings.

In Europe, similar endeavors have been undertaken, such as the one-volume *Kompendium Feministische Bibelauslegung*, edited by Luise Schottroff and Marie-Theres Wacker (Gütersloh, Gütersloher Verlagshaus, 2007), featuring German feminist biblical interpretation of each book of the Bible, along with apocryphal books, and several extrabiblical writings. This work, now in its third edition, has recently been translated into English.[14] A multivolume project, *The Bible and Women: An Encylopaedia of Exegesis and Cultural History*, edited by Irmtraud Fischer, Adriana Valerio, Mercedes Navarro Puerto, and Christiana de Groot, is currently in production. This project presents a history of the reception of the Bible as embedded in Western cultural history and focuses particularly on gender-relevant biblical themes, biblical female characters, and women recipients of the Bible. The volumes are published in English, Spanish, Italian, and German.[15]

Another groundbreaking work is the collection The Feminist Companion to the Bible Series, edited by Athalya Brenner (Sheffield: Sheffield Academic, 1993–2015), which comprises twenty volumes of commentaries on the Old Testament. The parallel series, Feminist Companion

---

14. *Feminist Biblical Interpretation: A Compendium of Critical Commentary on the Books of the Bible and Related Literature*, trans. Lisa E. Dahill, Everett R. Kalin, Nancy Lukens, Linda M. Maloney, Barbara Rumscheidt, Martin Rumscheidt, and Tina Steiner (Grand Rapids, MI: Eerdmans, 2012). Another notable collection is the three volumes edited by Susanne Scholz, *Feminist Interpretation of the Hebrew Bible in Retrospect*, Recent Research in Biblical Studies 7, 8, 9 (Sheffield: Sheffield Phoenix, 2013, 2014, 2016).

15. The first volume, on the Torah, appeared in Spanish in 2009, in German and Italian in 2010, and in English in 2011 (Atlanta, GA: SBL). Four more volumes are now available: *Feminist Biblical Studies in the Twentieth Century*, ed. Elisabeth Schüssler Fiorenza (2014); *The Writings and Later Wisdom Books*, ed. Christl M. Maier and Nuria Calduch-Benages (2014); *Gospels: Narrative and History*, ed. Mercedes Navarro Puerto and Marinella Perroni (2015); and *The High Middle Ages*, ed. Kari Elisabeth Børresen and Adriana Valerio (2015). For further information, see http://www.bibleandwomen.org.

to the New Testament and Early Christian Writings, edited by Amy-Jill Levine with Marianne Blickenstaff and Maria Mayo Robbins (Sheffield: Sheffield Academic, 2001–2009), contains thirteen volumes with one more planned. These two series are not full commentaries on the biblical books but comprise collected essays on discrete biblical texts.

Works by individual feminist biblical scholars in all parts of the world abound, and they are now too numerous to list in this introduction. Feminist biblical interpretation has reached a level of maturity that now makes possible a commentary series on every book of the Bible. In recent decades, women have had greater access to formal theological education, have been able to learn critical analytical tools, have put their own interpretations into writing, and have developed new methods of biblical interpretation. Until recent decades the work of feminist biblical interpreters was largely unknown, both to other women and to their brothers in the synagogue, church, and academy. Feminists now have taken their place in the professional world of biblical scholars, where they build on the work of their foremothers and connect with one another across the globe in ways not previously possible. In a few short decades, feminist biblical criticism has become an integral part of the academy.

## Methodologies

Feminist biblical scholars use a variety of methods and often employ a number of them together.[16] In the Wisdom Commentary series, the authors will explain their understanding of feminism and the feminist reading strategies used in their commentary. Each volume treats the biblical text in blocks of material, not an analysis verse by verse. The entire text is considered, not only those passages that feature female characters or that speak specifically about women. When women are not apparent in the narrative, feminist lenses are used to analyze the dynamics in the text between male characters, the models of power, binary ways of thinking, and dynamics of imperialism. Attention is given to how the whole text functions and how it was and is heard, both in its original context and today. Issues of particular concern to women—e.g., poverty, food, health, the environment, water—come to the fore.

---

16. See the seventeen essays in Caroline Vander Stichele and Todd Penner, eds., *Her Master's Tools? Feminist and Postcolonial Engagements of Historical-Critical Discourse* (Atlanta, GA: SBL, 2005), which show the complementarity of various approaches.

One of the approaches used by early feminists and still popular today is to lift up the overlooked and forgotten stories of women in the Bible. Studies of women in each of the Testaments have been done, and there are also studies on women in particular biblical books.[17] Feminists recognize that the examples of biblical characters can be both empowering and problematic. The point of the feminist enterprise is not to serve as an apologetic for women; it is rather, in part, to recover women's history and literary roles in all their complexity and to learn from that recovery.

Retrieving the submerged history of biblical women is a crucial step for constructing the story of the past so as to lead to liberative possibilities for the present and future. There are, however, some pitfalls to this approach. Sometimes depictions of biblical women have been naïve and romantic. Some commentators exalt the virtues of both biblical and contemporary women and paint women as superior to men. Such reverse discrimination inhibits movement toward equality for all. In addition, some feminists challenge the idea that one can "pluck positive images out of an admittedly androcentric text, separating literary characterizations from the androcentric interests they were created to serve."[18] Still other feminists find these images to have enormous value.

One other danger with seeking the submerged history of women is the tendency for Christian feminists to paint Jesus and even Paul as liberators of women in a way that demonizes Judaism.[19] Wisdom Commentary aims to enhance understanding of Jesus as well as Paul as Jews of their day and to forge solidarity among Jewish and Christian feminists.

---

17. See, e.g., Alice Bach, ed., *Women in the Hebrew Bible: A Reader* (New York: Routledge, 1998); Tikva Frymer-Kensky, *Reading the Women of the Bible* (New York: Schocken, 2002); Carol Meyers, Toni Craven, and Ross S. Kraemer, *Women in Scripture* (Grand Rapids, MI: Eerdmans, 2000); Irene Nowell, *Women in the Old Testament* (Collegeville, MN: Liturgical Press, 1997); Katharine Doob Sakenfeld, *Just Wives? Stories of Power and Survival in the Old Testament and Today* (Louisville, KY: Westminster John Knox, 2003); Mary Ann Getty-Sullivan, *Women in the New Testament* (Collegeville, MN: Liturgical Press, 2001); Bonnie Thurston, *Women in the New Testament* (New York: Crossroad, 1998).

18. Cheryl Exum, "Second Thoughts about Secondary Characters: Women in Exodus 1.8–2.10," in *A Feminist Companion to Exodus to Deuteronomy*, FCB 6 (Sheffield: Sheffield Academic, 1994), 75–97, at 76.

19. See Judith Plaskow, "Anti-Judaism in Feminist Christian Interpretation," in *Searching the Scriptures: A Feminist Introduction* (New York: Crossroad, 1993), 1:117–29; Amy-Jill Levine, "The New Testament and Anti-Judaism," in *The Misunderstood Jew: The Church and the Scandal of the Jewish Jesus* (San Francisco: HarperSanFrancisco, 2006), 87–117.

Feminist scholars who use historical-critical methods analyze the world behind the text; they seek to understand the historical context from which the text emerged and the circumstances of the communities to whom it was addressed. In bringing feminist lenses to this approach, the aim is not to impose modern expectations on ancient cultures but to unmask the ways that ideologically problematic mind-sets that produced the ancient texts are still promulgated through the text. Feminist biblical scholars aim not only to deconstruct but also to reclaim and reconstruct biblical history as women's history, in which women were central and active agents in creating religious heritage.[20] A further step is to construct meaning for contemporary women and men in a liberative movement toward transformation of social, political, economic, and religious structures.[21] In recent years, some feminists have embraced new historicism, which accents the creative role of the interpreter in any construction of history and exposes the power struggles to which the text witnesses.[22]

Literary critics analyze the world of the text: its form, language patterns, and rhetorical function.[23] They do not attempt to separate layers of tradition and redaction but focus on the text holistically, as it is in

---

20. See, for example, Phyllis A. Bird, *Missing Persons and Mistaken Identities: Women and Gender in Ancient Israel* (Minneapolis: Fortress, 1997); Elisabeth Schüssler Fiorenza, *In Memory of Her: A Feminist Theological Reconstruction of Christian Origins* (New York: Crossroad, 1984); Ross Shepard Kraemer and Mary Rose D'Angelo, eds., *Women and Christian Origins* (New York: Oxford University Press, 1999).

21. See, e.g., Sandra M. Schneiders, *The Revelatory Text: Interpreting the New Testament as Sacred Scripture*, rev. ed. (Collegeville, MN: Liturgical Press, 1999), whose aim is to engage in biblical interpretation not only for intellectual enlightenment but, even more important, for personal and communal transformation. Elisabeth Schüssler Fiorenza (*Wisdom Ways: Introducing Feminist Biblical Interpretation* [Maryknoll, NY: Orbis Books, 2001]) envisions the work of feminist biblical interpretation as a dance of Wisdom that consists of seven steps that interweave in spiral movements toward liberation, the final one being transformative action for change.

22. See Gina Hens Piazza, *The New Historicism*, Guides to Biblical Scholarship, Old Testament Series (Minneapolis: Fortress, 2002).

23. Phyllis Trible was among the first to employ this method with texts from Genesis and Ruth in her groundbreaking book *God and the Rhetoric of Sexuality*, OBT (Philadelphia: Fortress, 1978). Another pioneer in feminist literary criticism is Mieke Bal (*Lethal Love: Feminist Literary Readings of Biblical Love Stories* [Bloomington: Indiana University Press, 1987]). For surveys of recent developments in literary methods, see Terry Eagleton, *Literary Theory: An Introduction*, 3rd ed. (Minneapolis: University of Minnesota Press, 2008); Janice Capel Anderson and Stephen D. Moore, eds., *Mark and Method: New Approaches in Biblical Studies*, 2nd ed. (Minneapolis: Fortress, 2008).

its present form. They examine how meaning is created in the interaction between the text and its reader in multiple contexts. Within the arena of literary approaches are reader-oriented approaches, narrative, rhetorical, structuralist, post-structuralist, deconstructive, ideological, autobiographical, and performance criticism.[24] Narrative critics study the interrelation among author, text, and audience through investigation of settings, both spatial and temporal; characters; plot; and narrative techniques (e.g., irony, parody, intertextual allusions). Reader-response critics attend to the impact that the text has on the reader or hearer. They recognize that when a text is detrimental toward women there is the choice either to affirm the text or to read against the grain toward a liberative end. Rhetorical criticism analyzes the style of argumentation and attends to how the author is attempting to shape the thinking or actions of the hearer. Structuralist critics analyze the complex patterns of binary oppositions in the text to derive its meaning.[25] Post-structuralist approaches challenge the notion that there are fixed meanings to any biblical text or that there is one universal truth. They engage in close readings of the text and often engage in intertextual analysis.[26] Within this approach is deconstructionist criticism, which views the text as a site of conflict, with competing narratives. The interpreter aims to expose the fault lines and overturn and reconfigure binaries by elevating the underling of a pair and foregrounding it.[27] Feminists also use other postmodern approaches, such as ideological and autobiographical criticism. The former analyzes the system of ideas that underlies the power and

24. See, e.g., J. Cheryl Exum and David J. A. Clines, eds., *The New Literary Criticism and the Hebrew Bible* (Valley Forge, PA: Trinity Press International, 1993); Edgar V. McKnight and Elizabeth Struthers Malbon, eds., *The New Literary Criticism and the New Testament* (Valley Forge, PA: Trinity Press International, 1994).

25. See, e.g., David Jobling, *The Sense of Biblical Narrative: Three Structural Analyses in the Old Testament*, JSOTSup 7 (Sheffield: University of Sheffield Press, 1978).

26. See, e.g., Stephen D. Moore, *Poststructuralism and the New Testament: Derrida and Foucault at the Foot of the Cross* (Minneapolis: Fortress, 1994); *The Bible in Theory: Critical and Postcritical Essays* (Atlanta, GA: SBL, 2010); Yvonne Sherwood, *A Biblical Text and Its Afterlives: The Survival of Jonah in Western Culture* (Cambridge: Cambridge University Press, 2000).

27. David Penchansky, "Deconstruction," in *The Oxford Encyclopedia of Biblical Interpretation*, ed. Steven McKenzie (New York: Oxford University Press, 2013), 196–205. See, for example, Danna Nolan Fewell and David M. Gunn, *Gender, Power, and Promise: The Subject of the Bible's First Story* (Nashville, TN: Abingdon, 1993); David Rutledge, *Reading Marginally: Feminism, Deconstruction and the Bible*, BibInt 21 (Leiden: Brill, 1996).

values concealed in the text as well as that of the interpreter.[28] The latter
involves deliberate self-disclosure while reading the text as a critical
exegete.[29] Performance criticism attends to how the text was passed on
orally, usually in communal settings, and to the verbal and nonverbal
interactions between the performer and the audience.[30]

From the beginning, feminists have understood that interpreting the
Bible is an act of power. In recent decades, feminist biblical scholars have
developed hermeneutical theories of the ethics and politics of biblical
interpretation to challenge the claims to value neutrality of most academic biblical scholarship. Feminist biblical scholars have also turned
their attention to how some biblical writings were shaped by the power
of empire and how this still shapes readers' self-understandings today.
They have developed hermeneutical approaches that reveal, critique,
and evaluate the interactions depicted in the text against the context
of empire, and they consider implications for contemporary contexts.[31]
Feminists also analyze the dynamics of colonization and the mentalities
of colonized peoples in the exercise of biblical interpretation. As Kwok
Pui-lan explains, "A postcolonial feminist interpretation of the Bible
needs to investigate the deployment of gender in the narration of identity, the negotiation of power differentials between the colonizers and
the colonized, and the reinforcement of patriarchal control over spheres
where these elites could exercise control."[32] Methods and models from
sociology and cultural anthropology are used by feminists to investigate

28. See Tina Pippin, ed., *Ideological Criticism of Biblical Texts: Semeia* 59 (1992); Terry
Eagleton, *Ideology: An Introduction* (London: Verso, 2007).

29. See, e.g., Ingrid Rose Kitzberger, ed., *Autobiographical Biblical Interpretation:
Between Text and Self* (Leiden: Deo, 2002); P. J. W. Schutte, "When *They, We*, and the
Passive Become *I*—Introducing Autobiographical Biblical Criticism," *HTS Teologiese
Studies / Theological Studies* vol. 61 (2005): 401–16.

30. See, e.g., Holly Hearon and Philip Ruge-Jones, eds., *The Bible in Ancient and
Modern Media: Story and Performance* (Eugene, OR: Cascade Books, 2009).

31. E.g., Gale Yee, ed., *Judges and Method: New Approaches in Biblical Studies* (Min-
neapolis: Fortress, 1995); Warren Carter, *The Gospel of Matthew in Its Roman Imperial
Context* (London: T & T Clark, 2005); *The Roman Empire and the New Testament: An
Essential Guide* (Nashville, TN: Abingdon, 2006); Elisabeth Schüssler Fiorenza, *The
Power of the Word: Scripture and the Rhetoric of Empire* (Minneapolis: Fortress, 2007);
Judith E. McKinlay, *Reframing Her: Biblical Women in Postcolonial Focus* (Sheffield:
Sheffield Phoenix, 2004).

32. Kwok Pui-lan, *Postcolonial Imagination and Feminist Theology* (Louisville, KY:
Westminster John Knox, 2005), 9. See also, Musa W. Dube, ed., *Postcolonial Feminist
Interpretation of the Bible* (St. Louis, MO: Chalice Press, 2000); Cristl M. Maier and

women's everyday lives, their experiences of marriage, child rearing, labor, money, illness, etc.[33]

As feminists have examined the construction of gender from varying cultural perspectives, they have become ever more cognizant that the way gender roles are defined within differing cultures varies radically. As Mary Ann Tolbert observes, "Attempts to isolate some universal role that cross-culturally defines 'woman' have run into contradictory evidence at every turn."[34] Some women have coined new terms to highlight the particularities of their socio-cultural context. Many African American feminists, for example, call themselves *womanists* to draw attention to the double oppression of racism and sexism they experience.[35] Similarly, many US Hispanic feminists speak of themselves as *mujeristas* (*mujer* is Spanish for "woman").[36] Others prefer to be called "Latina feminists."[37] Both groups emphasize that the context for their theologizing is *mestizaje* and *mulatez* (racial and cultural mixture), done *en conjunto* (in community), with *lo cotidiano* (everyday lived experience) of Hispanic women as starting points for theological reflection and the encounter with the divine. Intercultural analysis has become an indispensable tool for working toward justice for women at the global level.[38]

---

Carolyn J. Sharp, *Prophecy and Power: Jeremiah in Feminist and Postcolonial Perspective* (London: Bloomsbury, 2013).

33. See, for example, Carol Meyers, *Discovering Eve: Ancient Israelite Women in Context* (New York: Oxford University Press, 1991); Luise Schottroff, *Lydia's Impatient Sisters: A Feminist Social History of Early Christianity*, trans. Barbara and Martin Rumscheidt (Louisville, KY: Westminster John Knox, 1995); Susan Niditch, *"My Brother Esau Is a Hairy Man": Hair and Identity in Ancient Israel* (Oxford: Oxford University Press, 2008).

34. Mary Ann Tolbert, "Social, Sociological, and Anthropological Methods," in *Searching the Scriptures*, 1:255–71, at 265.

35. Alice Walker coined the term (*In Search of Our Mothers' Gardens: Womanist Prose* [New York: Harcourt Brace Jovanovich, 1967, 1983]). See also Katie G. Cannon, "The Emergence of Black Feminist Consciousness," in *Feminist Interpretation of the Bible*, ed. Letty M. Russell (Philadelphia: Westminster, 1985), 30–40; Renita Weems, *Just a Sister Away: A Womanist Vision of Women's Relationships in the Bible* (San Diego: Lura Media, 1988); Nyasha Junior, *An Introduction to Womanist Biblical Interpretation* (Louisville, KY: Westminster John Knox, 2015).

36. Ada María Isasi-Díaz (*Mujerista Theology: A Theology for the Twenty-first Century* [Maryknoll, NY: Orbis Books, 1996]) is credited with coining the term.

37. E.g., María Pilar Aquino, Daisy L. Machado, and Jeanette Rodríguez, eds., *A Reader in Latina Feminist Theology* (Austin: University of Texas Press, 2002).

38. See, e.g., María Pilar Aquino and María José Rosado-Nunes, eds., *Feminist Intercultural Theology: Latina Explorations for a Just World*, Studies in Latino/a Catholicism (Maryknoll, NY: Orbis Books, 2007).

Some feminists are among those who have developed lesbian, gay, bisexual, and transgender (LGBT) interpretation. This approach focuses on issues of sexual identity and uses various reading strategies. Some point out the ways in which categories that emerged in recent centuries are applied anachronistically to biblical texts to make modern-day judgments. Others show how the Bible is silent on contemporary issues about sexual identity. Still others examine same-sex relationships in the Bible by figures such as Ruth and Naomi or David and Jonathan. In recent years, queer theory has emerged; it emphasizes the blurriness of boundaries not just of sexual identity but also of gender roles. Queer critics often focus on texts in which figures transgress what is traditionally considered proper gender behavior.[39]

Feminists also recognize that the struggle for women's equality and dignity is intimately connected with the struggle for respect for Earth and for the whole of the cosmos. Ecofeminists interpret Scripture in ways that highlight the link between human domination of nature and male subjugation of women. They show how anthropocentric ways of interpreting the Bible have overlooked or dismissed Earth and Earth community. They invite readers to identify not only with human characters in the biblical narrative but also with other Earth creatures and domains of nature, especially those that are the object of injustice. Some use creative imagination to retrieve the interests of Earth implicit in the narrative and enable Earth to speak.[40]

## Biblical Authority

By the late nineteenth century, some feminists, such as Elizabeth Cady Stanton, began to question openly whether the Bible could continue to be regarded as authoritative for women. They viewed the Bible itself as

---

39. See, e.g., Bernadette J. Brooten, *Love between Women: Early Christian Responses to Female Homoeroticism* (Chicago and London: University of Chicago Press, 1996); Mary Rose D'Angelo, "Women Partners in the New Testament," *JFSR* 6 (1990): 65–86; Deirdre J. Good, "Reading Strategies for Biblical Passages on Same-Sex Relations," *Theology and Sexuality* 7 (1997): 70–82; Deryn Guest, *When Deborah Met Jael: Lesbian Feminist Hermeneutics* (London: SCM Press, 2011); Teresa Hornsby and Ken Stone, eds., *Bible Trouble: Queer Readings at the Boundaries of Biblical Scholarship* (Atlanta, GA: SBL, 2011).

40. E.g., Norman C. Habel and Peter Trudinger, *Exploring Ecological Hermeneutics*, SymS 46 (Atlanta, GA: SBL, 2008); Mary Judith Ress, *Ecofeminism in Latin America*, Women from the Margins (Maryknoll, NY: Orbis Books, 2006).

the source of women's oppression, and some rejected its sacred origin and saving claims. Some decided that the Bible and the religious traditions that enshrine it are too thoroughly saturated with androcentrism and patriarchy to be redeemable.[41]

In the Wisdom Commentary series, questions such as these may be raised, but the aim of this series is not to lead readers to reject the authority of the biblical text. Rather, the aim is to promote better understanding of the contexts from which the text arose and of the rhetorical effects it has on women and men in contemporary contexts. Such understanding can lead to a deepening of faith, with the Bible serving as an aid to bring flourishing of life.

## Language for God

Because of the ways in which the term "God" has been used to symbolize the divine in predominantly male, patriarchal, and monarchical modes, feminists have designed new ways of speaking of the divine. Some have called attention to the inadequacy of the term *God* by trying to visually destabilize our ways of thinking and speaking of the divine. Rosemary Radford Ruether proposed *God/ess*, as an unpronounceable term pointing to the unnameable understanding of the divine that transcends patriarchal limitations.[42] Some have followed traditional Jewish practice, writing *G-d*. Elisabeth Schüssler Fiorenza has adopted *G\*d*.[43] Others draw on the biblical tradition to mine female and non-gender-specific metaphors and symbols.[44] In Wisdom Commentary, there is not one standard way of expressing the divine; each author will use her or his preferred ways. The one exception is that when the tetragrammaton, YHWH, the name revealed to Moses in Exodus 3:14, is used, it will be without vowels, respecting the Jewish custom of avoiding pronouncing the divine name out of reverence.

---

41. E.g., Mary Daly, *Beyond God the Father: A Philosophy of Women's Liberation* (Boston: Beacon, 1973).

42. Rosemary Radford Ruether, *Sexism and God-Talk: Toward a Feminist Theology* (Boston: Beacon, 1983).

43. Elisabeth Schüssler Fiorenza, *Jesus: Miriam's Child, Sophia's Prophet; Critical Issues in Feminist Christology* (New York: Continuum, 1994), 191 n. 3.

44. E.g., Sallie McFague, *Models of God: Theology for an Ecological, Nuclear Age* (Philadelphia: Fortress, 1987); Catherine LaCugna, *God for Us: The Trinity and Christian Life* (San Francisco: HarperCollins, 1991); Elizabeth A. Johnson, *She Who Is: The Mystery of God in Feminist Theological Discourse* (New York: Crossroad, 1992). See further Elizabeth A. Johnson, "God," in *Dictionary of Feminist Theologies*, 128–30.

## Nomenclature for the Two Testaments

In recent decades, some biblical scholars have begun to call the two Testaments of the Bible by names other than the traditional nomenclature: Old and New Testament. Some regard "Old" as derogatory, implying that it is no longer relevant or that it has been superseded. Consequently, terms like Hebrew Bible, First Testament, and Jewish Scriptures and, correspondingly, Christian Scriptures or Second Testament have come into use. There are a number of difficulties with these designations. The term "Hebrew Bible" does not take into account that parts of the Old Testament are written not in Hebrew but in Aramaic.[45] Moreover, for Roman Catholics, Anglicans, and Eastern Orthodox believers, the Old Testament includes books written in Greek—the Deuterocanonical books, considered Apocrypha by Protestants. The term "Jewish Scriptures" is inadequate because these books are also sacred to Christians. Conversely, "Christian Scriptures" is not an accurate designation for the New Testament, since the Old Testament is also part of the Christian Scriptures. Using "First and Second Testament" also has difficulties, in that it can imply a hierarchy and a value judgment.[46] Jews generally use the term Tanakh, an acronym for Torah (Pentateuch), Nevi'im (Prophets), and Ketuvim (Writings).

In Wisdom Commentary, if authors choose to use a designation other than Tanakh, Old Testament, and New Testament, they will explain how they mean the term.

## Translation

Modern feminist scholars recognize the complexities connected with biblical translation, as they have delved into questions about philosophy of language, how meanings are produced, and how they are culturally situated. Today it is evident that simply translating into gender-neutral formulations cannot address all the challenges presented by androcentric texts. Efforts at feminist translation must also deal with issues around authority and canonicity.[47]

Because of these complexities, the editors of Wisdom Commentary series have chosen to use an existing translation, the New Revised Standard

---

45. Gen 31:47; Jer 10:11; Ezra 4:7–6:18; 7:12-26; Dan 2:4–7:28.

46. See Levine, *The Misunderstood Jew*, 193–99.

47. Elizabeth Castelli, "*Les Belles Infidèles*/Fidelity or Feminism? The Meanings of Feminist Biblical Translation," in *Searching the Scriptures*, 1:189–204, here 190.

Version (NRSV), which is provided for easy reference at the top of each page of commentary. The NRSV was produced by a team of ecumenical and interreligious scholars, is a fairly literal translation, and uses inclusive language for human beings. Brief discussions about problematic translations appear in the inserts labeled "Translation Matters." When more detailed discussions are available, these will be indicated in footnotes. In the commentary, wherever Hebrew or Greek words are used, English translation is provided. In cases where a wordplay is involved, transliteration is provided to enable understanding.

## Art and Poetry

Artistic expression in poetry, music, sculpture, painting, and various other modes is very important to feminist interpretation. Where possible, art and poetry are included in the print volumes of the series. In a number of instances, these are original works created for this project. Regrettably, copyright and production costs prohibit the inclusion of color photographs and other artistic work. It is our hope that the web version will allow a greater collection of such resources.

## Glossary

Because there are a number of excellent readily available resources that provide definitions and concise explanations of terms used in feminist theological and biblical studies, this series will not include a glossary. We refer you to works such as *Dictionary of Feminist Theologies*, edited by Letty M. Russell with J. Shannon Clarkson (Louisville, KY: Westminster John Knox, 1996), and volume 1 of *Searching the Scriptures*, edited by Elisabeth Schüssler Fiorenza with the assistance of Shelly Matthews (New York: Crossroad, 1992). Individual authors in the Wisdom Commentary series will define the way they are using terms that may be unfamiliar.

## Bibliography

Because bibliographies are quickly outdated and because the space is limited, only a list of Works Cited is included in the print volumes. A comprehensive bibliography for each volume is posted on a dedicated website and is updated regularly. The link for this volume can be found at wisdomcommentary.org.

## A Concluding Word

In just a few short decades, feminist biblical studies has grown exponentially, both in the methods that have been developed and in the number of scholars who have embraced it. We realize that this series is limited and will soon need to be revised and updated. It is our hope that Wisdom Commentary, by making the best of current feminist biblical scholarship available in an accessible format to ministers, preachers, teachers, scholars, and students, will aid all readers in their advancement toward God's vision of dignity, equality, and justice for all.

## Acknowledgments

There are a great many people who have made this series possible: first, Peter Dwyer, director, and Hans Christoffersen, publisher of the academic market at Liturgical Press, who have believed in this project and have shepherded it since it was conceived in 2008. Editorial consultants Athalya Brenner-Idan and Elisabeth Schüssler Fiorenza have not only been an inspiration with their pioneering work but have encouraged us all along the way with their personal involvement. Volume editors Mary Ann Beavis, Carol J. Dempsey, Amy-Jill Levine, Linda M. Maloney, Ahida Pilarski, Sarah Tanzer, Lauress Wilkins Lawrence, and Seung Ai Yang have lent their extraordinary wisdom to the shaping of the series, have used their extensive networks of relationships to secure authors and contributors, and have worked tirelessly to guide their work to completion. Two others who contributed greatly to the shaping of the project at the outset were Linda M. Day and Mignon Jacobs, as well as Barbara E. Bowe of blessed memory (d. 2010). Editorial and research assistant Susan M. Hickman has provided invaluable support with administrative details and arrangements. I am grateful to Brian Eisenschenk and Christine Henderson who have assisted Susan Hickman with the Wiki. There are countless others at Liturgical Press whose daily work makes the production possible. I am especially thankful to Lauren L. Murphy, Andrea Humphrey, Lauress Wilkins Lawrence, and Justin Howell for their work in copyediting.

# Acknowledgments

In my wildest dreams, I never imagined writing a commentary on the Song of Songs, much less being asked to do so. But however readers might judge the final product, the process of researching, pondering, and producing this volume has been one of the most enjoyable experiences of my professional life. I'm very grateful to the general editor, Barbara Reid, for inviting me to contribute to this monumental series and to the volume editor, Lauress Wilkins Lawrence, for her careful attention to the manuscript at every stage and her numerous insights that I gladly incorporated. Both of these scholars represent models of uncommon wisdom and unstinting support. While I have tried to heed their sage voices calling out at conferences (where we've met) and on the cyberstreets of email, I still have much to learn from them and other feminist scholars concerning this breathtaking "Holiest of Songs."

I also thank the amazing women's chorus of Contributing Voices (and Visuals), who enriched this commentary with their distinctive and wide-ranging offerings. It's been an honor and pleasure to work with each one of you.

My first deep dive into this book came a few years ago in a memorable seminar, "Sex and Song," at the Baptist Theological Seminary at Richmond, where I teach. I want to give a shout out to that exceptional group of students who worked with me: Josh Beeler, Blaine Britt, Ben Brown, Alice Cates, Joel Ingram, Joe Kendrick, Khan Naw, Tovah Nunez, Jeff Poythress, Tina Schilling, Catie Walsh, Jeff Walton, and Carolyn Williams. Thanks, gang, for your openness, enthusiasm, and sharp thinking throughout the course (even at 8:20 a.m., twice a week!).

Finally, and foremost, I thank my wife Janet, with whom I've shared over four decades of life, love, and learning. Though far from the young sweethearts of the Song, we're hanging in there and cherishing every moment of our lives together. She even hopes I've learned a thing or two from this project. We shall see . . .

# Author's Introduction

## *Playing the Song of Songs in a Feminist Key*

*Just an old fashioned love song*
*Comin' down in three-part harmony*
*Just an old fashioned love song*
*One I'm sure they wrote for you and me.*[1]

So crooned Three Dog Night in their 1971 smash hit written by
Paul Williams. Love songs have been in fashion a long time,
as long as people have been falling in love. Though only a select few
artists are gifted enough to compose good love songs, most of us have
the capacity to hear them as if they were written *for* us, "for you and
me," in perfect "harmony." Of course, the older the song, particularly
"comin' down" from antiquity, the less its love images speak to modern
sensibilities. But with some careful linguistic and historical work, ancient
tunes can be transposed fairly well into contemporary keys. And such
work is worth the effort with the most poignant love songs from any era
and environment. The classics, as they say, never go out of style.

---

1. Paul Williams, lyrics. "Just an Old Fashioned Love Song," in *Harmony*, by Three
Dog Night. Dunhill, 1971.

The Song of Songs in the Hebrew Bible is arguably the biggest block-buster love song ever composed, not just because it claims to be the top Song above all songs (שיר השירים; 1:1), but because it constitutes the singular example of sustained love lyrics in the Jewish and Christian scriptural canon known as the Bible, which has been a bestseller in the Western world for centuries. I doubt that the single biblical Song has been "played"—read, heard, voiced—as much as some hits of Sinatra or Elvis in modern America, but as part of the canonical collection, it enjoys an honored place within the #1 album of all time. Popularity, however, while intimating a certain universal appeal, is no guarantee of uniform interpretation. Quite the contrary. The more singers and hearers a song has, the more diverse viewpoints it attracts, all the more so concerning such a complicated and variegated emotion as romantic love, a "many splendored"—and splintered—thing.[2]

My prime concern in this commentary is to interpret the Song of Songs in a feminist key. But that is no simple transposition, like raising all the notes a full step from the key of E-flat to F. There is no definitive "F" key in feminist musicology—or F-sharp, as some critics might insist, naïvely dismissing all feminist criticism as acrimonious, prickly, "sharp." Contemporary feminism is as multidimensional and intersectional as love—a rich range of feminisms, a dazzling run of arpeggios up and down the keyboard. In all its varied manifestations, feminism does trumpet a programmatic theme of full equality and opportunity for all women throughout society. But this is more of a political orientation than a procedural policy: a core feminist manifesto, yes; a lock-step feminist methodology, not at all.[3]

2. See Aaron Ben-Ze'ev and Rouhama Goussinsky, *In the Name of Love: Romantic Ideology and Its Victims* (Oxford: Oxford University Press, 2006); Helen Fisher, *Why We Love: The Nature and Chemistry of Romantic Love* (New York: Henry Holt, 2004); Robert C. Solomon, *About Love: Reinventing Romance for Our Times* (Indianapolis: Hackett, 2006); Solomon, *Love: Emotion, Myth, and Metaphor* (Garden City, NY: Anchor/Doubleday, 1981).

3. See the concise, yet broad-based, definition of feminism offered by bell hooks. She writes, "Simply put, feminism is a movement to end sexism, sexist exploitation, and oppression. . . . Practically, it is a definition which implies that all sexist thinking and action is the problem, whether those who perpetuate it are female or male, child or adult. It is also broad enough to include an understanding of systemic institutionalized sexism. As a definition, it is open-ended" (*Feminism Is for Everybody: Passionate Politics* [Cambridge, MA: South End, 2000], 1). See also Naomi Zack, *Inclusive Feminism: A Third Wave Theory of Women's Commonality* (Lanham, MD: Rowman &

This lively interpretive array is just as true of feminist biblical criticism as of any other discipline. Introducing a multivolume essay series of "Feminist Companions to the New Testament," Amy-Jill Levine assesses the state of play in feminist biblical interpretation via an apt musical image for our interest in the biblical Song.

> The feminist choir no longer sounds the single note of white, Western, middle-class, Christian concerns; "feminist biblical studies" is now a symphony. It acknowledges the different concerns social location and experience bring to interpretation and recognizes the tentativeness and partiality of each conclusion: no instrument alone is complete; no two musicians play the music exactly alike. Feminist readers of Christian origins are so diverse in terms of approach (literary, historical, sociological, text-critical, ideological, cross-cultural . . .), focus (imagery, characterization, genre, plot, Christology, ethics, politics, polemic . . .), hermeneutics (of suspicion, of recovery . . .), identity (Womanist, Latina, African, Evangelical, lesbian, Jewish, Catholic . . .) and conclusions—namely, it is just like most biblical studies and indeed like most academic disciplines in the humanities and social sciences—that any single definition of what constitutes a "feminist reading" is necessarily reified.[4]

Inevitably, then, this commentary represents *my* feminist reading of the Song of Songs, more specifically, the reading of a white, late middle-aged, forty-plus-year-married American male, father of two young adult daughters, ordained Baptist minister, and seminary professor appointed to teach New Testament and biblical interpretation. You may be forgiven an incredulous reaction at this point. It's nice to have a large, welcoming feminist choir, but surely there are some standards! Did this guy really pass an audition? In good Adamic fashion, I will mostly blame the women editors of this series for their foolish choice and leave you to address all complaints to them (see the acknowledgments for how I really feel about

---

Littlefield, 2005); Jennifer Baumgardner and Amy Richards, *Manifesta: Young Women, Feminism, and the Future*, 2nd ed. (New York: Farrar, Straus, and Giroux, 2010); Chimamanda Ngozi Adichie, *We Should All Be Feminists* (New York: Anchor, 2015).

4. Amy-Jill Levine, "Introduction," in *A Feminist Companion to Matthew*, ed. Amy-Jill Levine with Marianne Blickenstaff, 13–24 (Sheffield: Sheffield Academic, 2001), 14. A valuable series on books in the Hebrew Bible that preceded this 2001 *Feminist Companion to* series has been edited by Athalya Brenner for Sheffield Academic, including two volumes on the Song of Songs co-edited with Carole Fontaine, *A Feminist Companion to the Song of Songs* (Sheffield: Sheffield Academic, 1993); and *A Feminist Companion to the Song of Songs*, Second Series (Sheffield: Sheffield Academic, 2000).

these extraordinary women scholars). But by way of brief apology, I simply appeal to my long-standing engagement with feminist biblical scholarship in both testaments. I have often found Hebrew Bible/Old Testament studies blazing the trail for my New Testament work. The mounting wisdom of a brilliant cadre of pioneering female feminist biblical scholars and a few male feminist associates over the past four decades has immeasurably enriched and challenged my thinking. Fortunately for me, the Song of Songs has been one of the most fruitful fields for feminist biblical commentary. My feminist reading of the Song is thus heavily derivative. The footnotes and bibliography represent more than academic convention; they reflect a confession of debt and gratitude that I can never fully repay.

That being said, this commentary is far from a compendium of contemporary feminist readings of the Song, still less a survey of the poem's long and rich reception history.[5] I make choices all along the way about what to highlight in the Song and how to interpret it within my understanding of the poem's unfolding meaning and relevance to feminist thought. Methodologically, I attend to linguistic and other literary features of the poem within its broad social and cultural milieu. I thus aim at a close, contextual reading of the Song. Though drawing on illuminating studies of comparative ancient Near Eastern artifacts and love lyrics, I try to keep the spotlight tightly trained on the Song itself. Ideologically—I assume that all interpretation is ideologically motivated to some degree—I'm motivated by my feminist commitments, mixed with all sorts of other social and political bents peculiar to my location, many of which I'm scarcely aware. But to borrow an image from the Song, the main "banner" (2:5) stretching across this volume is "My Feminist Commentary"—with due distinctive credits to the gifted guest "Contributing Voices," soloists that chime in from time to time.

The detailed proof of my particular literary and feminist performance of the Song will come through an attentive reading/hearing of this commentary. But it is worth offering by way of general orientation a kind

---

5. See Francis Landy and Fiona Black, *The Song of Songs through the Centuries*, Blackwell Biblical Commentaries (Malden, MA: Wiley-Blackwell, 2016). For thorough engagement with the history of Jewish interpretation, see Michael Fishbane, *Song of Songs*, JPS Bible Commentary (Lincoln: University of Nebraska Press, 2015); and Marvin H. Pope, *Song of Songs: A New Translation with Introduction and Commentary*, AB 7C (Garden City, NY: Doubleday, 1977), 89–229; for Christian interpretation, see Richard A. Norris, *The Song of Songs: Interpreted by Early Christian and Medieval Commentators*, The Church's Bible (Grand Rapids: Eerdmans, 2003).

of playbill of key features characterizing this work and setting it apart from others.

## Voices and Valence: The Choral Factor

The Song of Songs calls for two principal vocal parts, one female and one male, with occasional choral backup. It is a tour de force for the two lead singers, featuring their virtuosic talents sometimes in solo performance and other times in antiphonal response. They must have youthful, vibrant, electric voices appropriate to the passionate love lyrics they sing. Beyond this dominant duo, the Songstress periodically addresses a female chorus, known as the "daughters of Jerusalem," who may in turn voice a brief reply (Song 1:5-6, 12-15; 2:3-10, 15-16; 3:1-11; 5:1-9; 6:3; 6:11-13; 8:3-5, 8-12). She also occasionally references other influential figures in the couple's love story—namely, her mother and brothers, her lover's mother, and the city watchmen—but these have no voice of their own (1:6; 3:3-4, 11; 5:7; 8:1-2, 5, 8-9).

Within the Song itself, the featured woman and man share the stage much of the time with their comparably strong voices and presence. A case can be made, however, that the woman merits top billing. She has the first and last words in the Song, each with exclamatory force directing the man's actions.

> Let him kiss me with the kisses of his mouth! (1:2)
> Make haste, my beloved [man], and be like a gazelle or a young stag upon the mountains of spices! (8:14)

And throughout the intervening material, the woman's voice rings loud and clear with purpose and passion, intention and intimacy. She knows what she wants and is not afraid to say it. Though walls and flowers dot the landscape of the Song (1:14; 2:1, 9, 12; 4:12-16; 5:1, 5, 13; 6:2, 11; 7:12; 8:9), the Songstress herself is no wallflower (see 8:10). All in all, the young diva of the Song of Songs projects the most powerful female voice in the entire Bible. We might well call her the Woman of Women.

This star character has not escaped the notice of feminist interpreters hungry for gynocentric materials and positive female role models within a patriarchal canon and culture. Finally, a female biblical figure and an entire biblical book to be celebrated by feminist readers! For example, Athalya Brenner concludes the groundbreaking collection of feminist essays on the Song that she edits with a strong affirmation and a hopeful question. I track a singular female singer throughout the Song, whereas

Brenner interprets the Song as an anthology of multiple female voices (the feminist point works either way):

> After content and form have been taken apart and then made to coalesce again, there remain the images of the Song of Song [*sic*] women. They come across as articulate, loud, clear, culturally and socially undeniably effective—even within the confines and inner circle of their patriarchal society.
> A role model to identify with?[6]

Similarly, Marcia Falk asserts:

> Women's speech in the Song is hardly reserved or shy; on the contrary, it is uninhibited and even outspoken, and the Song's female speakers do not hesitate to initiate action. . . . Indeed, women may be seen as the Song's central figures primarily *because* of their full participation in both direct and indirect kinds of speech, including modes of self-address. . . . Unlike most of the Bible, the Song of Songs gives us women speaking out of their own experiences and their own imaginations.[7]

But before we throw a feminist parade with the Song of Songs as our marching anthem, we must address a critical question of vocal interpretation. Just because a woman (or women) is given a big part and sings it with gusto does not guarantee that *what* she sings advances women's best interests and represents women's honest perspectives. Further, it doesn't mean that she's performing lyrics and music that *she* composed or even endorses. Who's to say that she is not simply channeling another's voice and vision, even that of a man antithetical to women's concerns? Perhaps she's a hired vocalist, even one pressed into service against her will, a kind of musical whore, hardly a far-fetched notion in a patriarchal society. Or perhaps she is a more congenial accomplice, having thoroughly internalized the dominant social hierarchy and become happy, as far as she is aware, to play her assigned part. In any case, the problem of authentic women's speech persists, as deftly identified by Thomas Hardy's spirited heroine, Bathsheba Everdene: "It is difficult for a woman to define her feelings in language which is chiefly made by men to express theirs."[8]

---

6. For consistency, this last line should read, "Role models to identify with?" Athalya Brenner, "An Afterword," in *A Feminist Companion to the Song of Songs*, ed. Athalya Brenner and Carole R. Fontaine, 279–80 (Sheffield: JSOT, 1993), 280.

7. Marcia Falk, *The Song of Songs: A New Translation and Interpretation* (New York: HarperCollins, 1990), 117 (emphasis original).

8. Thomas Hardy, *Far From the Madding Crowd* (London: Penguin, 2000 [orig. 1874]), 308.

In the case of the biblical Song, there's much we do not know, including the composers and producers, authors and editors. Undoubtedly, most ancient writing and publishing were done by men, certainly in the fields of history, philosophy, and society. But if there were a literary-artistic opening for women, it would have been in the medium of love poetry. Women from a variety of cultures have been pouring out their hearts in song about love and other deep sentiments for centuries. Comparisons could be (and have been) made between the woman singer(s) in the Song and female poets in Egyptian, Greek (Sappho), Tamil, and Awlad 'Ali Bedouin traditions.[9] Fine, but broad parallels do not clinch the argument for female authorship or the authenticity of female voice(s) in the biblical love Song.

An honest and judicious literary- and feminist-critical hermeneutic acknowledges two interpretive ground rules succinctly identified by Cheryl Exum in her important article, "Ten Things Every Feminist Should Know about the Song of Songs":

1. There are no real women in this text.
2. The woman, or women, in this text may be the creations of male authors.[10]

"No real women in this text" reminds us that the Song is fundamentally a song about a woman (or women) in love *within* the text (lyrics) of the Song; it is not a journalistic account or verbatim transcription of any "real" particular woman's expressions of love. It may well have been inspired by an actual woman, but it does not emanate from that woman

9. See Michael V. Fox, *The Song of Songs and the Ancient Egyptian Love Songs* (Madison: University of Wisconsin Press, 1985); Richard Hunter, " 'Sweet Talk': *Song of Songs* and the Traditions of Greek Poetry," in *Perspectives on the Song of Songs*, ed. Anselm C. Hagedorn, BZAW 346 (Berlin: Walter de Gruyter, 2005), 228–44; Abraham Mariaselvam, *The Song of Songs and Ancient Tamil Love Poems: Poetry and Symbolism*, AnBib 118 (Rome: Pontifical Biblical Institute, 1988); Chaim Rabin, "Song of Songs and Tamil Poetry," *SR* 3 (1973–74): 205–19; Lila Abu-Lughod, *Veiled Sentiments: Honor and Poetry in a Bedouin Society*, 2nd ed. (Berkeley: University of California Press, 1999); cf. David M. Carr, *The Erotic Word: Sexuality, Spirituality, and the Bible* (New York: Oxford University Press, 2003), 91–93.

10. J. Cheryl Exum, "Ten Things Every Feminist Should Know about the Song of Songs," in *The Song of Songs*, ed. Athalya Brenner and Carole R. Fontaine, FCB, Second Series, 24–35 (Sheffield: Sheffield Academic, 2000), 27–29. These are #3 and #4 in her "Ten Things" catalogue. Exum works out these and many other points in her sterling commentary, *Song of Songs*, OTL (Louisville: Westminster John Knox, 2005).

or reflect her viewpoints in any unmediated sense. Elton John's "Candle in the Wind (Goodbye Norma Jeane)," co-written with Bernie Taupin, is a moving tribute to Marilyn Monroe (later revised for Princess Diana) but is clearly *his* interpretation of her: about "Norma Jeane" to some degree, but hardly capturing *her* identity. The biblical Song doesn't even come close to identifying the female figure(s), except via the enigmatic "Shulammite" designation in Song 6:13. All we have is a poetic persona, a literary construct of a passionate vocal woman. The Songstress exists only within the bounds of the Song and the minds of readers/hearers.

Accordingly, the Songstress may exist only "as a creation of male author(s)," as Norma Jeane's "candle" first flickers in Elton John's imagination, and then in the conjurations of the song's hearers. Even so, there remains the issue of lesser or greater resonance with the "real" woman. Presumably, millions of actual women and men, by virtue of their making John's song a blockbuster hit, have judged his musical portrait as reasonably authentic, by which they mean comparable, to their concept of the historical Marilyn Monroe—though such judgments are hugely complicated by the fact that Marilyn Monroe was a stage name, indeed, one of the most managed public names in entertainment history. Who knows what the "real" Norma Jeane would have thought about the song, written over a decade after her death? As for the biblical Song, though we have no named referent for the female star(s), we have a number of astute female readers who have carefully attended to what the woman actually says in the Song and how she says it, and they have detected a strong ring of authenticity to her voice that is in harmony with their own experiences of female love and sexuality. Many feminist biblical scholars, whether they hear one dominant voice or many female voices in the Song, concur with Falk's perspective. Expanding her statement cited above: "Unlike most of the Bible, the Song of Songs gives us women speaking out of their own experiences and their own imaginations, in words that *do not seem filtered through the lens of patriarchal male consciousness.* . . . In the Song . . . women are central, not peripheral, and I would add, their speech seems 'true,' not imitative."[11]

But not all critics are so sanguine. Two male scholars, each supporting feminist concerns, raise cautionary flags in the vein of a hermeneutic of suspicion. Donald C. Polaski, evoking the haunting image of Jeremy Bentham's "Panopticon" prison via Michel Foucault's postmodern theory, sees the lead woman of the Song caught in a web of power relations

11. Falk, *Song,* 117–18 (emphasis added).

that forge her self-identity (her "subject") through the threat of constant surveillance. However much she resists—and she does try to assert herself—she can't shake the feeling that someone is always watching her and monitoring her behavior, specifically, some male authority looking her up and down behind a one-way window to see if she's acting properly, if she's following the agenda he and his patriarchal cohorts have (con) scripted for her. Whether or not anyone is actually behind the looking glass at every moment, she always feels their judgmental gaze boring in, as if an electronic tracker has been implanted within her. Fight as she might, she cannot escape internalizing the dominant standard: "The constitution of the female Subject may be understood as the result of the internalization of the male gaze and the adoption of disciplinary practices which assume the presence of 'a panoptical male connoisseur.'"[12]

David Clines pushes beyond the pressures of internalization that impinge on the woman in the Song and that might still allow for some resistance on her part to a totalizing program of colonization executed by male writers, editors, publishers, and marketers solely for their profit and consumption. As Clines sees it, this commercial enterprise controlled by business*men* is the only way this Song could have survived as *the Song* above all songs—the "top of the pops"—in antiquity. Hence, the passionate woman in the Song is totally a male fantasy, the woman of every man's dreams, a perfectly designed love doll with pull-string cueing the perfectly scripted pillow talk delivered in the sexiest voice. Of course, to mitigate the blatant sexism for more sensitive tastes and to soften the pornography for more sophisticated types, the woman must appear to "want it," to be a happy and willing participant in the fantasy. That's all part of the marketing scheme: "So the Song is the dream of a dream. The male author is dreaming a love poem, and the love poem takes the form of a woman's dream, of a woman dreaming her male lover's words. It is a fetching ventriloquy, this voice that is doubly thrown."[13] So Clines

---

12. Donald C. Polaski, "What Will Ye See in the Shulammite? Women, Power and Panopticism in the Song of Songs," *BibInt* 5 (1997): 76–77. The final phrase derives from Sandra Lee Bartky, "Foucault, Femininity, and the Modernization of Patriarchal Power," in *Feminism and Foucault: Reflections on Resistance*, ed. Irene Diamond and Lee Quinby, 61–96 (Boston: Northeastern University Press, 1988), 72; Polaski (70) cites Bartky's fuller comment regarding "the panoptical male connoisseur who resides within the consciousness of most women."

13. David J. A. Clines, "Why Is There a Song of Songs and What Does It Do to You If You Read It?" in *Interested Parties: The Ideology of Writers and Readers of the Hebrew Bible*, JSOTSup 205, Gender, Culture, Theory 1 (Sheffield: Sheffield Academic, 1995), 104.

nails the Song of Songs with little room to move. This is what the Song *is*, period, and feminist interpreters should get in line with this position: "Even feminist critics sometimes ignore the fact that what we have in this book is not a woman, not the voice of a woman, not a woman's poem, not a portrayal of female experience from a woman's perspective, but always and only what a man imagines for a woman, his construction of femininity."[14]

So much for Falk's and other women scholars' more positive assessments of women's "true" experiences reflected in the Songstress's speech. Clines, normally sympathetic to feminist readings and a pioneer of postmodern biblical studies, seems to dismiss the prevailing feminist-critical appreciation of the Songstress with a definitive pronouncement of the "always and only" legitimate way to read the Song, that is, *not* "from a woman's perspective." But how does *he* know what a woman's perspective is on love and sexuality—or on anything, for that matter—or what a woman does (or should!) feel upon reading the Song of Songs? The only way I know for a man to know anything about what a woman thinks or feels about anything is to *listen* to what she says about her thoughts and feelings, dreams and aspirations. Of course, this doesn't rule out critical response. Indeed, feminist criticism(s) encourages open and honest dialogue, and problems of male cooptation of female voices and women's internalization of patriarchal voices and values are widely acknowledged by feminist critics. Further, most female feminist scholars welcome the engagement of male scholars who take feminism seriously. But until a perfectly equal, nonsexist utopian society dawns (and we remain a long way from that), priority should be given to women's opinions on women's issues, however much women can and will disagree among themselves. This has nothing to do with a man's virtuous humility or sensitivity, graciously giving the ladies a chance to speak, which only reinforces the hierarchy. It is a matter of social justice, but from a quite pragmatic standpoint; those given the greater voice should be those who know most what they're talking about.

So in this introductory section on the Song's vocal expressions and effects, I give the last word to Cheryl Exum, in fact her last point among her "Top Ten" feminist perspectives on the Song:

> *Feminists don't have to deny ourselves the pleasure of the text.* . . . . Why should an ancient author's intention matter? Let's assume for the sake

14. Ibid., 117.

of argument that Clines and Polaski are right, that the subject position
the Song constructs for women is one in which the woman is to see herself as the man sees her; in other words, that the text subtly encourages
women to adopt a male vision of woman. It does not follow that I have
to read it that way. Our protagonist is assertive, determined, and not
least important, vulnerable. This combination makes her an irresistible
subject for further feminist investigation.[15]

Are we (men) listening? Do we hear a Songstress that is "assertive, determined," *and* "vulnerable"? An irresistible feminist subject indeed.

## Harmony and Counterpoint: The Compositional Factor

Two aspects come into play related to the Song's unity and diversity:
the genre and the theme. While there is wide agreement among feminist interpreters concerning the Song's broad classification as erotic love
poetry, on the more particular level, these scholars divide between those
who assess the Song as a single composition reflecting the passionate
longings of the same couple throughout and those who regard it as an
anthology or album of multiple love lyrics from different artists about
different lovers. Again, in the absence of internal headings and copyright
information, this Song/Songs issue remains open to dispute and largely
a matter of reader/hearer-response: how an interpreter, feminist or otherwise, chooses to approach the text. It can be a valuable exercise to take
either stance and see where it leads, since both a single song and a song
collection can be either highly unified or multifarious. One song can be
so complex as to sound like a mixed tape on its own, and an album can
be so formulaic that to hear one song is to hear them all. But I will do well
in this commentary to follow one interpretive trail, and I have chosen
the more direct, one-lane road. Again, Exum nicely charts the way: "The
Song . . . *works* as a unity, so well, in fact, that distinguishing different
voices and attitudes is not easy, and nothing approaching a consensus is
in sight. Even commentators who see the Song as an anthology tend to
read it as though its attitude toward love is uniform and the protagonists
are the same two people throughout."[16]

Still the question of thematic harmony nettles, especially regarding the
equality and mutuality of the female and male lovers in the Song. Are
they blending their embodied voices together—"the two shall become

15. Exum, "Ten Things," 35 (emphasis original).
16. Ibid., 29 (emphasis original).

one flesh" (Gen 2:24)—with consummate balance and intimacy? A number of feminist critics well attuned to sexist biases throughout the Bible in fact hear predominantly egalitarian, Edenic strains of heterosexual harmony in the Song. In Falk's judgment:

> The equally rich, sensual, emotionally expressive, and often playful language of the Song's female and male voices . . . seems to evidence a nonsexist, nonhierarchical culture—unique in the Bible. Rather than offering a reversal of stereotypical male-female relations, the Song provides a different model, one in which *all* hierarchical domination is absent. Thus the Song expresses mutuality and balance between the sexes, along with an absence of stereotyped notions of masculine and feminine behavior and characteristics.[17]

Carol Meyers also affirms a "sustained sense of gender mutuality" in the Song and boldly contends: "In the erotic world of human emotion, there is no subordination of female to male."[18] And Phyllis Trible commends the consistent "depatriarchalizing" tone of the Song: "Like Genesis 2, Canticles affirms mutuality of the sexes. There is no male dominance, no female subordination, and no stereotyping of either sex. The woman is independent, fully the equal of the man."[19] These sweeping assessments of gender equality—using absolute "all/no/fully" language—from pioneering feminist writers in the 1970s and 1980s should not simply be chalked up to premature exuberance over finding something in the Bible for feminists to celebrate without demurral. These are reasoned assessments by thoughtful scholars, and others could be added. And in the feminist hermeneutical repertoire, vibrant moves of remembrance and celebration are just as critical as more cautious steps of resistance and suspicion, especially with such an iconic religious text as the Bible.[20] The vast majority of feminist biblical interpreters have been and remain women and men not just of good faith and integrity but of religious faith and spirituality, Bible-believers in some sense who care enough about the Bible and its God to wrestle with them, like Jacob, until they

---

17. Falk, *Song*, 118 (emphasis original).

18. Carol Meyers, "Gender Imagery in the Song of Songs," in *A Feminist Companion to the Song of Songs*, ed. Athalya Brenner and Carole R. Fontaine, The Feminist Companion to the Bible, 197–212 (Sheffield: Sheffield Academic, 1993), 211.

19. Phyllis Trible, "Depatriarchalizing in Biblical Interpretation," *JAAR* 41 (1973): 45.

20. See Elisabeth Schüssler Fiorenza, *Wisdom Ways: Introducing Feminist Biblical Interpretation* (Maryknoll, NY: Orbis Books, 2001), 1–19, 165–91.

shake out some "blessing." If the cheater-patriarch can do this, why not feminist critics?[21]

More recent feminist interpreters of the Song, however, more deeply informed by polyglot postmodern perspectives, doubt whether any two subjects can ever speak in perfect harmony, whether dialogue ever merges into monologue, whether two bodies ever become fully, equally "one flesh." At the heart of Exum's "Top Ten" list of feminist assessments of the Song, is her own "no" statement: *"There is no gender equality."*[22] The Song depicts no feminist Utopia or Eden. All is not bliss in the couple's love nest. The shocking scene of violence against the woman in the heart of the poem, however briefly narrated (5:7), is enough to scar the woman and her Song permanently. For these reasons, I give considerable attention to this "text of terror" in this commentary, and there are other twists, tensions, and turns worth investigating in the Song, though none, thankfully, quite as terrible as the beating episode.

Nevertheless, the world of the Song is far from Dystopia or Hell. The earlier feminist writers had a point, even if they carried it too far. Though not granting gender equality in the Song, Exum does recognize "gender bending. Erotic coding in the Song crosses conventional gender lines" in terms of common images, like deer and dove, which are applied to and by both male and female lovers (1:15; 2:9, 12, 14, 17; 4:1, 5; 5:12; 6:9; 7:3; 8:14). Thus, "one could argue on the basis of such gender symbolism that the Song destabilizes conventional biblical gender stereotypes."[23] But destabilization is not the same thing as equalization. Constitutional amendments, legislative acts, and Supreme Court decisions have certainly shaken the foundations of sexual and racial discrimination in the United States over the past century and a half and given liberationists much to sing about. But few would argue that America has achieved full social equality. There's a long way to go and much still to lament. But it's better to proceed with realistic hope than abject defeatism. I hear the Song as sounding many positive notes for feminists' interests in women's agency, opportunity, and equality, but not in some Pollyanna naïveté unhinged from reality. I attempt to follow the Song's score carefully

21. See the appropriation of the Jacob story as a model for feminist biblical criticism in Phyllis Trible, *Texts of Terror: Literary-Feminist Readings of Biblical Narratives*, OBT (Philadelphia: Fortress, 1984), 4–5.

22. Exum, "Ten Things," 30 (emphasis original).

23. Ibid.

from measure to measure, alert to discordant detours and minor-key modulations along the way.

## Score and Story: The Choreographical Factor

This matter of following the Song's score from measure to measure merits further explanation as an interpretive schema. This is a reading strategy, pure and simple, privileging no particular agenda, unless reading linearly from start to finish is considered an ideological move. This approach may yield insights with feminist implications, but it is not in and of itself more or less feminist than another literary method. Further, I do not claim this as the only way to study the Song, especially if one views the book as a montage of discrete poems, each demanding independent attention. And even taking the Song as a single entity, as I do, it can be instructive to focus on a particular verse or stanza in Janus-like fashion, correlating it with both preceding and succeeding developments in the Song.

I adopt a somewhat constricted approach of reader-response criticism that carefully tracks the reading process of a literary work sequentially, step-by-step from one segment to the next, resisting the urge to peek ahead and spoil the story's suspense.[24] I aim to let the drama unfold with fresh immediacy, as if experiencing it for the first time.[25] This is impossible to achieve fully with familiar works like the Song of Songs that have already been read or heard in whole or part many times. But for those most familiar with the Song and perhaps inured to its charms and challenges (how many classic hymns do we sing and hear automatically, without thinking?), it can be vital to slow down and try to encounter the Song anew, note-by-note, phrase-by-phrase, without jumping ahead too much. Such is the tour I try to lead in this commentary.

24. See Wolfgang Iser, "The Reading Process: A Phenomenological Approach," in *Reader-Response Criticism: From Formalism to Post-Structuralism*, ed. Jane P. Tompkins (Baltimore: Johns Hopkins University Press, 1980), 50–69; and in the same volume, Stanley E. Fish, "Literature in the Reader: Affective Stylistics," 70–100. Applied to biblical studies, see Robert M. Fowler, *Let the Reader Understand: Reader-Response Criticism and the Gospel of Mark* (Minneapolis: Fortress, 1991), 41–58 and *passim*.

25. This approach, however, is by no means a naïve reading, as it is sometimes called. While striving to maintain an open element of surprise and not to anticipate the story's ending, this reading strategy remains keenly informed by linguistic and cultural knowledge critical to understanding an ancient text.

But this approach to the Song can be problematic, since a progressive reading strategy is best suited for a plotted narrative, which the Song clearly is not. It doesn't even easily fit the category of narrative poetry, certainly not like Homer's epic-poetic sagas or others' countless love ballads, both ancient and modern. Though a few stanzas, like the dream sequence in Song 3:1-5, have an obvious story structure, the poem as a whole is more loosely episodic and quixotic, flowing down a winding stream of consciousness. As Exum discerns, "The Song is a poetic text of great lyrical power and beauty," a sterling model of "lyric poetry, which is essentially a discontinuous form . . . [in which] we normally do not expect the kind of linear unfolding of events that produces a plot." Yet she also acknowledges "the powerful readerly tendency . . . to read for the plot" and "to create a 'story'" for the sake of meaning, a tendency a number of recent commentators on the Song indulge to various degrees even as they admit a lack of overall narrative structure.[26] Ultimately, however, rather than accentuating the Song's narrative development and dynamic, Exum gives priority to its "poetic development" (blossoming images and symbols) and "circular dynamic" (thematic reinforcement). She cautions, "But tempting as it may be, we should be wary of looking for narrative progression in a lyric poem that meanders the way the Song does."[27]

I confess to succumbing to more than resisting the temptation to find narrative threads, however tenuous, holding the Song lovers' experiences together within their special love story, albeit an unending and often untidy one, as love stories tend to be. I grant that the Song's love dance—to shift the artistic image—is more improvisational than choreographed, more like a tango, though with the man and woman alternating lead positions, and less like a ballet pas de deux. But I still see the movement self-consciously moving somewhere rather than just hopping all over the dance floor. Or, to try one more metaphor, I interpret the Song as a series of broadly connected images, scenes, and slides, as in a PowerPoint presentation, rather than a more impressionistic, kaleidoscopic flash barrage, as in old MTV videos.

My motivation to narrativize the Song no doubt owes much, in Exum's terms, to my desire to impose meaning-making structure on the lovers' lyrics, to set these lyrics not simply to inspiring music but also to an informing

---

26. Exum, *Song*, 42. She cites the commentaries of Bergant, Weems, Munro, Landy, Fox, and Garrett (see "Works Cited" in the present volume) as examples of those who appreciate a "narrative dynamic" (42–45).

27. Ibid., 44–45.

storyline. I particularly appeal to the inherent narrative dimension of human emotion, not least that most intensive and pervasive emotion of love, perceived by some philosophers and psychologists. For example, the philosopher Peter Goldie argues, "Our thought and talk of emotions is embedded in an interpretive (and sometimes predictive) narrative which aims to make sense of an aspect of someone's life."[28] Applied to a couple's love life, a man's laconic "because I love her" explanation of any given affectionate gesture encodes a broader network of experience, encompassing "all the episodes of thought and feeling which are involved . . . placing them in the narrative as part of the love you have for her. The complex web of thoughts and feelings is thus summarized, or concertinaed, so to speak, into a simple explanatory phrase: 'Because I love her.' "[29] Similarly, the research psychologist and novelist Keith Oatley observes that emotions are not just random jolts or isolated impulses but "can be sequences of actions and events, based on scripts," especially storied scripts like various "falling-in-love" plots: "Scripts of the amorous enable us to visit worlds of love, and to take rides on the vehicles that transport us into those worlds. The idea of script works perfectly with the idea of story, which is also a sequence of actions and outcomes. . . . In psychological understandings of love . . . to understand anyone's love relationship, one has to understand what kind of story it has at its center."[30]

Again, I do not claim that the Song of Songs tells the love story of any "real" couple in ancient Israel. It is not a historical romance between Solomon and any of his wives or mistresses or between any other actual pair of lovebirds. Neither does the Song unfold an intricate tale of love with the narrative detail and psychological depth of a romantic novel, whether of the dime-store or highbrow variety. But as a passionate love song, the Song of Songs does draw us into a dynamic world of (e)motion, not simply moment, with elements of elation and frustration, fulfilled and unfulfilled longing, projected across past, present, and future time, though not in strict chronological sequence. This strong sense of move-

28. Peter Goldie, *The Emotions: A Philosophical Exploration* (Oxford: Oxford University Press, 2009), 103; and further: "Emotional experience cannot be adequately made sense of in abstraction from the narrative in which it is embedded" (45).

29. Ibid., 42.

30. Keith Oatley, *The Passionate Muse: Exploring Emotion in Stories* (Oxford: Oxford University Press, 2012), 74–75; for his final point about love, Oatley is indebted to Robert J. Sternberg, *Love Is a Story: A New Theory of Relationships* (Oxford: Oxford University Press, 1998); see also Nico H. Frijda, "The Laws of Emotion," *American Psychologist* 43 (1988): 349–58.

ment spurs us readers and hearers to follow the flow, erratic though it
may be, and to keep up as best we can.

Before leaving this brief discussion of the Song's framework, a quick
word is needed about how I've structured this commentary. After the
heading in Song 1:1, I have organized my analysis around fourteen
"stanzas," as I call them. I hasten to add, however, that these are simply
practical divisions for the sake of discussion rather than formal poetic
units. I pay attention to poetic techniques such as parallelism and framing devices, but I make no pretense of tracking the definitive structure
of the Song, of which there is no scholarly consensus, or revealing some
new grand scheme of things.[31] Along with the basic unit of "stanza," I
use common terms such as "segment" and "line" for parts of a stanza,
"Song" or "Poem" for the entire work, and "chapter" and "verse" for numerical references in the NRSV. All biblical citations are from the NRSV,
unless otherwise indicated, and I generally do not indicate where NRSV
versification differs from the Hebrew Bible or Septuagint. I do, however,
annotate the NRSV text printed at the head of each stanza with my judgments regarding who's speaking to whom, which are not always obvious
in English versions (and sometimes ambiguous in the Hebrew text). The
letters "W," "M," and "D" stand for the Woman/Female protagonist,
Man/Male protagonist, and daughters of Jerusalem, respectively, and
the flow of speech is represented by an arrow. Hence, [W → M] signals
the principal woman (Songstress) speaking to her male lover.

## Repertoire and Reputation: The Canonical Factor

Processes of canonization, of circumscribing an official corpus of "approved" writings, naturally capture the suspicious attention of feminist
critics, since canonical judgments are ultimately sanctioned by some authoritative body that is usually male-dominated and necessarily involve
some degree of exclusion since only the chosen few make the grade. More
often than not, women's interests fall outside the canonical circle. This is
certainly true concerning the Jewish and Christian scriptural canons with
most, if not all, books written by men for men in an ancient patriarchal

---

31. For a helpful survey of various proposed structures, see Exum, *Song*, 37–41;
on p. 39 she charts twelve different schemes! I should also say that my 14-stanza
scheme has no numerical significance (say, a "perfect" double-seven pattern) and no
particular correlation with Michael D. Goulder, *The Song of Fourteen Songs*, JSOTSup
36 (Sheffield: JSOT, 1986).

society. But the Bible, comprised of numerous writings composed over centuries, is not the narrowest canon one might imagine and does contain some memorable "women's books," like Ruth, Esther, Judith—and the Song of Songs. Of course, how women are treated in these relatively short pieces and how they fit with the other writings and within the prevailing culture are matters of intense debate. We've already hinted at the complicated issue of women's speech and action in the Song.

The pervasive erotic play and tension in the Song poses a special case in a sacred canon wary of sexual pleasure outside the bonds of marriage and the goals of reproduction, neither of which gets much play in this Poem. Ruth, Esther, and Judith all have their sexy moments, but nothing like the Songstress, and for the most part they stay within the bounds of "proper" conduct. They are all beautiful and desirable and know how to use their sexuality, if necessary, in the interests of national and familial security, but they are far from "loose" women like the prostitutes and adulteresses condemned in Proverbs. The passionate woman in the Song, however, operates more on the edge, dances dangerously close to more suspicious sides of the street(s). Any way you slice it, the Song's presence in the biblical canon flashes like a neon sign signaling its blatant oddity. As Daphne Merkin queries, "How did so conspicuously ungodly a composition—a piece of undeniable erotica, filled with enough sexual punning . . . to make Shakespeare blush—slip by the defenders of the faith, the old men with beards?"[32] Likewise, Ilana Pardes comments regarding the Song, "The canonization of a secular work in which female eroticism is presented so favorably—a rare phenomenon not only in the Bible, but in Western culture as a whole—remains an astonishing phenomenon."[33] So what gives? Did the Song just serendipitously squeak into the Bible as a canonical glitch or more conspiratorially as a deliberate oversight?[34] Did the religious authorities "discreetly look away, recognizing that a religion based on 613 commandments could do with a little leavening, a welcome touch of sensuality"?[35] Or did they suffer some inexplicable blindness when it came to the Song?[36]

---

32. Daphne Merkin, "The Women in the Balcony: On Rereading the Song of Songs," in *Out of the Garden: Women Writers on the Bible*, ed. Christina Büchmann and Celina Spiegel (New York: Fawcett Columbine, 1994), 238–51, at 244.

33. Ilana Pardes, *Countertraditions in the Bible: A Feminist Approach* (Cambridge: Harvard University Press, 1992), 128.

34. Merkin, "Women in the Balcony," 240.

35. Ibid., 244.

36. Pardes, *Countertraditions*, 128–29.

Merkin and Pardes ultimately propose more substantive answers to their canonical questions, each related, interestingly enough, to the city "watchmen" in the Song who "find" and briefly meet the woman out searching for her lover one evening and assault her on another (3:3-4; 5:6-7)! Merkin accentuates the harsh police action of the canonical guards: "Radical as its inclusion in the canon of Holy Scriptures may appear to be, I suggest it is less surprising if one sees this amorous dialogue in the form of a warning—a prophylaxis, as Gerson Cohen calls it: Caution ye seekers of passion, lest you end up lost and wandering, in a city with no name, reduced to calling on the help of anonymous and hostile 'watchmen.'"[37] Pardes, however, is more charitable toward the custodians of the canon and the sentinels of the city: "Why was the Song canonized? Let me suggest that . . . those who set the limits on the sacred corpus were in fact not unlike the keepers of the walls in the Song. Just as the guards in the Song are neither omnipotent nor innocent of desires, so the watchmen of Holy Writ could not fully prevent the admission of ideologically alien voices within the canon, especially those other voices which filled (unconscious) needs in the biblical array."[38]

Yet, however plausible these theories may appear, they remain speculative, since the process of biblical canonization is shrouded in mystery. It's difficult to believe that the early rabbis and church fathers signed off on the Song with a quick nod and wink or, worse, dozed off when the Song came up for discussion. Surely they knew the hot potato they had in their hands and gave it due attention. But we have scant evidence of the debate.[39] Our best clue comes from the testimony of Rabbi Akiva (c. 50–135 CE) in the Mishnah, asserting, "Heaven forbid!—No Israelite man ever disputed concerning Song of Songs that it imparts uncleanness to hands" (m. Yad. 3:5).[40] Here the notion of transmitting uncleanness has

---

37. Merkin, "Women in the Balcony," 249. The Cohen reference is to Gerson D. Cohen, *Studies in the Variety of Rabbinic Cultures* (Philadelphia: JPS, 1991), xv.

38. Pardes, *Countertraditions*, 142–43. In my judgment, however, the watchmen in the Song are thoroughly antagonistic characters (see commentary on 5:7).

39. See the helpful general discussions related to the Song's canonization in Exum, *Song*, 70–73; Fox, *Song*, 247–52; Pardes, *Countertraditions*, 118–43; Roland E. Murphy, *The Song of Songs*, Hermeneia (Minneapolis: Fortress, 1990), 5–7; Tremper Longman, III, *The Song of Songs*, NICOT (Grand Rapids: Eerdmans, 2001), 56–58; and Alicia Ostriker, "A Holy of Holies: The Song of Songs as Countertext," in *The Song of Songs*, ed. Athalya Brenner and Carole R. Fontaine, FCB, Second Series, 36–54 (Sheffield: Sheffield Academic, 2000).

40. Translation by Jacob Neusner, *The Mishnah: A New Translation* (New Haven: Yale University Press, 1988); cited in Exum, *Song*, 70–71.

to do with the book's powerful sanctity, not its impurity, as the "holiest" of all sacred writings. It is so holy in Akiva's view that all human hands, however well scrubbed, are automatically unclean in comparison and should handle the Song with only the greatest care or not at all; pointers or cloths could be used as intermediaries.[41] The fact, however, that Akiva felt compelled to deliver such a strong and sweeping apologia for the Song—he doth protest too much—suggests that some had indeed disputed his claim, perhaps contending that the Song itself was too dirty to handle. In all likelihood, then, the Song was just as controversial among early Jewish authorities as that other strange piece of wisdom associated with Solomon, the book of Qoheleth (Ecclesiastes), which Akiva acknowledges as a contested canonical candidate.

Another tradition attributes to Akiva a further cautionary word concerning the Song: "Whoever warbles the Song of Songs in a banquet hall, treating it like an ordinary song, has no share in the world to come" (t. Sanh. 12:10; cf. b. Sanh. 101a).[42] Again, the good Rabbi's admonition betrays a counter-opinion and probably a common practice of singing the Song in banquet halls and festival centers. What better accompaniment for such occasions than a lively love song invoking a banquet house setting (Song 2:4) and frequently celebrating the joys of rich food, drink, and fellowship? The Song of Songs may well have originated in such a venue as a piece of entertainment, but that doesn't mean it was a purely "secular" composition, still less a blue-movie sound track. The many festivals featured in the Jewish calendar have always blended secular/religious, ordinary/sacred, and bodily/spiritual elements in celebrating earthly life as a gift of the Creator God. Dualistic splits in cosmology and anthropology are largely creations of Western (Greek) thought. Hence, it's no surprise that the Song (or Canticles) came to be grouped with Ruth, Esther, Ecclesiastes, and Lamentations as the five *Megillot* or Festival Scrolls traditionally sung at respective annual festivals. The Song eventually became the anthem for the weeklong Passover holidays, which included many joyous indulgent festive events along with more contemplative acts of prayer, worship, and sacrifice.[43] Christian adherents so accustomed to associating Passover with Jesus' solemn Last Supper on Maundy Thursday, the eve of his crucifixion, can easily

41. Pardes, *Countertraditions*, 120.

42. Translation by Jacob Neusner, *The Talmud of Babylonia: An American Translation* (Chico, CA: Scholars Press, 1985); cited in Exum, *Song*, 70.

43. Fox, *Song*, 247–52; Exum, *Song*, 72.

lose sight of the larger Passover picture and wonder why in the world anyone would "warble the Song of Songs" on this occasion, as if it were a folk concert or a club set.

But Akiva's concerns ran in the other direction. He thought that the Song was appropriate *only* for the most sacred occasions and *never* for the banquet hall, even with its festive language. While the whole earth is the Lord's, there's an apt time and place for everything under heaven, as Qoheleth insisted in Eccl 3:1-15, and Akiva believed that the Song should never be performed in a banquet hall "like an ordinary song." Nothing wrong with love songs in general sung at celebratory feasts, just not this holiest of Songs. One needs to match the right music with the right ambience. The Lord lamented once to the prophet Ezekiel that the people were missing his serious message of judgment during a period of national crisis because they mistook him for "a singer of love songs, one who has a beautiful voice and plays well on an instrument; they hear what you say, but they will not do it" (Ezek. 33:32).[44] Again, love songs are ordinarily fine, just not, to return to Akiva, *this* Song at any ordinary time.

But Akiva's restriction doesn't solve the problem of the Song's lyrical contents, which, in their gushing about a torrid romance, reflect the longings of ordinary people about the most basic human drives for love and sexual intimacy, and never once (well, maybe once, 8:6) mention God! How can a book be holy without explicitly honoring God? (The book of Esther has the same problem.) Clearly, Akiva was convinced by some method of nonliteral, spiritual interpretation that the Song of Songs did honor the holy God through and through. What that method was we don't know, but it likely involved some type of allegorizing the lovers as God (male) and Israel (female), which became the standard Jewish approach until the modern era, matched by Christian adaptations of God into the Christ-figure and Israel into the church as the bride of Christ. So interpreted, the Song was best suited for cantors and choirs in synagogues and churches and fell off the repertoire of torch singers and jazz bands in banquet halls. That's the way it often goes as books and songs get into circulation; they take on a life of their own, whatever the composers' original intentions, and if they're lucky, like the Song of Songs, they keep being published for centuries, long past the time when authors have any say over their reception.

44. See Fox, *Song*, 248–49; Clines, "Why Is There a Song?," 101.

But whatever may be gained by such a dynamic process, a price is also paid: something is lost, perhaps even something vital to the work's core essence, which may still be argued for without claiming that it captures the only valid meaning. Regarding the canonical Song interpreted in purely spiritual terms, the casualty is sexuality and not only in its most worldly, carnal expressions but also in its more sublime, metaphysical aspects. Allegorical readings of the Song may efface its sexual dimensions as much as embroider them, if not more so. Clines contends "that the history of its interpretation is one of a massive repression of sexuality, of denial of the book's ostensible subject matter, a testimony especially to male fear of female sexuality."[45] That overstates the case, however. For medieval monks, the response seems less one of repression than redirection. The great twelfth-century theologian Bernard of Clairvaux, for example, spent eighteen years meditating on the Song's first two chapters and crystallizing his thoughts into eighty-six sermons.[46] This was no dry sermon series sketched out in a dusty cell because he happened, say, to be a scholarly specialist in the later Hebrew idiom of Song manuscripts. Brother Bernard was personally and passionately committed to the Song as a call to embodied passionate union with the incarnate passionate Christ as the highest and deepest experience of God's love. As William Loyd Allen concludes, "[Bernard] may have had a distorted view of human sexuality; he may have failed personally to love as he felt loved; but he did not fail to see the erotic ardor between a woman and a man as an ideal representation of the higher Truth from which it first sprang."[47] To make things even more interesting, we should not ignore that, in this intense nearly two-decades-long engagement with the Song, Bernard, like other monks, would have assumed the subject position of the Song's *woman* in relation to the loving male Christ figure. From the start, "Let him kiss me with the kisses of his mouth" (1:2) would mark for Bernard a longing for eroticized spiritual intimacy with Christ on a mystical, gender-bending, homosexualized plane, but no less fervently felt for its metaphorical state.[48]

45. Clines, "Why Is There a Song?,"113.

46. See Carey Ellen Walsh, *Exquisite Desire: Religion, the Erotic, and the Song of Songs* (Minneapolis: Fortress, 2000), 198–201; William Loyd Allen, "Bernard of Clairvaux's *Sermons on the Songs*: Why They Matter," *RevExp* 105 (2008): 403–16; and Kristin Johnston Largen, "The Erotic Passion of God," *Dialog* 49 (2010): 7–8.

47. Allen, "Bernard of Clairveaux's *Sermons*," 413.

48. See the provocative article by Stephen D. Moore, "The Song of Songs in the History of Sexuality," *Church History* 69 (2000): 328–49.

Nuns and other sisters of the church might have an easier, more "natural" entry into the love bond with Christ via the Songstress, but what about modern feminist women, whether professionally or personally religious or not? Feminism's fundamental commitment to embodied female life in all its facets—not least female sexuality—free from the stifling stays of male oppression and repression does not sit well with exploitations of the female body for others' interests, whether subtle or overt, allegorical or literal. Such commitment to women's choice and agency holds even in the face of purportedly noble appropriations, as in the interest of knowing God or Christ with utmost intimacy.[49] Hence, I know of no feminist interpretation of the Song that does not appreciate its basic character as erotic poetry extolling the virtues and vicissitudes of natural, passionate human love. But a Jewish or Christian feminist reader of the Song may certainly *choose* to expand her (or his) interpretive horizon into the spiritual realm, to appropriate the book as a theological-spiritual resource in addition to or in tandem with its natural-sexual elements. Recalling Exum's tenth point, quoted above, feminists are free to sing the Song as they will. Exum chiefly has in mind reading against the grain of sexist (mis)readings, but she would doubtless allow for additive spiritual or devotional readings, though she herself rarely ventures into this territory in her commentary. Neither do I in the present volume, as I keep the spotlight trained on the "natural" plane of primary concern to most feminist interpreters. But other writers, on various points of the feminist-critical spectrum, happily engage in more multilevel reflections of this multifaceted Song.[50]

49. For a superb discussion of feminist theory's emphases on women's embodiment and agency and their implications for theological experience, see Serene Jones, *Feminist Theory and Christian Theology: Cartographies of Grace*, Guides to Theological Inquiry (Minneapolis: Augsburg Fortress, 2000), 1–68.

50. For thoughtful reflections on the spirituality and theology of the Song, see, from a Jewish view, the magisterial new commentary by Fishbane (*Song*), in which, following the traditional rabbinic "Pardes" method of scriptural interpretation, he tracks throughout the Song four levels of analysis: *peshat* (literal/plain meaning), *remez* (allegorical/symbolic approach), *derash* (comparative/midrashic reading), and *sod* (mystical/spiritual insights); Debra Band, *The Song of Songs: The Honeybee in the Garden* (Philadelphia: JPS, 2005), which is illustrated by the author with stunning color paintings, four of which appear in grayscale, with accompanying commentary, in the present volume; Ostriker, "Holy of Holies." From a Christian perspective, see Carr, *Erotic Word*; Walsh, *Exquisite Desire*; Ellen F. Davis, *Proverbs, Ecclesiastes, and the Song of Songs*, Westminster Bible Companion (Louisville: Westminster John Knox, 2000), 231–302; Stephanie Paulsell, "The Song of Songs," in, *Lamentations and the*

Carey Ellen Walsh strikes a particularly attractive tone that I think most religiously inclined feminists would appreciate, even if it doesn't reflect their main approach. Walsh envisions the Song as "a celebration of all things of human life. . . . [It] is in essence, a spiritual book . . . concerned with the responses of the soul to life and its pleasures. As such, it is neither secular nor religious, since these are modern categories and carriers of dualism."[51] Encountering this remarkable work thus "yields a renewed sense of the erotic as a human energy, a life-enhancing response to the world," what the modern poet Octavio Paz pinpoints as "the luminous side of eroticism, its radiant approval of life."[52] More fully, Walsh expounds her holistic take on the Song:

> Discerning the spiritual dimension of the Song is potentially the most rewarding part of the investigation. For if there can be a unity of the spiritual and sexual impulses, then we have come a long way toward healing the rift between religion and sex, between the spirit and the body. And we catch biblical testimony to the sheer glee of being human, without caveat or reflex, religious promises to keep trying harder. Religion of the latter kind can wear one out. Sexual energy can wreak havoc, of course, but that potency itself does not make it sinful. The Song's unremitting, unabashed attention to desire provides a needed heuristic salve for those who have been emotionally splintered by religion.[53]

As one still picking out painful splinters from an early age, I can only say: Amen and Amen.

---

*Song of Songs*, Belief: A Theological Commentary on the Bible, ed. Harvey Cox and Stephanie Paulsell (Louisville: Westminster John Knox, 2012), 169–276; Christopher West, *Heaven's Song: Sexual Love as It Was Meant to Be* (West Chester, PA: Ascension, 2008); and Iain M. Duguid, *The Song of Songs: An Introduction and Commentary*, TOTC (Downers Grove, IL: InterVarsity Press Academic, 2015).

51. Walsh, *Exquisite Desire*, 191.

52. Ibid., 187; citing Octavio Paz, *The Double Flame: Love and Eroticism* (Orlando, FL: Harcourt Brace, 1995), 25.

53. Ibid., 193.

# Song of Songs 1:1

## *Heading*

This title, whether original or editorial, provides three guide-lines for interpretation. First, it assumes a singular song (שִׁיר) best heard, read, or sung as a whole, in one sitting. Though comprised of multiple stanzas featuring various voices and love themes in a panoply of luscious images, the Song brings all these elements together into one stunning performance. The rich tones, tensions, points, and counter-points of this complex symphony alternately thrill and chill, delight and disturb the hearer/reader.

Second, the heading dares to claim this Song as superlative: the "Song of Songs" (שִׁיר הַשִּׁירִים), that is, in the Hebrew idiom, the Song above all others, the "supreme song" or "songiest of songs," as David J. A. Clines quips.[1] The wide and long popularity of this book among Jewish and Christian commentators bears out its exalted title. Witness Rabbi Akiva's famous encomium: "For all the ages are not worth the day on which the Song of Songs was given to Israel; for all the *Ketuvim* are holy, but the Song of Songs is the Holy of Holies" (m. Yad. 3.5). Of course, the "holy

---

1. David J. A. Clines, "Why Is There a Song of Songs and What Does It Do to You If You Read It?," in *Interested Parties: The Ideology of Writers and Readers of the Hebrew Bible*, JSOTSup 205, Gender, Culture, Theory 1 (Sheffield: Sheffield Academic, 1995), 99.

*Song of Songs 1:1*

¹The Song of Songs, which is Solomon's.

of holies" comparison works best with an allegorical reading of the Song unfolding the covenantal love between God and Israel (or, for Christians, between Christ and the church). But even if we choose not to go that route, at least not as our primary interpretive path, the Song's soaring language and imagery lifts us above the banal puppy-love musings of a pop song into more hymnic and spiritual dimensions of dynamic love "strong as death" (Song 7:6).[2]

Third, the Song bears a Solomonic stamp; it is related to (ל-prefix) though not authored by Israel's renowned king. The Song names Solomon in three places (1:5; 3:7-11; 8:11-12), each reflecting his royal splendor, and refers to an unnamed "king" three other times (1:4, 12; 7:5). In all but one of these cases, the female protagonist extols her male lover; in the lone exception (7:5), the male speaker associates himself with a king "held captive" by the woman's luxurious locks. The persona of Solomon and the royal imagery characterizing both lovers—the woman is compared to a queen or princess in 6:8-9; 7:1—embroider the couple's relationship in the Song, but the Poem does not chronicle the amorous experiences of the historical Solomon. Rather, it evokes Solomon's iconic reputation not only for wisdom and power but also, in sharp counterpoint, for womanizing and exploitation.

With his thousand foreign wives and concubines, opulent self-indulgence, and forced labor of his own people as well as non-Israelites for his massive building projects (1 Kgs 5:13-18; 9:15-22; 11:1-13, 26-28; 12:1-11; cf. Eccl 2:1-11), Solomon is scarcely a feminist hero. He uses people, not least women, for his personal pleasures and profits—quite the opposite of the picture of mutual love that the Song supports. The Song may be viewed, then, in some sense as revising (redeeming) Solomon's notorious past or, perhaps, as returning to his humbler and wiser royal roots before accumulating extraordinary wealth and power (see 1 Kgs 3–4). But the full picture remains to be seen as we work through the Song. With feminist lenses firmly fixed, we read not only with hopeful anticipa-

---

2. On the spirituality of the Song, see the Introduction, lxiii–lxiv n. 50, and the related discussion.

tion—this is the Song of Songs!—but also with watchful reservation. We know how kings, real and imagined, can operate, not least in pursuits of love. We know how women under enormous societal pressures can internalize dominant perspectives to their disadvantage.[3] The Song must be sung—and suspected.[4]

3. On internalization of prevailing sexist values, see Phyllis Chesler, *Women's Inhumanity to Woman*, 2nd ed. (Chicago: Lawrence Hill, 2009), xxi, 1–34; Donald C. Polaski, "What Will Ye See in the Shulammite? Women, Power and Panopticism in the Song of Songs," *BibInt* 5 (1997): 68–81.

4. On the foundational hermeneutic of suspicion employed in feminist biblical interpretation, see Elisabeth Schüssler Fiorenza, *Wisdom Ways: Introducing Feminist Biblical Interpretation* (Maryknoll, NY: Orbis Books, 2001), 175–77; F. Scott Spencer, *Salty Wives, Spirited Mothers, and Savvy Widows: Capable Women of Purpose and Persistence in Luke's Gospel* (Grand Rapids, MI: Eerdmans, 2012), 24–54.

# Song of Songs 1:2-8

## *Comfortable (Mostly) in Her Own Voice and Skin*

The Song begins robustly in *medias res* with the lead voice of the woman addressing her male lover. She primarily speaks to him in the second person, with occasional slippage into a more formal, respectful third-person viewpoint: "Let him kiss me . . . for your love"; "Draw me after you. . . . The king has brought me" (1:2, 4).[1] The male voice is not heard until the final verse of this stanza (1:8).

While the intimate relationship of the couple forms the principal theme, a wider circle of interest soon becomes evident, encompassing the woman's female friends ("maidens," "daughters of Jerusalem" [1:5]) and brothers ("my mother's sons" [1:6]) and the man's male coworkers ("flocks of your companions" [1:8]). And while the overall tone is joyous and playful, certain ominous and hurtful strains darken the mood temporarily (1:5-6). The

---

1. On the issue of "grammatical person," see Michael V. Fox, *The Song of Songs and the Ancient Egyptian Love Songs* (Madison: University of Wisconsin Press, 1985), 97. Fox writes, "The lovers often address each other in the third person, sometimes switching back and forth rapidly from third to second person (e.g., 1:12; 2:1-3; 4:6; 6:9; 7:11). Third-person address carries a special tone of respect" (see 265–66). Passionate desire and considerate respect go hand in hand in the bedroom.

*Song of Songs 1:2-8*

**[W → M]**
²Let him kiss me with the kisses of
   his mouth!
For your love is better than wine,
   ³your anointing oils are fragrant,
your name is perfume poured out;
   therefore the maidens love you.
⁴Draw me after you, let us make
   haste.
The king has brought me into
   his chambers.
We will exult and rejoice in you;

we will extol your love more
   than wine;
rightly do they love you.
**[W → D]**
⁵I am black and beautiful,
   O daughters of Jerusalem,
like the tents of Kedar,
   like the curtains of Solomon.
⁶Do not gaze at me because I am
   dark,
   because the sun has gazed
      on me.

tension focuses on related optic, aesthetic, and somatic perceptions: how one views or "gaze[s] at" (1:6) and values the woman's body, especially her "dark" complexion. For the most part, she surmounts the narrow "beauty myths" of her society,[2] buoyed by the patent admiration of her lover. But the fact that she defends her beauty perhaps betrays an undercurrent of insecurity in the face of cultural stereotypes.

## Wining and Pining (1:2-4)

The lead woman vocalist eschews polite overture or foreplay, plunging right in to expressing her deep desire for her lover that brooks no delay: "let's run [רוץ]!" (1:4, CEB; similarly NJPS: "we will run after thee"). Her approach is unabashedly sensual, both in its erotic longing and in its somatic engagement of all five senses. Touch, taste, and smell are explicitly cited; hearing is presumed in the act of speaking/singing; so too, seeing is implied, but less strongly, as the pleas for contact—"Let him kiss me" (1:2); "Draw me after you" (1:4)—suggest a pining for intimate presence not currently realized. But this is no pure fantasy in the mind of a lovesick girl. She has previously experienced and enjoyed sexual relations with her "royal" lover—"The king has brought me into his chambers" (1:4)[3]—

---

2. See Naomi Wolf, *The Beauty Myth: How Images of Beauty Are Used Against Women*, 2nd ed. (New York: Harper Perennial, 2002); Ellen Zetzel Lambert, *The Face of Love: Feminism and the Beauty Question* (Boston: Beacon, 1995).

3. The Hiphil perfect form of בוא ("has brought") suggests causative, completed action.

My mother's sons were angry with me;
they made me keeper of the vineyards,
but my own vineyard I have not kept.

**[W → M]**

⁷Tell me, you whom my soul loves,
where you pasture your flock,
where you make it lie down at noon;

for why should I be like one who is veiled
beside the flocks of your companions?

**[M → W]**

⁸If you do not know,
O fairest among women,
follow the tracks of the flock,
and pasture your kids beside the shepherds' tents.

and she longs for more of the same. This happy yet poignant tension—at once pleasant and painful[4]—between love's anticipation and satisfaction as well as the lovers' presence and absence runs throughout the Song. A further tension simmers regarding the agency of the lovers. While the woman seems content to be wooed, "drawn," and "brought" by her male lover, she remains very active, collaborative (*"let us* run"), and directive (*"let him* kiss me") in the relationship. As the Song unfolds, both parties find themselves swept up in love's overwhelming currents beyond their total control. But neither surrenders personal agency altogether, and the woman may well be the strongest swimmer.

The woman conveys her passionate delight in bodily sensations in vivid language and imagery with no trace of prudery or disgust. Tactile experience leads the way with the woman's particular longing for multiple mouth kisses—no peck on the cheek will do—and her broader excitement about her lover's gestures of passion. "Your love[s]" (דדיך), which appears twice, framing the segment in 1:2 and 1:4, is plural in Hebrew and connotes the more physical activity of "love-makings" and "caresses" than the psychological attitude of love.[5]

4. See Aristotle's classic definition of emotions or passions (*pathē*) as a mix of pleasure and pain in *Rhet.* 2.1.8 (see 4 Macc 1:20-28).

5. Fox, *Song*, 97; J. Cheryl Exum, *Song of Songs*, OTL (Louisville: Westminster John Knox, 2005), 91; William J. Holladay, *A Concise Hebrew and Aramaic Lexicon of the Old Testament* (Grand Rapids: Eerdmans, 1971), 68. The LXX and Vg. mistranslate the term as "breasts." The Song will frequently refer to the allure of breasts in love-making, but usually applied to the woman's body.

Closely connected with tactile delights of lovemaking are gustatory sensations. Kisses "of his mouth" (פה, 1:2) are at once tasted as well as felt, and the woman extols her beloved's lovemakings as "better than wine" (1:2), whose piquant flavor immediately strikes lips, tongue, and palate, then "rightly" (1:4) or smoothly[6] flows down the throat and sends a tingle throughout the body. Of course, the delectable joys of wine owe in the first place to nature's fruitfulness. From the start, the Song celebrates holistic, interconnected experience of love between embodied persons grounded in God's good earth from which human life sprang and to which it will return (see Gen 2:7-9; 3:19).

The olfactory is the most sensitive of the five senses and most evocative after the initial scent has dissipated. Wine stimulates the nose even before it touches the lips, and at the heart of this segment are parallel lines announcing the lover's captivating fragrance. The woman recalls the bracing aroma of her lover's applied colognes mixing with his natural odors. Indeed, she only has to speak or think his name for his titillating smell to permeate or be "poured out" (1:3) into her environment.[7] The Song never reveals either lover's given name, but the pun on "name" (שם, *shem*) and "perfume" (שמן, *shemen*) suggests the "powerful sensual impact" of the male lover's person on the woman.[8] Moreover, his delicious scent is so pungent and pervasive that it wafts beyond the woman to stimulate other "maidens" (עלמות, young women, 1:3). Such shared experience at this stage, however, prompts neither competitive jealousy among the young women nor playing the field by the attractive man.

The erotic mix of senses celebrated here bears a provocative resemblance to the seductive charms of the "loose" or "strange" woman in Proverbs, variously cast as a prostitute or adulteress, who brazenly

---

6. Taking מישר (from the root for "straight") in 1:4 as "smoothly" rather than "rightly" (NRSV), in association with wine's smooth flow down the throat and lulling affect on the drinker, as in Song 7:9 and Prov 23:31; see Fox, *Song*, 99; John G. Snaith, *The Song of Songs*, New Century Bible Commentary (London: Marshall Pickering, 1993), 17.

7. The verb for "pour/empty out" (תורק) in 1:3 has a feminine subject that clashes with the masculine forms for "perfume" and "name" applied to the male lover. Most commentators acknowledge the awkwardness and leave it there; some, however, prefer various emendations, including the possibility that the term refers to a particular type of oil (תורק) or its native region (*Turaq*), otherwise unknown. See the discussion in Michael Fishbane, *Song of Songs*, JPS Bible Commentary (Lincoln: University of Nebraska Press, 2015), 29.

8. Marcia Falk, *The Song of Songs: A New Translation and Interpretation* (New York: HarperCollins, 1990), 167–68.

"seizes and kisses" (7:13) a vulnerable young man and lures him with "lips smoother than oil" (5:3) to her intoxicating perfumed bed, masking diabolical "chambers of death" (7:27; see 5:3-6; 6:24-29; 7:5-27). The woman who opens the Song matches the Proverbial loose woman's aggressive, sensual passion, but then, so does the "wise woman" and "good wife" of Proverbs (see Prov 1:20-33; 5:18-19; 8:1-21; 9:1-6).[9] The critical character distinctions have to do with the life-bringing or death-dealing ends of these figures' behavior, not their erotic means. The Song commences with no hint of death or deception. The tone is thoroughly exuberant, jubilant, and intoxicating in the best, invigorating sense of wine's beneficence.[10] Moreover, while the Song's male lover is enthralled by the passionate woman, he is not entrapped against his better judgment: he brings her "into *his* chambers" (Song 1:4; contra Prov 7:16-27).[11]

To be sure, the lack of marital language defining the relationship of the Song's lovers breaks the confines of the good wife's world. But this wider world of love is just as "good," if not "better" (טובים, Song 1:2-3) than any other arrangement. Even so, that doesn't mean all is bliss or without tension, as the next segment implies.

## Black but Beautiful (1:5-6)

The mood of communal exultation—"*we* will exult . . . *we* will extol" (1:4b)—suddenly modulates to the woman's more personal and polemical exhortation toward antagonists in her inner circle of friends and family. She still remains confident and assertive, but from a more defensive posture. The problem is not with her lover but with her female associates and her brothers, and the problem is not, in the first place, with her love but with her looks. So she flatly declares: "I am black, but beautiful!" (1:5, my translation; the verb-less Hebrew is crisper: "black-I-but-beautiful"). Since the woman makes this assertion to counter the disdainful glances and "gazes" she receives "*because* I am dark" (1:6), I favor reading the *waw* (ו) conjunction as adversative ("but, yet") rather than consecutive

9. See Gale A. Yee, " 'I Have Perfumed My Bed with Myrrh': The Foreign Woman (ʾiššâ zārâ) in Proverbs 1–9," *JSOT* 43 (1989): 53–68; *Poor Banished Children of Eve: Woman as Evil in the Hebrew Bible* (Minneapolis: Fortress, 2003), 149–58.

10. See Woman Wisdom's invitation: "Come, . . . drink of the wine I have mixed," (Prov 9:2, 6).

11. For a careful comparison of the portraits of the Song woman and both the "strange" and "good" women in Proverbs 1–9, see Kathryn Imray, "Love Is (Strong as) Death: Reading the Song of Songs through Proverbs 1–9," *CBQ* 75 (2013): 649–65.

("and").[12] But, as F. W. Dobbs-Allsopp argues, informed by the Algerian feminist theorist Hélène Cixous, the same protest can be lodged more positively and playfully with appropriate accentuation: "I am black *and* beautiful!"[13] Conversational tone can be tricky to detect in written discourse, especially when speakers first appear in a poem or narrative and we are just beginning to hear their voices and read their characters. Fundamentally, however, we encounter the Song as scripted discourse with no embedded notes about staging or oral performance within a scriptural canon that, as biblical scholar Lauress Wilkins Lawrence notes in her perceptive essay included here, "Beautiful Black Women and the Power of Love (Song 1:5)," periodically esteems lighter skin over blacker or, conversely, deems darker skin as inferior or suspect in some way (Job 30:30; Lam 4:7-8; Sir 25:17).

### Beautiful Black Women and the Power of Love (Song 1:5)

"No wonder," said Hagar. "No wonder."

"No wonder what?" asked Pilate.

"Look at how I look. I look awful. No wonder he didn't want me. I look terrible. . . . Oh, Lord. My head. Look at that." She peered into the compact mirror again. "I look like a ground hog. Where's the comb?"[14]

What African American woman has not, at some point in her life, experienced a moment of panic like Hagar did in Toni Morrison's *Song of Solomon*? Bombarded by advertising images and cultural icons of blue-eyed blondes with Barbie-like dimensions,[15] it is not

---

12. Following the Vg. (*nigra sum sed* [but] *formonsa*) against the NRSV and NAB ("and").

13. F. W. Dobbs-Allsopp, " 'I am Black *and* Beautiful': The Song, Cixous, and *Écriture Féminine*," in *Engaging the Bible in a Gendered World: An Introduction to Feminist Biblical Interpretation in Honor of Katharine Doob Sakenfeld*, ed. Linda Day and Carolyn Pressler (Louisville: Westminster John Knox, 2006), 128–40.

14. Toni Morrison, *Song of Solomon* (New York: New American Library, 1977), 312.

15. Naomi Wolf (*The Beauty Myth: How Images of Beauty are Used Against Women* [New York: W. Morrow, 1991]) offers an early discussion of a range of issues related to "the beauty myth" in Western culture. In addition, volumes of feminist criticism have been written about the deleterious impact that the iconic Barbie doll has had on women of all races. For example, see Mary Rogers, *Barbie Culture*, Cultural Icons Series (Thousand Oaks, CA: Sage, 1999); and M. G. Lord, *Forever Barbie: The Unauthorized Biography of a Real Doll* (New York: Avon, 1995).

uncommon for African American women, even in the twenty-first century, to have internalized "the beauty myth" that only women who are "White, young, slim, tall, and [from a socioeconomic] upper class" can hope to attain the standards of beauty operative in the United States and countries influenced by its culture.[16] According to the informal but very influential rules of that cultural framework, the only way an African American woman could be considered beautiful is "if her hair was straight, her skin light, and her features European; in other words, if she was as nearly indistinguishable from a white woman as possible."[17] No wonder Hagar, with her dark skin and kinky hair, thought that her efforts to attract her mate were doomed! What if she had had the self-knowledge and confidence expressed by the female lover (Scott Spencer's "Songstress") in the biblical Song of Solomon? Then would Hagar have known how truly loved and lovable she was? Would she have recognized and celebrated the beauty in her mirrored image, instead of being driven by that image tragically to her death?

Song 1:5 is the only verse in the Bible that juxtaposes the Hebrew terms שחורה ("black") and נאוה ("beautiful"). It's tempting, especially as an African American woman whose childhood coincided with the US Civil Rights Movement in the 1950s and 1960s, to embrace the NRSV's word choice of "and" instead of the equally correct "but" for the Hebrew ו that connects the two descriptors; hence, "I am black *and* beautiful" (Song 1:5; emphasis mine). But an affirmative reading of that ambiguous conjunction is not consistent with other biblical references to black (or blackened) skin. For example, in Song 1:6, the Songstress explains, in a tone that is defensive and almost apologetic, that her blackness (שחרחרת, "dark") is the result of having labored long hours in her brothers' sun-drenched vineyards. The book of Lamentations describes the skin of Zion's princes, which had been "whiter than milk" prior to Jerusalem's fall, but had become "blacker [שחור] than soot" as a result of postwar famine and disease (Lam 4:7-8). Similarly, a much-beleaguered Job laments, "My skin turns black [שחר] and falls from me, and my bones burn with heat" (Job 30:30). Darkened skin is even associated with moral evil, according to the author of the

16. Tracey Owen Patton, "Hey Girl, Am I More than My Hair? African American Women and Their Struggles with Beauty, Body Image, and Hair," *NWSA Journal* 18 (2006): 24–51 (esp. 30).

17. Michele Wallace, *Black Macho and the Myth of the Superwoman* (New York: Dial, 1979), 158; cited in Patton, "Hey Girl," 26.

book of Sirach, who declares that "a woman's wickedness changes her appearance, and darkens her face like that of a bear" (Sir 25:17)![18]

To be sure, these references indicate a temporary darkening of the skin due to challenging circumstances: manual labor outdoors, famine- or disease-induced blemishes, etc. The observation holds, however, that most biblical characters identified as of African descent (and presumably with African physiological features like dark skin) are also described in negative or at best ambivalent terms. For example, the Egyptian maid Hagar, for whom Morrison's character is named, is "abandoned" by Abraham,[19] to whom she has by force borne a son (Gen 21); Moses' wife Zipporah is ridiculed by his sister Miriam for her Ethiopian heritage (Num 12).[20] Pharaoh King of Egypt and his taskmasters and army defiantly oppress the Israelites until Israel's God crushes the Africans in a confrontation that is recounted frequently in the Deuteronomistic History and the prophetic corpus.[21] And Jeremiah famously refers to an Ethiopian whose skin cannot be washed white to illustrate the impossibility of purifying the character of those "who are accustomed to do[ing] evil" (Jer 13:23).[22] In short, though it's tempting to interpret Song 1:5 in a way that resonates with post–

18. In Sir 25:17, the Greek term for "darkens" (σκοτόω) is the same term used in Lam 4:8 and Job 30:30 (LXX). However, Song 1:5-6 (LXX) uses a different term, μέλαινα, which literally means "black" (see the contrasting word pair λεύκην/μέλαιναν [white-black] in Matt 5:36).

19. The name "Hagar" may be an apparent word-play on an Arabic term for "abandonment." See *Hebrew and English Lexicon with Appendix Containing the Biblical Aramaic* (Peabody, MA: Hendrickson, 1979), 212.

20. Though because of this "rebellion" against Moses' authority, Miriam, presumably somewhat dark-skinned herself, is punished with leprosy that makes her "as snow" (כשלג, NAB, NRSV, NIV), perhaps connoting "snow-white scales" (NJPS).

21. Notable exceptions to this observation include the Ethiopian Ebed-melech who rescues the prophet Jeremiah from unjust imprisonment and certain death in Jer 38, and the Ethiopian official in Acts 8, who is often associated with the spread of Christianity to the African continent. However, this figure is primarily identified in the text as an emasculated "eunuch" (five times), marking him out as a deviant, stigmatized figure in the ancient world.

22. Trying to wash an Ethiopian white (as a metaphor for the futility of trying to change one's essential nature) is often associated with Aesop (a contemporary of the biblical prophet Jeremiah), to whom a fable on this topic was attributed. See Karen Newman, "'And Wash the Ethiop White': Femininity and the Monstrous in *Othello*," in *Fashioning Femininity and English Renaissance Drama* (Chicago: University of Chicago Press, 1991), 71–93.

Civil Rights Era "Black Pride," it is unlikely that black skin was positively associated with beauty in the thought-world of the Song of Songs.

Even today skin color presents a challenge to self-esteem and social acceptance for many African American women. Research has demonstrated that not only is "the beauty myth" in the United States based on standards that elevate the physical features of Caucasian women but also that the more a woman's appearance deviates from those standards, the less likely it is that she will achieve higher socioeconomic status.[23] Furthermore, even within the black community, "skin color hierarchies" persist, as Morrison's frequent identification of characters in *Song of Solomon* as "dark-skinned," "light-skinned," and "high-yellow Negroes" reflects. Sociologist Maxine L. Hunter reports that light-skinned African American women tend to enjoy more privileges and opportunities for social advancement than their dark-skinned counterparts. Hunter traces this phenomenon back to the pre–Civil War period, when slaves with lighter complexions (usually as the result of their masters' having raped their enslaved mothers) often were

assigned less strenuous labor on the plantations than their darker-skinned counterparts. Hunter asserts that light-skinned African American women tend to be offered more and better educational and employment opportunities; in addition, they tend to appeal more to black men who, like Hagar's lover in Morrison's novel, tend to seek lighter-skinned (or even non-black) mates who can boost their chances for upward social mobility.[24]

Is it possible, then, as an African American woman, to read Song 1:5 in a way that remains true to the spirit of the biblical text while still affirming the truth of black beauty? Yes, it is, for two clear reasons. First, the King James Version (a Bible translation frequently read in English-speaking black churches) retains the challenging rendering of the ambiguous Hebrew conjunction ו as "but" instead of "and": "I am black *but* comely" (Song 1:5, KJV, emphasis mine). But when read in the context of a religious tradition that ideally preaches good news to the oppressed, that rendering invites black worshipers to redefine and re-valuate what it means to be black and what it is to be beautiful. The message of Song 1:5 is transformed into good

23. Maxine L. Hunter, "Colorstruck: Skin Color Stratification in the Lives of African American Women," *Sociological Inquiry* 68 (1998): 517–35.

24. Ibid., esp. 522–23.

news for black women and men: "I am black but [*contrary to the so-called beauty myth and the centuries-old racist ideologies of colonialism and slavery, 'black' is]* beautiful!"

Second, as an African American woman, I hear Song 1:5 as good news when I read it in light of later verses in the Song where the Songstress declares: "I am my beloved's, and my beloved is mine" (Song 2:16 ; 6:3; 7:10). That declaration evokes a refrain frequently heard in black churches where worshipers whose ancestors were sold as chattel remind each other about the truth of "who we are and Whose we are." We are not property of human slave masters nor commodities tested and approved according to human standards of skin color, hair texture, or the like. No! Our true selves are defined by the infinite love of a compassionate Creator who awesomely, wonderfully, yes, beautifully

has fashioned each of us in the sacred image (Ps 139:14; Gen 1:27). In a world where violence still compels us to assert that "black lives matter," it is important for us to remember why: because each of us is a beautiful, precious, deeply loved daughter or son of God.

And so it happens, in the final chapters of Morrison's *Song of Solomon*, that Hagar's grandmother, Pilate, whose "full lips [were] blacker than . . . [her] skin, berry-stained," eulogizes Hagar and, with her, African American women (and men) everywhere, with the good news and the truth about beauty in the biblical Song:

> "That's my baby girl. My baby girl . . ."
> . . . Pilate trumpeted for the sky itself to hear, "And she was *loved!*"[25]

*Lauress Wilkins Lawrence*

The Song woman's initial critical gazers are not crude, leering males but the "daughters of Jerusalem" (Song 1:5), probably the same group as the young women who admire the male lover (1:3) and likely among the female lover's cohort in age and interest. These "daughters" will be invoked several more times in the Song (2:7; 3:5, 10-11; 5:16; 8:4), but their precise relationship with the principal Songstress is only beginning to unfold. Are they her close girlfriends, more distant acquaintances, casual observers, congenial admirers, social critics, potential rivals, or some

25. Morrison, *Song*, 322–23 (emphasis original).

mix of these? The first impression they evoke falls on the more remote, judgmental side. The descriptor "daughters of Jerusalem" is rather formal, generic, and suggestive in this context of a privileged royal-urban circle into which the "king" has brought this dark-skinned, sun-scorched country girl. They're not quite sure what to make of her yet, but at first glance, she doesn't fit the part.

*"You Are Black,* **therefore** *Beautiful": The Un-"Fairness" of Skin Color*

I heard this for the first time during a visit to North America. Forgetting to thank the stranger for the compliment, I wondered in disbelief, "How can this be? I have only heard of being fair and lovely in India. Could I possibly be black and beautiful?" I quickly dismissed the thought, saying to myself, "Maybe the North American sun has not kissed me like the South Indian sun!"

Scorched by the blazing sun of South India, many women lighten their skin with the root spice turmeric (the source of yellow color in many curries). Turmeric complements feminine beauty, both as an antiseptic and a bleaching agent. Likewise, pregnant women hoping for a beautifully fair child drink warm milk spiced with saffron (also used to flavor rice). South Indian women, young and old, often covet fair skin. Fair maidens are deemed fittest to catch the most desirable grooms (see Song 2:15 on catching the "foxes"). Darker-skinned baby girls are more likely to be given up for adoption.

In Middle Eastern and South Indian cultures where marriage may be more of an economic transaction than a romantic enterprise, class discrimination besets society as much as, if not more than, racial prejudice. Historically, dark skin has been a sign of lower caste and material status. The dark-skinned Dravidian race was pushed aside by the white Aryan Hindus of the higher caste in India's early history. The lower the caste, the harder one worked under extreme conditions, including greater exposure to the sun, thus leading to darker skin. For generations families would be bound in the bondage of discrimination based on skin color. Song 1:5 potentially offers hope for economically disadvantaged dark-skinned women who, in the absence of help, servants, and slaves, do their own work; who, instead of bathing in milk and honey, moisturizing and maintaining their skin, toil under the blistering heat of the sun (1:6); who develop sun spots and wrinkles laboring for their families; whose profile pictures rarely make it on magazine covers or the desks of their lovers.

The Hebrew ו and Greek καί (LXX) in Song 1:5, normally

rendered "and," resist a discriminatory reading. The reader sees the possibility of the young woman's being both black *and* beautiful. We thus focus less on the brutal effects of the sun and more on the beautiful essence of the girl; less on her outer appearance and more on her inner strength. Nevertheless, in describing her skin color, not to her lover, but to the dissenting "daughters of Jerusalem," the woman hints at an alternative counter-reading: "I am black, *but* comely" (KJV, RSV). It is not surprising that this potential bride-to-be is concerned about her beauty viewed through the eyes of other women, for in a traditional, arranged marriage system, the opinions of mothers-in-law, sisters-in-law, aunts, and grandmothers are critical to the success of a marriage deal. Bottom line: a bride's personal value and the wealth of her family are calibrated by her skin color.

Consider, further, a third reading: "I am black, *therefore* beautiful." In evoking prospects of racial, gender, and familial discrimination in society, the Song's opening scene offers a time-tested platform on which to construct erotic love. What makes a young woman beautiful? Comparing her skin color and quality to rugged tents and shielding curtains, Song 1:5 prompts us not to disregard the skin embracing the soul, but to embrace the skin in all its protective power, which the pigment melanin provides. The tents and curtains were sturdy and durable, designed to weather the storms of life and to shield the domestic sphere from danger. Such is the tenacity of the Shulammite's dark, black, melanin-filled skin—a sign of inner strength and durability, characterizing women's worth and beauty which do not *fade* away.

*Jerusha Moses*

The woman's distinctive swarthy pigment that draws others' downward looks results less from ethnic heritage (most Middle Easterners would have darker skin than Europeans) than from the environmental effects of the sun looking down upon her. She is the object, then, of a double-gaze: by other women and by the sun. She is deeply tanned from daily toil in the vineyards (1:6), not from lolling on the beach. Aesthetics, not least standards of physical beauty, are culturally conditioned. Tanned skin of various shades, which is coveted by modern white American women of all classes and the men who look at them as a model of attractiveness, does not translate to the Song's ancient Near Eastern world—or to that of contemporary South India, as Jerusha Moses observes in her Contributing Voice essay, " 'You Are Black *therefore* Beautiful': The

Un-'Fairness' of Skin Color." Here the female protagonist's darker skin marks her as an underprivileged field hand, physically and socially distinct from the less dark-complexioned daughters of Jerusalem. But she also clearly stands out for her exotic beauty, which is appreciated by her gorgeous kingly lover, whatever anyone else might think. As for the daughters' inspections, they need not reflect sinister, piercing dirty looks or the envious, ill-wishing "evil eye" intent on sabotaging the woman's relationship with her lover. But they at least betray gawking curiosity and wide-eyed puzzlement that this different outsider has managed to catch such a desirable suitor. This relationship doesn't *look* quite right to them.

Feminist critics of film and literature have exposed the problem of the male gaze objectifying the female body and subjecting it to microanalysis and fantasy severed (disembodied) from women's subjectivity and agency.[26] The camera zooms in and slowly scans a woman's body from an ogling male perspective. Her form is captured—held captive—in the frame, and however artificial and airbrushed the scene might be, it reflects, reinforces, and reconfigures aesthetic standards and social locations from the male viewpoint, too often internalized by women who assume the position. The Song's leading woman, however, dares to protest, "Don't look at me like that!" She writes her own script, makes her own movie. She doesn't hide but rather reveals herself on her terms proclaiming her blackness beautiful—just "like the tents of Kedar, like the curtains of Solomon" (1:5). These ebony textile images merge two contrasting environments: the dark canvas dwellings of the Arabian tribe Kedar (קדר) whose name denotes "black"[27] and the elegant black draperies in Solomon's Jerusalem palace.[28] Thus collapse foreign/domestic, tribal/

---

26. See the pioneering article by Laura Mulvey, "Visual Pleasure and Narrative Cinema," *Screen* 16 (1975): 6–18; repr. in Mulvey, *Visual and Other Pleasures*, 2nd ed. (Houndsmill Basingstoke, U.K.: Palgrave Macmillan, 2009), 14–27.

27. See the related noun קדרות in Isa 50:3 meaning "blackness." Roland Murphy comments that "the tents of these Bedouin would have been made from black goat skins" (*The Song of Songs*, Hermeneia [Minneapolis: Augsburg Fortress, 1990], 126).

28. As Exum (*Song*, 104–05) observes, though Solomon's curtains evoke a different setting from Kedar's tents, both could have been fashioned from black goats' skins into distinctively beautiful materials. Not satisfied with this broad connection, however, some interpreters forge a tighter parallelism by revocalizing the consonants for Solomon's name to render Salmah, the name of another Arabian tribe evidenced in some sources. See also Fox, *Song*, 100, 102; Snaith, *Song*, 18; Marvin H. Pope, *Song of Songs: A New Translation with Introduction and Commentary*, AB 7C; (New York: Doubleday, 1977), 291, 320.

royal, rustic/urbane, nomadic/monarchic binaries under a thick coat of beautiful black paint. And thus our blackened vineyard woman finds a welcome home in the black-shaded chambers of her kingly lover. For an actual painting that suggestively coordinates images of picked grapes and dark curtains from 1:5-6, along with a weathered mosaic panel, with that of the striking tanned woman, see the illumination and commentary by the contemporary artist and Contributing Voice, Debra Band.

### Illumination 1 Commentary
*(The depicted Hebrew text is 1:5-8)*

A picked-at cluster of grapes— invariably symbolizing joy and sanctification in Jewish lore—still looks juicy and sweet, and a mosaic of grapevines has lost some tiles yet remains bright and colorful. While the young woman worries that her dark skin renders her undesirable to her lover, she asserts defiantly that the tan is not her fault, that she is beautiful nonetheless. In spite of the moment of self-doubt, she remains confident that the apparent flaw will not prevent the union with her lover. The midrashic, philosophical, and kabbalistic interpretations of the passage play on the notion of desirability despite unwitting imperfection. Putting the same argument into the mouth of Israel, cast here in female form, rabbinic legend compares the contrast of light and dark to the contrast of good and evil deeds. Song of Songs Rab. 1:5 reminds the reader that Israel has swung repeatedly between obedience to and rebellion against God: in Egypt, at the crossing of the Red Sea, in reaction to the spies' report, and on several other occasions. Finally, Israel declares, "I am black in this world and comely in the world to come," that is, after the dreamed-of union with the Divine beloved.[29] The same curtains seen in Illumination 3[30]

---

29. Ezra ben Solomon of Gerona, *Commentary on the Song of Songs and Other Kabbalistic Commentaries* (Kalamazoo, MI: Western Michigan University Press, 1999), 53.

30. See Band's commentary on 7:6-9a below, pp. 188–89.

sway in the breeze. The dark and light layers of drapery reinforce the same theme, that the evil impulse which separates Israel from God can be conquered, that goodness can indeed supplant evil and bring about the union of God and Israel.

In Gersonides' Aristotelian analysis of divine wisdom, the woman becomes the human soul restrained by the material intellect from union with wisdom: "The material intellect said to the other faculties of the soul that ab initio she is *black* since she lacks any intelligibles but is nonetheless comely because of her disposition to receive every intelligible when she will be stimulated to do this."[31]

In the Kabbalistic interpretation of 1:6, the Shekhinah, the feminine divine emanation closest to the human realm, asserts that after descending to Egypt along with Jacob, she participated in Israel's exile (thus separated from the higher levels of the Godhead), "complain[ing] and thunder[ing] forth about her being in exile," as she longs for reunion with the higher emanations.[32]

*Debra Band*

But the native home of the Songstress has proven not so hospitable. In particular, her brothers, though identified as "my mother's sons,"[33] have not treated her well; they have betrayed or taken advantage of the familial bond. Being "angry" with her, the brothers made their young sister "keeper of the vineyards" (1:6). This anger term (חרה) connotes a burning, boiling emotion;[34] its hot-headed force thus functionally coincides in the present case with the high-voltage energy of the sun irradiating earth's

31. Levi ben Gershom (Gersonides), *Commentary on the Song of Songs*, trans. and ed. Menachem Kellner, YJS 28 (New Haven, CT: Yale University Press, 1998), 27.

32. ben Solomon of Gerona, *Commentary*, 43.

33. Chana Bloch and Ariel Bloch explain, "A term for full brothers, brothers of the same mother [that] sometimes implies a sense of special closeness" (*The Song of Songs: The World's First Great Love Poem* [New York: Modern Library, 1995], 141). See Gen 43:29; Judg 8:19; Ps 50:20; 69:8. Alternatively, Robert Alter notes that the sister's identification of "my mother's sons" rather than "my brothers" marks "a certain distancing from them" (see *Strong as Death Is Love: The Song of Songs, Ruth, Esther, Jonah, and Daniel: A Translation with Commentary* [New York: Norton, 2015], 9). In any case, the way they treat her scarcely befits true brotherly love.

34. Matthew R. Schlimm, *From Fratricide to Forgiveness: The Language and Ethics of Anger in Genesis*, Siphrut 7 (Winona Lake, IN: Eisenbrauns, 2011), 197–98; Ellen van Wolde, "Sentiments as Culturally Constructed Emotions: Anger and Love in the Hebrew Bible," *BibInt* 16 (2008): 7–17.

fields and those who toil in them.[35] The brothers' blazing anger caused their sister's sunburned condition. Beyond that, by overburdening her with tending the family vineyards (pl.), the hostile brothers prevented her from keeping her own vineyard (sg.). She decries this loss in the most emphatic terms: literally, "My vineyard—which [belongs] to me [שלי]—I have not kept" (1:6).[36]

At this point, we face the first of many interpretive decisions on the literal-figurative spectrum. Of course, the poetic genre of the Song demands a keen figurative imagination, but not an unbridled one. Most contemporary scholars, for example, resist a thoroughgoing allegorical reading so favored by patristic and medieval interpreters. For example, the picture of the woman as darkly stained by sin but made beautiful by God's redemptive grace imposes a narrow theological template on the Song persuasive to few modern readers, not least feminist readers attuned to the deleterious effects of depicting women, especially sexually active women, as prototypes of human sinfulness.[37] The image of the vineyard (כרם) is a well-known symbol for Israel in prophetic literature (Isa 5:1-7; 27:2-6; Jer 2:21; Ezek 19:10-14; Hos 10:1; see also Ps 80:8-16) and for the woman's sexuality in the Song (1:14; 2:15; 7:13; 8:11-12). But any effective metaphor trades on reality, and poetic imagery typically evokes multiple associations.

Simply to substitute "the female sex" for every use of "vineyard" across the Song is reductionist. In the present scenario, the woman might be admitting that she has not "kept" her sexuality—that is, not maintained her virginity. She has taken a lover before marriage, seemingly without personal shame or regret. Perhaps it is such shameless disregard for sexual-marital convention that sparks her brothers' anger. As older male siblings protective of socioeconomic as well as more personal interests related to their sister, hoping to obtain an optimal bride price and marriage contract for her (see Song 8:7-12), they try (unsuccessfully!) to rein in their wild sibling with forced labor. This plausible scenario, however, is not made explicit; we are not privy to what provoked the brothers' ire against their sister, only to her conscripted labor that resulted.

---

35. Fox, *Song*, 102.

36. Or "my vineyard, mine" (Bloch and Bloch, *Song*, 141).

37. On patristic interpretation, see the stimulating article by Mark S. M. Scott, "Shades of Grace: Origen and Gregory of Nyssa's Soteriological Exegesis of the 'Black and Beautiful' Bride in Song of Songs 1:5," *HTR* 99 (2006): 65–83.

It is also possible that the woman laments the neglect of her property, that is, an actual vineyard to which she feels entitled. With multiple living brothers, it is doubtful that she legally owned any parcel of the family estate. But this need not stop her from desiring some financial independence, a piece of land to call her own ("my vineyard") apart from fraternal exploitation, like the capable woman of Proverbs (though admittedly a wife) who "considers a field and buys it; with the fruit of her hands she plants a vineyard" (Prov 31:16).[38] At this early point in the Song, it seems best to take the woman's "vineyard" as representing her own multifaceted interests, including sexual and socioeconomic aspects. The celebratory joy of the Song is forged out of the woman's struggle to control her own life.

### Hiding and Seeking (1:7-8)

Impinged by withering looks from Jerusalem's daughters in the city and by the whip-cracking of her mother's sons in the vineyard, the woman seeks respite and refuge in her lover's pastures. In reflecting on her vulnerability to others' power plays and honor games, she shifts her lover's image from a king in palatial chambers to a shepherd in bucolic fields. The potential exploitative dimensions of royal rule give way to or, better, blend with gentler associations of pastoral care and protection from blazing midday heat. "Lying down at noon" in green pastures (Song 1:7) provides a soothing contrast to laboring in the sunbaked vineyards.[39] In the literal and figurative dance of the Song, we need not settle the male lover's actual occupation (king or shepherd? both or neither?) nor imagine two distinct suitors. The woman projects an ideal composite picture of her beloved as a shepherd/king-type, on the order of Solomon's father David at his best—protecting family flocks (1 Sam 16:11; 17:34-35) and composing Ps 23, *not* cruelly seizing another man's dear "ewe lamb" (2 Sam 12:1-15).

The activity of "pasturing" or "grazing" flocks (רעה, *ra'ah*)—pursued by both male and female protagonists (she too has goat "kids" to feed

---

38. On this text in the context of women's property rights and opportunities in the ancient Near Eastern world, see Christine Roy Yoder, "The Women of Substance (אשת־חיל): A Socioeconomic Reading of Proverbs 31:10-31," *JBL* 122/3 (2003): 444–45.

39. The Hiphil form of רבץ used in 1:7 means "make lie down" (NRSV), stressing the causative agency of the kindly shepherd in resting his flock (see Ps 23:1), in contrast to the angry brothers who press their sister into harsh fieldwork.

[Song 1:8]) and by other male shepherds (1:8)—evokes a homophonic link with the daughters of Jerusalem's looking/gazing (ראה, *raʾah*) and what will soon emerge as the man's favorite pet name for his dearest "love" (רעיה, *raʿyah*) (1:9, 15; 2:2, 10, 13; 4:1, 7; 5:2; 6:4).[40] As the woman is the object of both looking and loving, she also appears in some sense as the object of the man's grazing or tending. She is his "fairest" (1:8), most beautiful (יפה), most precious lamb or kid; she anticipates his laying her down at noon (1:7), his resting and eating with her in erotic refreshment.[41] She is a willing, pursuant partner in this arrangement, seeking out his pastoral location where she may actively feed her needs. As a lovemaking picture, the al fresco setting both extends and complements the bedchamber in 1:4. Our couple's love longs for free, unfettered expression in harmony with nature's open environment.

But pastoral romance in the Song is not wholly idyllic. It poses its own teases and tensions as others encroach on the lovers' meadow. Other shepherds, the man's male "companions" (1:7), graze their flocks and pitch their tents. We don't know how close these other men are to the woman's lover, just as her relationship with the "daughters of Jerusalem" remains ambiguous, but they do not appear overtly hostile as the woman's brothers have been. Still, they constitute a crew of field-working men. An attractive woman appearing in their midst is bound to draw a few lewd glances and rude advances. Far from being threatened by this prospect, however, the woman cleverly turns it to her advantage to prompt her lover's protective guidance. She questions the prospect of "veiling" herself in the shepherds' company, either to shield herself from their unwelcome glances or to pique their desire to see what lies behind her gossamer mask. Either way, she tantalizes her lover in a "mock pout" with this scenario.[42] Does he want her receiving all this public attention? Why should she be so exposed?

In response, he treats her query more playfully than seriously, matching her primary concern with seeking-and-finding him rather than fending off dirty looks and come-ons from other shepherds. And he presumes that she knows exactly where to find him—perhaps at their favorite trysting spot—but prefers to keep him wooing her and worrying that,

---

40. Fox, *Song*, 103.

41. Noting that רעה may mean "eat" (intransitive use) as well as "feed" (transitive), Fox (*Song*, 103) aptly remarks: "She desires him and he her, and he 'eats'—enjoys sexual pleasures—with her."

42. Dobbs-Allsopp, "'I am Black'," 133.

if she takes a notion, she just might wander into other men's tents. In other words, she's playing coy and hard to get, and in turn he tries to play it cool and aloof: "Well if you don't remember, my dear, where to find me, go ahead and follow any tracks that strike your fancy and try your luck with any shepherds you happen to meet" (1:8, my paraphrase). Ah, the courting games young lovers love to play. No surprise here. The cheeky banter only makes the inevitable rendezvous more delicious. But teasing—the playful as well as hurtful kind—trades on real possibilities. While in this situation the woman does not appear seriously to fear for her safety—because she knows where to reach her lover who desires her deeply and will defend her, if need be—she still must make her way in a precarious, male-dominated public world. She has to watch her step and track her course judiciously. An undertone of vulnerability never fades completely from the Song.

# Song of Songs 1:9–2:7

## *Looking at the Lovers' Nest— and Letting It Be*

Overall this stanza further develops the outdoor landscape: the couple's natural love nest amid luscious greenery of various plants and trees and pleasant habitats of peaceful doves, gazelles, and wild does. This erotic environment is evocative of fertile areas in Israel (En-gedi and Sharon) and redolent with fragrant oils distilled from imported plants (nard and myrrh; Song 1:12-14; 2:1). Suggestive exceptions to this verdant love-nest ambience are the opening segment's equine-martial imagery associated with Pharaoh's chariots (1:9-11) and the description of the meeting place as a "house" (בית; 1:17; 2:4).

The man's initial comparison of his lover to a mare among stallion-driven chariots (Song 1:9) forms a zoological frame with the woman's final adjuring of the daughters of Jerusalem "by the gazelles or the wild does" (2:7) around the central botanical portrait. While the man's conjuring up of powerful horses and the woman's summoning of gentle deer may seem to reflect gender-stereotyped sensibilities, the picture may be more fluid.[1] Both types of animals excel in dynamic movement, and in

---

1. On the poetic technique of "conjuring," see J. Cheryl Exum: "Conjuring seeks to make immanent through language what is absent, to construct the lovers as 'real'

25

*Song of Songs 1:9–2:7*

**[M → W]**

⁹I compare you, my love,
  to a mare among Pharaoh's
    chariots.
¹⁰Your cheeks are comely with
    ornaments,
  your neck with strings of jewels.
¹¹We will make you ornaments of
    gold,
  studded with silver.

**[W → D(?)]**

¹²While the king was on his couch,
  my nard gave forth its fragrance.
¹³My beloved is to me a bag of
  myrrh

that lies between my breasts.
¹⁴My beloved is to me a cluster of
    henna blossoms
  in the vineyards of En-gedi.

**[M → W]**

¹⁵Ah, you are beautiful, my love;
  ah, you are beautiful;
  your eyes are doves.

**[W → M]**

¹⁶Ah, you are beautiful, my beloved,
    truly lovely.
  Our couch is green;
¹⁷the beams of our house are
    cedar,
  our rafters are pine.

a high-jumping contest, the gazelle would beat the horse every time. Of course, a deer couldn't pull a wagon or chariot, but then again, unlike the horse, the deer resists all manner of domestication and servitude. In this sense the woman's "wild doe" is wilder than Pharaoh's stallions, and the mare in 1:9 may be viewed as a wild filly that drives the steeds wild (see more below). In any case, the mobile menagerie infuses the rustic love scene with mutual energy and passion; this is not simply a leisurely campout in the woods.

On the second matter, concerning the mix of outdoor and indoor settings, the domestic imagery in Song 1:17 where "the beams of our house are cedar, our rafters are pine" and in 2:4 when "he brought me to the banqueting house" easily elides into the rustic. The wood-based dwelling reinforces the dominant tree house or greenhouse structure with an elegant touch, cedar being the material of choice for royal buildings (1:16-17). The "banqueting house" (2:4) is literally the "house of wine" (בית היין) and can thus suggest a vineyard setting for a picnic where wine is enjoyed (1:14) as well as a more formal occasion at a "banquet" table.

---

(that is, present before us) and endow them with meaning" (*Song of Songs*, OTL [Louisville: Westminster John Knox, 2005] 6-7); and Exum, "How Does the Song of Songs Mean? On Reading the Poetry of Desire," *SEÅ* 64 (1999): 51–56. A modern analogy to the gender-stereotyped imagery of war horses and peaceful deer might be men's love of monster trucks and fast cars contrasted with women's preference for graceful ballet and soft romantic music.

²:¹I am a rose of Sharon,
a lily of the valleys.
**[M → W]**
²As a lily among brambles,
so is my love among maidens.
**[W → D]**
³As an apple tree among the trees
of the wood,
so is my beloved among young
men.
With great delight I sat in his
shadow;
and his fruit was sweet to my
taste.
⁴He brought me to his banqueting
house,
and his intention toward me
was love.
⁵Sustain me with raisins,
refresh me with apples;
for I am faint with love.
⁶O that his left hand were under
my head,
and that his right hand embraced me!
⁷I adjure you, O daughters of
Jerusalem,
by the gazelles or the wild
does
do not stir up or awaken love
until it is ready!

Still, the conflation of rural and regal structures under the "banner"² of love further enhances the Song's holistic, harmonious atmosphere and resists restrictive configurations of a woman's place.

The back-and-forth dialogue between the couple also solidifies the sense of their mutual intimacy. But once again, the picture is not as simple as that. Other characters continue to come into play, not necessarily to interfere, yet the presence of other viewers and hearers (including us readers) cannot help but affect the experience. In Song 1:11, the man includes himself among a group of jewelers as "we" who will adorn his beloved "mare" (1:9). And the woman speaks not only *to* her lover (1:16–2:1) but also *about* him to a wider audience (1:12-14; 2:3-7), again identified as the "daughters of Jerusalem" (2:7). The stanza climaxes with the woman beseeching these other women *not* to affect her lovemaking in some way, which I will explore below. In any event, some potential "disturbance" concerns the female protagonist.

She may also be worried about her self-image, as we might call it, particularly concerning her physical appearance. Body-beautiful, somatic-optic perspectives predominate in this stanza, with plenty of compliments heaped on the woman by her lover. But she may not be so convinced in her own mind, perhaps suffering from a wallflower syndrome she can't quite shake: "I'm just another common wildflower

---

2. See below on reading "banner" instead of "intention" (Song 2:4 NRSV).

dotting the countryside" (Song 2:1; my paraphrase). Moreover, she may be insecure about keeping up with her vigorous lover and subject to breathless swoons: "I am faint with love" (2:5). While these are by no means necessary interpretations, they are scarcely fanciful readings of the text. Feminist antennae finely tuned to gender-based power relations will pick up signals here that beg for careful investigation. The woman's apparent vocality, agency, and potency can mask a strong undertow of vulnerability, insecurity, and dependency that strengthens more than subverts conventional gender polarities; in other words, the undertow ultimately sucks the Song's woman down into its androcentric vortex, leaving the surface of traditional society undisturbed. Or maybe not. To reprise an image used above, the woman may be a strong enough swimmer to chart her own course. We must continue to navigate carefully these deep waters with her.

### Here's Looking at You (1:9-17)

The man addresses the woman with his favorite term of endearment (רעיתי), meaning "my love" (Song 1:9), "my darling" (NJPS), or, more casually but no less intimately, "my friend, companion, neighbor" (πλήσιον, LXX). Though resonant with roots for "graze" and "see," this term appears in the Hebrew Bible outside the Song only in the tragic incident of Jephthah's daughter, who laments with her female "friends" before her execution (Judg 11:37). In that horrific story, the daughter finds no love or support in the masculine world, least of all from her father, whose rash vow sealed her death. By contrast, the Song's woman enjoys abundant love from her male partner exceeding that of her female companions, though perhaps his way of expressing it leaves something to be desired.

The man's opening line in Hebrew ending with "my love" begins with "to my mare" (לססתי; Song 1:9). To be sure, it's not to any old nag that he compares his lover, but rather to a mare "among/in the chariots of Pharaoh," which were typically driven by stallions. Noble company, but to what end? The finest and fittest horses selected to pull royal chariots were commonly bedecked with luxurious ornamentation draped about the head and neck.[3] Analogously, the woman's gorgeous cheeks and neck are perfect settings for jeweled adornment. Her own accessories set off

---

3. See the illuminating discussion and ancient artistic reproductions in Othmar Keel, *The Song of Songs: A Continental Commentary*, trans. Frederick J. Gaiser (Minneapolis: Fortress, 1994), 56–59.

her stunning features nicely (1:10), but she merits more than she can afford. So her lover schemes to enlist a team of craftsmen ("we") to fashion gold- and silver-studded necklaces and earrings for her (1:11). Whether he actually has the clout and means to pull this off is questionable, but he likes to play the kingly role she has assigned him. As Solomon lavished special gifts upon Pharaoh's daughter, his first wife (1 Kgs 3:1; 7:8; 9:24; 11:1), the Song's male lover hopes to spoil his lovely Pharaoh's mare.[4]

While the horse-and-chariot image highlights the woman's facial beauty, it does so in tandem with strength and stateliness. Her mien cannot be reduced to pixie cuteness. She can proudly and elegantly pull her weight alongside any man (stallion); she is every bit her lover's match, and he loves her for it. But is there more to the picture than a robust aesthetics? Although an ancient Near Eastern royal couple might have gone on a leisurely chariot jaunt through the countryside, the ancient equivalent of a Sunday drive,[5] horse-driven chariots were chiefly designed as war machines fueling the expansion of imperial power. And from the standpoint of Israel's historians and prophets, they were instruments of foreign, godless pride, greed, and oppression. At the height of his exploitative rule precipitating the fissure in his kingdom, Solomon amassed a bevy of "chariots and horses"—many imported from Egypt (1 Kgs 10:26-29)—against the explicit interdict in Deut 17:16. The leaders of God's people must depend on God for their security, not on Egypt's horses and chariots designed to enslave colonized peoples and ultimately destined to drown in turbulent waters (see Exod 14:21-31; Isa 31:1-3).

But the Song's kingly lover does not seek to emulate Solomon's acquisitive lust for either horses or women. He desires but one "mare" (Song 1:9), which in the world of warfare, may operate more to discomfit than support military operations; let loose among a phalanx of chariots, a mare in heat could incite steeds to break their reins and cripple battle plans.[6] But the last thing the Song's "king" (1:4, 12) wants to do is to set his beloved loose in a dangerous world. She drives him wild and at the

4. I take the possible allusion to Pharaoh's daughter, Solomon's favored wife, in broad suggestive terms. For a tighter identification of the Song's desirable "dark lady" with Pharaoh's daughter, see Victor Sasson, "King Solomon and the Dark Lady of the Song of Songs," *VT* 39 (1989): 407–14.

5. Keel, *Song*, 57–58.

6. For a lively, detailed explanation of this military scenario or "horse sense" (his phrase), see Marvin H. Pope, *Song of Songs: A New Translation with Introduction and Commentary*, AB 7C (Garden City, NY: Doubleday, 1977), 338–40.

same time reins in his desires for her alone in their peaceful love nest, far away from the battlefield. He affirms the woman's sexual power to make love, not war.

The woman's response to her lover's compliments is not directly antiphonal: she speaks of him in third person and shifts the symbolic ambience from the exotic equestrian world of Pharaoh to the more intimate aromatic atmosphere of lovemaking (Song 1:12-14). But she is as passionately, though differently, taken with him as he is with her. While the man looks at her with consummate admiration, she pulls him close in erotic embrace enhanced by sweet fragrances of nard, myrrh, and henna. Her senses of touch and smell again predominate; in 1:16 she will also engage her sense of sight. And most significantly, from the standpoint of the woman's agency, she strongly asserts how her lover meets *her* needs: she is not saddled or bridled by his desires. In parallel lines, she announces: *"My* beloved is *to/for me"* (דודי לי; 1:13-14). As he favors calling her "love" (רעיה; 1:9, 15; 2:2) or darling with shades of friendly companionship, she favors calling him "love" or "beloved" (דוד; 1:14, 16; 2:3) with shades of familial commitment ("brother, kinsman"; ἀδελφιδός, LXX) and echoes of previous references to amorous caresses (דד; 1:2, 4). More specifically, the woman's lover is to her and for her a "bag of myrrh" (1:13) between her breasts and "cluster of henna blossoms in the vineyards of En-gedi" (1:14).[7]

| Male<br>*"My lover is a . . ."* | Female<br>*". . . to/for me"* |
| --- | --- |
| Sachet of myrrh | Between my breasts |
| Spray of henna blossoms | In the vineyards of En-gedi |

The erotic nature of the breast-focused image is unmistakable, but again, the focus is *hers*, though we can also assume the man's delight in being nestled in his lover's bosom. The parallel construction suggests "the vineyards of En-gedi" (Song 1:14) as another image of the woman's erotic body. As En-gedi designates the lush, vivacious oasis on the western bank of the salty Dead Sea, the woman's body provides a wet, sweet garden of refreshment for her lover. Whereas his comparison to a sachet

---

7. Jill M. Munro, *Spikenard and Saffron: A Study in the Poetic Language of the Song of Songs*, JSOTSup 203 (Sheffield: Sheffield Academic, 1995), 50.

or pouch (צרור) of myrrh (1:13) evokes an image of his head, the picture of a spray or cluster (אשכל) of henna flowers is more suggestive of his hair. Likewise, the flourishing of his florid hair in her vineyards intimates his erotic entanglement in her hair, possibly in the pubic area, because of the wet-garden setting of En-gedi.[8] This is the woman's second self-reference to "vineyards." I suggested above that the initial usage may refer to her oppressive labor in her brothers' literal "vineyards" (1:6). But in 1:14, the En-gedi vineyards are transformed into a figurative site for lovemaking, which may function poetically as an oasis from her harsh real-life vineyard work. This conjured vineyard—a luxuriant blend of body and botany, that is, her sexual body within a fragrant, verdant environment—she can be the "keeper" of (1:6) and draw her lover into as she wills.

At first blush, the woman's further staging of her love scene with "the king . . . on his couch" (Song 1:12) may seem to evoke a domestic setting rather than the rustic ambience of a henna field or vineyard. Of course, poetic drama allows for a kaleidoscope of shifting images. The word for "couch," however, does not necessarily denote a piece of indoor furniture; derived from the verb for "surround" (סבב), it generally refers to a type of "enclosure."[9] It thus suits a bed within which lovers lie, a banquet table around which diners recline (ἀνακλίσει, LXX; see 2:4),[10] or, combining these possibilities in an outdoor scene, a blanket of cloth or leaves surrounding lovers' amorous and festive picnic activities. The latter picture is reinforced by the woman's subsequent description of "our couch" (ערש; "bed, divan" [1:16], a different term from the "couch" in 1:12) as "green" or "leafy" (רענן; "our couch is in a bower," NJPS), nestled within a cedar-beamed and cypress-raftered "house" (1:17).[11] Though royal palaces and temples, like David and Solomon's, may sport cedar appointments and other expensive woodworks (2 Sam 5:11; 7:2;

---

8. A less moist, less intimate (though still romantic) image may be in view, reflecting the practice of Middle Eastern women adorning their heads and chests with sprigs of henna; see Munro, *Spikenard*, 50; and Harold N. Moldenke and Alma L. Moldenke, *Plants of the Bible* (Mineola, NY: Dover, 1952), 124–25.

9. Roland E. Murphy, *The Song of Songs*, Hermeneia (Minneapolis: Fortress, 1990), 131.

10. "Circle of feasters," according to William J. Holladay, *A Concise Hebrew and Aramaic Lexicon of the Old Testament* (Grand Rapids: Eerdmans, 1971), 203.

11. The NRSV is unusual in pairing cedar with pine in 1:17. Most versions follow the LXX in reading "cedar (κέδροι) beams" and "cypress (κυπάρισσοι) rafters" (NAB, NIV, NJPS, CEB). Holladay (*Lexicon*, 48) renders the Hebrew ברות as "juniper." Moldenke and Moldenke (*Plants*, 175–77) prefer "fir" for the second wood type.

1 Kgs 5:6-10; 7:1-12; 9:10-11; 10:17), the green, leafy place of repose in the Song suggests a bucolic backdrop, a makeshift love cabin in the woods, an arbor or bower.

As with the accumulation of horses and chariots, the proliferation of palatial cedar- and cypress-adorned structures (the temple excepted), whether by Israelite, Judahite, or foreign rulers, often drew the ire of biblical prophets as a mark of pretentious human sufficiency destined to crumble under divine judgment (2 Sam 7:7; 1 Kgs 10:26-27; 2 Kgs 19:21-28; Isa 2:11-13; 37:21-29; Jer 22:11-23; Ezek 17:24; 31:1-18; Amos 2:9). In their natural love nest, however, the Song's couple makes no claims to power, except the power of their love for each other. Moreover, their imagined tryst among the trees has no scent of Israel's acts of idolatrous, whorish worship under every "leafy tree" (רענן), against which the prophets also inveighed (Deut 12:2; 1 Kgs 14:23; 16:4; 2 Kgs 17:10; Isa 57:1-5; Jer 2:20; 3:6-13; 17:1-8; Ezek 6:13). The Song's characters offer no sacrifices to any god, engage in no cultic ritual, yet their simple lovemaking in the woods represents a deep act of faithful devotion—to each other.

This mutual devotion is rhetorically reinforced in Song 1:15-16 by matching expressions of each lover's beauty (my translation):

> *Man to Woman*: "Just look at you [הנך] my beautiful darling [יפה רעיתי]."
> *Woman to Man*: "Just look at you [הנך] my beautiful love [יפה דודי]."

The woman is multisensual, as we have seen, and though not as preoccupied with visual stimuli as the man, she is by no means aesthetically blind. Both lovers enhance their "beautiful" assessments, though the man offers a more specific description; he is particularly taken with her attractive dove-like eyes, whereas she simply adds, "you are lovely [or pleasant] indeed [אף נעים]" (my translation). Doves routinely graced ancient love poetry, providing apt images for lovers' eyes due to their oval shape, gray color, monogamous mating habits, general peaceful demeanor, or some combination of these traits. Comparing the woman's pretty eyes to a peaceful dove counterbalances the man's previous association of her striking cheeks and neck with a war horse. If a stunning mare helps win the battle by disrupting enemy chariots (see above), a gentle dove signals the promise of peaceful restoration (Gen 8:8-12).[12]

---

12. On the significance of doves in the biblical world, see Debbie Blue, *Consider the Birds: A Provocative Guide to Birds of the Bible* (Nashville: Abingdon, 2013), 1–18; Alice Parmelee, *All the Birds of the Bible: Their Stories, Identification, and Meaning* (New York: Harper, 1959), 53–58; Elizabeth A. Johnson, *Ask the Beasts: Darwin and the God of Love* (London: Bloomsbury, 2014), 139–40.

## How Do I Look? (2:1-4)

The woman's speech dominates this segment, with the exception of one line where the man answers her self-description (Song 2:2). Botanical images—rose, lily, apple tree—fill out the verdant love scene, now spiced with gustatory as well as optical experience (2:3-4).

Reminiscent of Song 1:5, the woman makes another personal "I am" evaluative comment. She is not afraid to express her own identity, which is affected, but not wholly absorbed by, her lover's opinion of her. Here, she asserts, "I am a rose [חבצלת] of Sharon, a lily [שושן] of the valleys" (2:1). In modern Western thought, roses and lilies rank among the most precious and pulchritudinous of flowers, the former signifying the classic love gift on Valentine's Day. Though "rose" has been the traditional English rendering since the KJV, the Hebrew term likely designates the more common "crocus"[13] that dotted Israel's fertile coastal area of Sharon; likewise, lilies naturally sprouted in valleys.[14] The woman is thus not claiming uniqueness, as if she were a one-of-a-kind beauty pageant winner—à la Esther (Esth 2). But neither is she bemoaning her ordinariness. The landscape of Sharon mirrors En-gedi: a lush area in an otherwise arid territory, arrayed with lots of beautiful flowers, each one no less beautiful than its clustered companions. The Song's woman does not seek to set herself apart from her beautiful sister-friends, but she does stake her claim to their company; she, too, has a rightful place in the blooming Plain of Sharon and valleys of lilies. A certain tension may underlie her assertion, much like her "I am black and beautiful" statement (1:5). Others might question her place among the "beautiful people" of society, but she can hold her own, buoyed by her regal lover's consummate admiration. If she's now fishing for his further compliments, it's only in a playful sense, not out of a sense of quivering insecurity, though a feminist analysis judiciously appreciates women's ongoing struggles with self-confidence in the face of oppressive cultural-aesthetic norms.[15]

---

13. See NRSV textual note b for Song 2:1.

14. See Michael V. Fox's translation: "I'm (just) a crocus of Sharon, a valley-lily." He further notes that the singular "lily" with the plural "valleys" (העמקים) stresses commonality—a flower typically found in any Palestinian valley—rather than uniqueness, "for a single lily could only be in one valley" (*The Song of Songs and the Ancient Egyptian Love Songs* [Madison: University of Wisconsin Press, 1985], 106–7).

15. See Ellen Zetzel Lambert, *Face of Love: Feminism and the Beauty Question* (Boston: Beacon, 1995); Jennifer Baumgardner and Amy Richards, *Manifesta: Young Women, Feminism, and the Future*, 2nd ed. (New York: Farrar, Straus, and Giroux, 2010), 126–66, 191–200.

In any case, the male lover promptly obliges and ups the ante. To him, his lover ("my darling") *is* one of a kind among all "daughters" (בנות), "a lily among brambles" (2:2). Not that she doesn't merit a home in Sharon, but in his eyes she so outshines the other flowers as to render them little more than thornbushes. The only other reference to "crocus" (חבצלת) in the Hebrew Bible appears in the context of restoration of hope, where Israel blossoms again "like the crocus" within the desert, where their wilderness experience of exile gives way at last to the renewed "majesty of Carmel and Sharon" (Isa 35:1-2). Likewise, in the Song the female lover instantly transforms any place where she blooms, even the most desolate, into a luxurious paradise.

The woman returns the favorable comment, singling out her lover "among young men/sons [בנים]," like a sweet-producing, shade-providing apple tree among a thicket of otherwise nondescript woodlands (Song 2:3).[16] She also further depicts their love nest as a banner-festooned "banqueting house" or house of wine (2:4). As mentioned above, this "house" need not shift the festivities indoors; wine may be enjoyed just as well outside, especially in an environment associated with vineyards, orchards, flowers, and bowers. The NRSV's idiosyncratic substitution of "his *intention* toward me was love" (2:4) for "his *banner* [דגל] over me was love" seems based on an Akkadian cognate form (*diglu*) meaning "intention."[17] But the emendation is not necessary to make good sense. The "love banner" erected over the woman by her lover may be purely figurative—she feels secure under his canopy of love—but it also easily fits into the arboreal scene, as if he had carved the word "love" or "X loves Y" in a thick overhanging branch. Moreover, later in the Song, the man compares his lover's "terrible" beauty to a national banner or standard under which an army fights (6:4, 10), and the book of Numbers repeatedly refers to regional banners marking out the various tribes

16. Standard lexicons and most English versions render תפוח as "apple tree." Since apples were not indigenous to biblical Palestine, however, some scholars prefer "apricot" (Fox, *Song*, 107; Moldenke and Moldenke, *Plants*, 184–88) or "quince" (Robert Alter, *Strong as Death Is Love: The Song of Songs, Ruth, Esther, Jonah, and Daniel: A Translation with Commentary* [New York: Norton, 2015], 14; Marcia Falk, *The Song of Songs: A New Translation and Interpretation* [New York: HarperCollins, 1990], 174) in 2:5; 7:8; 8:5, though Falk translates the term more broadly as "sweet fruit tree" in 2:3. I retain the traditional "apple," but the type of fruit tree does not significantly affect interpretation.

17. Fox, *Song*, 108; Pope, *Song*, 375–77; supporting the "banner" reading, see the helpful discussion in Exum, *Song*, 115.

of Israel.[18] Martial-patriotic strains continue to resound in the Song as signals of the lovers' strong personalities and the strength of their love, but with a telling twist: they march under the banner of LOVE; again, they are consumed with making love, not war.[19]

## Look, But Don't Touch! (2:5-7)

The woman concludes this stanza where she began, speaking of her lover in third person, and in Song 2:5 she explicitly addresses a wider audience: "Let *them* sustain me with raisins" (my translation). Though the plural pronoun suffixes in 2:5-7 are masculine, the addressees throughout are "the daughters of Jerusalem" designated in 2:7. Michael Fishbane suggests that this gender mix reinforces the "generic" thrust of the "oath formulary" invoked by the woman in 2:7 and may also indicate a greater flexibility in pronoun usage in later Hebrew style.[20] The woman pleads with her female friends concerning two key aspects of this lovemaking scene (2:5, 7), spliced with an expression of deep longing for her beloved's embrace (2:6).[21] The focus is now on action rather than ambience; the flow has now reached the point of climax.

In the first instance, the woman seeks fruitful fortification (raisins, apples) to fulfill her intense amorous desires. She confesses she has become "faint" or "weak" (חלה) with love (Song 2:5). In addition to implying flagging physical strength (such as Samson faces with shorn hair [Judg 16:7, 11, 17]), the term often refers to debilitating illness and occasionally to sword-inflicted battle wounds (1 Kgs 22:34).[22] Hence the woman's

---

18. For example, Num 1:52; 2:2, 3, 10, 17, 25, 31, 34; 10:14, 18, 22, 25. Outside of Numbers and the Song, the only other reference to דגל in the Hebrew Bible occurs in Ps 20:5, also involving the image of a military banner or standard.

19. Keel (*Song*, 85) writes, "The banner erected over the female . . . carries the symbol 'Love.' 'Love' is her mission and her patron goddess. A concrete image for this symbol could well be the dove."

20. Michael Fishbane, *Song of Songs*, JPS Bible Commentary (Lincoln: University of Nebraska Press, 2015), 65; 228 n. 156. The woman also addresses the daughters with masculine pronouns in 1:6; 3:5; 5:8.

21. Again, incorporating a wider audience does not presuppose a literal crowd at the love nest; their presence draws the hearer/reader in more intimately in a voyeuristic but not illicit sense. Theirs is a special love, inviting our comparison and contrast with other loves; see Exum, *Song*, 7–8, 116.

22. The LXX of Song 2:5 reads "wounded (τιτρώσκω) with love." The verb could connote a physical wounding, as in battle (Deut 1:44; 1 Kgs 22:34; Jdt 16:12; 2 Macc 11:9) or a psychological anguish (2 Macc 3:16). The love-struck woman in the Song

condition might be aptly diagnosed as "lovesick" or "love struck." She is clearly affected by love on a deep, somatic level: this is no casual, merely titillating, affair. But we need not assume a stereotypical image of the fair, weak-kneed damsel who swoons in the presence of powerful men, as the Greek Esther faints before the fearsome Persian king (Esth 15:1-7, LXX). A better royal analogy would be the Queen of Sheba's rapt response to Solomon's overwhelming wisdom and wealth, such that "there was no more spirit in her" (1 Kgs 11:15). But she doesn't literally faint, and she holds her own with Solomon with her incisive questions and lavish gifts (11:1-13). The Song's woman, too, is no impressionable young romantic who has taken leave of her senses; indeed, as we have seen, she takes full measure of her senses in her rich experience of love. Now, sensing that she's approaching the limits of her vigor, she pleads for energy-boosting raisins—or raisin cakes—and apples.[23] Though such fruits were common accoutrements of lovemaking, the woman does not seek them as aphrodisiacs per se. From the opening line of the Song, she has been fully charged with desire.[24] She simply longs to maintain her passion to the end, more like a powerful distance runner needing mid-race refueling snacks from friends on the sidelines.

As with the leafy trees implied in Song 1:16-17, "raisin cakes" (אשׁישׁות) were associated with cultic as well as erotic rituals; raisin cakes appear in positive contexts of Israelite worship (2 Sam 6:17-19; 1 Chron 16:3) and in foreign, idolatrous scenarios (Isa 16:7; Hos 3:1). But in any case, once again the activity of the Song's lovers, while illustrative of intense devotion, focuses wholly on their human, embodied relationship with each other rather than with the divine. A broader theological perspective may assume God's delight in their bond and, broader still, their reflection of God's perfect love as God-imaged beings, but these are secondary readings. The primary world of the Song is unabashedly natural and human.

Before she makes her final and most solemn plea to her daughter-friends in Song 2:7, the woman describes the lovemaking position with her partner: "his left arm is under my head, and his right arm embraces

---

notably contrasts again with the "strange" licentious woman of Proverbs who "has wounded (τιτρώσκω) and laid low" many young men (Prov 7:26, NETS).

23. Fishbane (*Song*, 62) notes, "This edible [raisin cake] was thus some kind of 'energy booster,' and is used here to suggest some support for or inducement of love."

24. Supporting a non-aphrodisiac interpretation of raisin cakes, see Fox, *Song*, 109; Murphy, *Song*, 136–37; Exum, *Song*, 116.

me" (2:6, NIV; see also 8:3).[25] This common erotic posture stresses rapt—
and wrapped—intimacy: tight and secure envelopment, like a Russian
nesting doll-couple within the concentric outer enclosures of the "couch"
(1:12) and the bower (1:16-17).[26]

The woman's second summons to her companions seems to soar to
the intense form of an oath-bound entreaty—"I adjure you" or "You
must swear to me"—with two typical components: (1) the witnessing
and enforcing *authority* behind the oath and (2) the specific *responsibility* being demanded of the oath-taker (what must or must not be done
on penalty of perjury). It is possible, however, that the woman employs
this legal formula more playfully than seriously, more on the order of a
"pinky swear" among girlfriends in modern American life.[27] She is after
all in a love nest, not a courtroom.

The authorities she invokes to adjudicate her adjuration appear to support a more frivolous environment: "I adjure you . . . by the [female]
gazelles or the wild does" (Song 2:7). Such forest creatures hardly inspire
fear and trepidation. Quite the opposite, they evoke images of lithesome
grace and natural beauty, perfectly suited for poetic love scenes set in
the fields and woodlands, as we have in this Song stanza. Still, lurking
behind these winsome zoological figures may be more fearsome theological associations. The terms for "gazelles" (צבאות) and "wild/field does"
(אילות השדה) bear close resemblance to powerful divine titles—the Lord God
of "[Military] Hosts" (צבאות), especially in the prophets Isaiah, Jeremiah,
and Amos, and "God Almighty" (אל שדי) (see Gen 17:1; 28:3; Exod 6:3; and
frequently in Job). A feminist reading might celebrate a female speaker's

25. The NRSV features the man's hands instead of his arms and treats the statement as a wish rather than an observation: "O that his left hand were under my
head, and that his right hand embraced me." The Hebrew simply reads "right" and
"left" without designating "hand" or "arm." But "arms" are more appropriate to the
picture of full "embrace" (NIV, CEB). Alternatively, some versions opt for a mixed
image: "his left *hand* is under my head and his right *arm* embraces me" (NAB, NJPS,
NASB). Chana Bloch and Ariel Bloch read it as "his right hand beneath my head, his
left arm holding me close" (*The Song of Songs: The World's First Great Love Poem* [New
York: Modern Library, 1995], 57, 151–52). While the utterance may be taken as a plea
for future experience, the grammar does not demand such a reading. The only verb
in the sentence (חבק, "embrace") is in the imperfect form and may suggest a future
(LXX) or present scenario (NIV, NAB, CEB, KJV); see Exum, *Song*, 117.
26. On the parallel "reclining" of the couple on the (1) "couch/bed," (2) in the
"house," and (3) in each other's "embrace" in 1:12–17 and 2:4–7, see Fox, *Song*, 107.
27. Exum (*Song*, 119) takes the oath as "light-hearted, not solemn."

invocation of such authoritative divine names, normally pronounced by patriarchs, male prophets and sages, and even God "himself" (Gen 17:1; 35:11; Exod 6:3). Naomi stands out as an exception to this pattern, but her perceived experience of the Almighty is decidedly oppressive: "The Almighty [שדי] has dealt bitterly with me. . . . the LORD has dealt harshly with me, and the Almighty [שדי] has brought calamity upon me" (Ruth 1:20-21). By contrast, if the Song's woman in fact alludes to the Almighty Lord of Hosts, she boldly assumes this divine figure is on her side against any who might thwart her intentions.

Still, we must remember that she addresses her charge to "the daughters of Jerusalem." While we have observed a degree of tension between her and these women, it is scarcely a pitched battle. They remain her associates throughout the Song, though with elements of conflict and suspicion that can complicate any relationship. The Song's female protagonist is an intelligent, passionate woman, but no theologian or prophet, and her circle of companions is not a religious conventicle or prayer group. Wordplays between frolicking deer and ferocious deity are just that: *playful* uses of language befitting the intense and intimate—yet pleasing and teasing—play of love, as if the woman says tongue-in-cheek: "Listen up, ladies: if you mess with this love between me and my man, you will gosh darn have hell to pay!"

But what is it exactly that the woman is asking her friends—and by extension, us readers—*not* to do? This same adjuration appears twice more in the Song at climactic points (3:5; 8:4; see 5:8), signaling its importance in understanding the entire Poem. The interpretive options boil down to two antithetical concerns: either "Do not push or rush into love prematurely, before it's ready to *start*"; or "Do not interrupt or impede love before it's ready to *stop*."[28] In the first case, the sign on the door (or banner on the bower) might be, "Slow Down: Dangerous Curve Ahead!" The second might warn, "Love in Session: Do Not Disturb!" In both cases, the object of concern is Love itself (האהבה) in powerful, personified presence: "Do not wake or rouse Love until it pleases" (2:7; NJPS).[29] With a mind of its own, Love operates as a volatile force, opting to move slowly or quickly as it wills to both the frustration and delight of lovers swept up in its impulsive current. Best to let it be and run its course.

---

28. I simplify here. For a helpful sketch of eight interpretive options, see Brian P. Gault, "An Admonition against 'Rousing Love': The Meaning of the Enigmatic Refrain in Song of Songs," *BBR* 20 (2010): 161–84. Several of these options are closely related, however, with only slight variations and nuances.

29. Exum, *Song*, 118.

But doesn't this personification—and virtual coronation—of Love effectively disempower the woman (and the man) and dissipate her agency regarding her amorous experience? What's a poor girl to do in the throes of Love's overwhelming force but give in, for good or ill? Her body is not her own. At this point, feminist interpreters would mount a strong critique, by exposing the Song's reductive stereotype of a weak, helpless woman, lovesick in the most shallow, feeble sense, with no power to resist Love's assault, and love struck in the most abusive, violent sense. But as we have seen throughout this love-nest scene, the woman has actively embraced her passionate experience with her self-determined body, voice, mind, and will. She has proven herself every bit a match for her strong male lover and for the mighty wave of Love.

Moreover, interpreting the stanza of Song 1:9–2:7 as a poetic-narrative account of the couple's enacted lovemaking—not simply its anticipation—tilts the climax in 2:7 toward the second option: "Love in Session: Do not Disturb!" But while the context favors this reading, the immediate text pushes back with the key repeated verb עור, meaning "arouse, awaken" from a state of rest. Hence, it's certainly plausible that the woman pleads for her friends not to "wake up" dormant Love before it's ready to ignite the couple's passionate union. But then, back to context, what exactly have they been up to in their love nest, if Love has been asleep and not aroused or awakened? They've certainly not been woozily napping on separate sides of the bed waiting for something to stimulate them! But neither have they been stoked in a nonstop frenzy of lovemaking. Their elegantly expressed passion, while rich and strong, has also been deeply reflective and restful. The woman basks in her lover's calm nuzzling between her breasts (1:13), and his two-armed envelopment of her (2:6) suits a posture of pre- or post-coital cuddling as well as more intense erotic stimulation. Love has its rhythms of arousal and release, energy and rest, and it is this whole love experience that the woman wants to enjoy undisturbed and undiminished until it has spent its full desire.[30]

---

30. Supporting the "Do Not Disturb" reading, see Fox, *Song*, 107, 109–10; Gault, "Admonition" and "A 'Do Not Disturb' Sign: Reexamining the Adjuration Refrain in Song of Songs," *JSOT* 36 (2011): 93–104. Gault's articles are especially helpful, supporting his thesis: "The literary structure [of the Song] contains cycles in which the lovers progress from separation to reunion, at rest in each other's arms. Perhaps the poet intentionally uses עור as a metaphor, portraying the lovers at rest and cautioning others from disturbing this love" (" 'Do Not Disturb'," 103).

# Song of Songs 2:8-17

## *Viewing, Cooing, and Wooing*

From the setting of the bucolic love nest and wine hut that the couple shares, the stage shifts to the woman's house from which the man seeks to draw her into the luscious vernal hillside bursting with fresh botanical life. The architectural and geological images in this stanza mark boundaries separating the male and female, though these are hardly insuperable. The man bounds "over the hills . . . like a gazelle" (Song 2:8-9) and beckons to the woman beyond the wall (2:8-12, 17), while the woman, for her part, though momentarily ensconced in her house like a dove in a rock crevice (2:9, 14), is more than capable of flight to her lover. Moreover, the "little foxes," whatever persons they might represent (see below), typify wild, agile, resourceful animals capable of burrowing under fence lines and breaking into vineyards (2:15). This stanza negotiates the tension between boundary and autonomy, with a heavy tipping toward the freedom pole. The flora springs forth from its earthen tomb, and the fauna flits about through land and sky with reckless abandon.

*Song of Songs 2:8-17*

| [W → D] | [M → W (in W's self report)] |
|---|---|
| ⁸The voice of my beloved! | "Arise, my love, my fair one, |
|    Look, he comes, |    and come away; |
| leaping upon the mountains, | ¹¹for now the winter is past, |
|    bounding over the hills. |    the rain is over and gone. |
| ⁹My beloved is like a gazelle | ¹²The flowers appear on the earth; |
|    or a young stag. |    the time of singing has come, |
| Look, there he stands | and the voice of the turtledove |
|    behind our wall, |    is heard in our land. |
| gazing in at the windows, | ¹³The fig tree puts forth its figs, |
|    looking through the lattice. |    and the vines are in blossom; |
| ¹⁰My beloved speaks and says to |    they give forth fragrance. |
|    me: | Arise, my love, my fair one, |

### Imagery

| Architectural/Geological | Botanical (Flora) | Zoological (Fauna) |
|---|---|---|
| Wall | Flowers | Gazelle/Young Stag |
| Window | Fig Tree | Dove |
| Lattices | Vines/Vineyards | Foxes |
| Earth/Land | Lilies | |
| Rock (cleft) | | |
| Mountains/Hills (clefts) | | |

From the opening lines—"The voice [קוֹל] of my beloved! Look [הִנֵּה] he comes" (Song 2:8)—acoustic and optic experiences predominate. The lovers' longings crystallize into deep desires to hear each other's sweet voice and to see each other's lovely face (2:14). While the entire stanza seems to be spoken by the woman, a substantial segment at the heart of the unit presents the man's words of supplication to the woman mediated (focalized) through her narrative voice (2:10-14). We the hearers/readers, via the implied audience of the Jerusalem daughters, thus encounter the woman's memory or imagined script of her lover's entreaty or, to add another interpretive level, the Poet's version of what she or he constructs as the woman's recollection or invention of the man's speech. This issue of "whose voice is it, anyway?" persists throughout the Song and poses a special concern for feminist interpreters sharply aware of the power

and come away.
¹⁴Oh my dove, in the clefts of the
      rock,
   in the covert of the cliff,
let me see your face,
   let me hear your voice;
for your voice is sweet,
   and your face is lovely."
**[W → D (?)]**
¹⁵"Catch us the foxes,
   the little foxes,
that ruin the vineyards—

for our vineyards are in blos-
      som."
¹⁶My beloved is mine and I am
      his;
   he pastures his flock among
      the lilies.
**[W → M]**
¹⁷Until the day breathes
   and the shadows flee,
turn, my beloved, be like a gazelle
   or a young stag on the cleft
      mountains.

of voice (who has the right to speak for whom?) to shape self-identities and social relations.

Speaking to and for women has been a major tool of domination and oppression of women in patriarchal cultures.[1] In a suggestive twist on this pattern in Song 2:10-14, the female lover speaks for her male suitor to herself, though presumably within overhearing earshot of her girlfriends. But is her self-reporting authentic, however that might be judged? Does her recitation reflect a legitimate, self-affirming "woman's viewpoint" concerning how she wants to be courted? Is it significant that she speaks directly to the man only in the stanza's final line (1:17b), shifting to second masculine singular imperative? Of course, given the impossibility—and essentialist arrogance—of defining a generic "woman's viewpoint," not to mention the social pressures impinging on her perspectives, these questions defy confident answers. But they remain worth considering in our assessment of the Song woman's agency and autonomy in relation to her male partner.

## The Gazing Gazelle (2:8-9)

Having just summoned a herd of gazelles and wild does to guarantee and guard, as it were, the couple's pastoral love nest (Song 2:7), the woman now envisions her lover as a frisky gazelle or "young stag" (2:9)

---

1. See the section on "Voice and Rhetoric" and "Power and Experience" in F. Scott Spencer, "Feminist Criticism," in *Hearing the New Testament: Strategies for Interpretation*, 2nd ed., ed. Joel B. Green (Grand Rapids: Eerdmans, 2010), 295–304, 311–18.

pursuing her in her house. The porous boundaries between city and countryside remain in view, with the woman now situated inside an urban walled dwelling and the man approaching her from the hillside. He pursues her with unbounded energy that is at once passionate and playful, befitting the youthful cervine imagery. He can scarcely contain himself in a rapid sequence of motions tracked in two participial triplets: coming/leaping/bounding (2:8) and standing/gazing/looking (2:9). The first triad swiftly brings the man to the woman's town and residence. The second triad slows him down somewhat, restraining him from bounding right through her door! But he remains taut with desire and keeps pressing closer with increasing visual intensity, which, however, he seems intent on concealing from his beloved. He wants to see her without being seen, proceeding from (1) surveying her house from behind the *wall*, to (2) gazing inside through the *windows*, to (3) peering in more closely through the *lattice*.[2]

Why all this stealth and stalking? Why not simply knock on his beloved's door and speak with her? Is he afraid that he might not be able to control himself, that he might come on too strong and pounce right on her? Possibly, but his feelings are not the main focus here. Recall that this part of the Poem is being sung by the woman, chiefly reflecting her perceptions of the man's approach. She calls for her chorus attendants to look with her as she looks at the man looking at her. Thereby the potentially threatening scenario of a dangerous stalker or "peeping Tom" is defused.[3] The woman's keen surveillance of her lover's movements pulls down the walls and opens up the windows separating them. He stands fully exposed before her, not as a prowling lion but as a prancing gazelle—her "beloved" and beautiful gazelle (צבי is a homonym denoting both "beautiful" and "gazelle"). Their gamboling hide-and-seek game is in full play again (see 1:7-8), and the woman has the advantage that she is delighted to share with her friends.

A feminist perspective, however, as noted earlier, remains wary about women serving as the object of the male gaze, even in playful contexts—

2. This scenario presents a notable inversion of the male sage in Proverbs 7 looking out—both curiously and disapprovingly—through his window/lattice at the street prostitutes' seduction of impressionable young men (7:6-23). In the Song, the young man is the peering seeker and the woman, the watchful yet welcoming lover (but no prostitute or adulteress) inside her home; see further connections with Proverb 7 in the next Song stanza (3:1-5).

3. On the male "lover . . . playing the peeping Tom," see Marvin H. Pope, *Song of Songs: A New Translation with Introduction and Commentary*, AB 7C (Garden City, NY: Doubleday, 1977), 392.

and maybe especially there, since such contexts can downplay serious issues. Voyeuristic male attention, a staple of modern crime and horror shows, is typically a prelude to assault and functions to indulge base male fantasy and to reinforce female vulnerability. This is not to take all the fun out of the Song-lovers' courting romps in which the woman is fully aware and welcoming of the advances her lover makes. But it does keep readers, male and female, from blithe naïveté that the dance of love always trips along blissfully. The world of the Song is not all fun and games, as we have seen and as will soon become more evident. Preying foxes and eyeing sentinels lurk in the shadows (Song 2:15; 3:3; 5:7), with potential for harming the woman.

## The Cooing Dove (2:10-14)

Any illusion of a surprise ambush by the man is broken when he calls out to his lover from outside her window. He wants her to know he's there, and by all accounts she's delighted to hear the voice of her beloved whose advances she's been tracking. Recall again that the man's speech is filtered through the woman's report: she controls the message and fully engages its summons. The fact, however, that the man calls to the woman from outside her house still suggests a private communication or secret assignation. They seem to be colluding in the hiding game against monitors who might wish to thwart their escape: the woman's controlling brothers (Song 1:6), perhaps, or even her mother at this stage (1:6; see also 3:4, 11; 6:9; 8:1-2). The man is wooing the receptive woman to make a furtive nocturnal getaway before the day dawns and the shadowy night dissipates. To avoid detection and detention, they must flee before night's "shadows flee" (2:17).[4]

---

4. The time frame could be the break of dawn or dusk, but the language and context better fit a secret joint getaway after a night of trysting just before daylight. As Chana Bloch and Ariel Bloch write, "before day breathes; before the shadows of night are gone" (*The Song of Songs: The World's First Great Love Poem* [New York: Modern Library, 1995], 65, 157). Robert Alter puts it, "Until morning's breeze blows and the shadows flee," with the comment, "she clearly invites him to spend the night." (*Strong as Death Is Love: The Song of Songs, Ruth, Esther, Jonah, and Daniel: A Translation with Commentary* [New York: Norton, 2015], 18). For the opposite view see Marcia Falk who translates, "Until the day is over and the shadows flee," with the comment, "the female speaker banishes her beloved until nighttime" (*The Song of Songs: A New Translation and Interpretation* [New York: HarperCollins, 1990], 179); and Axel Van de Sande argues that הצללים always refers to daytime shadows cast by the sun (*ombres du soleil*) ("Le souffle du jour et la fuite des hombres en Ct 2:17 [4:6]: matin ou soir?"

### The Song and Ecofeminism
### (2:8-17)

Ecofeminism acknowledges interconnections between the exploitation of the earth and the oppression of women. But ecofeminism is a diverse inquiry characterized by various questions: Is the female body parallel with the earth? Are such parallels empirical-historical (e.g., women working closely with/in land), conceptual-symbolic (e.g., women symbolically linked with land), or epistemic (e.g., women possessing greater knowledge of land and implicated in its destruction)? Does the text evidence a dualistic substructure, such as nature/ culture, man/woman, mind/ body, that needs to be overcome? Is there evidence of domination or exploitation of the land? Of women? Do such dominations intersect with race or class?

One way to consider the relationship between women and land is to explore the question of voice, a traditionally important topic for feminist inquiry and one that extends to the landscape here. In Song 2:8-17, the Hebrew word קוֹל ("voice, speech") is used four times, applied to the woman, the man, and the turtledove.

First, the poem is cast in the voice of the woman. She speaks: "The voice [קוֹל] of my beloved!" (Song 2:8). The man's voice is embedded in her speech, and in a sense authorized by it. In this poem, the land also "speaks": This verse (2:12) marks the only place the word אֶרֶץ ("land," "earth") occurs in the Song. But it doesn't mean "earth" in a universal or impersonal way; the phrase "in our land" (בְּאַרְצֵנוּ) reveals a sense of identity with the land and attendant notions of responsibility and care. The man says, "The voice [קוֹל] of the turtledove is heard in our land" (2:12). Some scholars have interpreted this as an instance where earth "raises its voice in celebration," or "finds its voice."[5]

---

*VT* 62 [2012]: 276-83). The pun on the couple "fleeing" before the shadowy evening "flees" is mine and pushes the Hebrew some. The term for "come away" (הלך) in Song 2:10 and 13 is a common verb of motion ("come, go, walk") without the immediate urgent connotations of "flee" (נוס). But in the present setting, the man doubtless pleads for the woman to "come away" with due haste—to "run away with him," not walk!

5. Norman C. Habel, ed., *Readings from the Perspective of Earth*, Earth Bible 1 (Cleveland: Pilgrim , 2000), 24; The Earth Bible Team, "The Voice of Earth: More than Metaphor?," in *The Earth Story in the Psalms and the Prophets*, ed. Norman C. Habel and Shirley Wurst (Sheffield: Sheffield Academic, 2001), 23–28; Francis Landy, *Paradoxes of Paradise, Identity and Difference in the Song of Songs*, BLS 7 (Sheffield: Almond Press, 1983), 17. See also Hendrik Viviers, "Eco-Delight in the Song of Songs," in *The Earth Story in Wisdom Traditions*, ed. Norman C. Habel and Shirley Wurst (Sheffield: Sheffield Academic, 2001), 152.

But if we readers perceive the voice of the earth here, it is by peering through a latticework of textual representation: the earth's "voice" is embedded in the man's "voice," which is embedded in the woman's "voice." The woman remains the principal agent and authority. The passive verbs further embed the earth in human perception: the blossoms "are seen" (נראו); the voice of the turtledove "is heard" (נשמע). The flourishing of the landscape, in this poem, is a tertiary experience and a human evaluation.

In this way, the poem compels the reader to acknowledge that human experience is inseparable from experience within the landscape. The Song consistently blurs boundaries between land and lovers, making us wonder where one ends and the other begins. The boy is imagined as a gazelle: is the sound of his approach his voice or hooves rustling the brush? The woman is described as a dove: is her sweet voice human speech or birdsong? Such details hint at a non-dualistic understanding of the human situation, in which the flourishing of the land and human flourishing are inextricable. By the Song's own terms, what is truly good for women also benefits the larger ecological order. This reading of voice resonates with ecofeminist concerns about non-domination and participation in the landscape and shows how the Song can be a resource for resisting dualisms in the Western tradition.

*Elaine T. James*

The man clearly declares his intentions for his lover in framing impera-tival pleas: "Arise, my love, my fair one, and come away" (Song 2:10, 13). Within this frame he paints a beautiful picture of the blossoming spring season the lovers can enjoy together in the countryside when the day breaks. Erotic and ecological elements coalesce.[6] As the dark shadows of night give way to the fresh morning air (2:17), so the cold showers of winter give way to fragrant vernal ambience (2:11-13). Budding botanical and animal figures fill out the springtime environment (2:12-13):

Blooming flowers "on the earth/land" (ארץ)
   Cooing turtledove "in our earth/land" (ארץ)
Blossoming fig trees and grapevines

Between identifying the flowers and the turtledove is an announcement of the coming "time of הזמיר" (2:12), from the root זמר, which can denote

6. See "The Song and Ecofeminism" by Elaine James, pp. 46–47.

either "pruning" or "singing." Cleverly, both ideas may be in view, providing an elegant bridge between the flowers and turtledove: the *pruning* of the former for maximum flourishing and the *crooning* of the second to attract the most desirable mate.[7]

If a choice must be made, the singing or cooing of the turtledove seems primary, elaborating on its "voice [קוֹל] heard in our land" (Song 2:12) celebrating the end of its migratory return to Israel, the beginning of spring, and the longing for a love-match. Its cooing typically stretched across the day, from dawn to dusk, in persistent outcall.[8] The shift from budding flowers "on *the* earth/land" in the opening line of 2:12 to singing doves "in *our* earth/land" in the last line may signal the human lovers' close identification with a pair of amorous turtledoves calling to each other. Though the male voice takes the lead, the female chimes in with a kind of ventriloquist echo. From their perspective, this is altogether *our* Song in *our* world.

The male lover extends the central image of the dove in Song 2:14, but with notable twists. The terminology shifts from the specific turtledove (תּוֹר, used only in 2:12) to the more generic dove (יוֹנָה) featured repeatedly in the Song. The woman has already compared the man's lovely eyes to doves (1:15; see also 5:12), and the man will soon return the favor (4:1; see also 5:2; 6:9). Here, however, the man can neither directly see the woman's beautiful dove-like eyes nor clearly hear her mesmerizing voice because she is ensconced in a cliff-side crevice. His desire for unimpeded intercourse with her still awaits fulfillment. His dove—"*my* dove" now, in anticipation but not yet consummation of "*our* love" in our land—is presently concealed in her rock-nest.

But while she may be playing coy with her lover, she's not really hiding from him. He knows where she is, and she knows that he knows this. She's not run off from him to some cavern hideout; this is her natural "dove" habitat, the metaphorical equivalent to being inside her walled, windowed home. She's happy that her lover has come to call, but he

---

7. See Michael V. Fox, *The Song of Songs and the Ancient Egyptian Love Songs* (Madison: University of Wisconsin Press, 1985), 113; Pope, *Song*, 395–96; Bloch and Bloch, *Song*, 154–55.

8. Alice Parmelee writes, "By sheer repetition the turtledove attracts attention to its song. Softer and sleepier than the song of other pigeons, it is described as a purring '*roor-r-r*'" (*All the Birds of the Bible: Their Stories, Identification, and Meaning* [New York: Harper, 1959], 172–73); see also E. F. F. Bishop, "Palestiniana in Canticulus," *CBQ* 29 (1967): 25–26.

must still woo her outside. And he must assure her that she will be safe and secure with him, protected from unwanted advances and potential attacks; for, as Debra Band's painting hauntingly illustrates, the shadowy threat of predators ever lurks outside the woman-dove's alcove. The Songstress is scarcely a quivering, skittish little bird, but she does have to remain alert to threats in her environment.

### *Illumination 2 Commentary*
*(The Hebrew text depicted is Song 2:14)*

In this flirtatious passage, the man compares his girl to a dove hiding from predators in a rock cranny. The man's cupping hands offer protection to a dove, half-hidden in an alcove of the garden wall while a hawk casts its threatening shadow against the stones of the wall nearby.

Beneath the light tone is a plea for trust: the woman's trust of her lover, Israel's trust in God. Midrash compares the people of Israel to a gentle dove; just as the Israelites seek shelter from enemies ranging from Pharaoh's charioteers to the Amalekites (not to mention the Roman government of the Mishnaic period), a dove seeks protection from a pursuing hawk above and a snake below.[9] Hence, in the miniature above the text, the man's cupped hands rise to a niche in the stone wall where the dove is half-hidden. The shadow of the hawk that the dove flees is visible on the wall nearby. Tossed onto the gold background (in the original color version) are caper branches, which still sprout from crannies of stone walls and dusty corners throughout Jerusalem. The caper was prized for the agricultural value of its buds, berries, and tender new leaves, and celebrated in the Talmud for its ability—like Israel itself—to persevere through even the most

---

9. See Debra Band, *The Song of Songs: The Honeybee in the Garden* (Philadelphia: JPS, 2005), 21.

hostile conditions with no visible support, only invisible Divine loving kindness.

The philosophical interpretation suggests that the dove's hiddenness resides in its dependence on the senses of sight and sound, while logically derived knowledge rises above the limitations of material senses.[10]

*Debra Band*

So the male lover tries again, this time with more urgency. Notice the progression from the simple summons of Song 2:10, 13 to the more intense and intimate entreaties of 2:14.

| Song 2:10, 13 | Song 2:14 |
| --- | --- |
| Arise<br>My love<br>My fair one<br>Come away | Let me see your face<br>Let me hear your voice<br>Your voice is sweet<br>Your face is lovely |

The man now expresses his longing for a full visual (facial) and aural (vocal) experience of his beloved. Instead of gawking and speaking at her as an object of attention, he wants to receive her as her own subject: to see *her* face and hear *her* voice. The Qal imperatives of 2:10, 13, commanding the woman to act ([*You*] Arise/Come away) as *his* (*my* love/fair one) subject or subjected one modulate to the causative Hiphil imperatives of 2:14, imploring the woman-dove to *let herself* be seen and heard by him in complete control of *her* agency (*your* face/voice). Thus, the "me/your" perspective of 2:14 blends nicely with the mutual "our" viewpoint of 2:12b.

Moreover, as I've already stressed, the significance of *voice* ranges beyond a simple tonal characteristic (sweet/raspy, high-/low-pitched, soprano/alto) to represent personal substance and authority. So too, the notion of *face* constitutes more than an assemblage of pretty or ugly anatomical features above the neck: weak chin, luscious lips, pointed nose, droopy eyes, etc. Actually the Hebrew term מראה, rendered "face" or "countenance" in several versions of Song 2:14 (NRSV, NIV, NAB,

---

10. Levi ben Gershom (Gersonides), *Commentary on the Song of Songs*, trans. and ed. Menachem Kellner, YJS 28 (New Haven: Yale University Press, 1998), 45.

NJPS, KJV), more properly denotes "form" (NAB) or " 'appearance,' " which includes the total visual impression."[11] Chana and Ariel Bloch translate the two "face" lines as "Let me see you, all of you!/I love to look at you," and further comment that "the lover wants to see the [woman] from every side."[12] Likewise, Cheryl Exum tersely captures the desire for a personal, subjective I-you encounter: "Let me see you/you are lovely."[13] Here, the gazing man does not want to look his lovebird up and down or even just around her face, as if taking an inventory of parts to describe to his buddies after work. He simply, yet passionately, wants to see her as she is.

We may stick with the focus on the "face" if we understand it as a prime revealer of our emotional selves, as Charles Darwin and others have demonstrated,[14] or as the window to the "soul" or reader's guide to the "embodied subject," as the philosopher Roger Scruton has argued.

> The face . . . is the threshold at which the other appears, offering "this thing that I am" as a partner in dialogue. This feature goes to the heart of what it is to be human. Our interpersonal relations would be inconceivable without the assumption that we can commit ourselves through promises, take responsibility now for some event in the future or the past, make vows that bind us forever to the one who receives them, and undertake obligations that we regard as untransferable to anyone else. *And all this we read in the face.*[15]

Scruton continues, with special application to erotic relations:

> Especially do we read those things in the face of the beloved in the look of love. Our sexual emotions are founded on individualizing thoughts: it is *you* whom I want and the type or pattern. This individualizing intentionality does not merely stem from the fact that it is persons (in other words, individuals) whom we desire. It stems from the fact that

---

11. Pope, *Song*, 401.

12. Bloch and Bloch (*Song*, 61) also note that the first use of מראה in 2:14 is plural ("let me see your *sights, views*"). "The plural is meaningful and fully motivated: the lover wants to see the Shulamite from every side" (156).

13. J. Cheryl Exum, *Song of Songs*, OTL (Louisville: Westminster John Knox, 2005), 120.

14. Charles Darwin, *The Expression of the Emotions in Man and Animals*, 4th ed. (Oxford: Oxford University Press, 2009 [1872 orig.]); Paul Ekman, *Emotions Revealed: Recognizing Faces and Feelings to Improve Communication and Emotional Life*, 2nd ed. (New York: St. Martin's Press, 2007).

15. Roger Scruton, *The Soul of the World* (Princeton: Princeton University Press, 2014), 104 (emphasis added).

the other is desired as an embodied subject, and not as a body. *And the embodied subject is what we see in the face.*[16]

Above all, the wooer desires to look his beloved and lovely dove "in the I."[17]

## The Spoiling Foxes (2:15)

The meaning of this verse about "little foxes" as field raiders is difficult to decipher despite the clarity of the image and the continuity with blossoming vines from 2:13. But who's asking whom to "catch" these creatures and for what purpose remains ambiguous. Something sinister seems to threaten the springtime idyll: these foxes, however small, aim to "ruin" ("corrupt," "spoil") the vineyards. But how precisely do our lovers fit into this picture? Or put another way, how might these pesky foxes spoil their plans?

The verse begins with a notable shift in address from singular to plural. Suddenly the focus expands beyond the one-to-one exchange between lovers. The imperative form changes to masculine plural; some *group* of fox hunters is being summoned on behalf of *us*: "[You all] catch [for] us the foxes" (Song 2:15). The "us" may refer to the two lovers, connecting back to their anticipated dove-like mating in *"our* land" (2:12) and forward to their ripening revelry in *"our* vineyards" in the last line of 2:15, expanding from *"the* vines" in 2:13. In some sense, then, the foxes potentially affect the relationship between the couple. Accordingly, one member of the couple must be the supplicant on behalf of their bond. The woman has been the narrator throughout the stanza, though reporting the man's desires in 2:10-14. The shift in audience in 2:15 seems to break this segment and return the woman to her own unmediated voice spoken to her group of choral companions; recall that the "daughters of Jerusalem" are sometimes addressed as a masculine-plural grammatical unit. Given the multiple number and slippery tactics of "little foxes," however, the woman may also be calling more widely to any and all available fox

16. Scruton, *Soul*, 104 ("you" emphasis original; other emphasis added). Scruton also notes, "A body is an assemblage of body parts; an embodied person is a free being revealed in the flesh. When we speak of a beautiful human body we are referring to the beautiful embodiment of a person, and not to a body merely considered as such" (40) in *Beauty: A Very Short Introduction* (Oxford: Oxford University Press, 2011).
17. Scruton, *Soul*, 75.

catchers, and she may be as concerned about potential vulpine threats to all women (or the "daughters" more particularly) as to herself.[18]

So who do these vine-munching foxes represent and why do they need nabbing? An obvious place to begin is the widespread symbolic fox-sex link. Unlike in modern American parlance, however, where "foxy" primarily designates a sexually attractive and aggressive woman (a vixen; "little fox" morphs into "sex-kitten"), in ancient culture exemplified in Egyptian love songs and Greek poetry (Homer, Theocritus), fables (Aesop), and vase iconography, foxes represented frisky, lusty young men on the prowl for the budding fruit (grapes/vines) of luscious nubile women.[19] Most likely, then, the woman in the Song issues a lookout notice to her lover and/or girlfriends for roguish youths on the make. But to what end and at what threat level?

At first blush there's nothing surprising here: boys will be boys and will chase girls. Most women (I think) don't mind the chase if it doesn't get out of hand and violate their veto power. No need to round up and get rid of all these foxes; keeping a close eye on them should be sufficient. Though the woman does call for someone to "catch" them, the verb אחז can refer to a more benign, though still aggressive, "holding" or "grasping" as well as a hostile "seizing" or "trapping." In fact, it refers elsewhere in the Song to each lover's passionate embrace or holding of the other: "I *held* him, and would not let him go" (3:4); "I will climb the palm tree and *lay hold* of its branches" (7:8). Perhaps, then, the woman is urging her friends to latch onto one of these foxy suitors as she has snagged her beloved one. Favoring this scenario, Exum notes the wide disparity in freedom in this society, allowing men to roam about as they will while carefully circumscribing women's movements, largely within domestic space.[20] So the best women can do is trap and tame a wild man. Of course, Exum in no way endorses this arrangement as a

18. Othmar Keel asserts, "It would be best to think of an indeterminate addressee—something like, 'Won't someone catch us the foxes?' " (*The Song of Songs: A Continental Commentary*, trans. Frederick J. Gaiser [Minneapolis: Fortress, 1994], 108).

19. On foxes' associations with sexuality in the ancient world, see the sketches from the thirteenth–twelfth century BCE reproduced in Keel (*Song*, 109). See the discussion of Greek literature and iconography (on vases) in Anselm C. Hagedorn, "Of Foxes and Vineyards: Greek Perspectives on the Song of Songs," *VT* 53 (2003): 337–52. See also the imagery in Egyptian love songs in Fox (*Song*, 10–11, 78, 114), e.g., Egyptian Song no. 4, with a female speaker: "My heart is not yet done with your lovemaking, my (little) wolf cub."

20. Exum, *Song*, 130.

feminist ideal, since, if pressed to its conclusion, it feeds into the "ball and chain" stereotype. It simply reflects social realities of the day and does, at least, encourage women's agential working within the system to their advantage.

On a more playful note, which the Song is happy to employ from time to time, the woman may again be teasing her lover about his competition, namely, the bevy of "little foxes" sniffing around her, akin to his ogling shepherd-companions in Song 1:7. She has no interest in these inferior "little" pursuers but neither does she want her chosen man to take her for granted. For "us"—that is, for the sake of their enduring relationship—he and his posse should "catch" his foxy rivals and kick them out of their love-vineyard.[21] As we have seen, however, it's difficult to know how far to press the Song's playful themes. While undeniably celebratory and optimistic, the Song does not reduce to a little love ditty or romantic romp. The party can be crashed, the love nest "disturbed" (2:7), and the fresh spring air choked by an unseasonable chill. In the present case, the lustful foxes, for all their littleness, still have the power to burrow under the walls and fences and *"ruin/corrupt* [חבל] the vineyards" (2:15) of women's sexual identity, either by the personal violation of sexual assault or by interference with the woman's current, committed relationship. The foxes are not only impish "free-running admirers"[22] but also impudent, self-serving predators meriting cautious surveillance by women and by men respectful of women's interests. A hermeneutics of suspicion stays alert for foxy intruders.[23]

This is not to suggest that the Song's star female vocalist cowers in fear or cannot manage volatile male sexuality. The "little" adjective cuts the menacing foxes down to size. Moreover, while they can do real damage, they are not capable of breaking a woman's will and destroying her life, especially her love life. In mocking the wall around Jerusalem being constructed by Nehemiah, the Ammonite Tobiah quips that "any fox

21. For various examples of a teasing, playful interpretation, see Fox (*Song*, 114), Keel (*Song*, 110), and Roland E. Murphy, *The Song of Songs*, Hermeneia (Minneapolis: Fortress, 1990), 141.

22. Keel, *Song*, 108, 110.

23. See Falk's (*Song*, 178) perception of the dangerous elements in this little fox scene: "The . . . 'foxes' are hostile marauders; they seem to represent male figures who are as threatening in this context as are the city guards in poem 19 [Falk's numbering = 3:1-5]. . . . danger lurks in the background of several poems in the Song; this one in particular [2:15] seems to be a mood piece—or perhaps a fragment—emphasizing ominous undercurrents in the collection."

going up would break it down!" (Neh 4:3). In other words, though pesky and predatory, foxes hardly rise to the status of marauding armies; they might burrow underneath or wriggle through cracks in the walls, but they can't smash them down. Of course, they can wreak more havoc on budding vines than stone walls. But still, the woman in the Song, while alert to her and other women's precarious positions in society, remains optimistic that ominous stalkers can be caught and neutralized.[24]

## The Grazing Gazelle (2:16-17)

As the woman opened this stanza with a triple characterization of "my beloved" (דודי, 2:8, 9, 10), so she concludes with a double declaration of this favorite pet name (2:16, 17; see also 1:13). But whereas she formerly described her "beloved" as coming and speaking to her through various barriers, now she announces their intimate union with pristine simplicity: "My beloved is mine and I am his" (2:16) or, more succinctly, "My beloved to/for me [לי] and I to/for him [לו]." The line accentuates the mutuality of their relationship. Yet the order of the woman's claim should not be missed: she embraces him as her own *before* she surrenders herself to him. Her agency receives priority. She has caught her fox.

The woman then reprises pastoral imagery from earlier stanzas, now figuring her lover as one who "pastures his flock among the lilies" (Song 2:16). Recall that the verb for "pasture" or "graze" (רעה) puns on similar sounding words for "see/gaze" and "love/darling," his pet name for her, and that the shepherding meadow represents a trysting tract for the Song's lovers (see 1:7-9). Moreover, the pastoral-romantic landscape has been furnished with an array of flowers, among which the man esteems the woman, "my love" (רעיתי), as the fairest "lily" (שושן) in the land (2:2). Therefore, the woman's second line in 2:16 appears to envision her lover's "grazing" (and gazing) among the delights of her lily-like body. She is the blossoming field and vineyard where he nibbles at her behest, where she draws him to her and opens herself to him.

All the intense wooing and longing of Song 2:8-15 seems to have led to an idyllic match. But suddenly the woman injects a final note that keeps the scene taut with anticipation. She returns to the gazelle/young stag

---

24. See the paraphrase of the woman's thoughts in Alter (*Strong as Death*, 17): "There are in the world pesky agents of interference that seek to obstruct love's fulfillment, as foxes despoil a vineyard, but our own special vineyard remains flourishing and intact, our love unimpeded."

image of her "beloved" with which she began this stanza, but only now, at the very end, does she address him alone, imploring him to "turn" (סב, imperative) before the day breaks and to leap "like a gazelle . . . on the cleft mountains" (2:17). The intent of the woman's plea is tantalizingly ambiguous, turning on various meanings of the verb סבב: "turn about, go around, surround." The problem is determining the direction of the turning: whether the woman is imploring her lover to turn *away* from her ("Go back to your mountains for now and call on me later"), *toward* her ("Come closer"), or *back around* to her ("Hey, where are you going? Don't give up now, when I'm ready to receive you!").

Other "turning" (סבב) points in the Song attest to variable usage:

- The woman *goes about* the city streets and squares in search of her lover (3:2).
- The sentinels find the woman as they *go about* the city (3:3).
- The sentinels find the woman (again) while *making their rounds* in the city (5:7).
- The male lover pleads for the woman to *turn away* her eyes due to their overwhelming beauty (6:5).

The first three references depict a general "going about" town, trading on the circular, roundabout nuances of the verb but with an aim to find someone along the way. The last reference parallels 2:17 most closely, though with a reversal of speakers. In 6:5 the man begs the woman to divert her eyes from him, but in no way rejecting her. Quite the opposite: the couple is entangled again in their lily-studded, grazing pasture (6:1-3 marks a close parallel with 2:16-17). Since the piercing beauty of her gaze is more than he can stand, however, he simply requests that she glance away before he melts (6:5). Otherwise, he continues to revel in her presence and extol her many charms (6:6-10).

Although certainty eludes us, as always, in interpreting the Song's allusive language, both the immediate and larger contexts of 2:17 suggest that the woman is not dismissing her suitor. From her secure station within her walled, rock-hewn house and with her possible teasing about rival "foxes," she may not have provided the clearest signals of receptivity to her lover's nocturnal advances. So before the night "shadows flee" (2:17) and blow his cover, he may think it prudent to turn away, even trudge away in disappointment, and try his luck another evening. But having pushed her wooer to the limit, the desirous and desirable woman calls him to turn back around and resume his spirited, gazelle-like bounding—not, however, back to the distant mountains whence he came (2:8), but to *her* "cleft mountains" (2:17).

Commentators debate the meaning of this last phrase, with some opting for a literal-topographical reading: "mountains of Bether" (בתר). But no such location, mountainous or otherwise, is known. A more promising tack keys off the meaning of the root as "piece, part," the verb form of which conveys the act of "cutting/cleaving into two pieces" (see Gen 15:10). Applied to "cleft mountains," it suggests two peaks separated by a ravine or valley. It takes little imagination to associate these mountains with the woman's breasts (cleavage), which she again invites her lover to enjoy, though now with more exuberant cavorting than calm nestling, as in Song 1:13. But as Roland E. Murphy comments, the "mountains of Bether" may be a more inclusive "symbol of her own person, . . . of the woman herself," rather than one "part" of her.[25] In any case, she ultimately calls her lover to leap around, about, and "on" her. She urges him to come inside her dwelling, to squeeze with her in her cozy cliff crevice (2:14).

25. Murphy, *Song*, 139, 142. See the more extensive discussion on 4:1-7 concerning the Song's portrayal of the woman's body.

# Song of Songs 3:1-5

# *Seeking and Seizing Her Lover*

If the woman indeed urges her antsy, happy-footed gazelle-lover to turn back around to her in close embrace at the end of the courtship in Song 2:9-17, the Song does not allow us to bask in this union very long. The chase continues, and the longing lingers in the anxious, yet anticipatory, gap between presence and absence.

While my reading of the Song may impose a tighter narrative framework at various points than other critics would allow, most agree that the short stanza in Song 3:1-5 follows a simple plotline, though not at the expense of lyrical expression.[1] The story unfolds in a three-part circular journey from bed → city → bed:

1. In *her bed* at night, the woman longs for her lover and seeks to draw him to her by telepathy, so to speak, or imaginative conjuring. The NRSV, following the LXX, adds that she also "calls out" (καλέω) for him. But he does not respond (3:1).

---

1. Tod Linafelt classifies the Song overall as lyric rather than narrative or dramatic poetry; however, "In the night scenes . . . the narrative impulse is, unusually for the Song of Songs, actually quite strong, even if it serves lyrical ends" ("The Arithmetic of Eros," *Int* 50 [2005]: 251).

*Song of Songs 3:1-5*

**[W → D]**

3:1Upon my bed at night
    I sought him whom my soul
       loves
I sought him, but found him not;
    I called him, but he gave no
       answer.
2"I will rise now and go about the
    city,
    in the streets and in the
       squares;
I will seek him whom my soul
    loves."
    I sought him, but found him
       not.
3The sentinels found me,
    as they went about in the city.

"Have you seen him whom my
    soul loves?"
4Scarcely had I passed them,
    when I found him whom my
       soul loves.
I held him, and would not let him
    go
    until I brought him into my
       mother's house,
    and into the chamber of her
       that conceived me.
5I adjure you, O daughters of
    Jerusalem,
    by the gazelles or the wild
       does;
do not stir up or awaken love
    until it is ready!

2. The woman then decides on a more active pursuit, rising and going about *the city* in search for her lover. She enlists the aid of night watchmen, but they do not respond (3:2-3).

3. Soon the woman finds her lover on her own, clasps him, and brings him back to *her mother's bed*, from where she again enjoins the daughters of Jerusalem not to disturb her lovemaking (3:4-5).

Whether this reflects a dream sequence or real event, singular or recurrent night after night, matters little in imaginative poetic discourse.[2] In the world of the Song, the woman's nocturnal quest for her lover represents a deeply felt, lifelike (if not actual life) experience.

Four times in this stanza, she identifies the object of her devotion as "him whom my soul loves" (3:1-4). The Hebrew term נפש rendered as "soul" in the NRSV should not be interpreted along dualistic Greek

---

2. The "night" term in 3:1 is plural (לילות), suggesting either an iterative meaning "night after night, nightly" (Michael Fishbane, *Song of Songs,* JPS Bible Commentary [Lincoln: University of Nebraska Press, 2015], 83; Michael V. Fox, *The Song of Songs and the Ancient Egyptian Love Songs* [Madison: University of Wisconsin Press, 1985], 117–18) or a generalized singular connotation "during the night [watches]" (Roland E. Murphy, *The Song of Songs,* Hermeneia [Minneapolis: Fortress, 1990], 145).

philosophical and popular Christian lines as some inner psychic essence separate from flesh, blood, and feeling. Rather, נפשׁ encompasses one's entire being, the total embodied "self" or "life" created by God (see Gen 1:20-21, 24, 30; 2:7, 19).[3] The woman passionately longs for her lover's presence with every fiber of her being, with her very life, with all that she is, body-and-"soul."

While the action revolves around the woman from her viewpoint as reported to the Jerusalem daughters, she brings two other characters into the picture in addition to her desired lover. First, in her search mission around the city, she meets, or rather is met by, some "sentinels" or night watchmen making their rounds. They appear quite incidental to the scene, as they have no reply to the woman's request for information about her lover, whom she soon finds on her own. But their watchful police presence in the middle of the night raises the specter of danger: they are not out for an evening stroll but on the lookout for potential threats to the city and its people. The woman scarcely poses any security threat, but she is out of place at a precarious time and risks harm to herself in this environment. Lucky that she runs into these patrollers to shield her from nefarious forces of the night. Or is it? Again, we don't know how the watchmen respond or what they're thinking about this frantic woman roaming the dark streets, perhaps in her nightclothes. Are they trustworthy guardians? Could they take advantage of the situation? All we know is that they are watching her—indeed, they "found" her (Song 3:3). She quickly "passed them" this time (3:4), but she remains on their watch list, and she might do well to watch out for them in future perambulations about town (see 5:7).

Second, the woman mentions her "mother," more specifically, her "mother's house" and bedchamber to which she brings her captured lover (Song 3:4). Moreover, the woman stresses that this is the very place where her mother conceived her (3:4). Nothing in the Song thus far has anticipated this maternal reference. The only prior mention of

---

3. See the helpful entry on various usages of this term in William J. Holladay, including anatomical references to "throat" (Isa 15:4), "neck" (Ps 105:18), and "breath" (Job 41:21—"what makes man & animals living beings . . . to be sharply distinguished from Greek idea of soul") as well as broader meanings of "person," "life," and "desire" (*A Concise Hebrew and Aramaic Lexicon of the Old Testament* [Grand Rapids: Eerdmans, 1971], 242–43). See also Linafelt ("Arithmetic," 256): "we should not imagine the *nepeš* [*nephesh*] as a sort of platonic soul or spirit that is opposed to or separate from the flesh, but rather as seat of appetites, desires, and passions."

the woman's mother focused on her mother's sons' angry treatment of their sister (1:6). Labeling these brothers as "my mother's sons" reveals little about the mother and doesn't even guarantee that she is still alive. Except for bucking her brothers' restraints, the female lover has operated unencumbered by family interests. So why does she bring up her mother now, and, more specifically and strangely, her mother's coital, gestational bed? Is this the same bed she left to search for her lover? Is her mother dead or alive? Have we and her lover suddenly discovered her ultimate goal: to carry on her mother's—and women's—tradition to catch her man, marry him, and bear children by him? Again, we could have scarcely conceived of this agenda until now.

The introductions of night watchmen and birth mother into the Song seem more than incidental. But precisely what they signify and how much they affect the Song's main love match remains to be explored below.

### Wishing Aloud in Her Bed (3:1)

The curtain to this scene opens "at night" with the woman in her bed. Though the hour is not specified, the mood reflects more of a dark middle-of-the night struggle than a ripe edge-of-dawn blooming (2:17). The woman is neither peacefully asleep nor pleasantly awakening to a new day. She is caught in the throes of unfulfilled longing for her lover. She seeks for him, yearns for him with her whole embodied emotional being (נפשׁ), though not yet motivated physically to get out of bed and hunt for him. At this point, she aims to attract him by a kind of animal magnetism. He has, after all, played the part of the lusty, frisky gazelle poised to pounce on her at the slightest encouragement from her, which she has been happy to provide (2:16-17). But this time, he's not prancing around or peering through her window. He's not around at all, leaving the woman as the prime seeker but with no teasing foreplay or taste of fulfillment: for all her seeking, "she found him not" (3:2).

As noted above, the LXX adds a vocal component to her visceral longing: "I called him." The NRSV's inclusion of this reading makes good sense, supporting the stress on the lovers' voiced interaction in the Song overall and in this stanza in particular. When the woman takes her search out into the city, she asks the sentinels if they've seen her lover (3:3), and finally she adjures her girlfriends not to bother her once she's realized her quest (3:5). The woman is not one to hold her tongue or keep her feelings inside. So we would not be surprised if she cries out for her lover from her bed. But again her outreach is unrequited: "he gave no answer" (3:1). While we have become accustomed to a playful hide-and-seek tension between the couple, this eerie absence and silence strikes a different tone. The woman reaches a new level of frustration in the Song.

## Wandering about the Streets (3:2-3)

She is not, however, paralyzed by this disappointment. She takes resolute and somewhat risky action to get what she wants, to find whom she seeks. She puts feet to her feelings, motion to her emotions.[4] She determines to "rise *now* [נא]"—urgently, insistently, not waiting, as prudence might dictate, for daylight—and "go about [סבב] the city" through its narrow, private streets as well as its open, public squares (3:2). She doesn't search out houses or other structures. She assumes he's out there somewhere at night, either roaming about trying to find her house or camping in some corner or portico waiting for daylight. But doesn't he know where she lives? Or why has he suddenly become shy about approaching her at night? These and other questions lie on the periphery of the poetic scene and should not distract us from the main feeling they stoke concerning the elusiveness of the woman's lover. She deeply senses his restlessness, aimlessness, even homelessness, which she longs to tame in her embrace. It's not that he's trying to avoid her or that he doesn't long for her as much as she for him, but the volatile forces of love disorient and disperse as much as they arrange and attract. By definition, desire, not least erotic desire, yearns for what it does not have and cannot fully possess. It is inherently bittersweet.[5] Absence makes the heart groan with anxiety as much as grow fonder.

This aching absence is only exacerbated by the patrolling presence of the night watchmen. As Tod Linafelt comments, these guards are

---

4. On the motivational, "action tendency" of emotions, see Nico H. Frijda: "Action tendency . . . appears to be the core concept toward which expressive behavior is pointing. Action tendencies are states of readiness to execute a given kind of action" (*The Emotions: Studies in Emotion and Social Interaction* [Cambridge: Cambridge University Press, 1986], 70; see also 69–93; 231–41). See further Richard S. Lazarus, *Emotion and Adaptation* (New York: Oxford University Press, 1991), 59, 87, 97–98, 114–15, 197, 226–27.

5. Anne Carson writes, "The Greek word *eros* denotes 'want,' 'lack,' 'desire for that which is missing.' The lover wants what he does not have. It is by definition impossible to have what he wants, if as soon as it is had, it is no longer wanting what he does not have" (*Eros the Bittersweet* [Princeton: Princeton University Press, 1986], 10). Carson is also cited in Linafelt, "Arithmetic," 253. Kathryn Harding adds, "Desire, by its very nature, depends upon a deficiency, a lack, a need" ("'I sought him but I did not find him': The Elusive Lover in the Song of Songs," *BibInt* 16 [2008]: 45–46).

highly "emblematic" figures who "evoke the emotional charge of eros, inasmuch as that charge depends on the presence of a third party that triangulates and intensifies feeling."[6] And such feeling is fraught with tension. On the night beat, these men enforce border control: controlling who has a right to be where with whom. Their mandate is to ensure public safety according to the rule of law. They are fundamentally *keepers* (שמרים): keeper-protectors of law-abiding citizens and keeper-prosecutors of law-flaunting transgressors.[7] Thus they keep safe those who stay *in* their proper places by keeping *out* nonconformist aliens and keeping *apart* unsavory alliances. In her "nocturnal egression," the streetwalking woman falls wildly out of bounds both temporally and spatially, and her searching for a night-roving male lover only ratchets up the suspicious scenario.[8] If the keepers were to find the male drifter as they have "found" (מצא) the woman,[9] the couple would have a lot to answer for and would find their love plans more frustrated than fulfilled.

From the watchers' viewpoint, this looks bad. In fact, it looks very much like the proverbial prostitute's or adulteress's nighttime trawling "now in the street, now in the squares" for a john, whose life she seeks to pull down with her to Sheol (see Prov 7:6-27; esp. vv. 12, 27).[10] Of course, Woman Wisdom and her "servant-girls" also call out to young men on busy street corners and plazas, seeking to draw them into her life-giving embrace and invigorating banquet hall (Prov 1:20-23; 3:13-18; 8:1-12; 9:1-6). But they do so in the full light of day and within the model of marital faithfulness. Woman Wisdom is conceived in the image of the perfect wife who does her husband "good, and not harm, all the days of her life" (Prov 31:10-12).[11]

---

6. Linafelt, "Arithmetic," 253.

7. שמר is associated in the Bible with a wide range of "keeping" ("guarding") activity, including (1) keeping God's Torah/commandments (e.g., Exod 20:6; Deut 5:1; 6:2-3; Josh 1:8; 24:17; Neh 1:5, 7, 9); (2) keeping the garden of Eden (Gen 2:17); (3) keeping sheep (1 Sam 17:20); and even (4) keeping a harem (Esth 2:3, 8, 14-15).

8. See Fiona Black, "Nocturnal Egression: Exploring Some Margins of the Song of Songs," in *Postmodern Interpretations of the Bible: A Reader*, ed. A. K. M. Adam (St. Louis: Chalice, 2001), 93–104.

9. Note the woman's mixed experiences of "finding" (מצא) in 3:1-4: on the one hand, as *active subject*, in which she seeks to find her lover, first to no avail (3:1-2), but ultimately succeeding (3:4); on the other hand, as *passive object* found by the night watchmen (3:3).

10. Lindsay Andreolli-Comstock addresses this in "Sex Trafficking" in this volume on pp. 65–66.

11. See in this volume p. 9, notes 9 and 11.

### Sex Trafficking

In Song 3:1-5, the reader is introduced to a woman on a mission to find her cherished lover. Though her quest is motivated by true love, the image of her searching the streets and back alleys for a man conjures up images of the proverbial "nighttime trawling" prostitute seeking to lure and trap a man with her seductive attire and forward advances. While this scenario often plays out in Hollywood films and on late night television, reality is actually quite different.

Many people believe that sex workers and prostitutes choose the sex work profession and participate of their own free will. The seductive and sometimes aggressive advances displayed by sex workers on street corners and in topless bars add to the general public's misunderstanding about sex work. While voluntary sex workers do exist, estimates indicate that a large percentage of women in the sex industry do not participate voluntarily and are essentially slaves to the pimps and madams that own them. Pimps and madams use manipulative practices and forceful threats, like assigning women to specific street corners, hotels, or storefronts where they must fulfill nightly quotas of clients and profits, thus exploiting their fear and keeping the women bound by the industry. Failure to maintain a nightly visible presence in the appointed location and to satisfy requisite quotas too often results in beatings, rapes, withholding food and other necessities, and a range of other penalties, including death.

The Trafficking Victims Protection Act of 2000 explains that human trafficking is "the recruitment, harboring, transportation, provision, or obtaining of a person for labor or services, through the use of force, fraud or coercion for the purpose of subjection to involuntary servitude, debt bondage or slavery." The US Department of Health and Human Services notes, "Sex trafficking is a modern-day form of slavery in which a commercial sex act is induced by force, fraud, or coercion, or in which the person induced to perform such an act is under the age of 18 years."[12] The International Labour Organization estimates that 2.4 million people throughout the world are lured into forced labor.[13] In 2005, the total market value of human

12. U.S. Dept. of HHS, "Trafficking Resources," *Office of Refugee Resettlement*, Administration for Children and Families, 6 Aug 2012 and 2 Aug 2012, http://www.acf.hhs.gov/programs/orr/trafficking-resources.

13. ILO, "A Global Alliance against Forced Labour: Global report under the follow-up to the ILO Declaration on Fundamental Principles and Rights at Work.

trafficking was 32 billion US dollars, according to the United Nations. Sex trafficking, while only one form of human trafficking, is the fastest-growing and second most profitable crime on the planet.

*Lindsay Andreolli-Comstock*

The single woman of the Song is obviously not seeking her husband in the dead of night; still less is she burning the midnight oil at her "distaff and spindle" (Prov 31:18-19). And her night-wandering lover is no respected elder "known in the city gates" (31:23). Again, this would-be liaison looks bad, really bad, from the traditional watchtower. But why must this or any other woman be bound by the binary badges of devious whore or dutiful wife? Why can't a "good" woman move freely about the city, night and day, seeking her unmarried lover to whom she is not yet espoused and with whom there may be no marriage plans? Must she automatically be suspected as a man-deceiver and -destroyer, a home-wrecker and societal menace? Freedom always chafes against culturally defined spatial, temporal, and social boundaries. And historically, women have felt the greater pinch. The woman of the Song pushes back, determining to bust these stays, if only in her "dreams." Again, whether she speaks from "actual" experience is irrelevant. Her vivid lyrical language conveys a passionate sense of movement: that is, deeply moving feelings within—and pushing outside—normative social-narrative structures.

## Winding Back to Mother's House (3:4-5)

Any potential questioning or arresting by the night watchmen is thwarted by the woman's advance past the unhelpful sentinels and her discovery and apprehension of her lover, all of which happen in swift succession:

Scarcely had
   I passed them . . .
   I found him . . .
   I held him . . . (Song 3:4).

---

Report of the Director-General, 2005, " International Labour Organization, 01 Mar 2005, http://www.ilo.org/global/publications/ilo-bookstore/order-online/books /WCMS_081882/lang--en/index.htm.

The final component of this triple action is intensified by "and would not let him go" (3:4). After all she's gone through to realize her dream, she will not risk being subverted by meddling watchmen or a meandering lover. She's got this matter well in her hands and aims to see it through to the end. And that end is not simply contact but intimate connection.

The woman does not loosen her grip on the man or her control of the situation "until [she has] brought him" back home (Song 3:4). Heretofore, the man "has brought" her to his bedchamber (1:4) and to his wine-house (2:4).[14] Now the initiative is all hers and the locus of love is her house and bed. This is *her* arrangement, albeit with a notable twist in the form of an important associate. The woman's love plans and indeed her very life are wrapped up in her mother who conceived her in the very spot she has brought her lover (3:4). Another threefold sequence may be plotted, this time pulling the man closer—in progressively more intimate enclosures—along with her mother in a provocative threesome.

> I brought him
>> into my mother's *house*
>> into the *chamber* of her . . .
>> that conceived me [my mother's *womb*] (3:4).

The house → bedroom → womb ingressions into increasingly tighter, self-controlled boundaries reverse the house → streets → squares egressions into more precarious, socially controlled borders. Yet the internal space also has its "sentinel," its overseer and potential meddler, in the person of the woman's mother. Whether alive in body or memory, the mother seems to hover over her daughter's love life in the daughter's mind.

To what end? A familial convention, as recognizable in the modern world as in antiquity, is maternal pressure on daughters and daughters-in-law for grandchildren. To this point, however, the principal Songstress has exhibited no trace of personal reproductive desire or duty. She and her lover happily frolic in the robust, fecund environment of nature, but it is their love—their ripening relationship with each other—that is burgeoning in the fertile world, not their progeny. Likewise, on the other end of the moral spectrum, a major taboo (still in force today) proscribes ménages à trois, especially among kin. Whatever other boundaries the Song's leading woman may break, this is not one of them: she wants nothing to come between her and her lover, no one—including her

---

14. The Hiphil of בוא ("has brought") occurs in all three references.

mother—to disturb their lovemaking in any way, physically or emotionally, as her repeated adjuration underscores (3:5; 2:7). A more promising symbolic reading envisions the two lovers enveloped together, twinning and intertwining within the warm, nurturing cocoon of a mother's womb, safe and secure from outside interference.[15] No one—no watchmen and not even the woman's girlfriends or mother—has any right to hurry their lovemaking along, to deliver it prematurely before "it is ready" (3:5) to face the rude realities of the outside world and certainly not to abort it.

Finally, then, the woman has found, claimed, and locked on to the man she loves with all her being against anything and everyone that might weaken their bond. She has realized her dream all by herself: her active, subjective "I" drives every line of this stanza. To whatever extent she might enlist her mother's support, including in memoriam, she operates under no patriarchal restraint—she never mentions her father throughout the Song.[16] So we might well celebrate Song 3:1-5 as a feminist mini-manifesto. But maybe not so fast. There remain disturbing indications that this little stanza is not "ready" for laminated placards.

While the woman repeatedly asserts her self, her "I," her נפש, this self-identity is thoroughly enmeshed with the personality of her lover for whom she so desperately longs. Everything she says and does, night and day, is for him and toward him. She is "hopelessly devoted" to him (cue Olivia Newton John in *Grease*) and cannot conceive of life without him. And what is more (and worse), the present stanza intimates that, on this evening at least, her desire for him is not wholly reciprocated, or as she might say in the stark words Roland Barthes puts in the mouth of

---

15. Linafelt ("Arithmetic," 247) writes, "The mother's house . . . a symbol of safety and intimacy in the face of the outside world, is turned . . . into an image that is both a focused and intensified version of that desire for seclusion (an inner sanctum *within* the house) . . . with the chamber of conception shading into the womb where the two lovers are twins—bone of bone and flesh of flesh—within the single, encompassing body of the mother."

16. On a particular strand of feminist social ethics that stresses the vital importance of maternal-style care in critique of patriarchal authority, see Nel Noddings, *Caring: A Feminine Approach to Ethics and Moral Education*, 2nd ed. (Berkeley: University of California Press, 2003); Virginia Held, *The Ethics of Care: Personal, Political, and Global* (Oxford: Oxford University Press, 2006); Sarah Blaffer Hrdy, *Mothers and Others: The Evolutionary Origins of Mutual Understanding* (Cambridge: Harvard University Press, 2009); Carol Gilligan, *Joining the Resistance* (Cambridge, U.K.: Polity, 2011).

one confronting "amorous absence": "I am loved less than I love."[17] On this night, the man is not bouncing toward her and wooing her attention but rather aimlessly hanging about town without notifying her of his whereabouts. She's waiting by the phone, as it were, for him to call her back, and he couldn't care less. He puts up no fight, it seems, when she finally finds and seizes him. But why would he? Does he not find his subconscious dream coming true in her conscious dream-action? Is a common male fantasy not on parade here, as a lovely woman whom the man loves—though not as fervently as she loves him—throws herself at him and virtually throws him into her bed? She's not a prostitute or another man's wife: that can get complicated, even dangerous (see Prov 5, 7 and Joseph's treatment by Mrs. Potiphar in Gen 39). This is safe sex, easy sex, and hot sex to boot, with his girlfriend. What more could a man want? Here the seductive nature of the Song takes a potentially antifeminist turn, as Cheryl Exum and others have cautioned. Whose dream is really being realized here? The Song threatens to seduce readers into thinking that the woman gets her way and satisfies her longing for her man when in fact she is simply internalizing his fantasy, playing her scripted part in his screenplay, which now borders on a cheap blue movie or soap opera.[18]

But have we not drifted back into binary mode that fails to do justice to the richly textured tensions and nuances of the Song couple's relationship? Just as the woman is neither the man's wife nor his whore, so

---

17. Roland Barthes, *A Lover's Discourse: Fragments*, trans. Richard Howard (New York: Hill and Wang, 1978), 14. This comment appears in Barthes' chapter on "The Absent One" (14–17) under the headline definition of "absence": "Any episode of language which stages the absence of the loved object—whatever its cause and duration—and which tends to transform this absence into an ordeal of abandonment" (17). See the incisive discussion of Barthes in relation to the Song in Harding ("'I sought him,'" 49, 53–55). We might also consider the pain of loved-less biblical women like Leah (Gen 29:15-35) and both Peninnah and Hannah, to some extent (1 Sam 1:1-8), whose husbands are emotionally absent in favor of more beloved co-wives.

18. J. Cheryl Exum, "Ten Things Every Feminist Should Know about the Song of Songs," in *The Song of Songs*, ed. Athalya Brenner and Carole R. Fontaine, FCB, Second Series (Sheffield: Sheffield Academic, 2000), 28–29; See David J. A. Clines, "Why Is There a Song of Songs and What Does It Do to You If You Read It?," in *Interested Parties: The Ideology of Writers and Readers of the Hebrew Bible*, JSOTSup 205, Gender, Culture, Theory 1 (Sheffield: Sheffield Academic, 1995); Donald C. Polaski, "What Will Ye See in the Shulammite? Women, Power and Panopticism in the Song of Songs," *BibInt* 5 (1997): 76–77. Further, see discussion below on possible pornographic elements in Song 7:1-9a.

she scarcely reduces to either sovereign or slave. Her agency, like that of all mortals in a complex world of competing wills, remains limited and variable. And, as Kathryn Harding proposes, it retains in the current night scene an adaptive-assertive resistance to vulnerability. Yes, the woman is beside herself with overwhelming desire for her lover, a melding of her identity with his and a melting of an independent sense of self, made all the more tragic by the "unequal love" he reciprocates. She is all but lost—has all but lost her self—in a dark, dangerous city. But she finds some measure of herself as she finds her lover; she holds on not only to him but to some discrete image of herself, however fragile and conditioned it might be. She faces her fears and dares to mitigate them with poetic passion. As Harding states, "By imagining that her lover is absent, affecting their separation, the female protagonist displays a degree of resistance to the merging of her identity and her lover's that is evident elsewhere in the Poem, severing their interdependence, if only momentarily."[19] She knows that her absent lover—by virtue of his elusive nature—is distant, distinct, and different from her and her from him. Such knowledge provokes not only her pain but also her purpose. Her "soul" need not waste away in pathetic longing; it can spring into willful action and claim what (whom) she desires as her own.

19. Harding, "I sought him," 53.

# Song of Songs 3:6-11

# *Look Who's Coming to Town*

In this passage of the Song of Songs, the woman continues to address her Jerusalem daughter-friends (3:10-11), but from a different viewpoint. From speaking as the subject-participant "I" in 3:1-5, she shifts to the more distant-observer mode: she exhorts her companions to "look" (3:7, 11) *with her* at the stunning procession that approaches. But she stands out as a keen observer and well-informed reporter, shading into a personally invested admirer. Her rich description intimates that this procession, more than just passing by her group, comes especially *to* her, *for* her.

So exactly "what is that coming" her way (Song 3:6)? Though she knows the answer, she creates suspense for her audience and reflects her own mounting anticipation by teasing out her perceptual process in increments, from the hazy wilderness horizon (3:6) to progressively clearer and narrower features of the caravan: from the large entourage (3:7-8) to the central structure—described from the outside moving in (3:9-10)—to the principal person inside, with special focus on his head (3:11).[1] Using the headings presented below, we may eye-chart the movement toward the woman as follows:

Column of Smoke → Cavalcade of Swordsmen → Carriage of Splendor
→ Crown of Solomon

1. J. Cheryl Exum, "Seeing Solomon's Palanquin (Song of Songs 3:6-11)," *BibInt* 11 (2003): 302.

*Song of Songs 3:6-11*

**[W → D]**

<sup>6</sup>What is that coming up from the
  wilderness,
  like a column of smoke,
Perfumed with myrrh and frankin-
    cense,
  with all the fragrant powders of
    the merchant?
<sup>7</sup>Look, it is the litter of Solomon!
Around it are sixty mighty men
  of the mighty men of Israel.
<sup>8</sup>all equipped with swords
  and expert in war,
each with his sword at his thigh
  because of alarms by night.

<sup>9</sup>King Solomon has made himself
    a palanquin
  from the wood of Lebanon.
<sup>10</sup>He made its posts of silver,
  its back of gold, its seat of purple;
its interior was inlaid with love.
  Daughters of Jerusalem,
    <sup>11</sup>come out.
Look, O daughters of Zion,
  at King Solomon,
at the crown with which his
    mother crowned him
  On the day of his wedding,
  On the day of the gladness of
    his heart.

This is the *one* with the beautifully adorned head the woman longs for and looks at most excitedly.

Such personal interest fits the opening interrogative pronoun מי (Song 3:6), which normally references "Who?" instead of "What?" But the associated demonstrative pronoun זאת ("Who is *this*?") is *feminine* in gender, which doesn't fit the Solomon figure. This peculiarity might suggest the woman's imagined presence *in* the royal carriage that she invites her girlfriends to see, on the order of "Hey, Look at me!"[2] But the grammar and narrative logic of the stanza makes better sense by matching the feminine pronoun "this" with the feminine noun for "lit-ter" (מטה; 3:7), which represents an object—technically "what" rather

2. Jill M. Munro writes, "A number of interpretations suggest themselves, depen-dent on whether it is the woman borne by the litter, or the litter itself, which the epithalamium [wedding ode] describes" (*Spikenard and Saffron: A Study in the Poetic Language of the Song of Songs,* JSOTSup 203 [Sheffield: Sheffield Academic, 1995], 40–41). Some commentators bracket out the "Who is this [woman] coming?" query in 3:6 from the description of Solomon's litter in 3:7-11, viewing it as a stationary rather than processional bedchamber in this scene where the lovers lie (e.g., Michael V. Fox, *The Song of Songs and the Ancient Egyptian Love Songs* [Madison: University of Wisconsin Press, 1985], 120–24; Chana Bloch and Ariel Bloch, *The Song of Songs: The World's First Great Love Poem* [New York: Modern Library, 1995], 160–63).

than "who"—but one whose significance relates to *who* occupies it: it is "the litter *of Solomon*" or, more literally, "*his* litter that is *for Solomon*."[3]

The woman continues the poetic fiction, launched in the opening stanza, of casting her lover in royal-Solomonic terms (Song 1:4-5; see 1:12). He is *her* king, whose bed and chambers she longs to share, ultimately in marriage we now learn for the first time—and last time, as it happens. For the present scene represents some kind of wedding march (3:11), though the details remain fuzzy and are never elaborated in the balance of the Song. But at least for now the woman dreams of a wedding celebration and marital union with her man as splendiferous in her mind as anything the real Solomon might have staged.

This sudden epithalamium (nuptial ode) may strike the reader as an awkward intrusion at this juncture of the Song, if not in the composition altogether.[4] It is not unusual, however, in a passionate love song, for images to shift in kaleidoscopic fashion. But even with this variability, a thread connects with preceding material, not only the Solomonic strains, but, more immediately, the woman's quest for her flighty, elusive lover since Song 2:8. As he has bounded in and out from the mountains like a frisky gazelle (2:8, 16) and sojourned somewhere in the city like a homeless man awaiting her discovery (3:1-5), so he now parades from the distant wilderness to the city like a royal bridegroom (3:6-11). Though each scene leads to some kind of connection between the two lovers, the linkage is not fully secure or enduring. The tense dance between absence and presence, distance and intimacy, continues apace. And other parties continue to clutter the scene and potentially threaten it.

In fact, a company of guards and a mother once again come into the picture, just as in Song 3:1-5. This time the watchmen are Solomon's bodyguards, sixty strong, all armed with swords and alert to "alarms" of the night (3:7-8), as in the previous nocturnal scenario. And this time, the man's (Solomon's) mother is featured, not the woman's (3:11; cf. 3:4). The woman herself is under no threat in this vision; in fact, here *she* plays the role of the sentry at the watchtower, keeping an eye peeled to

---

3. Alternatively, the litter could be "his" in the sense that Solomon owns it and had it built (3:9-10) for someone else, namely, the woman. But the scene more naturally suggests that the litter is his because he's on it!

4. Athalya Brenner asserts, "The wedding procession referred to in ch. 3, if taken at face value, would have served better as a plot climax. Placed where it is, it has no clear plot function" ("To See Is To Assume: Whose Love is Celebrated in the Song of Songs?," *BibInt* 1 [1993]: 267).

the horizon for approaching enemies: "What is that coming up from the wilderness?" (3:6).[5] Though she quickly discerns the sweet fragrance of the distant smoke cloud, sparking tremulous joy rather than terror, the scene remains charged with tension and potential complications. So too with the man's mother, who seems innocent enough with her crowning activity (3:11). But recall that this is the *queen mother* in a royal portrait, reflective of some sense of power and influence over her son, as Bathsheba exerted in Solomon's accession to the throne (1 Kgs 1:11-31; 2:13-25). While a bride's mother-in-law might be problematic in any marital arrangement, one assuming regal-matriarchal authority might prove especially troublesome.[6]

## The Column of Smoke (3:6)

At the farthest edge of her field of vision in the direction of outlying wilderness, the woman sees smoke rising in a column-like formation.[7] Since this smoky pillar is advancing or "coming," it does not represent a smoldering battle site, though it could signal a torched earth military march. Less literally, the picture may reflect upheavals of dust or sand, appropriate to the desert source. If so, the fact that the dust cloud rises in tall and thick columnar fashion suggests a fast and formidable convoy. In any case, this is a prodigious procession, worthy of awe and possibly alarm.

Quickly, however, the woman's olfactory sense clarifies her optic perception, as she takes in a deep breath of "all [כל] the fragrant powders" (Song 3:6) on the market. Salient in this odiferous orgy is the waft of "frankincense" (לבונה). Is this the smoke she sees, the aromatic output of a magnificent burning incense candle's smoke column swirling into the heavens? At any rate, the sweet perfumed scent evokes a titillating romantic atmosphere (1:2-3, 12-14; 2:13), neutralizing any hints of quaking dread, at least for the moment.

---

5. Roland E. Murphy notes, "The question in itself, from a form-critical point of view, can be considered as a cry of a watchman on the wall to the guards, or also as a challenge to an approaching party to offer some sign of identification" (*The Song of Songs*, Hermeneia [Minneapolis: Fortress, 1990], 149).

6. See discussion on 3:11, pp. 79–80.

7. The plural form of "column" used here is likely a "plural of generalization," as Murphy (*Song*, 149) interprets it, evoking the dominant, overall impression of the image.

## The Cavalcade of Swordsmen (3:7-8)

But as the procession comes closer, the woman's visual sense takes over again, with mixed effects—and affects. First she recognizes with exhilaration ("Look!") that this is "the litter of Solomon!" (Song 3:7). That is, the magnificent aromatic caravan bears her lover-king on his bed or couch. She can't quite make out yet the contours of the lover or his litter, but the broad outline and accoutrements of the scene make clear who and what lie at its center. Though the reclining furniture term is different here, the association with previously imaged regal love nests—bed, couch, chambers—is obvious (1:2-4, 12-14, 16-17; 2:4-6; 3:1, 4). In the woman's looking, we feel her longing to rejoin her lover on his litter, a longing intensified by his long absence from her as a consequence of whatever drove him out toward the wilderness from which he now returns. In light of the previous searching scene, we may wonder if she's about to run toward the smoky pillar and latch on to him in his travel quarters.

But she now shows more restraint, content to let him come to her, though still strongly attached to him through her intense peering into the distance, as if to compel him to her with her magnetic laser eyes.[8] And as she waits, she takes in the larger picture, more visible from afar than from the litter, of the entourage that attends—and guards—her reclining lover. He is surrounded (סביב) by a crack troop of sixty warriors with hands clasped around (אחז) thigh-holstered swords, poised to strike in an instant against any nocturnal ambush (Song 3:7-8).[9] While these are sworn protectors of the king and thus allies of the woman who desires that he arrive safe and sound to her, they also represent barriers to her free access. They form an intimidating ring of iron, a human fortress around the king.

8. The poetic technique of "conjuring" again figures prominently; see J. Cheryl Exum, *Song of Songs*, OTL (Louisville: Westminster John Knox, 2005), 140–45; and "Seeing,"140–45; 302–3. The Song woman's longing look for her lover's homecoming and conjuring up a fulfilling vision of his glorious approach represents a dramatic contrast to Sisera's mother's tragically unrealized vision for her son's return from battle: "Out of the window she peered, the mother of Sisera gazed through the lattice: 'Why is his chariot so long in coming? Why tarry the hoofbeats of his chariots?'" (Judg 5:28). All the conjuring in the world, however, will not bring the brutally killed general back home (5:24–27).

9. The NRSV's "equipped with swords" doesn't fully capture the meaning of אחז as "grasp" or "hold." The LXX is closer to the mark: "All of them are holding (κατέχοντες) a sword."

In this martial scenario, the woman cannot just climb into her lover's bed anytime she wants and curl up in his arms in a tight love coil (Song 1:12–2:7). That innermost circle of intimacy is now not merely disturbed but distended in a hard outer crust penetrable only by special permission of the king and his security forces. At least in the preceding precarious scene, the woman managed to circumvent the watchmen making their rounds (סבב; 3:2-3) and grab hold (אחז; 3:4) of her lover and bring him into her chambers. But if she now wants to come to her beloved, especially at night, she must breach a cadre of threescore sword-grabbing "mighty men" (3:7). Of course, kings do summon their beloved queens for erotic pleasure now and again, as the Persian monarch Ahaseurus demonstrates in the book of Esther. But it's a scary proposition when even the favored Esther dares to approach the king on her own, a move potentially as shameless as her ousted predecessor Vashti's refusal to come when the lusty king called (Esth 1:10-21; 4:9-17).

Given her "king's" previous wooing of her, the Song's woman has every reason to anticipate another welcome visit to his chambers, under special escort this time, we may surmise, from the royal honor guard. But while these soldiers would treat the king's woman with utmost respect, they reinforce her subordinate and marginal position. The more powerful the male lover's portrayal, barricaded by muscular masculine force, the more precarious the woman's place. Fantasies of royal dalliances, even weddings, come at a price. The woman may land the man of her dreams, the mightiest man in the realm, but she must never forget her weaker status in the arrangement. She must tread carefully, watching her step and her tongue. Whereas in his bounding gazelle persona, her lover playfully espies her behind her wall (Song 2:9) and seeks to draw her out into the countryside (2:10-14), in his parading royal guise, he stands, or rather reclines, as the object of her outside-in gaze. He's ensconced in his stately couch buttressed by a bevy of brawny bouncers. While he can summon the woman at any time, he can also avoid her as long as he wishes. He can take long excursions with his men—and without her. In this imagined role, she waits entirely on him.

## The Carriage of Splendor (3:9-10)

Ahh . . . but isn't it worth the wait, given the luxurious prize in view? As the procession moves closer, the woman focuses on the larger structure housing the recumbent king, borne by attendants, perhaps a subunit of the armed guards. The briefly mentioned "litter" is now described with another term (אפריון), used only here in the Hebrew Bible. It is perhaps a Greek loanword from φορεῖον that appears in the LXX version of Song 3:9 and elsewhere denotes a "cot" or "stretcher" for casualties of war (2 Macc 3:27; 9:8).[10] In the Song setting, however, a more elaborate conveyance is clearly in view: some sort of "palanquin" (3:9), a canopied, box-like enclosure supporting the royal couch. So the king is further shielded from the public—including the woman! But what a magnificent showcase-shield it is: paneled with the finest wood from Lebanon (לבנון) redolent of *lebonah* (לבנה), the frankincense spicing the procession (3:6), stabilized with silver-embossed posts, and adorned with gold-laced backings, perhaps curtains or coverings.

And then the woman-reporter takes us inside the canopied chamber to see the king's chariot seat and the room's flooring. While these features may have been common knowledge, they afford an insider's perspective via either hearsay or eyewitness account. Have the woman and/or the daughters of Jerusalem been here before? The woman has certainly been no stranger to the "king's" couch (Song 1:12). Is this not another figuration of the lovers' trysting place, a different angle on the leafy bower (1:16-17) and banqueting house (2:4)?[11] This is by far the most ornate love nest, so much so that commentators compare it to a stately, palatial mansion on the order constructed by Solomon (1 Kgs 7:1-12; 10:18-20) or Ahaseurus (Esth 1:5-6).[12] But a lover's imagination can run wild, and the woman's is taking full flight here. Whatever the barriers—military, structural, material, or social—she excitedly transports herself and her female attendants right inside the king's quarters, sharing his royal "seat of purple" placed on the floor "inlaid with love" (Song 3:10).

This last phrase is problematic, suddenly breaking the string of material accoutrements—wood, silver, gold, purple—with the relational concept of "love" (אהבה; Song 3:10). Scholars have suggested various emendations to yield more appropriate construction materials of "stones," "ebony," or "leather."[13] But the image of a "love-floor" or "love-base" fits perfectly

---

10. See Marvin H. Pope, *Song of Songs: A New Translation with Introduction and Commentary*, AB 7C (Garden City, NY: Doubleday, 1977), 441; Fox, *Song*, 125–26.

11. See Fox, *Song*, 123.

12. Pope, *Song*, 441–42; Michael Fishbane, *Song of Songs*, JPS Bible Commentary (Lincoln: University of Nebraska Press, 2015), 96; Bloch and Bloch, *Song*, 163–64.

13. Fox (*Song*, 121, 126) opts for "stones"; William J. Holladay (*A Concise Hebrew and Aramaic Lexicon of the Old Testament* [Grand Rapids: Eerdmans, 1971], 5) for "leather" (see Hos 11:4); see discussion in Pope, *Song*, 445–46.

in this love Song, accorded special emphasis by its fresh imagery at the end of a descriptive chain.[14] Love represents the foundation and final goal of the whole procession. As the banner over the rustic wine-house is love (אהבה; 2:4), so too is the base under the royal bedchamber; and as the love banner deconstructs and reconfigures a standard symbol of war,[15] so too the love base of the palanquin, perhaps engraved with erotic images, disarms the sixty swordsmen, at least inside the carriage. In short, they will not be allowed to disturb the lovemaking couple (2:7; 3:5).

A final question remains concerning what the daughters of Jerusalem have to do with this love-floor. Though obscured in the NRSV, the grammar suggests that "the interior was inlaid with love *from the daughters of Jerusalem*" (Song 3:10). The מ prefix (representing מִן), though often meaning "from," attached to בנוה ("daughters") may suggest here the construction of the love-pavement *by* or *for* them.[16] If the floor represents their work ("by" them), this scarcely identifies them as artisans or masons who laid the floor; more likely, they would have provided some decorative touches or polishes.[17] If "for" them, the carriage's base reflects an amorous ambience pleasing to many women, whom the Solomon figure romances there. But whereas the historical Solomon had his myriad wives and concubines (1 Kgs 11:3), the Song's "king" is a one-woman man. And in the present "wedding" scene, unique in the Song, the "daughters" appear not as antagonistic rivals but rather as friendly attendants or ladies in waiting of the female protagonist. If they had a hand in preparing the palanquin's chamber, she is happy to admire their work, and in any case she happily invites them to look at it with her.

14. Robert Alter, writes, "There is no need to emend the noun [love] here. As Zakovitch notes, the sequence here exhibits a familiar biblical pattern of three similar terms and then a switch: silver, gold, crimson, love. The effect of surprise at the end is exquisite" (*Strong as Death Is Love: The Song of Songs, Ruth, Esther, Jonah, and Daniel: A Translation with Commentary* [New York: Norton, 2015], 22).

15. See above, Song 2:4, pp. 34–35.

16. "By" appears in the NASB, NJPS, and Bloch and Bloch, *Song*, 165. The KJV reads "for."

17. Drawing on ancient Mesopotamian architectural and epigraphic evidence, Hayim Tawil proposes that אהבה is used here as a "double entendre, to connote 'love' as well as 'attractiveness, luxuriance,' i.e., 'sumptuous decorations' . . . which artistically was executed by the choicest handicrafts women from Jerusalem" ("Paved with Love [Cant 3,10d]: A New Interpretation," *ZAW* 115 [2003]: 266–71, at 270).

## The Crown of Solomon (3:11)

With a final click of the telescopic lens, the woman zooms in for a close-up of her beloved "king's" crowned head. But this is not the typical royal diadem placed by a high priest or state official at an inaugural ceremony. This headdress, possibly a floral wreath, is affixed by the king's mother "on the day of his wedding" (Song 3:11). As noted above, the woman suspends identifying the nuptial purpose of this procession until the end of her report, though the "love" reference in 3:10 tilts toward it, and once mentioned, talk of a "wedding" (חתנה) never arises again in the Song. Indeed, this particular term is unique in the Hebrew Bible. The Song, while providing suitable wedding accompaniment, is not primarily a Wedding Song; the present little stanza could be dubbed "Here Comes the Bride*groom*," but that's all the march-music we get. While open to marital plans, the woman is clearly not obsessed with them. As we have seen, her visions of erotic union with her singular love-mate thrive in both outdoor and indoor venues *outside* the proper bounds of traditional lovemaking. While not promiscuous, she is scarcely the model of primness.

What of the queen mother's involvement? No known custom requires the mother's crowning or garlanding her son at his wedding, still less of her anointing him for kingship. But the historical example evoked of Solomon's mother, Bathsheba, is telling, both for her unconventional path to the royal palace and for her eventual power in getting her son on the throne. She is an outsider, married to a Hittite and perhaps a foreigner herself, forcefully appropriated by King David through sexual conquest and violent elimination of her husband (see 2 Sam 11). Her position in the king's household remains precarious until she maneuvers David on his deathbed to name their son Solomon as successor (1 Kgs 1:11-40; see 2:13-25). Her example of an outsider's resilient, resolute action mirrors that of the Song's woman in some respects (see 1:5-8; 3:1-5; 5:2-8). But while such proactive, provocative, even subversive responses merit admiration, the unstable subject locations these women inhabit still inhibit their freedom and agency, as Melissa A. Jackson notes in "A Subversive Song."[18] She also claims, however, that the Songstress takes the cake among "her sister subversives," deliciously pushing the patriarchal limits as far as possible. The male monarch, real or fictive, holds the trump cards, with particular power over women, including—and maybe especially—mothers, wives, and other female intimates.

---

18. See her essay below, p. 80.

### A Subversive Song

Throughout this commentary, Spencer points out a number of places in the Song that can be described as comic, for example, in texts that reflect wordplay and in texts with a general tone of "playfulness." Defining "comedy" or "the comic" with precision is elusive; however, a broad consensus does exist asserting that the experience of comedy involves perception of some *incongruity*—what one expects is not what one gets. A woman in the Hebrew Bible, with a voice, who uses that voice to express herself openly, boldly, and lengthily of love, lover, and lovemaking is a portrait of this incongruity. Yet, this portrait is not merely expectation left unmet; it is expectation that is upended, that is *subverted*.

In exploring intertextual connections between the Song and other Hebrew Bible texts, Spencer recalls the names of several subversive women, women who, in counter-expected ways, slip out from under the control of patriarchy. Ruth, Jael, Tamar of Genesis 38, and Bathsheba of 1 Kings 1–2 are each a version of comedy's "anti-hero," a marginalized figure who prevails using the unconventional weapons that are available to her: wits, savvy, and sexuality.[19]

Yet, even as the women listed here subvert structures of patriarchy, they simultaneously uphold them, as each one acts ultimately for the benefit of Israel and Israel's sons. Any benefit to herself is a fortunate byproduct. It is at this point that the woman of the Song emerges as an incongruity among the incongruous, even more subversive than her sister subversives. Certainly, the metaphorical world of the Song's poetry has its feet rooted in a patriarchal reality, harshly evident in texts such as 1:6; 5:7; and 8:8-9. However, even among these brief texts, the voice that remains dominant in the Song is the unfettered self-expression of sexuality without concern for those bonds of patriarchy that require her to exist as a sexual being strictly for the (patriarchal) purposes of marriage and motherhood. Laughing lustily along with the woman of the Song is to join the subversion of the highly regulated, tightly controlled, male-negotiated sexuality that is the substance of most of the rest of the Hebrew Bible's sex texts.

*Melissa A. Jackson*

19. See Melissa A. Jackson, *Comedy and Feminist Interpretation of the Hebrew Bible: A Subversive Collaboration*, Oxford Theological Monographs (Oxford: Oxford University Press, 2012).

Whatever the queen mother's status before her emperor son, how might she relate to the bride who awaits his coming? The creational ideal of a man's "leaving father and mother" notwithstanding (Gen 2:24), ancient Near Eastern custom often dictated the groom's extracting his new wife from *her* family and incorporating her into *his* extended household, with his mother and father's continued oversight and potential meddling as long as they lived. Female in-law relations, especially across social lines, could be quite fraught.[20] Rebekah, for example, was beside herself with Esau's wearisome Hittite wives (Gen 27:46). Naomi and Ruth represent a famous counterexample, but their solidarity is forged in the common crucible of childless widowhood (Ruth 1). As for the present poetic scenario, which only mentions the mother's crowning action on her son's wedding day and nothing of subsequent marital life, there is no hint of tension between the king's mother and his bride. The stanza concludes on a joyful note, though with accent on the "gladness of *his* heart" (Song 3:11). But in her singing the woman shares in this joy and seems to feel no threat from her imagined mother-in-law. This bond is not as closely knit as with her own mother in the previous stanza (3:4), but it is congenial as far as it goes.

20. Renita J. Weems writes, "In a patriarchal culture . . . it was signally important to have the mother-in-law's blessing, since brides upon marriage moved to their husband's locality, frequently in the compound where the mother and father lived" ("The Song of Songs: Introduction, Commentary, and Reflections," in *Introduction to Wisdom Literature, The Book of Proverbs, The Book of Ecclesiastes, The Song of Songs, The Book of Wisdom, The Book of Sirach,* NIB 5, ed. Leander E. Keck [Nashville: Abingdon, 1997], 400).

# Song of Songs 4:1-7

# *Formidable Beauty and Fearful Symmetry*

After an extended run of the woman's speech in Song of Songs (2:3–3:11), much of it pertaining to her elusive, migratory lover, the man stops to address the woman in the most intimate terms, concentrating on her alluring body that he longs to pursue (4:6). Not for the first time her beauty or fairness (יפה) overwhelms him (1:8, 15; 2:10, 13), though he frames the present portrait with special redundancies and intensifiers:

> Look at you, my beautiful [יפה] darling. Ah, just look at you, beautiful [יפה]! (4:1).
> Every bit of you is beautiful [יפה], my darling. No blemish [מום] is in you! (4:7, my translation).

The double "look at you" (הנך) from the outset conveys a startling sense of "Wow," as F. W. Dobbs-Allsopp aptly puts it.[1] The man already knows the woman is attractive, but he's never seen her in quite this brilliant

---

1. F. W. Dobbs-Allsopp, "The Delight of Beauty and Song of Songs 4:1-7," *Int* 59 (2005): 262. Elaine Scarry comments further on the arresting and overwhelming impact of beauty: "The beautiful thing seems—is—incomparable, unprecedented; and that sense of being without precedent conveys a sense of the 'newness' or 'newbornness' of the entire world. . . . It is the very way the beautiful thing fills the mind and breaks all frames that gives the 'never before in the history of the world' feeling" (*On Beauty and Being Just* [Princeton: Princeton University Press, 1999], 22–23).

*Song of Songs 4:1-7*

[M → W]

4How beautiful you are, my love,
    How very beautiful!
Your eyes are doves
    behind your veil.
2Your teeth are like a flock of
        shorn ewes
    that have come up from the
        washing
all of which bear twins,
    and not one among them is
        bereaved.
3Your lips are like a crimson thread,
    and your mouth is lovely.
Your cheeks are like halves of a
        pomegranate
    behind your veil.

4Your neck is like the tower of
        David,
    built in courses;
on it hang a thousand bucklers,
    all of them shields of warriors.
5Your two breasts are like two
        fawns,
    twins of a gazelle, that feed
        among the lilies.
6Until the day breathes
    and the shadows flee,
I will hasten to the mountain of
        myrrh
    and the hill of frankincense.
7You are altogether beautiful, my
        love;
    there is no flaw in you.

light. She continues to stun him with her striking beauty, which he can only approximate in verbal expression. The pileup of "*a*" vowels in 4:1 sonically reinforces his sense of wonder and bliss ("Aaah") in contemplating his beloved's gorgeous appearance.[2]

The final summation of her comprehensive (כל, "all/every bit"), unsullied beauty projects an image of utter perfection, completeness, without any lack. Internally, the stanza fleshes out this flawless pulchritude in praise of seven bodily features arranged in symmetrical fashion (4:1b-5).

A Eyes are doves

   B Hair like goats moving down the slopes of Gilead

      C Teeth like ewes bearing twins coming up from washing

         D Lips/Mouth like crimson thread

      C' Cheeks like halves of a pomegranate

   B' Neck like tower of David

A' Breasts like twin fawns/gazelles feeding among lilies

2. Sarah Zhang, "The Canvas of Emotion," paper delivered at annual SBL meeting, San Diego, CA, 2014; see also Zhang's contribution to this commentary, "The Emotional Timbre of the *Wasf*," pp. 90–91.

The symmetrical design, a common cross-cultural standard of human beauty,[3] is reinforced by the perfectly paired eyes and breasts (A/A') and twinning teeth and cheeks (C/C'). Overall the portrait forms a circle bisected in the center by the horizontal axis of the red lips/mouth (D), with the vertical axis running downward from head to chest, accentuated by elongations of hair and neck (B/B').

As much as it conveys a beautiful balance of the woman's upper physique, this description also conveys a *fearful symmetry*, recalling William Blake's famous ode, "The Tyger." The woman's form is formidable. She is no tigress, to be sure; the faunal images (doves, goats, ewes, fawns), like the floral images (pomegranate, lilies), are winsome, not wild. But the one image that breaks the idyllic-pastoral pattern (and deviations from carefully constructed templates are most telling) stands out for its stalwart strength and protective prowess: her neck is like a royal armory tower supporting a thousand military shields (Song 4:4). This is no weak woman to be trifled with or scanned up and down with leering lust. While she may welcome admiring looks, especially from her lover, her bearing demands that she be treated with respect, even fear. Echoing the poet-artist Blake, philosophers Edmund Burke and Immanuel Kant expose the ominous, terrifying, overwhelming dimensions of beauty, especially in the natural world (e.g., the vast ocean deep): the awe-full, sublime edge of aesthetics as well as the softer side.[4] The sublime body of the Song's woman transmits the warning "Beware" as much as the invitation "Behold."

Further signs of the woman's powerful transcendent beauty emerge in the man's descriptive stylization of her features. He starts with a simple metaphor that he has used before—"Your eyes are doves" (Song 4:1; see 1:15)—but quickly finds this approach inadequate. This time her eyes are veiled, which hints there is much more to them than meets his eye. So he turns from metaphor to a series of six more allusive similes: the best he can do is suggest what his lover's features are "like" (כ), since

3. On symmetry and beauty, see Nancy Etcoff, *Survival of the Prettiest: The Science of Beauty* (New York: Anchor, 1999), 15–17, 161–63, 185–87; cf. da Vinci's famous sketch of "Vitruvian Man."

4. Edmund Burke, *A Philosophical Enquiry into the Origin of our Ideas of the Sublime and Beautiful and Other Pre-Revolutionary Writings*, ed. David Womersley (London: Penguin, 1998 [orig. 1757–1759]), 49–199; Immanuel Kant, *Observations on the Feeling of the Beautiful and Sublime and Other Writings*, trans. and ed. Patrick Frierson and Paul Guyer (Cambridge, U.K.: Cambridge University Press, 2011 [orig. 1764–65]), 11–204. See the discussion of these works in Roger Scruton, *Beauty: A Very Short Introduction* (Oxford: Oxford University Press, 2011), 61–63.

language and imagery can at most approximate the grandeur of her body. Moreover, while the man seeks to capture the woman's stunning visage in a still-life portrait—"Let me look at you"—he in fact cannot contain her boundless beauty within a single snapshot. Poetic words, whether sung into the air or inscribed on a page, push the limits of language in creative ways, but they only go so far. In the present stanza, the male vocalist tries to depict his darling's dynamic essence in moving images— descending goats, ascending ewes, feeding fawns—that in turn spark his urgent desire to move toward her and join with her before she slips away (4:6). But these images, like the marvelous woman herself, remain as elusive as they are allusive, threatening to leap beyond the score or script and out of her lover's grasp.

While the form and content of this *wasf* (the Arabic term, meaning "description" and denoting a lyrical catalogue of a lover's body) work together to reveal a woman of consummate (perfect) and commanding (powerful) beauty, some less salutary elements potentially deconstruct or at least complicate this profile from a feminist perspective. Consider the barbed pests of (1) universal idealism, (2) surgical grotesquerie, and (3) somatic objectification buzzing around this *wasf* nest.

### Universal Idealism

Beauty standards, though variable across cultures, tend to ossify within a given society into an ideal form, not least with respect to women's bodies: the virtual cover girl and construct of male fantasy. Isn't that what the man creates in the present Song stanza: the ideal, flawless feminine physique, which is nothing but a mystique or mirage that no "real" woman, including his lover, can match?[5] Not necessarily. Apart from

---

5. My "mystique" reference plays on the classic work of first-wave feminism by Betty Friedan, *The Feminine Mystique* (New York: Norton, 2013 [orig. 1963]). Offering a trenchant critique of the model 1960's American woman promoted in *McCall's* magazine, she states, "In the magazine image, women do no work except housework and work to keep their bodies beautiful and to get and keep a man" (27). What a contrast this poses to the Song's woman, whose initial perception (protest) of her beauty appears in a context of her intense, forced labor (Song 1:5-6)! See also the modern feminist critiques of glossy media images of women's beauty, persisting to the current day, in Naomi Wolf, *The Beauty Myth: How Images of Beauty Are Used Against Women*, 2nd ed. (New York: Harper Perennial, 2002), 61–85; Ellen Zetzel Lambert, *The Face of Love: Feminism and the Beauty Question* (Boston: Beacon, 1995), 23–30; Jennifer Baumgardner and Amy Richards, *Manifesta: Young Women, Feminism,*

the fact that this is a lyrical, not literal, rendering—a more mosaic set of images than a polished (airbrushed) portrait—it is also a very *particular, concrete* (like her stone-pillared neck!) configuration of *this* woman's beauty by *this* man. As Dobbs-Allsopp remarks, "Indeed it is the very particularity of this woman and the beauty she embodies that should first claim our attention. She is no 'Everywoman' and her beauty is site specific. The female subject imagined . . . is singular."[6] Accordingly, this peculiar *wasf* allows for multiple, diverse notions of female beauty from a variety of viewpoints and beholders.

## Surgical Grotesquerie

But to ask another niggling question: isn't the present description of the woman's body so particular as to become partitioning, dismembering, a mechanical assemblage of parts?[7] To make matters worse, the parts seem chosen willy-nilly from the world's junkyard and sutured together in Frankenstein (not frankincense!) fashion: a pile of goat hair framing pomegranate-slice temples and red-thread lips perched atop a brick-layered neck. A quick internet search will turn up all sorts of artist caricatures of the Song woman's freaky features. Of course, these largely miss the point of poetic description—the woman wears no actual goat-hair wig. But, nevertheless, effective metaphors and similes trade on a degree of verisimilitude, which, in the present case, retain a degree of grotesquerie set at odds with the perfect symmetrical dimensions sketched above.

To what end, however? Intense passion can easily get carried away and drift apart from neat literary schemas: forgive the besotted male viewer if he gets all tangled up in awkward images and jumbled feelings. But maybe the man's chop-shop approach is, on some subliminal

---

*and the Future,* 2nd ed. (New York: Farrar, Straus, and Giroux, 2010), 87–125; Susan J. Douglas, *Enlightened Sexism: The Seductive Message that Feminism's Work Is Done* (New York: Times Books, 2010), 1–22, 159–67, 214–41.

6. Dobbs-Allsopp, "Delight of Beauty," 264.

7. On "dismembering," Lambert (*Face of Love*, 37–38) writes, "Operating as they must through the medium of time, words necessarily 'dismember' the image, constrain us to see it piece by piece. . . . Literary artists . . . can find ways, when they wish to do so, of creating the 'painterly' effect of a body seen whole. But [still] . . . 'dismembering' describes so well what these portraits in many ways do to their subjects. Which is why women feel, when they are objectified by this sort of masculine gaze, as though they were being dismembered: they are."

level, a flailing attempt to subdue the sublime terror the woman's beauty evokes, to "tame the tiger," as it were, cutting it down to parodied size(s), teasing it into funny shape(s), poking gentle fun at it. The perceived threat of women's bodies to male security, in particular their voracious man-eating sexualized bodies, is common currency in the androcentric biblical and modern worlds. Marking off and mocking up isolated parts of the beastly beauty can keep her at a safer distance. But that in fact is not what the male lover in the Song aims to do. Rather, he desires to "go to" her (Song 4:6), not pull away from her, and to take her in "altogether" (4:7), not subdivide her. He views her not as a collection of body parts, but as an *embodied person*—a glorious "you/thou" (4:1, 7) incarnation.[8]

But the effects (and affects) of grotesque bodily description, variously experienced as "playful, disconcerting, unsettling, dangerous,"[9] cannot be completely glossed over in the Song's *wasfs*. As Fiona C. Black reveals about "textures of desire," following her acute analysis of the grotesque elements in the Song: "If I am subjected to the itemization of my body by my lover (here I mean a real flesh-and-blood lover, not a textual one), even if it is a gentle teasing, I must recognize that amid all the fun, there is still the potential risk of ridicule, the threat of exposure, no matter what level of trust exists between us."[10]

## Somatic Objectification

Whether considered in parts or as a whole, the female body remains a problematic site to the extent that women's identities are reduced to outward physical appearances apart from social-psychological capabilities and character virtues. The Bible, while appreciating the beauty of all God's creation, also suspects beauty's potential superficiality (only skin deep) and deceptiveness. Eve is overwhelmed by the forbidden fruit's

---

8. Scruton (*Beauty*, 40) notes, "A body is an assemblage of body parts; an embodied person is a free being revealed in the flesh. When we speak of a beautiful human body we are referring to the beautiful embodiment of a person, and not to a body considered merely as such."

9. Fiona C. Black, "Beauty or the Beast? The Grotesque Body in the Song of Songs," *BibInt* 8 (2000): 311.

10. Ibid., 320; see also Black, *Artifice of Love: Grotesque Bodies in the Song of Songs*, LHBOTS 392 (London: T & T Clark, 2009); "Unlikely Bedfellows: Allegorical and Feminist Readings of Song of Songs 7:1-8," in *The Song of Songs*, ed. Athalya Brenner and Carole R. Fontaine, FCB, Second Series (Sheffield: Sheffield Academic, 2000), 104–29; and discussion below on 7:1-8.

eye-catching "delight" (Gen 3:6). Even the normally astute Samuel is captivated by the good looks of Jesse's eldest son until the Lord reminds him that "mortals . . . look on the outward appearance, but the LORD looks on the heart." The Lord's anointed successor to the disastrous tall and handsome Saul is not the tall, attractive Eliab, but the little shepherd boy David who will prove to be the "man after [God's] own heart." For good measure, however, it happens that David also "had beautiful eyes and was handsome" (1 Sam 9:1-2; 13:13-14; 16:6-13). The most beautiful of David's sons (not Solomon!) also turns out to be the most corrupt and devious: "There was no one to be praised so much for his beauty [יפה] as Absalom; from the sole of his foot to the crown of his head there was no blemish [מום] in him" (2 Sam 14:25). Of course, Eliab and Absalom are males; but if beautiful male physiques can mask deficient, even ugly, hearts, how much more pretty female bodies! The "unblemished" or "flawless" (מום) beauty of Absalom perfectly matches the description of the woman in Song 4:7.

So what should we think of the Songstress's character? Ellen Zetzel Lambert captures the conundrum:

> On the one hand, it seems to me there's nothing intrinsically shameful about the pleasure one takes in having one's body looked at and admired. Shouldn't one be able to enjoy getting back the image of oneself as a beautiful, desirable object in the eyes of another? . . . I wonder whether we, as the representatives of the first generation of feminists, have not done our daughters a disservice in teaching them that such pleasures are suspect. Yet then I hesitate. For those feelings *are* often suspect. . . . To the extent that [young women see] themselves as mere objects of another's gaze they [see] themselves as depersonalized. And surely something *is* wrong if one feels that as soon as one opens one's mouth and reveals oneself as a person (a thinking, feeling person) the pleasure evaporates. Something *is* wrong if the pleasure in being looked at seems to deny rather than confirm one's sense of one's own individuality.[11]

While a focus on beautiful bodies can serve a "cultural pathology,"[12] it doesn't have to if kept in proper perspective. The problem again comes with a surgical demarcation, this time not between body parts but between body and soul, flesh and spirit. A sharp anthropological dualism that privileges either side at the expense of the other misses the fundamental point of unitary human life. We are, again, *embodied selves*, with embodied minds, hearts, and everything else. There is no thinking,

---

11. Lambert, *Face of Love*, 29 (emphasis original).
12. Dobbs-Allsopp, "Delight of Beauty," 266.

feeling, or doing outside the body and no empty-headed or -hearted bodily shell, except in a vegetative state. Though we may try to disguise our internal attitudes by putting on a "good face," inevitably our faces give us away with telltale signs of our thoughts, feelings, and characters, both good and bad.[13] And numerous studies have demonstrated that forcing a smile, putting on makeup, looking the part—or receiving a loved one's sincere compliments about our looks—brightens our moods and sharpens our minds.[14] So the man's elaborate description of the Song woman's face and upper body, even for all of its odd elements, may well reflect a true life-affirming and -enhancing perspective for both parties.

This extended discussion of physical beauty serves as an introduction to the Song's several *wasfs*, beginning with the present stanza (4:1-7; see 5:10-16; 6:4-10; 7:1-9). Sarah Zhang's essay, "The Emotional Timbre of the *Wasf*," provides further insights on the genre. In one of these *wasfs* (5:10-16), the woman will extol the man's body, affording us the opportunity to compare and contrast distinctive gender viewpoints.[15] But for now, we unpack more fully the various components of the man's catalogue of the woman's body, remembering all the while that these are features of a whole beloved person.

### The Emotional Timbre of the *Wasf*

As an Arabic lyric genre, *wasf* characterizes the individual features of things, animals, and people for evaluation. In the Song there are four such poems: 4:1-7; 5:9-16; 6:4-10; 7:2-6. In the past, scholarly attention has often been given to the characterization of individual features in these poems, so the saliency of *wasf* has been defined narrowly as "description." Etymologically, though "description" is the core meaning of the nominal *wasf*, the form I verb of *wasf* (*waṣafa*) means both "to describe" and "to praise, laud, extol." The distinctive verbal meanings suggest an intertwined texture: describe to extol and extolment by description. According to

---

13. See notes 14 and 15 above on Song 2:8-17, p. 51.

14. Scruton (*Beauty*, 59) notes, "There is truth in Oscar Wilde's quip that it is only a shallow person who does not judge by appearances. For appearances are the bearers of meaning and the focus of our emotional concerns."

15. In "Beauty or the Beast?" and *Artifice*, Black examines both the woman's and the man's descriptions of each other's bodies in the Song.

Akiko Motoyoshi Sumi's study on the Arabic *wasf*,[16] the most important aspect of this genre is to transport the audience into a state of *tarab*, that is, a "strong emotion of joy or grief." A *wasf*, in other words, emulates not only the qualities of the object but also their affectivity. In this sense a *wasf* resembles rhetoric in its "art of seduction," the difference being that it stirs the audience not into accepting an idea or action but into a mode of emotion. A proper appreciation of the *wasf* in the Song, therefore, would include both its descriptive and, in terms of the evaluation and the rhetoric goal of *tarab*, emotional aspects. Or more precisely speaking, the reader is expected to see the described features (and their corresponding similes) through the lens of the intended emotion. Now common sense has it that intense emotions may cause exaggeration and incoherence in language; needless to say that poetry has the "poetic license." Hence, if interpreters were to put on the "objective" glasses that shield them from emotional effects, they may transcribe the extravagance of the lover's impression embodied in the poem as the ridiculousness of the beloved's qualities. Conversely, if the reader understands the making of a *wasf* as a case of *impression* turned into *expression*, which is particularly pronounced in love lyrics, one may follow the emotional footprints of the *wasf*: as the inflowing sensation provoked by the beautiful beloved, after vivifying the lover, reverts to an outpouring of exuberant praises, the reader also catches fire of the delight through encountering the poem and thus being provoked into the *tarab*—the joy of love.

*Sarah Zhang*

## Beauty and the Beasts (4:1-2)

As already noted, the animal imagery applied to the woman's body hardly suggests fierceness: instead of tiger-like fiery eyes, flaming fur, and fanged teeth, she has eyes of a dove, hair like goats, and teeth like ewes. But each of these creature features appears in a setting that enhances not only their descriptive power but also, by analogy, the woman's power.

---

16. Akiko Motoyoshi Sumi, *Description in Classical Arabic Poetry Waṣf, Ekphrasis, and Interarts Theory* (Leiden: Brill, 2004), 6.

- Her dove eyes appear "behind a veil" (Song 4:1). Such cloaking recalls the woman's imaged seclusion like a dove (in whole, not part) in the clefts of the rock, from which the man sought to draw her out, face-first (2:14). She is not automatically available to his beck and call or his look and gaze. She retains not simply her modesty but also her independence. Moreover, assuming a translucent veil, the woman's eyes would only be partially visible, mostly in terms of their general size (large or small), color (light or dark), and movement (still, blinking, or flitting). The latter characteristic seems particularly fitting for the active, darting tendencies of doves, prompting Dobbs-Allsopp to remark: "The look of this woman betokens a vibrant, knowing agency—one who knows her mind and acts on it."[17]

- Her hair is like goats in transit "down the slopes of Gilead" (4:1). Comparing a lover to an individual goat—You look and smell like a goat, my dear—was probably no more romantic in the Song's ancient Near Eastern world than in our own. The poet offers no close-up comparison, however, but rather a panoramic view of a flock of dark-coated goats (typical of Gilead) proceeding down these Trans-Jordanian heights. The animals merge together in this motion picture to illustrate the woman's "wavy black tresses cascading over head and shoulders."[18] One may even imagine her bouncing curls and flowing locks as she moves. In any case, the image evokes energy, vitality, and perhaps even a degree of wildness associated with the more remote and rugged Gilead setting.

- Her teeth are like "shorn ewes" emerging from bathing pools (4:2). Color again comes into play, this time accentuating the whiteness of the woman's teeth, like the smooth, glistening hides of shorn sheep "coming up from the washing." Contrast this image with that of grimy, woolly sheep before shearing and cleaning and of most people's teeth in this era before advanced dental hygiene. Likewise, note the exceptional nature of the woman's perfectly aligned teeth in this pre-orthodontic culture, as if each ewe-like one had borne its own identical twin. Elements of purity, symmetry, fecundity ("bearing"), and security ("not one . . . is bereaved") coalesce in this stunning pastoral-dental image.

17. Dobbs-Allsopp, "Delight of Beauty," 269–70.
18. Michael V. Fox, "The Song of Solomon," in *The HarperCollins Study Bible*, rev. ed., ed. Harold W. Attridge (New York: HarperCollins, 2006), 907.

## Beauty in Red (4:3)

The "color and contour"[19] of the woman's body parts—dark draping hair, white matching teeth—continue to captivate the male viewer.
Now the bold color red pops out in the lovely, thin-lined crimson lips
framed by pomegranate-like features evocative of the fruit's red peel,
white flesh, and red seeds. Pomegranates were also common fare in
ancient erotic settings, similar to strawberries in American culture.[20]
The woman's lips, though thin, stand out for their striking natural
redness; no lipstick needed. The parallel descriptor, "your mouth is
lovely" (Song 4:3)—not a separate simile—doubles the effect of the
beautiful lips or even thickens them, we might say. But it also injects a
linguistic surprise, in that the term for "mouth" (מדבר) is a homonym
for "wilderness," the most common meaning by far in the Hebrew
Bible, as in the "wilderness" origin of the palanquin's journey in the
previous Song stanza (3:6; see also 8:5). Again, a subtle wildness may
affect the man's perception of his lover's body, perhaps suggesting
that her taut ruby lips are driving him wild with expectation of more
intimate, openmouthed contact.

The pomegranate-like sidebars probably refer to the woman's temples
rather than her cheeks (NRSV). Indeed, the only other biblical use of
this term outside the Song (see also 6:7) denotes the temples of General
Sisera through which Jael hammered a tent spike, nailing his head to
the turf (Judg 4:21, 22; 5:26)! These are fragile, delicate parts, even for a
powerful military leader. The Song discloses that the woman's temples,
like her eyes, are secluded behind her veil, to be approached with care
and tenderness (no tent pegs allowed!). As far as what the man can see
through her veil, Marcia Falk imagines the sliced pomegranate picture
projecting "a gleam of red seeds through a net of white membrane"
translating into the woman's "ruddy skin glimpsed through a mesh of
white veil."[21] More particularly, the red seeds could suggest freckles or,
more pejoratively, pimples: "not a glowing but a more spotty, adolescent

19. Marcia Falk, "The *waṣf*," in *A Feminist Companion to the Song of Songs*, ed. Athalya
Brenner, FCB (Sheffield: Sheffield Academic, 1993), 230.
20. On pomegranates, see Jill M. Munro, *Spikenard and Saffron: A Study in the Poetic
Language of the Song of Songs*, JSOTSup 203 (Sheffield: Sheffield Academic, 1995), 85–86;
Othmar Keel, *The Song of Songs: A Continental Commentary*, trans. Frederick J. Gaiser
(Minneapolis: Fortress, 1994), 143–47.
21. Falk, "*waṣf*," 230.

complexion."[22] A case of teenage acne, however, hardly fits the final diagnosis of the woman's flawless beauty. This is a youthful lover's erotic
vision, not a dermatologist's examination. If any "objective" blemishes
mar the woman's "real" complexion, her lover doesn't see them. She
appears altogether perfect in his eyes.

## Beauty in the Stones (4:4)

In the notable shift from animal and agricultural imagery to an architectural picture, the man likens the woman's neck to the Tower of David.
While no such designated structure is known from the historical record,
it suits various watchtowers and walled fortifications protecting the city
of Jerusalem during David's reign. It is an unmistakable symbol of rock-
solid military defense, built out of stones arranged in "courses" or "tiers"
(תלפיות)[23] and adorned with a thousand shields that were brandished by
"mighty men" (גבורים) functioning as a massive "No Trespassing" sign.
If sixty armed "mighty men" guard Solomon's carriage (Song 3:7), a
regiment sixteen times that size secures David's capital. Applied to the
woman's body from the man's perspective, the message seems less as-
suring of "safety and shelter for her lover"[24] than warning him against
improper or uninvited advances. The mien of her stately neck supporting her lovely head conveys a strong sense of self-prepossession and
-protection. If the thousand hanging shields represent a dazzling array

22. Black, "Beauty or the Beast?," 311.

23. The term תלפיות, used only here in the Hebrew Bible, is of uncertain meaning.
A good case can be made for viewing the image as architectural, describing a tower
constructed in rows or courses of stones; see Marvin H. Pope, *Song of Songs: A New
Translation with Introduction and Commentary,* AB 7C (Garden City, NY: Doubleday,
1977), 465–68; Roland E. Murphy, *The Song of Songs,* Hermeneia (Minneapolis: Fortress, 1990), 155; Michael V. Fox, *The Song of Songs and the Ancient Egyptian Love Songs*
(Madison: University of Wisconsin Press, 1985), 130–31. Michael Fishbane acknowledges a likely connection with "courses or layers," but prefers a translation focused
on the tower's function—"built to hold weapons"—parallel to the next line, "hung
with a thousand shields" (*Song of Songs,* JPS Bible Commentary [Lincoln: University
of Nebraska Press, 2015], 109). Chana and Ariel Bloch provide a more aesthetic (and
adverbial) reading of "raised in splendor" and "built magnificently, to perfection"
(*The Song of Songs: The World's First Great Love Poem* [New York: Modern Library, 1995],
73, 170–72); similarly, Robert Alter translates, "built gloriously" (*Strong as Death Is
Love: The Song of Songs, Ruth, Esther, Jonah, and Daniel: A Translation with Commentary*
[New York: Norton, 2015], 24).

24. Dobbs-Allsopp, "Delight of Beauty," 267.

of jewels gracing the woman's neck (2:10; 4:9), as many have suggested, this imagery only intensifies the woman's power with stunning beauty.

And so we return to the notion of the sublime, that fearsome cocktail of force and fancy, of masculine military strength and feminine physical splendor in the present configuration. Ezekiel's oracle against the powerful city of Tyre closely matches the mix of martial and aesthetic images in the Song, albeit to lamentable rather than admirable effect:

> Paras and Lud and Put were in your army,
>     your *mighty warriors;*
> they hung *shield* and helmet in you;
>     they gave you *splendor.*
> Men of Arvad and Helech were on your walls all around;
>     men of Gamad were at your *towers.*
> They hung their quivers all around your walls;
>     they made *perfect your beauty.* (Ezek 27:10-11)[25]

In Tyre's case, as Ezekiel sees it, all of this masculine military magnificence—embodied in rapacious kings—will soon come crashing down on its neck in divine judgment (Ezek 27:25-36). By contrast, the Song's deployment of military imagery, as we have seen, serves the interests of love and peace, not war and strife, though with sober awareness of lurking threats and tensions. Though our Songstress is no naïve Pollyanna or helpless damsel in distress, she is also no warrior Deborah, Jael, or Judith—or Xena, Buffy, or Katniss Everdeen.[26] She more subverts than co-opts the masculine martial model. As Carol Meyers concludes:

> The Song . . . presents a significant corpus of images and terms derived from the military—and hence the male—world. Without exception, these terms are applied to the female. Since military language is derived from an aspect of ancient life almost exclusively associated with men, its use in the Song in reference to the woman constitutes an unexpected reversal of conventional imagery of stereotypical gender association.[27]

25. On this intriguing Ezekiel cross-reference, see Bloch and Bloch, *Song,* 173; and Carol Meyers, "Gender Imagery in the Song of Songs," in *A Feminist Companion to the Song of Songs,* ed. Athalya Brenner, FCB (Sheffield: Sheffield Academic, 1993), 203.

26. On the popularity and influence of the modern television series *Xena: Warrior Princess* and *Buffy the Vampire Slayer* (and others) featuring sexy kick-ass heroines, see the trenchant chapter "Warrior Women in Thongs" in Douglas, *Enlightened Sexism,* 76–100.

27. Meyers, "Gender Imagery," 204.

## Beauty and the Breasts (4:5)

Drawn down the bejeweled neckline to the woman's cleavage, the male admirer returns to pastoral imagery, all of which has been used before in the Song. Intimidated by her formidable neck, he retreats to the more familiar nest of her breasts characterized as twin fawns of a gazelle grazing among lilies. The fawns are "young stags" (תאומי, masculine plural) borne by a "gazelle" doe (צביה, feminine singular; Song 4:5). Previously the woman depicted her male lover as a bounding "gazelle or young stag" that she invites to her "cleft mountain"–like breasts.[28] Now the man compares her breasts to youthful, energetic male fawns. Rather than "bouncing" around, however, they are contentedly moored among the lilies, munching on the surrounding grass. In both male and female voices, the woman herself, not merely her chest, has been cast as a luscious lily (2:1-2, 16). Her breasts thus adorn her entire embodied person.

The notion of feeding, fawn-like breasts—that is, breasts that *eat!*—conveys a suggestive sense of self-nurturing from organs so intimately connected with nourishing others. But the identification of the woman's breasts with masculine animals probably hints more strongly at the man's desire to merge as closely as possible with her breasts, to nestle and nibble among them, as she earlier welcomed him (Song 2:13). Gender bending and blending terminology serves in part to entwine the lovers in "one flesh" union. The triangular maternal element also sneaks in again, this time in the form of the twin-bearing gazelle doe, comparable to the ewes in 4:2 and the lovers' mothers in 3:4 and 3:11, respectively. Touches of fruitfulness and tenderness accent the beautiful picture—with a notable absence of patriarchal tones.

## Beauty on the Hill (4:6-7)

Before wrapping up his portrait of the woman's consummate beauty (Song 4:7), the man can't resist expressing his desire to come to her, to move behind the easel, as it were, so that he can embrace his gorgeous "model." While brimming with passion, however, he is not planning to pounce on her, as the NRSV rendering, "I will hasten to [her]," might suggest. The term (הלך) is the common verb of motion, simply meaning "go, come, walk." But he does feel a sense of urgency to reach her before the day dawns, precisely echoing the woman's prior summons of him

---

28. See above discussion on 2:9, 17 at pp. 43–44, 57.

"until the day breathes and the shadows flee" (2:17). The prospect of the day's "breathing" with fresh life may also signal his "breathless" anticipation of touching her. Moreover, this nocturnal time-note functions somewhat like the veil, setting off her brilliant features in sharp relief; her incredible beauty shines through the night shadows.

The fragrant myrrh and frankincense on the prominent destination of mountain or hill of the woman's body may be her delightful breasts, which the man last fixed upon in Song 2:5 (see also 1:12-13; 2:17). But the use of the singular "mountain/hill" in synonymous parallelism, rather than the plural "breasts" or "cleft mountains" more likely reflects his interest in the lower area of her pubic mound. Again, however, he aims no more to reduce her to this one erogenous zone than to any other body part. Ultimately, it is her beautiful embodied person that overwhelms him "altogether" (4:7).

# Song of Songs 4:8–5:1

# *The Precarious Path to Paradise*

From the man's anticipated advance *to* his lover's personal "mountain [הר] of myrrh and hill of frankincense [לבונה]" (Song 4:6), this scene quickly modulates: he now appears *with* the woman, summoning her to come "with me" down *from* the heights of Lebanon (לבנון) and the surrounding "mountain [הר, 'habitats'] of leopards" (4:8). It's as if he has come to lure her away from a remote lair. She's in no distress: she seems quite at home in a wild environment among the lions and leopards. Accordingly, the man is not trying to rescue her but simply to relocate her, it seems, to a more suitable, undisturbed setting for making love, specifically, a more garden-like paradise (4:12-15). In fact, however, the garden paradise the man seeks is not so much a new venue as the woman herself. She *is* the garden of delights (4:12, 16; 5:1), flourishing *within* the wilderness, redolent with the "scent of Lebanon" (4:11) and tapping into the "streams of Lebanon" (4:15). So ultimately, the man continues to come *to* his luscious lover (5:1), longing to be *with* her wherever she is.

She represents his mountain retreat, his oasis in the wilderness. In her, Eden and Lebanon wondrously commingle—but not without tension. The garden—*her* garden—remains locked up and sealed off from unwelcome predators that lurk about (Song 4:12). And she alone holds the key to her body. She will open herself only to whom she wills. Fortunately for the man, she invites him to "*my* garden," which she even dares to call

*Song of Songs 4:8–5:1*

**[M → W]**

⁸Come with me from Lebanon, my bride;
come with me from Lebanon.
Depart from the peak of Amana,
from the peak of Senir and Hermon,
from the dens of lions,
from the mountains of leopards.
⁹You have ravished my heart, my sister, my bride,
you have ravished my heart
with a glance of your eyes,
with one jewel of your necklace.

¹⁰How sweet is your love, my sister, my bride!
how much better is your love than wine,
and the fragrance of your oils than any spice!
¹¹Your lips distill nectar, my bride;
honey and milk are under your tongue;
the scent of your garments is like the scent of Lebanon.
¹²A garden locked is my sister, my bride,
a garden locked, a fountain sealed.

"*his* garden" in the only lines she delivers in this stanza (4:16). But these few choice comments are crucial to the whole scene, maintaining the woman's agency and control over her affairs in a diverse and potentially dangerous world. She may evoke the halcyon days of primeval Eden (see more below), but not all the wild beasts in the Song's environment lie down peacefully beside her and her flocks.

The garden-in-wilderness setting suits the rich sensations that flood this love scene: a mix of delectable tastes bursting from "choicest fruits" (Song 4:13, 16) and tantalizing smells wafting from "all chief spices" (4:14) distilled from exotic regions, like the forests of Lebanon. Altogether, the man conjures up a gustatory cornucopia to be enjoyed with his lover. Aptly, the chorus (likely the daughters of Jerusalem) concludes this stanza with a rousing exhortation: "Eat, friends, drink, and be drunk with love" (5:1). But again, the woman is more than a participant in this lush banquet: she herself is the main dish and drink! And so the man focuses on her parts—again, representative of the whole person—that are most delicious and fragrant: her nectar-producing lips, her milk-and-honey-dripping tongue, her juicy and spicy "fountain" and "channel" (4:10-15). An intense, delightful experience of oral sexuality—mutually enjoyed—is strongly suggested (4:16–5:1; see also 1:2-4; 2:3-5).[1]

1. On possible allusions to oral sex in the Song, see Jennifer Knust, *Unprotected Texts: The Bible's Surprising Contradictions about Sex and Desire* (New York: HarperOne,

<sup>13</sup>Your channel is an orchard of
    pomegranates
  with all choicest fruits,
  henna with nard,
<sup>14</sup>nard and saffron, calamus and
    cinnamon,
  with all trees of frankincense,
myrrh and aloes,
  with all chief spices—
<sup>15</sup>a garden fountain, a well of living
    water,
  and flowing streams from
    Lebanon.
**[W → M]**
<sup>16</sup>Awake, O north wind,
  and come, O south wind!

Blow upon my garden
  that its fragrance may be
    wafted abroad.
Let my beloved come to his garden,
  and eat its choices fruits
**[M → F]**
<sup>5:1</sup>I come to my garden, my sister,
  my bride;
I gather my myrrh with my
  spice,
I eat my honeycomb with my
  honey,
I drink my wine with my milk.
**[D → W/M]**
Eat, friends, drink,
  and be drunk with love.

Finally, in introducing this stanza, we should notice the new pet name the man uses to address his lover. Rather than his usual "my darling/my love" (רעיתי; see also Song 4:1), he now repeatedly calls her "my sister-bride" (אחתי כלה; 4:9, 10, 12; 5:1) and "my bride" alone (4:8, 11). Nothing in the Song suggests any biological sibling relationship between the lovers like that between Abraham and Sarah (Gen 20:12); and the man certainly doesn't fit the profile of the woman's natural brothers who treated their sister badly (1:6). A common trope of ancient Middle Eastern love poetry employed "my sister" and "my brother" as metaphorical terms of endearment.[2] While there is some leaning toward matrimonial

---

2011), 26; Fiona C. Black, "What Is My Beloved? On Erotic Reading and the Song of Songs," in *The Labour of Reading: Desire, Alienation, and Biblical Interpretation*, ed. Fiona C. Black, Roland Boer, and Erin Runions (Atlanta: SBL, 1999), 48–50. These scholars focus chiefly on 2:3 ("With great delight I sat in his shadow, and his fruit was sweet to my taste"), which I only briefly touched on above.

2. See J. Cheryl Exum, *Song of Songs,* OTL (Louisville: Westminster John Knox, 2005), 168–72; Michael Fishbane (*Song of Songs,* JPS Bible Commentary [Lincoln: University of Nebraska Press, 2015], 118) comments that "sister, bride" "is a figure of intimacy, perhaps taken from traditional marital epithets," similar to the use of "daughter" in Ps 45:10 within a royal wedding hymn. He also notes that the use of "sister" language for a cherished girlfriend was common in Egyptian love songs (p. 233 n. 75; see Michael V. Fox, *The Song of Songs and the Ancient Egyptian Love Songs* [Madison: University of Wisconsin Press, 1985], 14, 52, 66, 135).

union, most recently in the wedding march of the king's palanquin (3:11), nuptial imagery hardly pervades the Song, and the woman's "bridal" (כלה) identity only surfaces in 4:8–5:1. It thus seems best to interpret the man's sibling-spousal address as figuratively emblematic of his strong familial feelings for the woman, his "desire," as Cheryl Exum puts it, "to achieve oneness with the other"[3] and, we might add, to achieve a permanent "one-flesh" union as sister-bride relations especially connote. It may also assure the woman of his genuine fraternal care for her in contrast to her hostile brothers (1:6).

The question still remains, however: why interject these concerns this way at this point in the Song? Coming off the bold depiction of the woman's beauty via dynamic animal, botanical, and architectural images, perhaps the familial sister-bride designation serves to humanize and domesticate her somewhat, not in a diminishing and stultifying sense—he remains awed by her—but in the interest of bringing her closer to him, more on his lower level. It's hard not to be intimidated by a perfect lover. If he does long for more domineering control of the woman, as he would typically have over a sister or wife in this culture, he hardly expects it with *this* woman. If she can hold her own with her towering figure among the lions and leopards, she doesn't have to submit to him or anyone else.

### Wild Heights and Haunts (4:8)

As the male admirer traced the contours of the woman's body in figures related to mountains generally (Song 4:6) and the slopes of Gilead in particular (4:1), he now situates her among the heights of Lebanon and the associated peaks of Amana, Senir, and Hermon. All of these rise near the northern edge of Israel on the Syro-Phoenician border—the Lebanon range to the northwest (Phoenicia) and the others in the Anti-Lebanon mountains to the Trans-Jordanian northeast (Syria)—looking down on the land of Israel overall. Of course, in biblical topography, they are still looking *up* to Mount Zion in Jerusalem, however far south it might be and whatever its measurable height. But at this moment, the man's thoughts seem miles away from Jerusalem, as the present setting highlights the woman's lofty, edgy, exotic remoteness, even strangeness. Mount Hermon and the other summits in fact represent the highest points in the

3. Exum, *Song*, 172.

region, piercing into the clouds and projecting a "mysterious otherness" to onlookers and outliers.[4] The woman's glorious yet ominous beauty continues to impress all the more as we survey her mountain landscapes more closely.

As noted above, Lebanon remains prominent through this stanza after its double mention in the opening parallel lines (Song 4:8, 11, 15). Usually with the definite article, "the Lebanon" in the biblical world referred to the densely forested highland off the Phoenician coast, dominated by the powerful city-state of Tyre. The evergreen trees of this area—fir, pine, cypress, and especially cedar—were well known for their pleasant aromas and quality timbers, and the land also supported vineyards producing fine wine.[5] The following text from Hosea, revealing the Lord's plans to restore Israel's fortunes, plays on all these marvelous Lebanon amenities:

> I will be like the dew to Israel;
>> he shall blossom like the lily,
>> he shall strike root like the forests of Lebanon.
> His shoots shall spread out;
>> his beauty shall be like the olive tree,
>> and his fragrance like that of Lebanon.
> They shall again live beneath my shadow,
>> they shall flourish as a garden;
> they shall blossom like the vine
>> their fragrance shall be like the wine of Lebanon. (Hos 14:5-7)

Hermon and Senir appear to be different terms for the same mountain (Deut 3:8-9), known for its year-round snowcaps and dew drops (Ps 133:3). The less well-known Amana represents another nearby peak with the same name as a major river in Syria (2 Kgs 5:12).[6] Senir and Lebanon are closely linked in Ezekiel's lamentation over beautiful Tyre, the same oracle cited above featuring shield-festooned walls and towers, paralleling the description of the woman's formidable neck in Song 4:4.

> O Tyre, you have said,
>> "I am perfect in beauty."
> Your borders are in the heart of the seas;
>> Your builders made perfect your beauty.

---

4. Jill M. Munro, *Spikenard and Saffron: A Study in the Poetic Language of the Song of Songs*, JSOTSup 203 (Sheffield: Sheffield Academic, 1995), 136.

5. See Robert Houston Smith, "Lebanon," *ABD* IV (1992): 270–71.

6. See Ray Lee Roth, "Amana," *ABD* I (1992): 172; Rami Arav, "Hermon, Mount," *ABD* III (1992): 158–60; David W. Baker, "Senir," *ABD* V (1992): 1087–88.

> They made all your planks
>    of fir trees from Senir;
> they took a cedar from Lebanon
>    to make a mast for you (Ezek 27:3-5).

The trees from Senir and Lebanon furnished the timber forged into planks for Tyre's magnificent merchant fleet that fueled the city-state's booming trade business (Ezek 27:6-25). The forests controlled by Tyre thus epitomize the realm's coalition of ecological beauty and economic bounty. Such an alliance, however, is rarely balanced. Pride and greed, which eventually lead to the downfall of Tyre and other empires, commonly exploit natural resources and strip them of their beauty for the sake of expanding financial profit to obscene proportions.[7]

While the Song's lovers let their imaginations run wild with luxurious, regal musings, they are building no empires or enterprises. Feathering their mutual love nest is all that matters, whether envisioned as a campsite in the woods (Song 1:15–2:4) or a carriage made of wood (3:9). While comfortable in modest rustic and domestic environments, they happily imagine living together beyond their means, not through material acquisition, but through passionate communion. They are never richer than when they are together undisturbed, enjoying each other's embodied selves. True beauty and bounty blossom in loving harmony with each other and with all creation.

While the glory of the mountain forests and their romantic associations—both evoking the elusive remoteness of love and providing a secluded retreat for love—are not hard to see, the love-links with mighty feline beasts are not so clear. If the woman's proximity with lions and leopards somehow suggests her wild side, does this connection not play into the stereotype of women as "man-eating" sexual predators poised to divest a man of all his wealth and resources and ultimately devour his "flesh and body" (Prov 5:10-11)? Is this why the Song's man seeks to draw his lover away from her lair? We are back to Blake's fearful tiger. But recall the full picture of bright-eyed, fearful symmetry, a sublime, awe-full, perfectly designed majesty. A divine "glory" suffuses the wildest beasts as much as any creatures (Gen 1:24-25; 1 Cor 15:38-41). And

---

7. By the time of Hezekiah's reign in Judah, Lebanon had suffered considerable deforestation at the axes of Assyrian expansionists (2 Kgs 19:23; Isa 10:34; 37:24); see Smith, "Lebanon," 271.

in the male Singer's eyes, the woman marks the pinnacle of creaturely glory, replete with "terrible beauty."[8]

## Bold Tastes and Scents (4:9-11)

With frank honesty and vulnerability, the man now makes clear the woman's consuming effects on him: "You have ravished my heart with a glance of [one of ] your eyes, with one jewel of your necklace" (Song 4:9). The verb (לבב) builds on the term for "heart" (לב), the seat of thought, will, and emotion in ancient Hebrew anthropology. The Piel form of this verb, aptly rendered "ravish," connotes either an intensification ("you really touched my heart"; "you make my heart race with excitement") or privation ("you've stolen my heart"; "you make my heart skip a beat").[9] Either way, while his lover may not devour his heart like a wild beast, she certainly "captures" (CEB, NJPS) and overwhelms it with alarming ease—with but a glance from one of her eyes or a glint from one of her neck beads. He is thoroughly stunned and stricken by her.

As Exum has astutely observed, the male and female figures in the Song tend to convey their passionate experiences from different perspectives: while the woman typically expresses how *she feels* (within herself) about her lover and their love, the man expresses how *she makes him feel*. She thinks and speaks in more personal, connective terms; he in more power-oriented, hierarchical ones. Where she freely acknowledges feeling sick with love over him (Song 2:5), he more nervously reports being struck by her with love.[10] They conform to distinct "genderlects," as the social linguist Deborah Tannen has described common, cross-cultural variations of speech patterns between men and women.[11] Masculine

---

8. See Exum, *Song*, 169: "The awe the woman inspires is part of her attraction, and so her presence in this fantastic setting transforms it into a place of terrible beauty and enchantment."

9. See Dianne Bergant, *The Song of Songs*, Berit Olam (Collegeville, MN: Liturgical, 2001), 51–52; Exum, *Song*, 170–71. The full form in 4:9 for "you have ravished my heart," conveyed by a single Hebrew word (לבבתיני), is aurally consonant with *Lebanon* in the previous verse and its associations with mystery and awesomeness; see Munro, *Spikenard*, 136 n. 16.

10. Exum, *Song*, 171–72; see the introductory section on "Lovesick and Awestruck" (15–17).

11. Deborah Tannen, *You Just Don't Understand: Women and Men in Conversation* (New York: William Morrow, 1990), 42; see *Gender and Discourse* (New York: Oxford University Press, 1996), *passim*; and "The Relativity of Linguistic Strategies: Rethinking

language, especially in ancient Mediterranean contexts, tends to reflect agonistic jockeying for control, precisely what the Song's man senses he's losing to his lover! Given her consummate delights, this is a battle he's quite willing to lose, but it remains unsettling all the same. As Exum concludes, "As a man, he is used to feeling in control. Now it seems to him as though he has surrendered control, and his autonomy is thereby challenged. The feelings he is experiencing are wonderful and welcome but also unfamiliar and thus disconcerting. And so he is in awe of her."[12]

Any sting of his "surrender" is quickly anesthetized by the intoxicating tastes and scents of her love, flowing from her body and seeping into her clothing (Song 4:10-11). His esteem of her fragrant love as "better than wine" (4:10) echoes the woman's opening engagement with him (1:2-4). And he also matches her passion for kissing (1:2), while taking it to a deeper level. He now imagines the thin red line of her lips (4:3) swelling with luscious nectar and parting open to a rich reservoir of honey and milk pooling under her tongue—and waiting for him to wade in and drink (4:11).[13]

## Sealed Gardens and Fountains (4:12–5:1)

The man suddenly shifts from direct second-person speech to the woman in Song 4:8-11 to more distant third-person description of her as a fruitful and fragrant garden and fountain (spring) in 4:12, before returning to second-person address in 4:13: "Your channel." Notions of the woman's succulent wetness, sweetness, and spiciness persist in these parallel garden/fountain images (4:12, 15), which flow together to create a profusely watered garden paradise (4:13).[14] Less focused now on

---

Power and Solidarity in Gender and Dominance," in *Gender and Conversational Interaction*, ed. Deborah Tannen, Oxford Studies in Sociolinguistics (New York: Oxford University Press, 1993), 165–88. Though not advocating an innate, essentialist view of gender differences, Tannen's research has uncovered typical socialized linguistic patterns across many cultures, reflecting women's main interests in intimacy and connection counterpointed by men's speech-aims toward separation and dominance.

12. Exum, *Song*, 172.

13. Here we see another similar-yet-different juxtaposition of the Song's woman with Proverbs' "loose/strange" woman, whose lips also "drip honey" as sweet words beckoning sweet kisses, but for destructive as well as seductive ends (Prov 5:3); see Murphy, *Song*, 156.

14. In Hebrew: פרדס; in Greek: παράδεισος. This is a Persian loanword rendered "orchard" in the NRSV.

his beloved's individual parts or her isolated person, the man becomes enamored with the whole world, the entire environment, she evokes. And given this breathtaking landscape, he can scarcely take it (her) in or conceive of entering it (her), though he desperately wants to. He dares not presume free access, since it (she) remains "barred" or "bolted" (נעל, "locked/sealed") against trespass, as he mentions twice in 4:12 .[15] To be sure, the garden is so soaked with delights that it overflows its boundaries (4:15), and the woman explicitly invites her lover in to savor her paradisiacal pleasures (4:16). But he's not given a permanent passkey entitling him to barge in any time he desires. She happily shares the garden: "my garden" is "his garden" (4:16), and thus he can legitimately lay claim to "my garden" (5:1). But she has not thereby transferred ownership to him or surrendered her rights and privileges. They are partners, cohabitants of the garden, but she remains first among equals in the arrangement; this is first and foremost *her* garden estate, and she remains its principal landlady. She holds the master key.

All this talk of hetero-erotic relations in a garden paradise naturally invites a return to Eden. In a watershed study in feminist biblical interpretation, Phyllis Trible unpacked her bold intertextual thesis that "Genesis 2–3 is the hermeneutical key with which I unlock this garden . . . of delight" in the Song.[16] The parallel elements in the second creation account with the present Song stanza are clear, though Trible draws from the entire Song to make her case: streams of water flowing in and out of the garden (Gen 2:6, 10-14); groves of beautiful, fruitful trees for nourishment (2:9, 16); species of animals in harmony with humanity (2:18-20); and intimate "one flesh" union between man and woman (2:21-25). In Gen 3, however, paradise is lost: beauty and bounty prove deceptive as the couple eats of the one lovely yet forbidden fruit of the tree of life, prompted by the attractive yet subversive serpentine animal (3:1-14); the disobedient man and woman are expelled from the garden, their reentry now barred by a flaming sword (3:24); and their relationship with the natural world and each other is compromised, not least with

15. Francis Brown, S. R. Driver, and Charles A. Briggs, *The New Brown, Driver, Briggs, Gesenius Hebrew and English Lexicon: with an Appendix Containing the Biblical Aramaic* (Peabody, MA: Hendrickson, 1979), 653.

16. Phyllis Trible, "Love's Lyrics Redeemed," in *A Feminist Companion to the Song of Songs*, ed. Athalya Brenner, FCB (Sheffield: Sheffield Academic, 1993), 100–120, at 100; repr. from *God and the Rhetoric of Sexuality*, OBT (Philadelphia: Fortress, 1978), 144–65.

the consequent subjection of the woman's desires to those of the man, who will "rule over" her (patriarchy) (3:16).

But all hope is not lost. In love's lyrical discourse in the Song, Trible sees the primordial alienation from Eden "redeemed."[17] Mutual love returns to the garden; the flaming sword is doused and dulled in the fresh-flowing streams in and out of Paradise. The profusion of fruits, trees, and spices in Song 4:13-14 celebrates the lovers' unfettered freedom: "In their world of harmony, prohibition does not exist."[18] No serpent or any other beast infects the environment: "All animals serve Eros."[19] And most important, the Song's couple returns to prelapsarian, egalitarian sexual union: "In this [garden] setting, there is no male dominance, no female subordination, and no stereotyping of either sex."[20] In Trible's view, the Song trumpets a utopian theme, the loving way the world is meant to be.

But isn't this all a bit too idyllic, too good to be true? While commending Trible's careful reading and suggestive thesis, many critics hear more dissonance in the Song.[21] For my part, while I appreciate the Song's tight harmonious tones and counterpoints to patriarchal hegemony,[22] I have argued that the military and beastly images retain some of their masculine, muscular threat to the woman's security. While no flaming sword guards the woman's garden, the swords of the sixty

17. See the title of Trible's essay: "Love's Lyrics Redeemed."

18. Ibid., 112.

19. Ibid., 114.

20. Ibid., 119.

21. See the critiques of Trible's idealistic reading of the Song, though with appreciation for her connections between Genesis 2–3 and the Song by Francis Landy, "Two Versions of Paradise," in *A Feminist Companion to the Song of Songs*, ed. Athalya Brenner, FCB (Sheffield: Sheffield Academic, 1993), 129–42; repr. from *Paradoxes of Paradise: Identity and Difference in the Song of Songs* (Sheffield: Almond Press, 1983), 183–89, 269–70; Marvin H. Pope, *Song of Songs: A New Translation with Introduction and Commentary*, AB 7C (Garden City, NY: Doubleday, 1977), 205–10; repr. as "The Song of Songs and Women's Liberation: An Outsider's Critique," in *A Feminist Companion to the Song of Songs*, ed. Athalya Brenner, FCB (Sheffield: Sheffield Academic, 1993), 121–28; Ilana Pardes, *Countertraditions in the Bible: A Feminist Approach* (Cambridge: Harvard University Press, 1992), 118–43; and Danna Nolan Fewell, "Reading the Bible Ideologically: Feminist Criticism," in *To Each Its Own Meaning: An Introduction to Biblical Criticisms and Their Application*, 2nd ed., ed. Steven L. McKenzie and Stephen R. Haynes (Louisville: Westminster John Knox, 1999), 266–82.

22. See the woman's expression of mutual desire in Song 7:10, which overturns Gen 3:16.

mighty warriors surrounding her regal lover, though sheathed for now, still reflect a world of forcefully protected male power (3:7-9). While no serpent poisons the scene and pictures of doves, sheep, and goats depict a peaceable kingdom of love, cameos of little foxes, lions, and leopards (2:15; 4:8) still admit a wild strain threatening to spoil the garden of delight. And we must not forget the other people who intersect the lovers' world and at times disrupt it, especially the woman's brothers and the city's night watchmen (1:6; 3:3-4; 5:7; 8:8-10). Even the female supporting cast—the daughters of Jerusalem and the couple's mothers—represent potentially "disturbing" figures, especially in the adjuration refrain in 2:7; 3:5; 8:4. Finally, the lovers' teasing and chasing each other, while largely playful and exhilarating, evince some persisting sense of unease, of jockeying for position and negotiating tension in the relationship. In short, the Song's garden, while evocative of Eden's bliss and largesse, remains locked off to unwelcome predators and must be worked and tended—like the original paradigm! (Gen 2:15)—in order to maintain its idyllic state.

Within the main attraction of the watered garden, two particular features merit further attention. Consider first the woman's paradisiacal "channel" (שלח) of "choicest fruits" like pomegranates and seven types of "chief spices" stirred into the heady mix (Song 4:13-14). The unusual "channel" term is in fact plural and projects either a botanical or hydraulic image: "shoots" or "canals." Both ideas fit the cognate verb form שלח, meaning "send forth," as in vegetation shooting or sprouting out and water coursing or surging along, and the combined scenario of a garden inundated with "living water" and "flowing streams."[23] Plurals (again) and dynamic participles, all ending in *im* (ים), drive and drench the picture with "abundance and breathless proliferation":[24] "a fountain of gardens [*gannim*], a well of living waters [*mayim hayyim*] and flowings [*nozelim*] from Lebanon" (4:15, my translation). The rendering "your

23. See the helpful discussions in Munro, *Spikenard*, 106–7, 110–13; and Exum, *Song*, 176–77. Exum prefers the hydraulic image in Song 4:13 (see Neh 3:15), "refer[ring] to the watercourses of the sealed spring, which spill over into this verse from the previous one, in which the woman was metaphorically identified as a spring" (177); see Fox's (*Song*, 137) picture of "watered fields" or "irrigation channels"; he also resists taking water channels as a euphemistic reference to any particular part of the woman's body, like the womb or vagina, especially since the term is plural (137–38); contra Pope, *Song*, 453, 490–91: "Your groove a pomegranate grove," though this makes for a nice "groove/grove" wordplay in English.

24. Munro, *Spikenard*, 112.

limbs" in the CEB and NJPS of 4:13, instead of the NRSV's "channel," opts for the botanical-arboreal nuance but too readily suggests a limited anatomical association with the woman's "limbs" (arms and legs) rather than the entire garden environment she "channels" to her lover and, indeed, all creation.[25] Along with controlling subterranean and mountain waters, she also commands the north and south winds to aerate her garden (4:16). All elements of nature swirl together around the couple's erotic paradise.

Second, consider another running water source described as "a *well* [באר] of living waters" irrigating the garden and paralleling the "garden fountain" (Song 4:15). In the biblical world, wells functioned not only as a means of survival, providing water in an arid land, but also as a site of social congress, a meeting place (think office water cooler on a larger scale). Such associations with physical and communal life converged in the special significance of wells as prime loci for matchmaking, leading to marriage: boy meets beautiful girl at well, drawing water for her family or flock; boy asks girl for drink; girl runs home to report "proposal" to her father (or other male authority); father meets boy to seal the nuptial deal. So Isaac (represented by Eleazar), Jacob, and Moses find their wives (Gen 24:10-67; 29:1-14; Exod 2:15-22).[26] And so too, at Jacob's well in the New Testament, Jesus forges covenantal communion with the Samaritan woman and her people, promising her "living water . . . a fountain of water gushing up into eternal life" (John 4:10-13; see 4:4-42).[27] Though

---

25. Though opting for the translation, "Your limbs are an orchard of pomegranates," Fishbane (*Song*, 125) does not interpret this in an atomistic, anatomical sense relative to the woman; rather, he views "limbs" as broader image of "trees" that "indicates the maiden's uncovering of her [entire] body, which has the aroma of an orchard" (citing Ibn Parḥon). Note also the sage observation of Exum, *Song*, 177: "The focus continues on the metaphor of the garden and not its referent, the woman."

26. On this betrothal type-scene, see Robert Alter, *The Art of Biblical Narrative*, 2nd ed. (New York: Basic Books, 2011), 62–70; and Esther Fuchs, "Structure and Patriarchal Functions in the Biblical Betrothal Type-Scene: Some Preliminary Notes," in *Women in the Hebrew Bible: A Reader*, ed. Alice Bach (New York: Routledge, 1999), 45–51. See Prov 5:15–20, where a man's wife is identified as his "well" (באר) from whose waters he must exclusively drink lest his "streams" be wasted and ruined with "strange," adulterous women. In the Song, the man acknowledges the refreshing delights of the woman's "well waters" as *hers* to give, not his to imbibe at will ("*Your* channel/ watercourses . . . a garden fountain, a well of living water," 4:13–15).

27. The Greek terms for "well" (φρέαρ), "living water" (ὕδωρ ζῶν), and "fountain" (πηγή) in John 4:14 match those used in the LXX of Song 4:15. On the connections between Jesus' encounter with the Samaritan woman and biblical betrothal scenes,

trading on the courting, matrimonial language, and ambience of the biblical well type-scenes, Jesus proposes no actual marriage. Likewise, the lovers in the Song play with intimate marital scripts without necessarily envisioning an actual wedding. And most significantly in the present scene, the boy and girl seek no permission from family authorities or involve them in any way; no one's mother pops in this time. The polar winds are summoned to refresh the atmosphere (Song 4:16), and the choral friends chime in to encourage the couple's love feast (5:1). But the lovers themselves orchestrate the affair, as the woman's invocation of the man's advance is promptly answered by his passionate visitation.

> *She calls*: "Let my beloved come to his garden, and eat its choicest fruit." *He comes*: "I come to my garden, my sister, my bride. . . . I eat my honeycomb with my honey. I drink my wine with my milk." (4:16–5:1, fulfilling the desire of 4:11)

In tune with the whole world, they also create their own intoxicating world with each other.

---

see F. Scott Spencer, *What Did Jesus Do? Gospel Profiles of Jesus' Personal Conduct* (Harrisburg, PA: Trinity Press International, 2003), 110–12. For intertextual links between the Song and the Johannine Jesus' vineyard imagery (John 15:1-6) and garden meeting with Mary Magdalene (John 20:11-18), see David M. Carr, *The Erotic Word: Sexuality, Spirituality, and the Bible* (New York: Oxford University Press, 2003), 160–67.

# Song of Songs 5:2-8

## *Painful Pillow Talk*

After an extended block of the man's speech in Song of Songs 4:1–5:1 with a brief interlude by the woman toward the end (4:16) and a final choral refrain (5:1b), the woman finds her voice again and will predominate through 6:3. Since she has just been passionately praised and pursued by her lover and willingly engulfed in a smorgasbord of garden pleasures, we might expect her to be luxuriating in her love, basking in her sense of well-being. Delicious sleep could easily follow her satiated and "drunken" communion with her lover. Indeed, the first thing the woman reports is her state of sleeping, but *not* in the blissful mode we anticipate, as she is jolted awake by a mix of sensations, as throbbing and distressing as they are thrilling and enticing.

To track quickly the events of this startling stanza: The heart of the aroused woman pulses faster as her lover pounds on her door in the middle of the night. But just when she opens to him, he beats a hasty retreat, prompting her to beat a winding path around the city, where the night watchmen beat her and thwart the search for her flighty beloved. As Virginia Burrus and Stephen D. Moore tersely capture this tragic watershed, "The Song of Songs *bottoms out* at 5:6-7."[1] After this whirlwind

---

1. Virginia Burrus and Stephen D. Moore, "Unsafe Sex: Feminism, Pornography, and the Song of Songs," *BibInt* 11 (2003), 41 (emphasis original).

*Song of Songs 5:2-8*

**[W → D]**

²I slept, but my heart was awake.
Listen! my beloved is knocking.
"Open to me, my sister, my love,
    my dove, my perfect one;
for my head is wet with dew,
    my locks with the drops of the
        night."
³I had put off my garment;
    how could I put it on again?
I had bathed my feet;
    how could I soil them?
⁴My beloved thrust his hand into
        the opening,
    and my inmost being yearned
        for him.
⁵I arose to open to my beloved,
    And my hands dripped with
        myrrh.

my fingers with liquid myrrh,
    upon the handles of the bolt.
⁶I opened to my beloved,
    but my beloved had turned and
        was gone.
My soul failed me when he spoke.
I sought him but did not find him;
    I called him, but he gave no
        answer.
⁷Making their rounds in the city
    the sentinels found me;
they beat me, they wounded me,
they took away my mantle,
those sentinels of the walls.
⁸I adjure you, O daughters of Je-
        rusalem
    if you find my beloved,
tell him this:
    I am faint with love.

---

of shocking activity, the woman utters her final exhausted comment to her friends, which she instructs them to "tell" her man: "Smitten [sick, weak] with love am I" (Song 5:8; author's translation).

The parallels with the earlier nocturnal egression scene in Song 3:1-5 are obvious, but the darkness has now deepened: the sentinels have become violently abusive, not merely unhelpful toward the woman; and this time, rather than laying hold of her beloved, she returns home bereft of him, to say nothing of her dignity and her clothing (5:7). Whether or not this reflects an "actual" experience in the woman's life does not, in my view, significantly affect its interpretation. Poetry is the language of imaginative construal, not concrete replication, but the construal still constructs a poignant mental and emotional reality that confronts readers/hearers. Gripping poetry like the Song of Songs pulls audiences into fresh encounters with the world rather than naïve escapes from it. And "fresh" can mean "raw and exposed," like the stark experiences in the woman's present account that plunge her into the depths of an "extreme situation," as Sarah Zhang, drawing on Roland Barthes, describes it in her Contributing Voice essay, "Bold Enough to Be Vulnerable?," pp. 130–31.

Further, given the mid-night setting of disrupted sleep, these lines (like Song 3:1-5) may be envisioned as a dream report. But again, this "imaginary" portrayal re-presents, rather than replaces, "real" events in revealing ways. Current psychiatric practice informed by interpersonal neurobiology appreciates the function of dreams in "integrat[ing] memory and emotion," in forging "an amalgam of memories in search of resolution." During REM sleep stages and dream states, normal daytime "cortical inhibition is released enough to allow our subcortical limbic and brainstem regions to have a heyday with imagination and feeling."[2] And the heyday can become a horror show as repressed fears and traumas take center stage. Sweet dreams sour into nightmares. In the case of the Song's woman, her honey- and myrrh-dripping paradise, conjured by her lover (4:11, 14; 5:1), seeps into her dream world (5:5), only to drain out into the rough urban streets (5:7). The pleasures of garden and wilderness clash with the pains of the walled city. The woman's persisting terrors and vulnerabilities come to light in the dead of night—with her lover nowhere in sight.

Though not a *wasf*, this scene incorporates into its tense ambience a number of somatic-symbolic features pertaining to voices, hands, feet, and clothes.

## *Voices*

The importance of voice—signifying authoritative, influential speech, not merely a torrent of words—as a medium of social power is a staple of feminist criticism, not least because women's voices have too often been scoffed at, suppressed, and dismissed at all levels of society.[3] Many feminist biblical interpreters, however, have followed Phyllis Trible in extolling the Song as a salient exception to this rule: here, more than anywhere else in the biblical canon, the woman speaks in her own voice as much and as authoritatively as the man, if not more.[4] But the

2. Daniel J. Siegel, *Mindsight: The New Science of Personal Transformation* (New York: Bantam Books, 2010), 141–42.

3. See F. Scott Spencer, "Feminist Criticism," in *Hearing the New Testament: Strategies for Interpretation*, 2nd ed., ed. Joel B. Green (Grand Rapids: Eerdmans, 2010), 295–300.

4. Phyllis Trible, "Loves Lyrics Redeemed," in *A Feminist Companion to the Song of Songs*, ed. Athalya Brenner, FCB (Sheffield: Sheffield Academic, 1993), 100–120; see Marcia Falk, *The Song of Songs: A New Translation and Interpretation* (New York: Harper-Collins, 1990), 115–19; Carol Meyers, "Gender Imagery in the Song of Songs," in *A Feminist Companion to the Song of Songs*, ed. Athalya Brenner and Carole R. Fontaine,

present stanza complicates this assessment. While the woman indeed tells her story of love and longing, it is not an altogether pleasant one, not only because of the night watchmen's maltreatment, but also because of her lover's deceptive speech. From the start, she embeds in her report his demand for entrance: "Open to me, my sister, my love" (Song 5:2). When she awakes at this word and the knocking that accompanies it, she responds willingly but also obediently, opening herself to him (5:3-6a). But precisely at this point of her openness, the man recoils, turns away, and flees, prompting the woman to recollect, "My soul failed me *when he spoke*," and to launch her ill-fated search-and-call for him, to which he "gave no answer" (5:6b-7). I will elaborate on the woman's "failed" reaction below, but for now I simply register that within the woman's narration, the man's initiatory speech followed by his refractory silence controls her action and leads her astray. Here, feminist strains of the Song are eerily muted.

## Hands

Except for the woman's expressed desire to be enveloped by the man's two hands or arms (Song 2:6), this stanza contains the first references to the lovers' hands in the Song and the first uses of the basic "hand" term, יד (5:4-5). This lacuna of such a key, demonstrative body part is surprising, given its centrality to lovemaking and the close attention to the couple's other physical features. Waiting until now for the hand's grand entrance accentuates its importance in the present context.

Like vocal expression, manual action—which includes communication through gestures and sign language—channels power as in the familiar biblical idiom, "the right hand of power" and the English connotation of "manipulation." In his fascinating "philosophical inquiry into human being," the British medical scholar and philosopher Raymond Tallis explores the hand as the most distinct and dynamic organ of humankind or "manukind," as he riffs, the one component we must "come to grips with," as best we can, to understand ourselves and the world we inhabit—and manipulate.

---

FCB (Sheffield: Sheffield Academic, 1993), 197–212, at 207–12; Athalya Brenner, "Women Poets and Authors," in *A Feminist Companion to the Song of Songs*, ed. Athalya Brenner, FCB (Sheffield: Sheffield Academic, 1993), 87–91.

> This hand—this professor of grasping, seizing, pulling , plucking, pick-
> ing, pinching, pressing, patting, poking, prodding, fumbling, squeezing,
> crushing, throttling, drumming, shaping, lifting, flicking, catching,
> throwing, and much else besides—is the master tool of human life. The
> brain's most versatile and intelligent lieutenant, the master grasper, it
> is simply ungraspable. We may, however, try to bring its multifarious
> . . . faculties to some sort of order. . . . In the hand are combined an
> organ of manipulation, an organ of knowledge and an organ of com-
> munication: a three-in-one, it acts, knows and speaks.[5]

In the Song's bedtime drama, each lover extends a passionate hand
toward the other. The woman first recalls how her "beloved thrust his
hand into the opening" (Song 5:4a). Though this gesture is charged
with obvious erotic intent, its particular significance requires further
exploration.

But at the gut level of "my inmost being" (Song 5:4) or, literally, "in-
nards," the thrusting hand arouses the woman's deep desires for him that
well up within her and ooze out as "liquid myrrh" through her hands
and fingers as they seek to grasp "the handles of the bolt"—another
image dripping with sexual innuendo (5:5).[6] This profusion of perfume
lubricates the powerful engine of passion driving the lovers' hands:
we expect erotic sparks to fly! The man, however, suddenly makes a
counter–power play, pulling back his hand and leaving the woman wet,
weak, and set up for wounding by the city guards. His controlling upper
hand in this current encounter leaves her empty handed—and worse.
Though not referring explicitly to the watchmen's hands, the woman's
memory of their beating, wounding, and taking her mantle all focus on
their brutal manhandling of her (5:7).

5. Raymond Tallis, *The Hand: A Philosophical Inquiry into Human Being* (Edinburgh:
Edinburgh University Press, 2003), 22 (and *passim*).

6. Less poetically and operatively, we might imagine the woman simply dousing
her hands with liquid myrrh perfume as she dashes to the door to meet her lover.
Alternatively, the scene has sparked consideration of the *man's* drenching the external
door handles with his tears and / or unguents, following the *paraklausithyron* or "door
lament" trope, the pattern of a rejected lover in Egyptian and Greco-Roman amatory
poetry. But Song 5:5 clearly ascribes the "handling" activity to the woman's hands
and fingers. See the discussion in Marvin H. Pope, *Song of Songs: A New Translation
with Introduction and Commentary*, AB 7C (Garden City, NY: Doubleday, 1977), 521–24;
Michael V. Fox, *The Song of Songs and the Ancient Egyptian Love Songs* (Madison: University of Wisconsin Press, 1985), 282–83; Othmar Keel, *The Song of Songs: A Continental
Commentary*, trans. Frederick J. Gaiser (Minneapolis: Fortress, 1994), 189–94.

## Feet and Clothes

I treat these features together in keeping with their tight juxtaposition in Song 5:3. In preparation for bed, the woman has washed her feet and shed her "garment" (כתנת, NRSV) or "tunic" (CEB), a "close-fitting, ankle-length, shirtlike undergarment."[7] She thus sleeps in a state of purity and freedom, unencumbered by footwear and other clothing. But such a bare condition is also vulnerable to defilement and disturbance. Hence, when the woman is stirred by her lover's knocking and beckoning, she first reacts with cautious concern about getting up and answering his call: without tunic, "how could I put it on again?"; with washed feet, "how could I soil them?" More is at stake here than her basic comfort and hygiene: "I'm all cozy and clean in my bed here." Her nocturnal state of undress and exposed feet connote sexual availability, which is not to say that she goes to bed anticipating an erotic experience but that normal bedtime ablutions naturally prepare her for sex as well as for sleep.[8] Sexual images of "lying down at the feet," "uncovering feet," and "spreading over a cloak," familiar from Ruth and Boaz's midnight liaison on the threshing floor (Ruth 3:4-9, 14), resonate here, all the more so in the Hebrew canon, where Ruth immediately follows the Song of Songs in the *Megillot* section of the *Ketuvim* (Writings).

In Ruth's case, however, she takes the initiative, urged by Naomi: having washed, perfumed, and donned her finest clothes, she goes outside her home *to* Boaz and *rouses him* (Ruth 3:1-8). Though bold and brazen, Ruth remains an altogether "worthy woman" (3:11) striking an honorable bond with her "near kinsman" (3:13). But she does tread close to the line of propriety crossed by the wayward feet of the prowling prostitute in Proverbs:

> Then a woman comes toward him,
>> decked out like a prostitute, wily of heart.
> She is loud and wayward;
>> her feet do not stay at home;
> now in the streets, now in the squares,
>> and at every corner she lies in wait.

---

7. Keel, *Song*, 189; see also Roland E. Murphy, *The Song of Songs,* Hermeneia (Minneapolis: Fortress, 1990), 165.

8. Contra Michael V. Fox who writes, "The woman had prepared for the visit by anointing herself with perfumed unguents" "The Song of Solomon," in *The Harper-Collins Study Bible*, rev. ed., ed. Harold W. Attridge [New York: HarperCollins, 2006], 908). This suggestion that the woman anticipated (arranged?) her lover's nocturnal visit over-interprets the scene.

> She seizes him and kisses him,
> > and with impudent face she says to him;
> . . . "I have decked my couch with coverings,
> > colored spreads of Egyptian linen;
> I have perfumed my bed with myrrh, aloes, and cinnamon.
> Come let us take our fill of love until morning;
> > let us delight ourselves with love." (Prov 7:10-18)

Similarly, the fancy feet of the proud "daughters of Zion" are denounced in Isaiah:

> The LORD said:
> Because the daughters of Zion are haughty
> > and walk with outstretched necks,
> > > glancing wantonly with their eyes,
> mincing along as they go,
> > tinkling with their feet;
> the LORD will afflict with scabs
> > the heads of the daughters of Zion
> > and the LORD will lay bare their secret parts.
> In that day the LORD will take away the finery of the anklets, the headbands, and the crescents, the pendants, the bracelets, and the scarfs; the headdresses, the armlets, the sashes, the perfume boxes, and the amulets; the signet rings and nose rings, the mantles, the cloaks and the handbags; the garments of gauze, the linen garments, the turbans, and the veils.
> Instead of perfume there will be a stench;
> > and instead of a sash, a rope;
> and instead of well-set hair, baldness;
> > and instead of a rich robe, a binding of sackcloth;
> instead of beauty, shame. (Isa 3:16-24)

The collocation of these questionable women's pedal movements, along with various other body features like neck, eyes, face, and hair, and their sartorial accoutrements, including jewelry and perfumery (myrrh, aloes, cinnamon), echoes the manifold descriptors of the Song's woman even more than Ruth.

Yet along with Ruth, though in different ways, the Songstress avoids the shameless paths of Proverbs' loose woman and Isaiah's elite ladies, though still veering eerily close to the edge. She thinks twice about getting out of bed, donning her clothes (and myrrh?), and soiling her feet. Her hesitancy may reflect mixed feelings of nervous vigilance; is this really her lover calling on her at such an inopportune time? Or perhaps it's coquettish dalliance; since he's popped in so unexpectedly, he can cool his heels a little longer.[9] But in any case, her surging desire, aroused by her lover's call and proximity, predominates, prompting her to uncover her feet and "to open" herself to him (5:5). She is moved with passion to pad her barefooted way to let him inside her bedroom—but only in response to his initiatory pursuit. She seeks because she is sought.

But then, in the wake of the man's sudden aborting of his amorous mission and of his disappearance, the woman is impelled (again) into searching for him in the dark city streets, outside the safety of her dwelling. She sets to roaming about, perhaps still in her bare feet, though she does at least wrap herself in a "mantle" (Song 5:7), "shawl," or "large veil."[10] But she is by no means protected from the elements of the night, especially the watchmen on their beat. Instead of finding her lover— whom alone she seeks, quite the contrary to trolling the streets for any john, like the prostitute in Proverbs—she is "found" by these guards and brutally treated (5:7), unlike the tenderly cared-for Ruth or the wealthy strutters in Isaiah before the Lord knocks them off their feet.

In the course of beating and bruising her, the patrollers peel off her shawl, leaving her to run away to her daughter-friends, we may surmise, in her stripped condition; we're never told that she put on her undergarment before dashing outside. Although innocently, perhaps even foolishly, pursuing the lover who had pursued her, the woman winds up being abandoned by him to a band of official protectors turned thugs. If this is another hide-and-seek game the man is playing, this one turns disastrous for the woman and raises serious questions about his reliability and careful concern for her welfare. Likewise, her "lovesickness," unlike its pleasant overtures of infatuation in 2:5, becomes a debilitating affliction in this context. The mean city streets policed by unscrupulous watchers prove immeasurably less hospitable to the loving woman than the lush leafy bowers attended by gentle gazelles and wild does (2:5-7).

With this survey of the voices, hands, feet, and clothes featured in this noir vignette, we have uncovered the main contours of the woman's experience, both passionate and painful. And, as always in this erotic

9. On the woman's possible teasing or coquetry here, see Robert Alter, *Strong as Death Is Love: The Song of Songs, Ruth, Esther, Jonah, and Daniel: A Translation with Commentary* (New York: Norton, 2015), 30; Keel, *Song*, 189–90.

10. In the Hebrew Bible, the term רדיד is used only in Song 5:7 and Isa 3:23. In the latter reference, it refers to the Lord's stripping activity of Israel's haughty elite women mentioned above: "In that day the Lᴏʀᴅ will take away . . . the veils (רדידים)" (Isa 3:18-23; NJPS renders it: "In that day the Lᴏʀᴅ will strip off . . . the capes").

Song, we listen in and look on as voyeurs.[11] But in that position, we choose what we hear and see and how we listen and look. The present scene poses particularly stark choices. On the one hand, 5:7 may tempt some readers to salaciously indulge in sadomasochistic sexual fantasy as if watching a pornographic clip, though they would need to embellish considerably the violent snippet in 5:7, as bare in descriptive detail as the woman herself, to satisfy such desires.[12] On the other hand, readers *should*, in my judgment, sympathetically engage the woman's painful experiences of being abandoned by her lover after he had aroused her passionate interest and abused by the city's security forces. A feminist analysis reveals that the woman is the victim of a social system that privileges male mobility—the freedom to go and come, roam and range at will—and physical power over women.[13] In this case, she pays for her natural, legitimate, willing sexual desires with frustration (5:6), molestation (5:7), and debilitation (5:8).

---

11. I use "voyeur" here in the broadest sense of an outsider looking on a more private scene, comparable to an "eavesdropper" overhearing a personal conversation. Though the Song invites us readers/hearers to see/hear the love scenes, we inevitably retain our outsider position to some degree. How we respond to this voyeuristic status is a key component of reader response. For a narrower perspective on voyeurism focused primarily on the lovers' looks at each other within the poem, J. Cheryl Exum writes, "I prefer to distinguish between the gaze as voyeuristic, looking that intrudes upon that which is seen, and the look as erotic, looking that participates in that which is seen. Being looked at is not necessarily objectifying" (*Song of Songs*, OTL [Louisville: Westminster John Knox, 2005], 22–25, 190, 208–9). Overall, Exum interprets the lovers' viewpoints vis-à-vis each other as mutually respectful and engaging (erotic) rather than intrusive and exploitative (voyeuristic). I agree.

12. See the provocative (and excessive) treatment by Roland Boer, "Night Sprinkle(s): Pornography and the Song of Songs," in *Knockin' on Heaven's Door: The Bible and Popular Culture*, Biblical Limits, 53–70 (London: Routledge, 1999), 68–69; and the discussion of Boer's work in Burris and Moore, "Unsafe Sex," 44–45. I will further critique Boer's pornographic reading of the Song below regarding 7:1-9a on pp. 175–78.

13. Sara Ahmed comments, "Women's access to public space is restricted by the circulation of narratives of feminine vulnerability. Such narratives are calls for action: they suggest women must always be on guard when outside the home. They not only construct 'the outside' as inherently dangerous, but they also posit home as being safe. So women, if they are to have access to feminine respectability, must either stay at home (femininity as domestication), or be careful in how they move and appear in public (femininity as constrained mobility)" (*The Cultural Politics of Emotion* [New York: Routledge, 2004], 68–69). Here Ahmed draws on the work of Elizabeth Stanko, *Everyday Violence: How Women and Men Experience Sexual and Physical Danger* (London: Pandora, 1990).

Finally, I turn to fill out a few more details of this provocative picture as it develops in three stages.

## Soaked with Desire (5:2-6)

The opening bedroom scene quickly floods with passion that flows from each lover's body: the man's head/hair is "soaked" (CEB), "drenched" (NJPS, NIV, NASB), or "filled" (מלא) with night dew (Song 5:2), while the woman's hands/fingers are saturated with "flowing [עבר] myrrh" (5:5, NJPS, NIV, NASB). The desired product is a wet and sticky sexual brew, though the full mixture never occurs, as the man bolts at the last moment, leaving a puddle from his dewy locks in his wake.

Erotic experience in the Song, as we have seen, is often doused with fluids from the lovers' bodies ("your kisses," "his fruit," "honey and milk under your tongue," "your watercourses") and from the environment (oils, wines, fruits, washing pools). As the eminent cultural anthropologist Mary Douglas has theorized, bodily openings (mouth, pores, genitals, anus) that constitute ports for the traffic of viscous substances symbolize porous social borders in the body politic that must be protected from alien infection.[14] Hence, the many regulations and taboos associated with food, sex, skin diseases, and waste management. Bodily fluids like saliva, blood, semen, and urine coursing on the borders of life and death must be carefully monitored to maintain personal and societal health and cleanliness. And because sexual intercourse, in particular, is so integral to (re)producing life, it must be hyper-protected through carefully constructed gender roles. Women's potent fluids, which swell into wombs nurturing new life, merit special control (damming) in this construction lest they be breached (penetrated) by foreign agents or "stick" to unauthorized surfaces.[15] This sticky problem is most perilously embodied in the "strange," "loose" women who open their swirling floodgates to suck foolish men down into the "chambers of death" and in the incontinent men who shoot their "streams of water in the streets"

14. Mary Douglas, *Purity and Danger: An Analysis of the Concepts of Pollution and Taboo* (London: Routledge, 1966).

15. On the cultural significance of "sticky" substances, evoking the social emotion of disgust, see Ahmed, *Cultural Poetics*, 96–100; Stephen D. Moore, "More than a Feeling: Affect Theory and Biblical Studies," paper delivered at annual SBL meeting, San Diego, CA, 2014.

rather than channeling them exclusively into their "own cisterns/wells" afforded by their wives (see Prov 2:16-18; 5:15-20; 7:10-27).

From this fluid perspective of socially constructed, embodied gender norms, informed by the work of Mary Douglas and Judith Butler, Yael Almog interprets the Song as busting through conventional dikes: "The various descriptions in the Song . . . demonstrate the ways in which the appearance of liquid, blurring the borders between the body's insides and outsides, is drawn to subvert social law."[16] Wetness drips, oozes, and pours out of the bodies of both lovers in more or less equal measure, without the slightest tinge of disgust.[17] They stick here and there, now and then, to each other, without glomming onto the other in possessive paralysis. Their mutual passion has no bounds, freely flowing in and out toward the other, but resisting consummation that might drain them or confine them in stagnant cultural stereotypes. In the present scene, right on the verge of opening their gates and merging their waters, the course is reversed by the man (Song 5:6). There will be no climactic intercourse and certainly no reproductive insemination. The relationship remains open and fluid, though passionately engaged. Such is typical of the Song in Almog's reading: "The allusions to bodily fluids seem subversive of normative copulation with its strictly deterministic goal of reproduction; the sensual relations between the lovers in the Song exist within this realm of transgression."[18]

While I appreciate the sense of mutual play and dynamic freedom enjoyed by the lovers in much of the Song, I also detect signs of their pain and struggle, not only amid familial (brothers) and societal (watchmen) resistance to their love and pressures to conform to traditional "arranged" norms, but also between the lovers themselves as they negotiate the bounds of their passionate relationship. Covenantal boundaries typical of committed partnerships, marital or otherwise, need not be oppressive iron curtains enforcing narrow social roles. Indeed, they can provide safe space for optimal growth and flourishing. Boundless

---

16. Yael Almog," 'Flowing Myrrh upon the Handles of the Bolt': Bodily Borders, Social Norms and their Transgression in the Song of Songs," *BibInt* 18 (2010): 257–58.

17. On the common reaction of disgust to exposed bodily fluids and functions not kept in their "proper places" and reminding humans of our mortal, animal natures, see Ahmed, *Cultural Politics*, 82–100; Martha Nussbaum, *Hiding from Humanity: Disgust, Shame, and the Law* (Princeton: Princeton University Press, 2004; also Martha Nussbaum, *From Disgust to Humanity: Sexual Orientation and Constitutional Law*, Inalienable Rights Series (New York: Oxford University Press, 2010).

18. Almog, " 'Flowing Myrrh,' " 257.

freedom without responsibility risks chaotic confusion. Anarchy is a poor antidote to patriarchy. Transgressive actions can indeed be liberating, *if enacted together* in a relationship. But unilateral transgression inevitably transgresses *against* the left-behind party in the name of freedom as conceived by the transgressor. In the current stanza, as elsewhere in the Song, the man appears freer than the woman to chart his own movements with or without her. He pops in when he pleases and pads off when it suits him, even after arousing and reaching out to his lover, leaving her frustrated and vulnerable.

The juicy sluice of waters and perfumes in the present nocturnal setting recalls the preceding garden paradise (Song 4:10–5:1). Likewise both garden and bedroom ensconcing the woman are locked—by her choice, we may assume, as much as by societal convention, since the primary issue is access to *her* body to which *she* holds the key—with the man outside seeking entrance (4:12; 5:4-5). But there is a marked difference of respect by the man for the woman's boundary. In the garden scene, the woman's waters overflow her banks, and her words invite her lover in to feast with and upon her. Only then, as we have seen, does he come to "gather my myrrh . . . eat my honeycomb . . . drink my wine" (5:1). In the bedroom scene, however, the wet-headed man proves more aggressive, even intrusive, as he wakens his sister-love with his knocking and pleading for entrance. Following her hesitancy to get up, re-dress, and re-dirty her feet—though it's ambiguous whether she registers these concerns aloud in her dream event—and before she rises to open the door and herself to him, he "thrust his hand into the opening" (5:4). In other words, he tries to push or force his way in.

The verb שלח, aptly rendered "thrust" in this context (NRSV, NIV), means "send forth" and comes, as noted above, from the same root as the "shoots" or "water channels" in the woman's pomegranate paradise (Song 4:13). But this time, rather than waiting for the woman's strong currents to draw him in, the man propels his stiff hand and arm into the "opening" (חר), which typically designates a "cave" or "hole."[19] If the for-

---

19. Though most English versions portray the man as extending his hand "*through* (מן) the opening," the NJPS reads: "My beloved took his hand *off* the latch." Alter (*Strong as Death*, 31) suggests, "My lover pulled back his hand *from* the latch." This rendering reflects the common meaning of the preposition מן as "from." Spatially, however, מן "indicates beginning-point of motion, out of" or "away from" the subject (William J. Holladay, *A Concise Hebrew and Aramaic Lexicon of the Old Testament* [Grand Rapids: Eerdmans, 1971], 200). Hence, in the present Song context, the man extends

mer meaning is in view, perhaps it reflects a general move to ingress the woman's darkened quarters; if the latter, it alludes to a smaller, particular hole. But which one: (1) a gap in a window or lattice, as in 2:9, through which the man saw and spoke to the woman, hoping to lure her outside;[20] (2) a peephole, larger than modern counterparts, through which a man's hand might squeeze, but designed for the resident to assess prospective entrants;[21] or (3) a "latch hole" (CEB; similarly, NIV) in the door through which the man might try to dislodge the inside bolt-locks?[22] The last two options represent home security checkpoints that the man trespasses. They may also evoke the double entendre of the woman's most private vaginal opening, though only remotely, since the couple never makes physical contact in this scene, and the main body parts—hands and feet—make sense in the scene according to their usual functions, apart from euphemistic associations with primary sexual organs.[23]

Though a startling transgressive move on the man's part, his hand thrust, punctuating his initial knock and call, impels the woman's attempt to grasp his hand and grant him entrance. His brazen gesture has stirred her up with tense excitement, at once painful and pleasant. Her "awakened heart" races, we may presume, with a swirl of intense anxiety and anticipation. So she comes with sweaty, myrrh-lathered hands to clutch the door bolt with the man's hand penetrating through the latch hole, slip it off its mountings, and guide him inside. Again, the bolt-and-hand

---

his hand outward *from himself*, rather than drawing it back toward him; compare Song 2:9: "My beloved . . . gazing *in at* (מן) the window, peering *through* (מן) the lattice." See Chana Bloch and Ariel Bloch, *The Song of Songs: The World's First Great Love Poem* (New York: Modern Library, 1995), 154, 180. Michael Fishbane uses the NJPS as his primary English version, but grants the plausibility of understanding a "charged image" in 5:5 of the man's "stretching his hand *through* the door," since both the verb and preposition "convey penetration" (*Song of Songs*, JPS Bible Commentary [Lincoln: University of Nebraska Press, 2015], 138).

20. Fox, *Song*, 144.

21. Keel, *Song*, 190–92.

22. Bloch and Bloch, *Song*, 181.

23. The exposure of the Song woman's "feet" in the Song is not as obvious a euphemism as in Ruth 3, where the two lovers are actually in bed together. For a view of the man's "hand" as a phallic symbol and the "hole" as a vaginal metonym, together "suggestive of coital intromission," see Pope (*Song*, 519). On the use of double entendre in the Song, see the insightful article of J. Cheryl Exum, "In the Eye of the Beholder; Wishing, Dreaming, and *Double Entendre* in the Song of Songs," in *The Labour of Reading: Desire, Alienation, and Biblical Interpretation*, ed. Fiona C. Black, Roland Boer, and Erin Runions (Atlanta: SBL, 1999), 71–86.

mechanism may hint at a phallic counterpart to the vaginal hole, but the fit is only suggestive, not consummative, since at the moment of her opening, the woman discovers the man has withdrawn and turned away, hand and all—a preemptive interruptus before coitus or any bodily contact! In a jolting progression of movements, his initial *transgression* triggers her desire for his *ingression* to her bedroom—and body—which he abruptly aborts with his *egression* from the scene.

No explanation is given for the man's sudden retreat, and no interpretation satisfies or justifies, whether the patrolling watchmen—what does he really have to fear from them?[24]—or the poetic trope of the "excluded lover" (*exclusus amator*) pining at the doorstep for the teasing, hard-to-get woman and then trudging off in disappointment, leaving behind lavish gifts and ointments as calling cards.[25] As Roland E. Murphy notes, however, the Song's man offers no lyrical lament typical of this genre; he just turns and departs. But Murphy does add that "if there is a complaint, it seems to be perhaps implicit in the story as told by the woman, *almost blaming herself* for the trouble she had to undergo in her search for him."[26] Likewise, Chana Bloch and Ariel Bloch suggest that the woman's sad report of opening her door to her unexpectedly absent lover reflects "an expression of regret about her delay."[27] Such supposed self-blame over her dilatory response veers close to blaming the victim and letting the flighty man off scot-free: the teasing, dawdling woman made him leave; if she'd just come sooner, all this frustration could have been avoided.

But pulling the Adam "blame the woman" stunt works no better here than in Eden. To his credit, Othmar Keel recognizes that the male-biased labeling of this scene as "Punished Coyness" or "Love's Sorrow

---

24. Bloch and Bloch (*Song*, 182) suggest that the male "lover may have left abruptly because he was concerned about the watchmen making their rounds." However, he certainly would not have been as vulnerable to the watchmen's abuse as the woman would be and also more likely than she to get off with a warning.

25. See p. 117 n. 6 above on the *paraklausithyron* or "door lament" topos. Often cited as primary evidence is a portion of Lucretius (*The Nature of Things* [*De Rerum Natura*], trans. A. E. Stallings [London: Penguin, 2007], 142):

But the lover locked out, weeps, and strews the stoop with wreaths in bloom,
And anoints the haughty doorposts with sweet-marjoram perfume,
And presses his lips to the door, the fool—when if he were let in,
One whiff and he would seek a good excuse to leave again!
His long-rehearsed heartfelt lament would then come crashing down,
Right then and there he's cursed himself for being such a clown (4.1177–83).

26. Murphy, *Song*, 169 (emphasis added).

27. Bloch and Bloch, *Song*, 182.

through Rejection" could just as easily be flipped against the man in the counter-titles of "The Inconsiderate Lover" or "Love's Sorrow through Impatience." Nevertheless, Keel then quickly disavows blaming either party: "But the poem is not about determining guilt: it is about a recurrent and painful experience of people in love: their feelings do not always match."[28] Well, true enough—and so love often goes. But it also often goes there because of one party's greater negligence, selfishness, and insensitivity, and in the present scene that bill is filled by the man: he starts the whole erotic flow and then abruptly stops it on his end for no good reason, except his own whimsy, his irresponsible freedom to go his own way as he pleases.

And the woman is not happy about it. Her "soul failed" as the echo of his alluring voice now dissipates with his abrupt retreat (Song 5:6).[29] That is, her "entire being, her life essence [נפש] went out [יצא]."[30] The same words denote the death of Rachel upon birthing Benjamin (Gen 35:18).[31] While the woman in the Song does not literally die, her experience should not be trivialized into some kind of melodramatic hyperbole, like "I could have just died," or a weak-kneed swoon in the presence of a powerful king, like the Queen of Sheba before Solomon or the Greek Esther before Artaxerxes (1 Kgs 10:4; Esth 15:5-16, LXX). To sharpen the point already intimated, the Songstress suffers a poignant deathlike pain inflicted by the absence and silence of her lover. He has thereby hurt her, knocking the wind out of her after first knocking on her door and piquing her desire. Moreover, he leaves her at serious risk of suffering more pain, even unto death. Because of his callous abandonment at the critical point of love's tidal surge, she spills out into the city streets, seeking and calling for her lover, but finding—or rather being found by—only rapacious patrollers who take advantage of her, striking her and stripping her of her cloak and almost her life.

---

28. Keel, *Song*, 194.

29. The verb (דבר) for the man's action that precipitates the woman's anguish can mean either "speak" (most commonly) or "turn away." Either option works here: "My soul failed me when *he spoke*" (NRSV; so also NASB, KJV, LXX; Fishbane, *Song*, 140; Alter, *Strong as Death*, 31); "I nearly died when he turned away" (CEB; so also NJPS, NAB, NIV; Keel, *Song*, 194; Holladay, *Lexicon*, 66). I'm inclined toward a double-meaning here: the contradiction between the man's speech and action, between his summons, still ringing in the woman's ears, and his unexpected retreat when she answers his call intensifies her pain to the breaking point.

30. On נפש, see n. 3 and discussion on 3:1-5 above, pp. 60–61.

31. Fox, *Song*, 145–46; Bergant, *Song*, 65. See parallel passage in Ps 146:4: "their breath/spirit [רוח] departs [in death] [יצא]."

## Stripped with Violence (5:7)

This verse needs little exegetical commentary but much sober reflection. Its language is painfully clear without flowery imagery. Its bare form fits its stark content. Its brevity reflects its dissonance: the love Song cannot bear this violent counter-strain very long. But it cannot gloss over it either. For all its beauty, the woman's body retains this painful scar that no makeup can conceal; and for all the savory love the couple has enjoyed and anticipated, the bitter taste of this sour moment lingers in the woman's mouth. She recalls the traumatic scene in a quick succession of perfect (completed action) verbs, beginning with the passive "found"—she was set upon by attackers; this was not her choice or her fault—followed by three active assaults on the woman's body: in the absence of her lover, the sentinels "struck me, bruised me, stripped my shawl." The threefold repetition of the first-person singular suffix ("me/my") marks the seared memory of violation against her person. If she could have left this horror out of the Song, she would have. But some wounds never completely heal.

One element that we haven't yet considered merits mention: the last word in this verse clarifies the watchmen's duty as keepers "of the *walls*" (Song 5:7). This specification is not added to the parallel text in 3:3-4 but is likely implied there also. Sentinels had primary responsibility in watchtowers along the city walls for sounding the alarm against outside intruders. They may also "make rounds" within the city in search of infiltrators or troublemakers, but never at the expense of vigilance on the distant horizon. The Song's watchmen seem too preoccupied with internal security, more interested in roaming around the city looking for trouble—which they are apt to foment as much as prevent!—than in staking out their position on the walls, alert to advancing threats. Certainly in the present scene they readily light on the wandering cloaked—veiled? barefoot?—woman, whom they may take for a prostitute without bothering to investigate closely and, in any case, who poses no real threat to the city's safety.

Persisting injustices of double standard and victim blaming again lurk in the dark. Pertaining to the former, we ask, while knowing the answer: Why does the night-crawling male lover, who effectively drew the woman outside, draw no attention himself from the watchmen? And concerning the latter, we readily detect the judgment of conservative critics ringing in the background (though *not* in the text of the Song): "What did you expect, young lady, going out and about in the night streets dressed like that? Chastely confined within the walls of your house is the only proper place to be and the only place you can count on being safe—well, more safe than out there at least." Though assuming this oppressive state of affairs and not railing against it, however, the Song and its female protagonist do not simply accept the way things are with quiet resignation. The woman has something to say about all this to her female friends.

## Smitten with Love (5:8)

Once more the woman concludes a stanza by compelling the daughters of Jerusalem to take a solemn oath on her behalf—"I adjure you"—which befits the seriousness of the extreme situation and her resolve. But this adjuration sharply differs in tone from the others that cap off scenes of richly imagined presence with and embrace by her lover, from which the woman desires *not to be disturbed* (Song 1:9–2:7; 3:1-5; 7:10–8:4). In the present case, as we have stressed, she has already been vexingly disturbed by her flighty absent lover and the viciously present night watchmen. This is a nightmare from which she would be happily shaken. And so, rather than a negative plea to her friends—"Do not disturb!"—the woman gives a positive charge: "If you find my [absent!] beloved, [Do!] tell him this: I am faint with love." The construction is actually in the form of a question and answer, scripting the precise message the woman wants conveyed.

> Question: "What [מַה] shall you tell him?"
> Answer: "I am sick with love."

Ignoring the distinction between this and the other adjurations in the Song, Michael V. Fox argues, against most commentators, that 5:8 also reflects a *negative* mandate: "Do *not* tell him." While the interrogative construction can yield a negative response—"You won't tell him, right?"—it hardly suits the current context. Fox explains the woman's supposed reticence as follows:

> She has acted in a distraught manner, running about the city at night half-dressed, and she is embarrassed over her behavior. Her concern is like that of the Egyptian girl who tells how her heart flees from her and makes her foolish and erratic. She says to her heart, "O my heart, don't make me foolish! Why do you act crazy?"[32]

Ancient Egyptian amatory poetry provides useful intertexts, but not straitjackets, for interpreting the biblical Song. The Song's woman is not a ditzy love-crazed girl panicking over her boyfriend's opinion of her, especially

---

32. Fox, *Song*, 146.

not in the present case. She's deeply in love, yes, all but consumed by her passion for a man she has enjoyed before and anticipates enjoying again this night after he has aroused her. But then he leaves her in the lurch, which provokes her ill-fated search. Now she wants him to know the terrible consequences of his inconsiderate hide-and-seek game on this occasion, however playful it might have been at other times. She is saying, "If you find him—this disrespectful roué who loves to flit and bound about—tell him what happened to me. Tell him how I feel: I'm sick with this love!"

Her prior confession of lovesickness or faintness emerged in the pleasant milieu of the bower and wine-house tryst (Song 2:5). But again, the present nocturnal environment is quite different from that milieu, far more painful than pleasant. Recall from the discussion on 2:5 that the term for "sick" or "faint" (חלה) suggests weakness and wounding, even fatality, as in battle. Metaphorically in relation to love, "faint for love" may connote a willing and wonderful surrender as in 2:5: the winsome "Ahh . . . I could just die!" Or it could connote a more bitter and biting lament: "I'm sick *of* this volatile love. It's wearing me out, beating me down!" The latter nuance dominates in 5:8 on the heels of a patently abusive beating/wounding in 5:7. At the moment, the woman all but conjoins her lover and the patrollers; they have both hurt and harassed her, and her lover needs to know and face up to this ill treatment.

### Bold Enough to Be Vulnerable?

One who reads Song 5:2-8 as a narrative or, as Tod Linafelt proposes, as "pseudonarrative"[33] will be surprised by the silence after 5:7. There is no report of consequence or response to the atrocity in 5:7. The "I" who still speaks does not comment on the physical violence she experienced. Would not she be the first to speak out if justice is what the subject has in mind? What does she intend to express? I suggest that we take this physical violence as a poetic expression, the consequence rather than the cause of her trauma. First, through the optic of an "extreme situation," Roland Barthes has helpfully compared the trivial situation

33. Tod Linafelt, "Lyrical Theology: The Song of Songs and the Advantage of Poetry," in *Toward a Theology of Eros: Transfiguring Passion at the Limits of Discipline*, ed. Virginia Burrus and Catherine Keller, 291–305 (New York: Fordham University Press, 2006), 293, 299. In other words, though this lyric poem utilizes narrative elements, the atmosphere around the "What?" and "Why?" of the story is rarified.

of a lovesick subject and "one of the most unimaginable insults of History" that was inflicted on the inmates of Dachau.[34] The enormity experienced in both situations exceeds the measure of consciousness. For one who is drowning into what *to her* is a bottomless abyss, does it matter whether it is a pond or the Mariana Trench? "I am lost, forever." This irreversible point is the salient marker of an extreme situation—be it the lover's despondence or the watchmen's beating. Second, the watchmen's drastically different responses to the subject in the two night scenes (3:1-5; 5:2-8) are best explained through the different premises. In the first, the subject is determined to go find her lover; having found and brought him back, she thus fulfills the circle of desire. In the second, the lovers' shared attentiveness to oneself rather than the other (5:2-3) bodes for coming mishaps.

Finally, instead of justice, the responses of the subject— first silence, then the unique adjuration (2:7; 3:5; 8:4)—uncover her tenacious, unfailing love. Through the lens of the traumatic happening in 5:6-7 and in the context of her speech to the girls, the content of her adjuration reveals more than a self-diagnosis of her vulnerability. Indirectly, the subject utters the abated response to her wounding. Not anger, not accusation, not even disappointment, the saying that sustains her self-exposure of vulnerability is rather patience. As a sign of obsession, patience does not simply wait for a future time to satisfy her desire but presses for urgent responses from other subjects. It is with a love given without being able to hold back that the subject realizes her unicity as an "I," the word that begins and ends this poem.

*Sarah Zhang*

Though recognizing the stark difference between the lovesick settings in Song 2:5 and 5:8, with the man present in the former and absent in the latter, Tremper Longman fails to push the distinction far enough. He inexplicably surmises that the woman approaches her girlfriends in 5:8 "with no apparent effects from her beating by the city patrol."[35] But how can she *not* be profoundly affected by an ambush of beating, bruising, and stripping? She's a strong woman, but not Superwoman! Brushing off the effects, whether imaginatively conceived or "literally" reported,

34. Roland Barthes, *A Lover's Discourse* (New York: Hill and Wang, 1977), 48–49.
35. Tremper Longman III, *Song of Songs*, NICOT (Grand Rapids: Eerdmans, 2001), 169.

of brutal assault against this woman—"Shake it off, girl!"—is a curious and, frankly, callous interpretive move.[36] Longman proceeds to explain the woman's lovesickness, which she very much wants her beloved to know, as an expression of her continued longing for him: "She pines for him. She needs him desperately. Her message is an exclamation of desire and a plea for union."[37] While I agree that the woman has by no means written her lover off as a hopeless case, as the next stanza makes clear, I do not think that, at this moment, she is sending him a desperate love note via her friends. Moreover, while I agree with Zhang that the Songstress perseveres with remarkable patience after this terrible ordeal, waiting hopefully for her lover's response (she still wants this relationship to work!), I do not separate this patient reaction from stirrings of "anger . . . accusation . . . and even disappointment."[38] A mix of volatile emotions doubtless roils within the passionate, vulnerable woman; and through it all, I hear her putting her irresponsible male lover on notice: "You've left me, you've hurt me, and I'm not going to stand for that any more. I'm sick of *this kind* of love-tease, for which I'm unfairly bearing the heavier burden!"

36. I use strong language here to emphasize the point. I do not mean to suggest in any way that Longman doesn't care about the violence done to this woman, only that his commentary underplays the effects of the scene. The Song text's brief report of the woman's beating need not imply that she got over it quickly, though the more upbeat ensuing stanza starts leaning in this direction; see discussion below on 5:9–6:3, pp. 133–45. Rather, as I posited above, the bare description reinforces the horror of the experience—too painful to dwell on at length. Moreover, in the blurry spectrum of "reality" (event) and "fantasy" (dream) reflected within the Song's vivid "poetic imagination," the simple catalogue of assault (beat/wound/strip) without poetic elaboration or imagery tilts the incident toward the hard, "real" side.

37. Longman, *Song*, 169.

38. Zhang, "Bold Enough to Be Vulnerable," this volume, p. 131.

# Song of Songs 5:9–6:3

## *Playful Girl Talk*

While shifting quickly from a "painful" to a "playful" mood may seem to be an awkward, even unlikely, transition challenging our reading of the previous stanza, it actually makes good psychological sense, given the human propensity to repress bad memories, downplay the severity of problems, and move on as quickly as possible to more pleasant prospects. Such resilience can serve us well, keeping us pressing forward through life's difficulties; but it can also trap us in harmful patterns of self-delusion and rear up to bite us in periodic eruptions of unresolved trauma. Love relations prove particularly vulnerable to optimistic accordance of forgiveness and second chances, which, again, can be redemptive, since no one is perfect, or detrimental if we're coddling bad behavior. The former salutary effect, biblically grounded in God's restorative covenantal bond with often wayward Israel in a broken world, motivates the people's gracious dealings with each other in flawed relationships. But sadly, the latter harmful effect also persists, not least in the common cycle of domestic violence across many cultures, including modern America, where the woman readily takes back the abandoning, abusive man—"He didn't really mean it; he's not such a bad guy; he's under a lot of pressure"—only to suffer repeated beatings.

Thankfully, to peek ahead through the balance of the Song, the woman overcomes the odds and does not suffer again at the cruel absence or

*Song of Songs 5:9–6:3*

**[D → W]**

[9]What is your beloved more than
         another beloved,
    O fairest among women?
What is your beloved more than
         another beloved,
    that you thus adjure us?

**[W → D]**

[10]My beloved is all radiant and
         ruddy,
    distinguished among ten thou-
         sand.
[11]His head is the finest gold;

his locks are wavy,
    black as a raven.
[12]His eyes are like doves
    beside springs of water,
bathed in milk,
    fitly set.
[13]His cheeks are like beds of spices,
    yielding fragrance.
His lips are lilies,
    distilling liquid myrrh.
[14]His arms are rounded gold,
    set with jewels.
His body is ivory work,

presence of her lover or at the attacking hands of the night watchmen to the degree reported in Song 5:6-8. Love is resiliently restored between the couple and will resolutely not fail: it stands "strong as death" (8:6). But I wonder and worry: Is love perhaps too quickly restored here? Does the woman too easily let the man off the hook? Can there be true restoration without some evidence of genuine sorrow and change that signal true repentance on the man's part?

Spurred by her friends' query into the character of her beloved (Song 5:9), the woman in the Song launches into an encomium of his magnificent body. This is the only *waṣf* devoted to the man, compared to three focused on the woman's body (4:1-7; 6:4-10; 7:1-9). Whereas the man almost always praises the woman directly, shifting to third person only in 6:8-10, she speaks here exclusively in third person about him to her friends—of course, he's not around now to be spoken to![1] Her image of him is thus more distant and, in a sense, more truly imaginative: this is how she constructs her beloved, as much wishing what she would like for him to be as representing what he is. In this mode, she details the features of a wondrous golden boy who outshines "ten thousand" competitors (5:10-16). It doesn't get any better than him! And then, when the friends pipe up again and press her gently about her lover's absence—"Where has your beloved gone?" (6:1)—the woman imagines his return to their

1. Fiona C. Black, "Beauty or the Beast? The Grotesque Body in the Song of Songs," *BibInt* 8 (2000): 317–18.

encrusted with sapphires.
15His legs are alabaster columns,
    set upon bases of gold,
His appearance is like Lebanon,
    choice as the cedars.
16His speech is most sweet,
    and he is altogether desirable.
This is my beloved and this is my
        friend,
    O daughters of Jerusalem.
**[D → W]**
6:1Where has your beloved gone,
    O fairest among women?

Which way has your beloved
        turned,
    that we may seek him with you?
**[W → D]**
2My beloved has gone down to his
        garden,
    to the bed of spices,
to pasture his flock in the gardens,
    and to gather lilies.
3I am my beloved's and my be-
        loved is mine;
    he pastures his flock among
        the lilies.

idyllic garden, where they continue to enjoy the delights of their mutual love. What counts is: "I am my beloved's and my beloved is mine" (6:3). Nothing's changed about that (see 2:16). Maybe then the woman does bounce back from her beating more quickly than I granted above in my critique of Longman. At this point in her reflections, does she not seem to dismiss the preceding bad night as one of those unfortunate hiccups in life, a little bump on love's long road, no big deal? We may briefly chart the flow of dialogue as follows:

> *Girlfriends' Question*: What is your beloved more than another beloved,
> O fairest among women? (5:9)
> *Woman's Response*: My beloved is . . . distinguished among ten thousand. (5:10)
> *Girlfriends' Question*: Where has your beloved gone,
> O fairest among women? (6:1)
> *Woman's Response*: My beloved has gone down to his garden. (6:2)

Notice that the friends address their question each time to "O fairest/ most beautiful among women" (Song 5:9; 6:1). This echoes the man's description of her (1:8, 15, 16; 2:10, 13; 4:1, 7) and, in the present context, raises some disturbing doubts about their relationship. His latest behavior hardly reflects cherished care of this "fairest" one. This exceedingly lovely woman, so confirmed by her companions, deserves better treatment than this. To be sure, the "daughters" are not haranguing their friend about her loutish lover or encouraging her to dump him. The tone tilts more toward juicy girl talk than judicial grilling. But the friends are still making the main character think: "Tell us again: what exactly do you see in this guy of yours?" They thus prime her for the gushy portrait of her lover's body that follows. Alternatively, they also give her a chance to complain further about his recent negligence, if she chooses. But she opts only for the most positive reinforcement of her lover.

Within this interpretive space opened by the friends' inquiry, however, an overprotective paternalism toward young women and the feminist hermeneutic of suspicion find some surprising common ground in critical regard for the Songstress's best interests. So I ask again, in different terms: Is the woman perhaps too overconfident about the strength of her lover and the stability of their relationship? Does she perhaps overcompensate for her lover's shortcomings with unbridled fantasy? Does she too facilely assume a swift and full recovery from her recent bout of painful "lovesickness"? Are the effects (and affects) of her beating en route to find her elusive lover just too distressing, too depressing to keep acknowledging? Does she feel it's better to repress the pain and revise the story?

Yet while these questions may register legitimate concerns, they also throw wet blankets on this new generally playful, ebullient scene, prompting a set of ripostes: Must we take such a dour, critical tack? Can we not envision that, at least some of the time, true love "bears all things, believes all things, hopes all things, endures all things [and] never ends" (1 Cor 13:7-8)—or, as the Song woman later exclaims: "Love is as strong as death" (Song 8:6)? Can fierce passion not overcome rough patches—even violent ones—in a relationship? This tension between hopeful and doubtful readings of the present stanza is not easily resolved. We keep seeking for clues as the stanza unfolds.

### So What's So Hot about This Guy of Yours? (5:9)

Beyond what we've already discussed about the opening gambit by Jerusalem daughters in response to their girlfriend's reported nightmarish experience, we focus here on two matters. First, even within the pleasing and teasing circle of girl gossip, the daughters acknowledge an abiding strain of seriousness by making a direct connection with their friend's solemn charge in Song 5:7 that they tell her lover about how "sick with/ of love" she is. They ask, what is so special about "your beloved . . . *that you thus adjure us*?" (5:9). To fill out their thinking, they might be saying, "We don't swear each other to commitments about every little thing [even modern 'pinky swears,' which outsiders might regard as trivial, are significant to the pledgers]. So this *is* a big deal! This guy is really *the one*, isn't he? But you're so enamored with him that he's making you *sick*—and not always in 'good' ways! You just got beaten up, for goodness' sake, looking for him! Are you sure he's worth all this anguish? Remind us, again: What's so great about this guy? We love hearing all about him, but we need some reassurance."

### LGBTQI Matters

For the gay, lesbian, bisexual, transgender, queer, and intersex (LGBTQI) communities, the Song of Songs invites a different reading of gender and sexuality than most of the Old Testament. At first glance, the Song depicts a heterosexual love affair conveyed in hetero-normative language with traditional male-female subjects and pronouns. A closer examination of the text, however, offers two distinct areas of entry into the Song for the LGBTQI communities otherwise underplayed in Scripture.

First, the Song stands out as one of only a few biblical books reflecting a woman's perspective, at least in part. Feminist readers are forced to translate much of the patriarchal, male-centered biblical story through the lens of women's experience in order to hear and understand it from their own perspectives. While ostensibly heterosexual in orientation, the Song invites female and female-identified readers into a more intimate reading of the text by sharing the thoughts and feelings of a woman in love.

Periodic ambiguities in Hebrew pronoun usage and in speaker identification provide space for intimate dialogue among lovers of all genders and sexual orientations. While some English versions of the Song display chapter headers indicating a "Male" or "Female" speaker, the text itself is not so confining. These passages allow a same-gender or transgender loving reader to engage the text with a sense of inclusion.

Second, the Song does not accentuate marriage as a context for these sexual encounters (the wedding procession of 3:6-11 is exceptional). For LGBTQI communities who, until recently, were completely excluded from state-sponsored and federally recognized marriage equality, omitting the marriage covenant as a required context for loving sexual relations is noteworthy. A biblical expression of authentic, passionate, and deeply loving sexual relations outside the confines of what so many in the modern day have termed "traditional marriage" allows members of LGBTQI communities to situate their sexual lives within the sacred fold of God's enduring love.

As a married lesbian minister, I feel a particular connection to Song 5:9b: "How is your lover different from any other lover, that you make us swear a solemn pledge?" (CEB). Prior to the passage of US marriage equality on June 26, 2015, my wife and I were forced to travel two states away in order to be legally married. Upon returning home, despite having a federally recognized marriage certificate in hand, our home state upheld the right to deny us married couple benefits and state-recognition until the Supreme Court ruled in our favor months later. This Song passage reminds me of the private pledge my wife and I made to commit our lives to one another despite the lack of official state authorization at the time. Our story is representative of thousands of other same-gender loving couples who have clung to their intimate private commitments to one another as that which truly binds us together in love.

*Lindsay Andreolli-Comstock*

Second, the friends particularly want to know how the woman's lover stacks up against other men, other "beloved" prospects. There are lots of fish in the sea, especially for such a desirable woman. Is this the best she can do? Is she settling too fast? Here we see a kind of inversion of ancient Near Eastern cultural codes in which men typically jockeyed for superior honor by attracting and acquiring the most desirable women. But in the case of the girlfriends, it's not that they are competing with one another in some agonistic contest over who can land the best man. They will soon pledge to "seek" the woman's lover "with" her (Song 6:1). And the woman's status does not simply derive from the man she attracts (acquires). She has a dignity (beauty as substance and power) all her own that deserves fair and considerate treatment, not least by her lover.

## You Should See His Golden Body! (5:10-16)

The woman jumps on the cue provided by her friends to extol her lover's exceptional physique beyond myriad comparisons. Recalling our discussion above[2] of beauty, in its broadest form, as encompassing the character and virtues of embodied persons, this woman's ode to her beloved's body should not be regarded as a shallow preoccupation with

2. See commentary on 4:1-7, pp. 83–91.

his physical appearance alone. His body reveals how "altogether [כלו] desirable" he is (Song 5:16, "every bit of him," CEB). She uses a number of images that match his sketch of her body: flowing hair, dove-like eyes, wet and fragrant lips, along with a familiar descriptive repertoire of water springs, milk, lilies, Lebanon cedars, and various jewels and spices. The bodies of the woman and man beautifully flow together in a common pool of natural delights.

But while blurring their distinctive identities somewhat and resisting binary absolutes, this is no unisex portrait. In contrast with the man's picture of her in Song 4:1-7, the woman sculpts his body image with a greater array of jewels and minerals. Gold, that most precious substance coveted by kings, not only adorns the man in the woman's eyes but constitutes the essence of his exquisite frame from head to base, reinforced by gold-rod arms in between (5:14).[3] The richness of his solid gold state is amplified by three different terms the woman uses for the prized metal.

His head is gold [כתם], pure gold [פז] (Song 5:11, NAB)
His arms are rods of gold [זהב] (5:14, NAB, NIV)
His legs are . . . set on bases of pure gold [פז] (5:15, NIV)

The man's gold body is also studded with ivory, sapphires, and alabaster (5:14-15). This marvelous assemblage of gems and stones forms an impressive statue of royal splendor and rock-solid stability.

The regal dimension correlates with the woman's previous images of her lover: he is her king, her Solomon-style hero, standing head and shoulders above all men. His rock-like mien, however, is extolled for the first time here, in counterpoise with his immediately preceding liquid meltdown and running away from the scene. Is this wishful thinking on the woman's part, what she'd like for her man to be, or an honest assessment of his true nature? Her language inclines more to a confident assertion via direct metaphors—"his head *is* the finest gold"; "his body *is* ivory work" (Song 5:11, 14)—with fewer allusive similes than the man used in 4:1-7. This reflects who her lover *is* from her perspective. As noted above, the woman in the Song typically conveys her personal emotions and opinions about her lover in forthright fashion: this is what she thinks and feels about him *within herself*, not because he has swept her off her

---

3. The element of gold appears twice elsewhere in the Song: first, as material the man plans to use in fashioning jewelry for his beloved (1:11); and second, as part of Solomon's lavish palanquin (3:10).

feet, rendered her helpless, or "ravished her heart," as he says of her influence on him (4:9). Her recent admission of lovesickness, however, though still a considered statement of self-analysis that she owns up to ("I *am* sick with love"), shades into awareness of the man's causative role in her feelings: her sudden sickness arises as a consequence of his unexpected and irresponsible absence. But she quickly (again, too quickly?) returns to what *she* knows, steeling herself against contrary judgments: "My beloved *is* a rock—and altogether worthy of my trust and love."

To gain a better sense of this *wasf* in Song 5:10-16, we may sketch a descending vertical portrait from head to legs as a "perfect" series of seven central features framed by adulations of the man's embodied nature as a whole. The symmetrical and parallel architecture is not as tight here as we saw in 4:1-7, but everything is still "fitly set" (5:12) into a formidable framework, with the accent more on cohesive strength than delicate balance.

> **Whole**: All radiant and ruddy,
>
>   distinguished among ten thousand
>
> **Parts**: *Head/Hair*: finest gold draped with raven-black locks
>
>     *Eyes*: like poolside doves after a milk bath
>
>       *Cheeks*: like spice towers filled with fragrance
>
>         *Lips*: lilies dripping with liquid myrrh
>
>       *Arms/Hands*: gold rods studded with jewels
>
>     *Body/Belly*: sapphire-studded ivory plate
>
>   *Legs/Thighs*: alabaster-white pillars on gold pedestals
>
> **Whole**: Appearance like Lebanon, speech most sweet
>
>   altogether desirable

To clarify and briefly expand on the various elements seriatim:

- The introductory statement of the man's "radiant and ruddy" (Song 5:10) condition may be taken as an overall assessment of his luminescent handsomeness, outshining "ten thousand" lesser lights. Alternatively, it may focus more particularly on his skin or facial complexion ("clear-skinned and ruddy," NJPS). "Ruddy" (אדם) beauty is evocative of David's appearance in his youth before his ascension to the throne as an unlikely concomitant of his proven physical prowess:

Goliath underestimates David on first glance, deriding him as "only a youth, ruddy and handsome" (1 Sam 17:42; see also 16:12).

• The blackness (שחר) of the man's hair matches the woman's self-described beautiful skin tone in Song 1:5, mocked by some. The comparison to the "raven" (5:11), while an apt descriptor of hair color (blackness) and texture (sleekness), carries some overtones of the ominous and macabre associated with this predatory, "unclean" creature (Lev 11:13-15; Deut 14:11-14).[4] Its close mention with "doves," separated in the Hebrew text by only the single word "his-eyes," offers a jagged juxtaposition of wild and winsome images and a tinge of warning against the man's strike-and-fly potential (5:12).

• The milk-bathed, dove-like eyes set beside water springs (Song 5:12) evoke a depth of allure—she could get lost in his deep eye-wells—and perhaps the smooth milky whiteness of the eyes' rims. They are indeed "fitly set" as the NRSV and KJV render the last phrase, though its meaning is uncertain. The notion of "sitting" is clear in the first Hebrew word (ישב); but the second term (מלאת) is ambiguous, used only here in the Bible. "Fitly set" implies a jewel setting, made explicit in the NIV's "mounted like jewels." But many versions follow the LXX, which we may literally translate as "sitting on a plethora of waters" (πληρώματα ὑδάτων). This fits the aquatic imagery of the vibrant, deeply set eyes encircled in "brimming pools" (CEB, NAB, NJPS).

• Whereas the man described the ornament-graced beauty of the woman's cheeks (Song 1:10), the woman now concentrates on the spiced fragrance of the man's cheeks. She uses a double simile—the singular "bed of spice" (balsam) followed by the plural "towers [מגדלות] of spices"—reflecting a progressive hyperbole: "like a bed of spices, no . . . towers full!"[5] The man compared the woman's neck

---

4. On the raven in the biblical world, see Debbie Blue, *Consider the Birds: A Provocative Guide to Birds of the Bible* (Nashville: Abingdon, 2013), 191–202.

5. See Chana Bloch and Ariel Bloch, *The Song of Songs: The World's First Great Love Poem* (New York: Modern Library, 1995), 186; and CEB ("towers of spices"). J. Cheryl Exum grants the validity of this reading, but prefers to revocalize the MT noun ("towers") as a Piel participle of גדל: hence, "*pouring forth* perfume," paralleling the liquid image of lips "dripping flowing myrrh" that follows in 5:13 (*Song of Songs,* OTL [Louisville: Westminster John Knox, 2005], 184, 205). (See LXX, Vg., NRSV, NAB, NJPS.) I stick with the MT reading, however, reinforcing the dominant architectural imagery of this *wasf.*

to a shield-festooned guard tower (מגדל; 4:4; 7:5) and also applies the tower image to her breasts in 8:10. The element of stone-built strength associated with towers could nicely fit the woman's construction of the man's hard body if it suggests his chiseled cheek-bones and strong jaw. But she softens, or rather sweetens, that sharp look with a stockpile of perfume. These cheek-towers are not storing weapons and ammunition, but spices! They thus beckon the woman's close contact rather than putting her on alert.[6]

- The inviting nature of the man's sweet-smelling cheeks extends to his lily lips leaking liquid myrrh, luring the woman to kiss and taste him as he has longed to indulge in her (Song 4:10-11). The lily and liquid myrrh images more typically apply to the woman in the Song (2:1-2, 16; 4:10-11, 5:5; 6:2-3; 7:2), making this the point in the present *wasf* where gender most blurs and blends together in one flesh. If we accept the seven-part scheme sketched above for 5:11-15, as in 4:1-5, once again the horizontal lips transect the center of the portrait. It's at this thinnest, softest, most delicate juncture that the two bodies, each otherwise strong in its own way, find their most intimate and satisfying communion.

- The woman now moves downward from the man's head and face to depict his "hands" literally (יד), and by extension his arms, which better fit the descriptive imagery (Song 5:14). She returns to envisioning his golden essence, this time in the form of arms like "rods" (JPS, NASB, NAB, NIV) or "cylinders" (CEB) of gold adorned with jewels, much better than the NRSV's odd "rounded gold." However soft and luscious his lips, they quickly give way to solid and powerful hands/arms. Recall the significance of "hands" in the preceding scene, including the man's thrusting hand, at once inviting and invasive (5:4). The prospect of the woman resting her head on his left hand/arm while snuggling into the embrace of his right hand/arm (2:6; see also 8:3) becomes less comfortable when those hands/arms are jewel-studded gold ramrods!

---

6. Roland E. Murphy's view that the man's spice cheeks refers to his fragrant beard is speculative and not necessary to the image (*The Song of Songs*, Hermeneia [Minneapolis: Fortress, 1990], 166, 172). Marvin H. Pope entertains the "beard" notion but also notes that the term for "cheek" (לחי) "does not of itself denote the beard, but the cheek or jaw where the beard, if there is any, grows" (*Song of Songs: A New Translation with Introduction and Commentary*, AB 7C [Garden City, NY: Doubleday, 1977], 540). In any case, the extent of the young man's beard in the Song is unknown.

- While the next part normally describes gastrointestinal organs (מעה, "bowels," "intestines"), it must refer here to some corresponding external feature like "belly," "stomach," or, most likely, "abdomen," as the LXX takes it (κοιλία). The NRSV "body" is too general. Its "ivory" quality no doubt suggests its polished hardness rather than whiteness (Song 5:14).[7] Jill M. Munro imagines the man's entire "lumbar area (see Dan. 2.32) which is likened to a block of ivory."[8] We might modernize this into six-pack abs or a strong, solid core à la Pilates.

- A related description of the man's "legs" or thighs (Song 5:15) follows, comparing them to alabaster columns securely set in gold sockets. The words for "ivory" (שׁן, *shen*) and "alabaster" (שׁשׁ, *shesh*) sound alike, reinforcing their common strength and high value— and also their whitish hue. Though these materials could be used in making statues, Munro relates the alabaster leg pillars in particular to architectural components of Israel's most prominent buildings: the tabernacle (Exod 27:10, 11, 17; 36:38; Num 3:37), Solomon's palace (1 Kgs 7:2, 3, 6), and the Jerusalem temple (1 Kgs 7:15; Jer 52:20, 21; 1 Chr 18:8; 2 Chr 3:15, 17; Ezek 40:49).[9] In the woman's eyes, her beloved stands firm on a regal and stable foundation.

- The final pair of features in this paean breaks the head-to-toe catalogue and the gems-and-stone imagery pattern. First, the woman stands back and takes in the whole of the man's "appearance" or visage (מראה), picturing him as the stately cedar forest of Lebanon (Song 5:15). Several times the Song has evoked this sylvan region as a site of mysterious grandeur and source of enticing odors. Here, all of this comes together to typify the man's entire bearing in the woman's mind: she is awed and stimulated by his majestic presence and could easily and happily get lost in his rich density. Earlier the man longed to see the woman's lovely "appearance"—same Hebrew term, though rendered "face" in NRSV—more clearly outside the cliff-side crevice that shielded her (2:14).

7. As with the woman's teeth in 4:2; 6:4, appropriate to biblical Hebrew's use of the same word (שׁן) for "tooth" and "ivory."

8. Jill M. Munro, *Spikenard and Saffron: A Study in the Poetic Language of the Song of Songs*, JSOTSup 203 (Sheffield: Sheffield Academic, 1995), 62–63.

9. Ibid., 63. We made some of these same connections above in relation to Solomon's palanquin procession as a "column/pillar of smoke" (3:6). That scene also focused on men's "thighs" (3:8, though using a different term than that for "legs/thighs" in 5:15), specifically, those of Solomon's sixty warriors with swords strapped to their thighs, displaying a powerful, martial, regal image.

- Second, just before recapitulating the man's "altogether desirable" nature, the woman extols the man's exceptionally "sweet speech" (חֵךְ; Song 5:16a). The term in fact denotes another anatomical part—"mouth" or "palate"—which the Song elsewhere employs for the woman's (2:3) and man's (7:9) taste organs savoring each other's love. But it may also be metonymic for "speech" or "voice." Either way it breaks the flow of the current *wasf*, either going back up from the man's legs to his mouth, after already highlighting his cheeks and lips, or shifting from physical attributes to vocal quality. If the accent suddenly falls on the man's sweet speech, it not only disrupts the focus on his magnificent body but also strikes a dissonant chord with his most recent speech (5:2), which drew the woman out with its seeming sweetness, only to lead her—inadvertently no doubt, but still irresponsibly—into a night ambush.

In the transitional line setting up the Jerusalem daughters' second question, the woman addresses them by their group name with a final flourish, a kind of "Ta da!" invoking their appreciation for the wonderful portrait she has just unveiled: "There you have it my friends. This is my beloved [דּוֹדִי] and this is my darling [רֵעִי]" (5:16b, my paraphrase). She thus conjoins the favorite pet names each lover uses for the other in the Song. Her "beloved" is also her "darling"—the masculine form of the term of endearment he repeatedly calls her. Despite their recent misadventures, despite the pain it caused her, she insists that their bond remains strong and intimate.

## Where, Oh Where, Has He Gone? (6:1)

I comment on the daughters' query in Song 6:1 through paraphrase:

> Fine, then. He's still gorgeous, and you two remain as tight as ever. But, forgive us for asking, if all this is true, where is he now? Where has he gone? Why aren't you with him now instead of here with us? And to rub the sore spot a little rawer, remember that he recently turned away from you and left you stranded.[10] Where exactly, pray tell, did he go at such a critical moment?
>
> But, listen, we're really not trying to upset you. We believe you and are on your side. In fact, we're ready to walk side-by-side with you to

---

10. The verb for "turn away" (פָּנָה) in 6:1, though different from the term in 5:6, "but my beloved had turned [חָמַק] and was gone," conveys the same idea of retreat.

seek and find your lover. So let's go find and rein in this wonderful guy of yours!

## In His (My) Spice(y) Bed, If You Know What I Mean! (6:2-3)

Instead of welcoming her friends' offer, however, to accompany her on a search mission, the woman insists there is no need, since she knows precisely where her beloved has gone. He has returned to the paradisiacal "garden" and pastoral "flock" (Song 6:2) setting of their sweetest lovemaking amid beds of spices and lilies (1:7-8; 2:1-4, 16; 4:12–5:1). And it's as if he has gone *to her* and she is already *with him*, since she *is* his garden delight and most precious lily of the field. Aptly, then, she can intone the harmonious refrain: "I am my beloved's and my beloved is mine. He pastures his flock among the lilies" (6:3). This echoes 2:16, except for a telling switch of order in the opening phrases, now placing her commitment to her beloved ("I am his") *before* her claim upon him ("He is mine"). In their mutual relationship, she now reaffirms the priority of her willing surrender to his desires, a remarkable recommitment to her lover on the heels of his fickle nocturnal behavior. So much for teaching him a lesson and taking him back with caution.

# Song of Songs 6:4-10

## An Overwhelming Ode to Terrible Beauty

So, after all that's happened in the last two stanzas, with the pendulum swing from the man's night visit fiasco to the woman's unstinting ode to him, what does the man have to say for himself? Such a question may well be beside the point, however, pushing our more linear narrative reading of the Song beyond reasonable limits. A sense of plot has become rather tenuous, as the man now simply sings another paean to his lover's beauty in antiphonal response, as it were, to the woman's praise of his body. But unlike her speech, his praise of her answers no particular questions from the daughters of Jerusalem, which provided some narrative link to the woman's preceding nightmare on the city streets: "What is your beloved . . . that you *thus adjure us*?" (5:9); "Which way has *your beloved turned*?" (6:1). Now the man whom the woman has just located in his garden pasture (6:2-3) jumps into another encomium for his beautiful lover, even reprising part of his earlier *wasf* almost verbatim (6:5-7 = 4:1-3). He is hardly wracked with remorse about or even aware of the bad evening two stanzas before. It's just his turn to sing again, and he belts it out with great élan.

A feminist reading of the Song might long for more sober words from the man. His last appeal to the woman to "Open to me, my sister, my love, my dove, my perfect one" (Song 5:2) may sound similar to his

*Song of Songs 6:4-10*

**[M → W]**

⁴You are beautiful as Tirzah, my
    love,
    comely as Jerusalem
    terrible as an army with banners.
⁵Turn away your eyes from me,
    for they overwhelm me!
Your hair is like a flock of goats,
    moving down the slopes of
    Gilead.
⁶Your teeth are like a flock of ewes
    that have all come up from the
    washing;
all of them bear twins,
    and not one of them is be-
    reaved.
⁷Your cheeks are like halves of a
    pomegranate
    behind your veil.

**[M → D (and others?)]**

⁸There are sixty queens and
    eighty concubines,
    and maids without number.
⁹My dove, my perfect one, is the
    only one,
    the darling of her mother,
    flawless to her that bore her.
The maidens saw her and called
    her happy;
The queens and concubines
    also, and they praised
    her.
¹⁰"Who is this that looks forth like
    the dawn,
    fair as the moon, bright as the
    sun,
    terrible as an army with ban-
    ners?"

present adulation of "My dove, my perfect one, [who] is the only one" (6:9), but we know that they are separated by the tragic midnight interlude in which he treats his lover as anything but his perfect dove. Are his words, then, nothing more than callow cant? Perhaps, but the same could be said for much of the Song's speech uttered by the woman and man alike. The poetry of young, infatuated lovers tends toward naïve and flowery expression, though still full of intense feeling and not entirely void of serious reflection. Even older couples can get carried away in the flush of new love. While the Song's passionate love lyrics, as I've been arguing, reflect a loose narrative substructure of emotional experience, they also evince a certain palpable *immediacy*, a spontaneous sprouting of raw emotion. Without forgetting or excusing the traumatic attack of 5:7, the rawest event of the entire Song, I approach the man's present ode primarily as a fresh, and re-freshing, expression of his passionate admiration for his darling.

Consider three stylistic elements of this stanza: the frame, the diptych pattern, and the imagery. First, the frame elaborates on the woman's loveliness, bookending it in identical terms: "terrible as an army with banners" (Song 6:4, 10). The man again accentuates his lover's formi-

dable bearing, her sublime strength as discussed above on 4:1-7, a terrible, fearful beauty like a stone-terraced armory tower placarded with
a thousand glittering shields (4:4) or a well-appointed precision army
marching under glorious banners (3:7-8). Recall that the woman previously identified the man's "banner" (דגל) over her as "love" in a kind of
demilitarizing move, transforming the martial marquee into a love tent
(2:4). Here, however, the man maintains rather than mitigates the force
of the image in relation to the woman, and she remains a strong independent force to be reckoned with and respected, though not an indomitable
force, if I may be permitted another glance back to 5:7. There she could
have used his protective "banner" of love, as her own mantle proved no
barrier to the assaulting night watchmen.

The term for "terrible" or "fear-inspiring" (אים) appears only in Song
6:4, 10 and Hab 1:7 in the Hebrew Bible.[1] The Habakkuk context fills
out the connotations in reference to the dreaded Chaldean (Babylonian)
army threatening to advance against Israel and other nations.

> For I am rousing the Chaldeans,
> > that fierce and impetuous nation,
> who march through the breadth of the earth
> > to seize dwellings not their own.
> Dread (אים) and fearsome are they;
> > their justice and dignity proceed from themselves.
> Their horses are swifter than leopards,
> > more menacing than wolves at dusk;
> > their horses charge.
> Their horsemen come from far away;
> > they fly like an eagle swift to devour.
> They all come for violence,
> > with faces pressing forward;
> > they gather captives like sand. (Hab 1:6-9)

By associating the woman's embodied person with such conquering
military force, the man commends not only her individual strength but
also her capacity to "overwhelm" him (Song 6:5), to capture and captivate
him for her interests, a prospect he finds as terrifying as it is titillating.

Second, the stanza reflects a two-part, diptych pattern, with each half
extolling the woman's consummate beauty, but to different addressees.
In the first part (Song 6:4-7), the man speaks directly to the woman; in the

---

1. William J. Holladay, *A Concise Hebrew and Aramaic Lexicon of the Old Testament*
(Grand Rapids: Eerdmans, 1971), 13.

second part (6:8-10), he speaks about the woman in third person to a wider audience that, we might surmise, includes the daughters of Jerusalem. He also incorporates into his own speech the high praise other women express about his lover (6:9-10), perhaps including a direct quotation, as the NRSV indicates in 6:10. The result pushes against variable opinions about beauty as idiosyncratic to the eye of the beholder. In the man's view, though still biased, of course, all beholders, whether male or female, should agree on the exceptional perfection of his darling one (6:9). But whatever anyone else thinks, he certainly has no eyes for any other woman.

Third, the imagery the man employs to describe his lover soars to the highest levels. The military language we've already discussed in the frame accords with allusions to the capital cities of Tirzah and Jerusalem (Song 6:4) and to royal personnel like queens and concubines (6:8), leading up to the climactic invocation of celestial heights (6:10). The whole universe sings the woman's praises. But that world also still includes less lofty, more ordinary, elements, such as pastoral, natural-life goats, ewes, and pomegranates (6:5-7) and social-familial ties like maidens and mother (6:8-9). The man's love-struck head is not stuck so high in the courts and clouds that it has lost its solid earthy bearings.

## Capital Magnificence (6:4)

The man specifically associates his sublime, army-like darling with the cities of Tirzah and Jerusalem, where military forces would be stationed. Though Tirzah is much less well known and significant than Jerusalem, it did function as the capital of the Northern Kingdom (Israel) from the time of the schism by Jeroboam to the reign of Omri, who moved the capital to Samaria (1 Kgs 14:1-18; note v. 17; 15:21, 33; 16:6, 8, 15, 17, 23). Michael V. Fox suggests that the Song's reference to Tirzah at a time when that city no longer existed indicates the "half-legendary" status it had acquired closer to that of Jerusalem, the great Davidic and Solomonic capital of the Southern Kingdom (Judah).[2] By comparing his beloved woman to both capitals in the Divided Kingdom, the man may be extolling not only her grandeur but also her holistic perfection, her resistance to division, and her harmonizing of everything in his world as "the only one" that matters to him (Song 6:9).

---

2. Michael V. Fox, *The Song of Songs and the Ancient Egyptian Love Songs* (Madison: University of Wisconsin Press, 1985), 151.

Linguistically, Tirzah also appears related to the root for "be pleased with" (רצה), which aptly fits the present admiration of the woman's pleasing nature. The term for "comely" or "becoming" (נאוה) occurs three other times in the Song, all applied to the woman (1:5; 2:14; 4:4). The first reference is part of the woman's initial self-identification in response to implied detractors: "I am black, but beautiful [comely; נאוה]" (1:5). Now the man affirms her comeliness in the loftiest of terms with no trace of demurral.

## Facial Attraction (6:5-7)

From his opening assessment of his darling's alarming loveliness, the man shifts into the more familiar mode of describing her pleasant facial features: eyes, hair, teeth, cheeks (temples). But straining against the echo of previous pastoral and natural descriptors of these features is a marked intensification of the effect the woman's *eyes* exert on the man, bolstering his sense of her "intimidating beauty."[3] From their demure, yet tantalizing, dovish allure behind her veil (Song 4:1), to their heart-stopping jolt at but a glance (4:9), the woman's eyes as the man views them now so "overwhelm" him that he can scarcely stand them, pleading that she avert her gaze from him (6:5). The NRSV's "turn away" in 6:5 might be better rendered "turn back" or "turn around" (סבב), suggesting a sharp about-face that would completely block her stunning eyes from his view (6:5). "Of course," as Cheryl Exum discerns, "he does not really want her to look away; just the opposite! This is lovers' talk."[4] True enough, but his sense of being "awestruck" by her—Exum's apt term—is surging to the breaking point. He may quickly return to idyllic images of hillside goats, poolside lambs, and picnic-fare pomegranates (6:5b-7) to catch his breath and calm his palpitating heart.

The verb rendered "overwhelm" (רהב) in the Hiphil carries connotations of "cause to tremble or fear," that is "frighten" or "shake up."[5] The LXX and Vg. translators decided that the woman's potent eyes

---

3. Chana Bloch and Ariel Bloch, *The Song of Songs: The World's First Great Love Poem* (New York: Modern Library, 1995), 189 (on Song 6:5).

4. J. Cheryl Exum, *Song of Songs*, OTL (Louisville: Westminster John Knox, 2005), 220.

5. Fox, *Song*, 152; see Michael Fishbane, *Song of Songs,* JPS Bible Commentary (Lincoln: University of Nebraska Press, 2015), 163, citing Ibn Ezra's sense of the man describing the woman's eyes in Song 6:5 as "too strong for me." Interestingly, the only other Hiphil form of this verb in the Hebrew Bible refers to the Lord's dynamic infusion of inner strength or courage in answer to prayer (Ps 138:3).

make the man "fly away" (ἀναπτερόω; *avolare*), "due perhaps," Murphy remarks, "to the man's disappearance in chapter 5," another version of "the woman made me leave," though nothing is said about her unbearable eyes in that chapter.[6] In its Qal form רהב means "storm against," "oppress," "assault" (see Prov 6:3; Isa 3:5), which coordinates with the related noun, personified as the mythological sea monster *Rahab*, the chaotic antipode to orderly creation (Job 9:13; 26:12; Ps 87:4; 89:11; Isa 30:7; 51:9).[7] Perhaps, then, thoughts of the woman's watery depths surface again. Her ominous oceanic eyes threaten to suck in and swallow the man whole, a prospect at once wondrous and terrifying.

## Royal Distinction (6:8-9)

As he turns to a broader audience, the man also returns to loftier political images in praising his beloved. Specifically he invokes the world of royalty, which she has repeatedly applied to him. But whereas she has unabashedly claimed him as her "king," he does not explicitly call her his "queen," though he does address her as a "queenly maiden" in Song 7:1. This is not to demean her in any sense, however; in fact, in the man's estimation, the woman stands uniquely above and apart from the female royal court, which typically included multiple queens and consorts. The arrangement in 6:8 reflects the hierarchy of ancient Near Eastern kings' harems, descending from queens to concubines, to maidens or young female attendants of the royal women.[8] With the higher ranks constituting a more selective group, the numbers conversely ascend from sixty queens (primary wives) to eighty concubines ("secondary wives," 6:8, CEB) to innumerable maidens (servant girls). It's not quite up to Solomon's thousandfold harem of princesses and concubines and no telling how many attendants (see 1 Kgs 11:3), but it's impressive enough.

And more impressive, still, is the Song woman's salience beyond the whole lot as "the perfect one, the only one," so esteemed not only by the man but also by the entire female court (6:9). This exceptional woman stands under the spotlight on center stage, as the very structure of 6:8-9 illustrates:

---

6. Roland E. Murphy, *The Song of Songs*, Hermeneia (Minneapolis: Fortress, 1990), 175.

7. Marvin H. Pope, *Song of Songs: A New Translation with Introduction and Commentary*, AB 7C (Garden City, NY: Doubleday, 1977), 564; Murphy, *Song*, 175.

8. See Tremper Longman III, *Song of Songs*, NICOT (Grand Rapids: Eerdmans, 2001), 181–82; Dianne Bergant, *The Song of Songs*, Berit Olam (Collegeville, MN: Liturgical, 2001), 78–79.

Queens

↓

Concubines

↓

Maidens

↓

**My Dove, My Perfect One, the Only One**

↑

Maidens

↑

Queens

↑

Concubines

Closest to the woman in her central position and affirming her consummate status is yet another female figure, one we have met before: her mother. As the woman is uniquely adored by the man, she also represents the special "darling" (literally, "the one") of her mother, the "flawless" ("pure," ברה; "chosen, choice," ἐκλεκτή, LXX) one "to her that bore her" (Song 6:9). Elsewhere the woman also refers to her mother conceiving (3:4) and delivering (8:2) her in the very room where she brings or longs to bring her lover. Though none of these references suggests the Song couple's immediate interest in having children, they all, as Phyllis Trible observes, "allude to the beauty of birth . . . [and] know nothing at all of the multiplication of pain in childbearing" Genesis describes as post-Edenic life (Gen 3:16).[9] The Song's lovers revel in their garden paradise as often as they can in the midst of a still precarious environment.

---

9. Phyllis Trible, "Love's Lyrics Redeemed," in *A Feminist Companion to the Song of Songs*, ed. Athalya Brenner, FCB (Sheffield: Sheffield Academic, 1993), 100–120, at 115.

## Celestial Brilliance (6:10)

Having asserted the fact of the royal harem's and the mother's high praise for the woman, the man proceeds to announce the content of their adulation, either through direct citation (NRSV, NAB, NASB) or his own paraphrase (NJPS, CEB, NIV). Either way, he claims to speak *for* other women concerning what *they think* of his lover. Since he reports the women's assessment in such glowing terms, this may seem beyond critique, except to say that he might exaggerate a tad in the swell of his besotted love. But who can blame him for that? Still, a feminist hermeneutic remains alert to male cooptation of female speech and opinion, a phenomenon that characterizes most, if not all, of the Bible written by men for men. The Song may represent an exceptional case of either female authorship or an unusually authentic mediation of female voice by a male writer, as some feminist critics argue.[10] But the provenance of an ancient anonymous book remains of necessity an open question. Whoever penned and/or edited the Song, the present lines demand to be heard, on their face, as women's speech focalized through a male point of view. This perspective raises its own questions, also unanswerable, but worth bearing in mind.

For one, how does the man know what all royal women "without number" (Song 6:8) think about anything, including his beloved girlfriend? Of course, this is hyperbolic, poetic language; the point is not that the male character has polled the world's royal female population. He might well be spinning his thoughts out of thin air, but, alternatively, we might presume that he's at least listened and paid attention to some female opinion, royal or not, which is the only way men can faithfully engage in "women-speak." Better that women speak for themselves, but still vitally important to the feminist enterprise—which seeks to bring all humanity into mutually supportive engagement—that men hear and take to heart what women have to say.[11] But has the male figure in the Poem really heard the harem's true evaluation of his lover? Is it likely they will all agree with the man and adore his blessed ("happy," 6:9, NRSV) woman, without a trace of critique, ambivalence, or jealousy?

In a fascinating personal account of life in a domestic harem in midtwentieth-century Fez, Morocco, Fatima Mernissi reminisces:

10. See discussion in Introduction to this volume, pp. xlv–liv.
11. See F. Scott Spencer, *Dancing Girls, "Loose" Ladies, and Women of "the Cloth": The Women in Jesus' Life* (New York: Continuum, 2004), 1–18.

Women's solidarity [in the harem] was actually a highly sensitive issue in the courtyard, since the women rarely sided all together against men. . . . In fact Mother accused women who allied themselves with men as being largely responsible for women's suffering. "These women are more dangerous than men," she would explain, "because physically they look just like us. But they are really wolves posing as sheep. If women's solidarity existed, we would not be stuck on this terrace."[12]

Another question we may ask from the man's side: Why does he care about what the harem thinks about his special lover? Within the royal fiction created in the Song, the man enjoys "king" status and is free to choose the most desirable woman for his principal "queen," as Ahasuerus chose Esther. And in the interest of maintaining peace in the court—in other words, keeping the women under wraps—and solidifying his power, he might prefer to imagine, and even impose, unanimous agreement with his choice. In this critical vein, then, he cares only about the opinions of his lesser queens, concubines, and maidens to control them for his own benefit. He can't afford dissension in the ranks from would-be Vashtis (see Esth 1:10-22).

Apart from the man's internal mediation of courtly women's viewpoints, his final statement regarding the superior beauty of his most beloved consort soars beyond the monarchical realm to astronomical heights (Song 6:10). Actually, the comment appears in the form of a rhetorical question: "Who is this?" (6:10). This is a familiar Song mode enhancing the dramatic splendor of the object whose identity is or becomes obvious (see 3:6; 5:9; 8:5). The choicest woman is now cast in luminescent and celestial terms as "the dawn" light or perhaps the "morning star" (6:10, CEB) shining out between the fair moon and "bright" or "pure" (ברה) sun, which matches her mother's evaluation of her in the previous verse. The action of "looking forth" is better rendered "looking down upon" (שׁקף) from majestic summits, as "the LORD looks down from heaven on earth" (Ps 14:2; 53:3; 85:12; 102:20).

Together, the sun, moon, and dawn span all of time, thus making the beloved woman the light of life—certainly the light of the man's life. Moreover, the image encompasses the entire celestial universe, the

---

12. Fatima Mernissi, *Dreams of Trespass: Tales of a Harem Girlhood* (Cambridge, MA: Perseus Books, 1994), 141; see the wide-ranging analysis of women's tendencies to undermine their "sisters'" interests in Phyllis Chesler, *Woman's Inhumanity to Woman*, 2nd ed. (Chicago: Lawrence Hill, 2009).

colossal "starry host" or "heavenly host" complementing and transcending the military host.[13] The banner might now headline "Light" as well
as "Love"—each an essential force of life with immense potential for
both tender nurture and terrible fierceness.

13. On the primary astronomical imagery ("starry host") here, see Longman, *Song*,
182–83; and Gary Alan Long, "A Lover, Cities, and Heavenly Bodies: Co-Text and the
Translation of Two Similes in Canticles (6:4c; 6:10d)," *JBL* 115 (1996): 703–09. Long
argues that the same Hebrew similes (אֲיֻמָּה כַּנִּדְגָּלוֹת), rendered identically as "terrible as
an army with banners" in the NRSV of 6:4 and 6:10, in fact have different comparative
"sight" referents for the man's beautiful beloved: first, comparing her to the majestic
"sights" of the capital cities (Tirzah and Jerusalem, 6:4); second, comparing her to the
cosmic "sights" of celestial bodies (moon and sun, 6:10).

# Song of Songs 6:11-13

# *A Flight of Fancy and a Campy Dance*

In lieu of a confident interpretation of this little stanza beginning in a nut orchard, I offer a pathetic pun: this is the toughest nut to crack in the entire Song. Pun aside, on the point of this being the most difficult part of the Poem to decipher, most commentators agree. The line in Song 6:12 is particularly intractable, so much so that the accomplished poet and translator, Marcia Falk, in her careful rendering of the entire Song, brackets out this verse without venturing a guess about its meaning: "I find it impossible even to offer a literal translation of this singularly garbled line; almost everyone agrees that, as it stands, it is unintelligible. . . . Admitting defeat, I omit this line from my translation."[1] Otherwise, across the three verses, it is hard to discern who's speaking to whom about what and whether these verses constitute a discrete unit. All or part of 6:13 may fit better as the introduction to the new *wasf* in 7:1-9, and in fact, 6:13 appears as 7:1 in Hebrew versions. If that's not enough to despair, the possible use of three obscure proper nouns makes matters worse. The double use of the epithet "Shulammite" (6:13) for

---

1. Marcia Falk, *The Song of Songs: A New Translation and Interpretation* (New York: HarperCollins, 1990), 187.

*Song of Songs 6:11-13*

**[W → D (?)]**
[11]I went down to the nut orchard,
  to look at the blossoms of the
    valley,
to see whether the vines had budded,
  whether the pomegranates
    were in bloom.
[12]Before I was aware, my fancy
  set me

in a chariot beside my prince.
**[D → W (?)]**
[13]Return, return, O Shulammite!
  Return, return, that we may
    look upon you.
**[M → D (?)]**
Why should you look upon the
  Shulammite,
  as upon a dance before two
    armies?

the female protagonist would afford welcome insight into her identity if we knew what the term meant! In addition, the NRSV renderings of "a chariot beside my prince" (6:12) with an annotation admitting "meaning of Hebrew uncertain" and "a dance before two armies" (6:13b) might read better as the "chariot of *Amminadib*" (NJPS, KJV) and "the dance of *Mahanaim*" (NIV, NJPS), respectively, but thereby provide no greater understanding.

So, under full disclaimer, I offer one possible perspective on this stanza, largely following the approach of Michael V. Fox, who himself freely acknowledges the interpretive problems these lines pose.[2] We may chart five quick movements in a lively imaginative scenario:

- The woman heads to a fertile valley to see the nuts and fruits grow-ing there.
- The woman is suddenly whisked away to a noble chariot seat.
- A group (likely the daughters of Jerusalem) summon the woman back from her flight of fancy so they may "look upon" her.
- The woman returns as requested.
- The man questions the onlookers about why they regard the woman as they would a camp dancer.

2. Michael V. Fox, *The Song of Songs and the Ancient Egyptian Love Songs* (Madison: University of Wisconsin Press, 1985), 154–58.

Natural elements like nuts, vines, and pomegranates and martial elements like chariots and army camps again coalesce with primary visual effect on the characters and readers. Perceptual experiences are key: the woman wants to "look at/see" (ראה, twice in Song 6:11) the fertile land, but before she "knows" (ידע) it, she's sitting in a chariot (6:12), and then the man and her companions "look upon/perceive" (חזה, twice in 6:13) her as in a dance. Precisely what they all perceive—and how we should review their perspective—is another conundrum of this stanza, which we seek to elucidate below.

## Checking Crops in the Valley (6:11)

While vines and pomegranates are common fare in the Song, this is the only valley setting for fruits and the only time we find nuts. The "valley" (נחל) is reminiscent of water-rich gardens, as it designates a ravine or *wadi* that courses with seasonal rains. The nut term (אגוז), appearing only here in the Bible, refers in postbiblical Hebrew to the walnut, a thriving crop in ancient Palestine, including, as some have thought, in Solomon's famous gardens.[3] Nuts generally have long been regarded as stimulating "love food," partly because of their iconic symbolization of sex organs; in modern colloquial parlance "nuts" still represent testicles. The open walnut, in particular, may conjure up images of the vulva. Marvin H. Pope, who otherwise marshals a wide array of ancient evidence surrounding the aphrodisiacal and "quasi-magical properties of the nut," makes a rather bizarre comparison to contemporary nut marketing, "as one may observe in the window displays and on the shelves of present-day 'organic' food shops."[4] I guess it depends on what kind of health food stores your neighborhood has.

While the picture of a budding love-nest is obvious by now in the Song, *who* is proceeding at this moment to check out the scene is not so clear. The "I" subject offers no grammatical clue of gender. Some commentators think that the man is speaking, echoing the woman's report of his last

---

3. See Harold N. Moldenke and Alma L. Moldenke, *Plants of the Bible* (Mineola, NY: Dover, 1952), 119–20; Marvin H. Pope, *Song of Songs: A New Translation with Introduction and Commentary*, AB 7C (Garden City, NY: Doubleday, 1977), 574; Josephus, *Jewish War* 3.516-17 (in Galilee); Debra Band, *The Song of Songs: The Honeybee in the Garden* (Philadelphia: JPS, 2005), 54–55.

4. Pope, *Song*, 577; see 574–79; John G. Snaith, *The Song of Songs*, New Century Bible Commentary (London: Marshall Pickering, 1993), 95.

whereabouts in Song 6:2-3. Just as she had informed her girlfriends, the man now confirms he has "gone down" to a favorite outdoor, garden-like, trysting site.[5] But the flow of this stanza, choppy as it is, favors the woman as the subject/actor, particularly the fourfold plea for her (the Shulammite) to "return" in 6:13. In order to return, she must have gone away somewhere.

But *why* is she heading to the nut grove and fruit orchard specifically to monitor their bloom status? Perhaps she is following through on her recent announcement to her companions that, whatever qualms they might have about her elusive lover, she knows that he has "gone down" to one of their luscious meeting places to prepare for lovemaking (Song 6:2-3). Moreover, he has just affirmed his passionate admiration and desire for her, concluding with the question, "Who is this magnificent one who *looks down* like the starry hosts?"—to which *she* is the answer (6:10). So, given their mutual desire—"I am my beloved's and my beloved is mine" (6:3)—what could be a more apt response than her *going down* to *look at/see* him in the fertile valley? But once again, there's a degree of tension, which never seems far from the surface in the Song. Note that the woman comes to see *whether* love is in bloom, *whether* the time is right.[6] A tinge of doubt and apprehension colors her hope and longing. She really wants this to work out, but she can't quite shake some nagging concerns. He's not always been there for her as she needed and expected, and at times she may not have been as ready as she thought for him and so let him slip away. Ah, the complicated dance of love and angst of desire.

Much of the anxiety—and excitement—of love comes from surprising twists and turns, moves that disrupt the tight choreography and set the heads (and sometimes feet!) of one or both lovers spinning. And so it happens again to the woman before she knows it (6:12).

---

5. On the man as the speaker and subject of the action here, see Chana Bloch and Ariel Bloch, *The Song of Songs: The World's First Great Love Poem* (New York: Modern Library, 1995), 192; Michael Fishbane, *Song of Songs*, JPS Bible Commentary (Lincoln: University of Nebraska Press, 2015), 169–70; Band, *Song*, 54; Othmar Keel, *The Song of Songs: A Continental Commentary*, trans. Frederick J. Gaiser (Minneapolis: Fortress, 1994), 222–26, though he sees a shift in 6:12 to the female subject; Jill M. Munro, *Spikenard and Saffron: A Study in the Poetic Language of the Song of Songs*, JSOTSup 203 (Sheffield: Sheffield Academic, 1995), 30; Carey Ellen Walsh, *Exquisite Desire: Religion, the Erotic, and the Song of Songs* (Minneapolis: Fortress, 2000), 99.

6. The conditional notion of "if" is conveyed by the interrogative ה in Hebrew, εἰ in LXX, and *si* in Vg.

## Riding Shotgun in the Chariot (6:12)

The surprise is not what awaits the woman in the nut orchard. It's not clear that she ever gets there; if she does, she doesn't linger long. "Before I was aware," that is, before she can take stock of the situation, she is transported to another venue. Literally, she states, "I did not know [it]" or "I did not know myself," if we take "my *nephesh* (נפשי)"—my thoughtful, willful, passion-filled self—as the object of the verb (though there is no object marker). The woman, for all her strength, energy, and agency, is not fully in control of her attitudes and emotions (who among us is?), especially in the throes of love that can produce a volatile mix of "great agitation" and "overwhelm[ing] excitement."[7] As kaleidoscopic images race rapid-fire across her mind, she finds it hard to focus. But the dizzying effect is not unpleasant; might as well let go and enjoy the ride.

The current ride now appears to spirit her away from the fresh nut and fruit groves of the valley to the fierce chariots of the battlefield. But given the muddled state of the Hebrew text, it's hard to uncover the precise image in view. The woman has been "placed" or "set" (שׂים) in some relation to chariots (plural). It is logical to infer that she envisions being set "on" or "in" one of these vehicles.[8] The agent who puts her in this place is unclear. The verb has a third feminine singular subject, creating the awkward sense of "*she* placed me," but who could this "she" be if the woman herself is the object? Many versions, including the LXX, take the feminine noun "my *nephesh*" as the subject, understanding the woman as generating her own fanciful scenario in which "my fancy set me in a chariot" (NRSV) or "my desire set me among the royal chariots" (NIV; so also NJPS). Cheryl Exum sees no problem with taking the woman's *nephesh* as both object of her mental confusion and subject of her chariot placement.[9]

---

7. Fox, *Song*, 156; see "ecstatic confusion" in Robert Alter, *Strong as Death Is Love: The Song of Songs, Ruth, Esther, Jonah, and Daniel: A Translation with Commentary* (New York: Norton, 2015), 40; "I am beside myself with joy" in Shalom M. Paul, "An Unrecognized Medical Idiom in Canticles 6,12 and Job 9,21," *Bib* 59 (1978): 547. Via an Akkadian parallel, Paul relates the language in Song 6:12 to a diagnosis of mental illness—"the loss of one's mental balance and normal composure." The mania can lead to feelings of extreme joy, as with the Song's lover, whom Paul takes to be the young man in 6:12, or unbearable pain, as with Job in Job 9:21 (545–47).

8. The -ב preposition ("on/in"), prefixed to "chariots" in some manuscripts, but not the MT, is not necessary to convey direction in verbs of motion; see Pope, *Song*, 586; J. Cheryl Exum, *Song of Songs*, OTL (Louisville: Westminster John Knox, 2005), 213.

9. So as not to repeat "myself," Exum (*Song*, 211, 224) adjusts the verb: "I did not know myself, *carried off* amid chariots," or in other words, "I lost my composure, my fancy *carried me off*."

But what is she doing with whom in or among a chariot(s)? A single compound word following "chariots" concludes this enigmatic verse. Some versions prefer simply to transliterate it as the proper noun *Amminadib* (LXX, KJV, NJPS), suggesting the woman's association with someone by that name. But who that person is and what he has to do with chariots is anybody's guess. A better approach focuses on the *nadib* (נדיב) part of the word, meaning "noble, princely." Soon the man will praise the woman as "daughter of a noble one" (*bat-nadib*, בת־נדיב) or a "noblewoman" (7:1). The *ʿammi* (עמי) part may be related to "people" (*ʿam*, עם) or, with emendation, to "with" (*ʾim*, אם), suggesting either "among the chariots of my *royal people*" (NIV) or "in a chariot *with a nobleman*."[10] The NRSV follows the latter option in different words: "in a chariot beside my prince," which we might paraphrase as "riding shotgun in my prince's chariot."

Presumably, the woman's noble prince is her lover, who previously associated her with royal chariots and came to her in a majestic palanquin (Song 1:9-11; 3:6-11). At least now the woman appears seated in the chariot rather than pulling it or prancing around it as a "mare" in heat (1:9)! As mentioned above, both horse-drawn chariots and servant-borne carriages could be sites of courting and lovemaking.[11] In any case, they reinforce regal status. In the present scene within the Song's fictional royal narrative, the woman imagines herself as the choice princess beside her prince, befitting his recent note of her acclamation by the harem (6:9). She thus takes her place, as Fox comments, among the "aristocracy of lovers."[12] Whatever her social status in the "real" world, whoever might look down upon her for whatever reason (1:6; 2:1-2), she can be assured of her noble position in her lover's eyes and by his side.

But for all its amorous and aristocratic nuances, a chariot, distinct from a wedding palanquin, stands out more as a war machine than a love wagon. We might combine the two elements—the martial and the sexual—as Carey Ellen Walsh paraphrases: "I am trembling, you have made me as eager for love as a chariot driver is for battle." Walsh at-

---

10. The latter reading is found in Fox, *Song*, 154. The singular "nobleman" or "prince" is also favored by Exum (*Song*, 211, 225) as "amid chariots with a prince" and by Tremper Longman III, "in a chariot with a noble man" (*Song of Songs*, NICOT [Grand Rapids: Eerdmans, 2001], 184–87).

11. In *The Song of Songs*, Berit Olam (Collegeville, MN: Liturgical, 2001), 80, Dianne Bergant remarks, "Both the litter and the chariot are majestic vehicles of transportation, vehicles that provide ample opportunity for the passengers to engage in lovemaking."

12. Fox, *Song*, 155.

tributes this statement to the man, but it could apply just as well to the woman.[13] But whether the chariot image suggests the driving force of passion, the unconquerable strength of the couple's love bond, or something else, it retains some sense of powerful and precarious movement, as in battle. It's a wild ride on which the woman must hold on tight.

## Appearing as a Dancer in the Camp (6:13)

The military angle may persist into the final verse of this odd stanza by way of allusion to an army camp. The scene begins with a plural group, plausibly the daughter-friends, bringing the woman, addressed for the first time as "Shulammite," back from her junkets to the nut orchard and chariot seat or "back to reality" from her rapt daydreaming "before I was aware" of these events (Song 6:12). The ladies call their friend to "return" so they might "look upon" her (6:13). But no sooner do they express this intention than the man, whom I take to be the speaker, challenges the way they seem to look upon the Shulammite, as if she's dancing before a troop of soldiers. But once again, the language admits to various possibilities begging for commentary.

First, we investigate the Shulammite epithet that is applied to the woman only here in the Song, though it has become a common way of referring to her in popular and academic discourse, as if "the Shulammite" were her principal moniker. Apart from the problem of its rarity, however, is its clarity. The "-ite" ending suggests a gentilic term like "Israelite" or Canaanite," though nothing is known of a place called "Shulam" (or "Shulem," NJPS) comprised of "Shulammite" people. But the close variant "Shunem" is attested: a city in the Jezreel valley inhabited by Shunammites (Josh 19:18; see also 1 Sam 28:4; 2 Kgs 4:8). As it happens, the featured "Shunammites" in the Bible are both women: the beautiful virgin Abishag who attended the dying David and served as a bargaining chip in the succession struggle between Solomon and Adonijah (1 Kgs 1:1-4, 15; 2:17-22); and an anonymous wealthy woman, whose deceased only son was raised up by Elisha (2 Kgs 4:8-37). While the lovely Abishag's task of lying with King David in Jerusalem may suggest some parallel to the Song woman's imaginative royal experience, the latter has no interest in a purely chaste bed-warming of a geriatric, impotent monarch (see 1 Kgs 1:2-4). And, of course, there's still the lexical problem of Shu*n*em, even if its difference is only a single letter.

13. Walsh, *Exquisite Desire*, 99.

Without adjusting the spelling, we focus on the triliteral root of "Shu-lammite," *sh-l-m* (שלם), conveying the idea of "peace, perfection, whole-ness," as in *shalom*, derived from the same root. Thus, as Fox prefers, the term may reflect the woman's character instead of her origin—"O perfect one"—which coordinates nicely with similar descriptions in other words (5:2; 6:9).[14] Alternatively, we might cast the woman as the "peaceful one." If we push the "-ite" form to refer to a place and its people, the best op-tion, given the Song's orientation around Jerusalem, may be to play up the *-salem* part of that city name as resonant with *shulam*. Hence Shulam-mite might serve as a variant for Jerusalemite, that is, "of Jerusalem," like the "daughters of Jerusalem." If so, it might intimate the woman's present association with Jerusalem "city folk" like the "daughters" and her "prince-king" more than her apparent rural origination (1:5-8). A fur-ther homophonic stretch might also bring "Solomon" into the picture.[15]

In any case, the "Shulammite" address by friends and lover seems consistent with their admiration for her (it's not a derogatory term) and her role in a royal drama. But there's still the question of her focal posi-tion under the spotlight. Why all this interest in "looking upon" her? Of course, this is nothing new in the Song; she has been thoroughly looked up and down before. But why now and to what end? Like different ways of touching, there are good and bad ways of gazing. While the woman's daughter-friends have provided a broadly appreciative and supportive circle around her, they have not simply functioned as her fan club or back-up singers. They've asked their questions, voiced their concerns, posed a certain threat of disturbance (Song 2:7; 3:5), and, in fact, already gazed upon her with some suspicion related to her dark complexion and perhaps social location as a common field-worker (see 1:5-6). But they've also recently acknowledged her extraordinary beauty, calling her "fairest among women" (5:9; 6:1), albeit in an interrogative context. Now they want to examine their friend again after the man's stunning tribute to her (6:4-10). Perhaps they simply want to confirm the endorsement of her formidable beauty that the man registers for them (6:9). Or perhaps they want to offer their own nuances, even a bit of critique, which the man is unable to see in his enthralled state. Maybe they want to bring her back down to earth a little after the man's gushy praise song and her Prince Charming fantasy, or even knock her down a peg or two out of jealousy

---

14. Fox, *Song*, 154, 157–58.

15. Alter (*Strong as Death*, 41) notes, "The most probable derivation is from *Shalem*, a shortened form of 'Jerusalem,' though one should not exclude a punning association with Solomon (שלמה, *Shelomoh*, in Hebrew) and with the verbal root that suggests wholeness."

or a streak of meanness. Who knows? The truth is this: we're not privy to their thoughts and motives, because *before we and they know it*, to reprise the surprise of the preceding verse, the man interjects a challenge question.

Whatever the friends' "real" intentions, the man seems to presume some kind of pejorative, indecorous viewpoint on their part. Of course, this may reveal as much about his judgment as theirs; we're back to the problem of a man knowing what women "really" see, think, and feel. His query implies a critique of the audience for looking upon the woman "*as a dance*"—or logically, by extension, as a danc*er*. The clear simile prefix (-כְ, "as, like") indicates that the woman is not actually dancing, though it doesn't preclude her moving or whirling with excitement in a way that inspires the comparison. But what's wrong with dancing, actual or fig-urative? This is not a strict Baptist group, if I may say so. It all depends on what kind of dancing is imagined, and in this case, the man identifies the routine as the "dance of *Mahanaim*" (מחנים), the place most famously named by Jacob where he meets with God's angels and prepares to meet his angry (he presumes) brother Esau. But Jacob does no dancing, though he does do some strategic maneuvering, such as dividing his large family and herds into "two companies/camps" to provide a more diffuse target for Esau to attack (Gen 32:2, 7-8; 33:1-3). This offers the most direct con-nection to "Mahanaim," which literally means "two camps" (not exactly "God's camp," as Jacob first exclaims in 32:2; there's no "God" or "Lord" or "Yah" component in "Mahanaim"). The simple, non-dual form *mahanah* (מחנה) refers to a "camp," most commonly a *military* camp.

So the man may be upset about the woman being looked upon *as if* she were involved in some sort of "dance of two army camps." Even so, the meaning remains far from clear. But we might sharpen the picture by envisioning her dancing *in front of* or *between* two army camps, with the men cheering her on and no doubt jeering and leering at her as well. Whether more like a USO entertainer or a less decorous gentleman's club dancer, this is no way for a noble queen or princess to carry on—or more correctly, in the present context—for her to *be viewed* by onlookers. This is certainly not how her lover, who desires exclusive access to her, wants her to be viewed.[16] He's no Ahaseurus who, by contrast, longed to

---

16. Fox (*Song*, 158) writes, "The youth rebukes the girl's companions for looking upon her disdainfully as if she were a common dancer who roams the camps of the soldiers (or, possibly, the shepherds)." Munro agrees (*Spikenard*, 31, esp. n. 18), though she takes the callers in 6:13a to be a *male* chorus egging the woman to dance before them. Munro further notes that, while women might properly dance in public to celebrate military victories or to adulate conquering warriors (Exod 15:20; Judg

parade his stunning queen Vashti before his lusty cronies (Esth 1:10-12; similarly, Mark 6:21-23).

Now again, if we give the man's judgment the benefit of the doubt, it's still far from obvious why the woman's friends might eye her as a common camp-dancer, even if they wanted to demean her somehow. In the flush of her love fancies, maybe she "returns" with too much strut and swagger, flaunting her romantic exploits with too much relish before her companions, prompting them in turn to shoot her some sharp visual daggers with the scurrilous subtext, "What a slut!" Women are not beyond such petty pursuits, just as men have their own mean streaks, but we hardly have enough evidence of that here. It's just as reasonable that the ill-informed man is making up his own story, seeing what he wants to see, driven by his overwhelming obsession to look privately on his beloved ("for his eyes alone")[17] and his overweening bravado to defend his princess against all prying eyes and alien forces. If so, I'm afraid he doth protest too much in compensating for his shameful behavior on that fateful recent night, when he abandoned her to hostile eyes and hands.

---

11:34; 1 Sam 18:6-7), the dancing role envisioned for the Song woman in the present scene is for pure entertainment and/or mockery; hence the audience's ogling "attention is inappropriate."

17. Munro, *Spikenard*, 31 n. 18.

# Song of Songs 7:1-9a

# *The Dynamic Delights of Statuesque Beauty*

From his querying of the audience's untoward (from his perspective) gaze at his beloved (Song 6:13), the man quickly turns to his third praise song of the woman's body, as if to say, "This is how you all *should see* my beautiful darling." But he's not all that concerned with engaging the onlookers in any debate on the matter; in fact, he rather squeezes them out. While they may remain in the background, the man turns his full attention to the woman, on whom he claims exclusive viewing rights. As in the previous *wasfs*, he begins by addressing her directly; yet unlike the most recent example (6:8-10), he never turns aside to let a wider group into the picture, perhaps because of their tendency to turn critical in ways he doesn't appreciate. As in 4:1-7, the only focal shift he makes is to zoom in closer to the woman, intensifying from "you" description to "I" action, from compliment to contact, from seeing her to touching, smelling, and tasting her (7:8-9; similarly, 4:6).

Since this is the final ode to a lover's body for either party in the Song, it is useful to consider the basic elements of this example in comparison with the others. This is the only one to scan up the lover's body rather than from the head/face downward, thus completing the picture of the man's intense visual preoccupation with "looking her up and down,"

*Song of Songs 7:1-9a*

**[M → W]**

¹How graceful are your feet in
    sandals,
  O queenly maiden!
Your rounded thighs are like jewels,
    the work of a master hand.
²Your navel is a rounded bowl
    that never lacks mixed wine.
Your belly is a heap of wheat,
    encircled with lilies.
³Your two breasts are like two
    fawns,
    twins of a gazelle.
⁴Your neck is like an ivory tower.
Your eyes are pools in Heshbon,
    by the gate of Bath-rabbim
Your nose is like a tower of Leba-
    non,
  Overlooking Damascus.

⁵Your head crowns you like Carmel,
  Your flowing locks are like
    purple;
  A king is held captive in the
    tresses.
⁶How fair and pleasant you are,
  O loved one, delectable
    maiden!
⁷You are stately as a palm tree,
  and your breasts are like its
    clusters.
⁸I say I will climb the palm tree,
  and lay hold of its branches.
O may your breasts be like clus-
    ters of the vine
  and the scent of your breath
    like apples,
⁹and your kisses like the best wine
    . . .

as the modern idiom goes. Beginning in this case with the woman's feet (Song 7:1) follows naturally from the man's preceding concern over what he regards as inappropriate eyeing of the woman as if she were a dancer (6:13). But just as we noted above that the woman does not have to be performing an actual dance to draw such looks, so the man's ensuing description need not be a review of her ongoing dance routine, as some commentators think.[1] While some movement might be associated with some body parts (e.g., "flowing locks," 7:5), the overall portrait is more static than dynamic, more statuesque than choreographic. And the present context suggests resistance to the dancer image altogether more

---

1. For example, Athalya Brenner, " 'Come Back, Come Back, the Shulammite' (Song of Songs 7:1-10)," in *A Feminist Companion to the Song of Songs*, ed. Athalya Brenner, FCB (Sheffield: Sheffield Academic, 1993), 243–54; Chana Bloch and Ariel Bloch, *The Song of Songs: The World's First Great Love Poem* (New York: Modern Library, 1995), 200; Dianne Bergant, *The Song of Songs*, Berit Olam (Collegeville, MN: Liturgical Press, 2001), 80–88; Robert Alter, *Strong as Death Is Love: The Song of Songs, Ruth, Esther, Jonah, and Daniel: A Translation with Commentary* (New York: Norton, 2015), 41–42.

than classing it up from a common camp twirler to a nobler "queenly" exhibition, whatever the ancient equivalent of a slow waltz might be. High-class royal ladies might watch an elegant ballerina-type performer, but they would never take the stage themselves.[2]

From the feet, the man proceeds upward in his description to the woman's head and hair, making this the most complete sketch, running from toe to head. The woman comes close in her ode, reaching down to the man's legs, but not his feet (Song 5:15). The other two *wasfs* are bust portraits of the woman, featuring head, face, and breasts (4:1-5; 6:5-7). But, as Athalya Brenner has observed, none of these catalogs, including the present one, is remotely complete.[3] Even moving from toe to head, the man's description represents but a small selection of the woman's anatomy. Again, this approach may owe less to a dismembering analysis of beauty than to a sampling of the woman's charms as representing her whole embodied person; after his ascending itemization of parts, the man steps back and takes her all in: "How fair and pleasant *you are*, O loved one" (7:6). Even so, this remains the man's very skewed and selective perception of his darling. This is the beauty *he* beholds.

So how might we best characterize what the man sees here in the woman? Provocative answers have been floated in relation to genres of grotesquerie, parody, and pornography. Each of these perspectives complicates the aesthetic and erotic dimensions of the picture. Is this woman in this context really as beautiful and desirable as many interpreters contend and, if so, at what price?

Extending our brief discussion of "surgical grotesquerie" in relation to Song 4:1-7, it may appear that the current assemblage of female body parts tilts more toward the grotesque than the previous incarnations. Though still selective rather than comprehensive, the examples in 4:1b-5, on our reading, unfolded in a nicely symmetrical sevenfold pattern within the 4:1a/6-7 frame accentuating the totality of the woman's beauty. The present portrait, however, is cluttered with more elements less neatly arranged. A pairing pattern begins to emerge (feet/thighs, navel/belly, two breasts), only to be broken by an odd triad (neck/eyes/nose) bracketed by "tower" images (neck, nose) (7:4). And the man's exclamation of his lover's overall beauty in 7:6 doesn't so much cap off

---

2. See more on dancing below at pp. 172–74, 179–80.

3. Brenner ("Come Back," 235) writes, "If we look closely enough . . . no 'description' is actually obtained: by the end of the poem we still have no idea what the loved person looks like, in the sense that no *complete* image is communicated" (emphasis original).

his description as interrupt it, before he zooms back in for a second look at her breasts and face (7:7-8). Moreover, as Fiona Black has observed, by the end the woman has grown to "giant" or "gigantic" proportions.[4] The single references to Mount Gilead and David's tower in 4:1-5 have stretched to two towers amid two topographical heights (Lebanon, Carmel), three municipal structures (Heshbon pools, Bath-rabbim gate, Damascus tower), and a tall palm tree or giant beanstalk, as it were, that this "Jack" aims to climb (7:4-8).

The woman is a colossus, but hardly the smooth, stately, symmetrical, larger-than-life yet true-to-life bronze statue commemorating classic mythological and monarchical figures. Her combination of altitude with the "amplitude" of broad-cupped navel, thick belly, and juicy breasts suggests to Black a precariously unstable structure: a base of shapely though shaky legs and feet trying to support an engorged torso connected to a long, thin neck "topped by its Carmalesque head. The woman is more like a biblical Barbie—though much less alluring—for she appears so ill-proportioned that she could not stand."[5] The caricature of enormity is further distorted by an incongruent hybridity of floral-faunal and martial-architectural images that we've seen before: What are fawn-dwelling, lily-hedged wheat fields doing abutted right up to city gates and military watchtowers? It's an image that evokes horrid modern thoughts of shooting Bambi.[6] If all that's not grotesque enough, add in bloody mixes of menstrual "wine" fluids flowing profusely from the dilated vulva ("navel"), over the lips and teeth, and down the gullet of the sexually voracious man or, alternatively, sucking him into her menstrual maw or *vagina dentata*.[7]

If we go with this grotesque reading, we should move, as with any reading, to ask how it functions in the present setting. Why would the Song's man or the woman channeling the man represent his beloved so grotesquely? I will discuss some possible answers in the next paragraphs in relation to parody, a type of grotesquerie with more comedic flavor.

---

4. Fiona C. Black, "Unlikely Bedfellows: Allegorical and Feminist Readings of Song of Songs 7:1-8," in *The Song of Songs*, ed. Athalya Brenner and Carole R. Fontaine, FCB, Second Series (Sheffield: Sheffield Academic, 2000), 121.

5. Fiona C. Black, "Beauty or the Beast? The Grotesque Body in the Song of Songs," *BibInt* 8 (2000): 312; for further "Barbie" associations, see the Continuing Voice essay by Lauress Wilkins Lawrence, "Beautiful Black Women," this volume, pp. 10–14.

6. The hybridity point is Black's ("Beauty or the Beast?," 319–23); the silly Bambi quip is mine.

7. Black, "Beauty or the Beast?," 314–15.

But for now I will foreclose this grotesque journey, since I think, in this case, it functions more as a side path than as the main interpretive route. Black herself makes clear how "elusive," "slippery," and quite impossible, as in "never" possible, it is to "wrap up" the grotesque "in a neat tidy package." She also acknowledges that a literary-critical study of the grotesque is a reader-oriented enterprise, not least with regard to the highly elusive and slippery imagery of the Song: "Readers are compelled by certain features, and repelled by others."[8] Like beauty, grotesquerie is in the eye of the beholder. And while I'm intrigued by Black's provocative analysis, I don't really see it in the present *wasf*, at least not to a great extent, not because I'm overly squeamish or romantic, but because of the way I read the context and language.

As already indicated, I take this final praise ode to be something of an *apologia*: the man's defense against what he regards as unacceptable ways of viewing his lover. To turn around and mock her or distort her, even playfully, seems out of kilter here. Moreover, as I will expand below, I think the body-part images, strange though some may be, make good sense more or less as they stand, without resorting to extreme euphemistic transfer. A navel, for example, can be sexy, even in bowl-like depiction, without making it into a vulva. Yes, a number of images go big, or more specifically tall (I see less indication of "fat"), into mythic Amazon dimensions, and the images do not convey the realistic grandeur of a Helios or Nero in classic sculpture. But while far from an actual statue, I still envisage the present portrait of the Song's woman as statuesque and stately more than grotesque. The prevailing picture of "heights" is predominantly honorific, symbolic of royal figures of lofty status and authority, like the princess displayed here, not in photographic or chiseled artistic form, though artisan imagery is used, but in lyrical expression, a verbal representation of the visual, which of necessity remains provisional, allusive, and variegated. Of course, the man could simply say, "You are so elegantly tall and regal, my dear." Nice try, but hardly high poetry.

But who says the Song has to be high poetry composed by and for elites? The continuing tension between rustic and royal, rural and urban environments and the woman's ostensible "country girl" background fit well in a more folk or populist literary setting; and women singing and gossiping about love—including what silly men think about the

---

8. Ibid., 309, 319; Black, "Unlikely Bedfellows," 115.

subject—is the stock-in-trade of women's conversation at all levels of society.[9] Likewise, men of every type hardly need encouragement to kibitz about women, not least about women's sexualized bodies. And amid all such common talk about the opposite sex can be heard plenty of snickering and snarkiness, good- and not-so-good-natured exaggeration, and embellishment: in genre terms, *parody*—which is precisely what Brenner thinks the Song's final *wasf* represents. In comparison with the previous serious odes to beauty and love, this one, in Brenner's view, pushes harder against the boundaries of good taste in the direction of a jocular tease, even striptease.[10] The tone is more burlesque than grotesque. The intent remains complimentary, but in a more casual, less idealistic form. While, as Black comments, the grotesque blends the "funny and frightening,"[11] parody tilts toward the funnier side with a more lighthearted tinge of mockery.

So what's so parodic in the present stanza? Brenner's analysis builds on the premise that the man reviews the woman as she enacts a live public dance performance. He clearly enjoys the show, but more as a nightclub or army camp exhibition with a few (or many!) drinks in him than as a formal court ballet. Things start innocently enough with comments on the woman's sandaled feet and shapely thighs but then quickly pick up steam(iness) at the juicy vulva-like "navel" and wavy pubic hair or "heap of wheat," none of which can be easily inferred through clothing. Hence, except for her sandals—though maybe she's kicked them off by now—the woman dances nude. Yes, it's that kind of "gentleman's" club. And she does so with great joy and abandon and a refreshing lack of self-consciousness—even about her less than perfect, ideal body shape. The undulating, "heaping" belly suggests a "dancing damsel that is far from slim" or, well, we might as well say it, as Brenner soon does: "The dancer is, frankly, fat, her belly in dance motion is big and quivering, much like an unstable mound of wheat."[12] Ahh, but perhaps men back then loved big, thick, jiggly belly dancers. No doubt some did, but we have no evidence that this was a beauty standard

---

9. See Lila Abu-Lughod, *Veiled Sentiments: Honor and Poetry in a Bedouin Society*, 2nd ed. (Berkeley: University of California Press, 1999), xvii–xxiii, 171–272; *Fatima Mernissi, Dreams of Trespass: Tales of a Harem Girlhood* (Cambridge, MA: Perseus Books, 1994).

10. Brenner, " 'Come Back.' "

11. Black, "Unlikely Bedfellows," 116; cp. "Beauty or the Beast?," 310.

12. Brenner, " 'Come Back,' " 247–48.

then any more than now. The woman's shaking it up probably inspired as much laughter as lust, as many hoots and hollers as "Bravas." And what's a little belly-shaking without some breast-shimmying, which Brenner thinks the "frolicking fawns" represent (Song 7:3)? Moreover, the woman's Heshbon pool eyes, far from suggesting clear shimmering lakes, are more like dirty watering holes or mud pits suitable for what else but sweaty, dirty dancing![13] Brenner continues through the stanza in this mode, but we have the idea by now.

Recall that the purpose of this raunchy parody, in Brenner's reading, is still, in the man's mind at least, more appreciative than derogative. This is not biting satire aimed to overthrow elite sensibilities or undermine women's dignity, certainly not this beloved woman's. As Brenner sums up the parody's result: The man "has laughed at the dance without undue reverence not because he does not respect [the woman]—we know nothing of that, one way or the other. He laughs at her because she is comical—even ridiculous—as well as sexy. One response does not cancel out the other—on the contrary! Ultimately, it is the sexy-sensual side that prevails."[14] Some men, like the country song puts it, happen to "like their women a little on the trashy side."[15] Brenner further entertains the notion that a woman or women may have composed this ode because she knows all too well how her man and how men in general think about her.[16] She may not be thrilled about his cruder side, but she can handle it, be amused by it even, and poke her own fun at him in return—really now, how can you ever eat a wheat bagel again after such absurd, dirty thoughts?

It will come as no surprise that I don't fully buy into Brenner's interpretation, as stimulating as it is, any more than Black's—but not for the reasons Brenner adduces. She specifically calls out resistant readers of her essay as enmeshed in (1) a fastidious view of Scripture and biblical love that forecloses from the start any playful, humorous, ribald treatment of sexuality, especially in a book like the Song so often interpreted in spiritual, allegorical terms; and (2) the same straitlaced view of any love literature worthy of the name, secular or religious, if such works

13. Ibid., 248–50.
14. Ibid., 252.
15. "Trashy Women," written by Chris Wall and recorded by the band Confederate Railroad in 1993.
16. Brenner, "'Come Back,'" 256–57.

"are not to be demoted from eroticism to pornography."[17] But I have no problem detecting the human tendency to joke and tease about the pleasant, yet also scary and serious, subject of sex in the Song or in other parts of the Bible or other literature.[18] I've noted playful elements at various places myself. Indeed, poking fun is a useful way of masking and surmounting the fear! But once again, I don't see parody as the prime mover *in this scene*. As with Black's reading, Brenner's depends too much on genital euphemisms that are questionable in the text, but more than that, Brenner's approach requires the woman to be onstage as a performing dancer, a rather low-class one at that, for maximum effect. Such a scenario, however, in my take on Song 6:13, is precisely what the man wants to close the curtain on. Rather than seeing her gyrating on a stage (or bar counter or around a pole), he tries to set her in more statuesque form on a pedestal. Yes, she teeters there a bit as he fumbles for the right words and images, and he will win no art prizes for his work. But he tries to admire her, adore her even, and keep her away from more critical eyes.

Of course, it's often said that the male gaze tends toward a vicious polarity, viewing women as either chaste virgins on a pedestal or churlish whores in the gutter. Such a dichotomy is behind Brenner's labeling of love depictions in the popular imagination as either eroticism or pornography. To avoid such a strict binary is partly why I see the Song's man placing his beloved on a shaky or shallow pedestal. He exalts her and makes exclusive claims on her love, but hardly regards her as a sexual innocent by this point in the Song. And though not shaking up a dance storm, she is scarcely frozen in place or petrified like some mechanical doll. The man is not "putting her on display" for others for his own exaltation, though ironically, the "fixing" of this ode in hard textual form has kept her on display for centuries. She retains control over her own body—and the man's to a great extent. As "kingly" as he may be, he is captured in her flowing tresses (Song 7:5). I think the man knows and respects the fact that the Song's female protagonist would happily echo the classic feminist lyrics by John Madara and David White recorded in

---

17. Ibid., 254.

18. See F. Scott Spencer, "Those Riotous—yet Righteous—Foremothers of Jesus: Exploring Women in Matthew's Comic Genealogy," in *Are We Amused? Humour in the Biblical World*, ed. Athalya Brenner, LHBOTS 383 (London: T & T Clark, 2003), 7–30; also in *Dancing Girls*, 24–46.

1963 by the popular singer Lesley Gore: "And please, when I go out with you / Don't put me on display, 'cause / You don't own me."[19]

But if we knock the woman too far or too hard off the pedestal, do we risk her—and the males who ogle her—dropping into the gutter, into pornographic degradation? A few critics have recently wondered if the Song doesn't project exactly that X-rated image, which we're just too afraid or ashamed to see and thus effectively censor through our allegorical and spiritual or literal and romantic readings, insisting the Song is not about sex at all, or it's about nice, loving sex.[20] Critical debates about pornography inevitably entangle us in thorny questions of aesthetic definition and political freedom: When does legitimate art shade into illicit smut? Who gets to decide where to draw the line? A male magistrate, perhaps, who "knows it when he sees it"?[21] What right does the government or any institution have to regulate sexual preference, provided it doesn't hurt anyone? Of course, this matter of "no harm, no foul" (maybe she "enjoys" S/M) or so-called victimless actions of prostitution and pornography (maybe she "chooses" to do it) is an extremely dubious supposition. But it continues to generate considerable heat even among feminist social critics. As Burrus and Moore summarize: "At least since the 'sex wars' of the 1980s, anti-porn feminists who favor censorship have been knocking heads with sex radicals of various stripes, many also strongly aligned with feminism. Feminism—scarcely a monolith as either a political or an intellectual phenomenon—has thus produced not only some of the toughest critiques of pornography but also some of the toughest critiques of censorship."[22]

---

19. John Madara and Dave White, "You Don't Own Me," *Lesley Gore Sings of Mixed-Up Hearts*, Mercury, 1963. Perhaps better known for another number, "It's My Party (and I'll Cry if I Want To)," Gore died on February 16, 2015, a few days before I drafted this portion of the commentary.

20. Roland Boer, "Night Sprinkle(s): Pornography and the Song of Songs" in *Knockin' on Heaven's Door: The Bible and Popular Culture*, Biblical Limits (London: Routledge, 1999), 53–70; David J. A. Clines, "Why Is There a Song of Songs and What Does It Do to You If You Read It?," in *Interested Parties: The Ideology of Writers and Readers of the Hebrew Bible*, JSOTSup 205, Gender, Culture, Theory 1 (Sheffield: Sheffield Academic, 1995); see the penetrating discussion in Virginia Burrus and Stephen D. Moore, "Unsafe Sex: Feminism, Pornography, and the Song of Songs," *BibInt* 11 (2003), 30–49.

21. I play here, of course, on Supreme Court Justice Potter Stewart's famous judgment about obscenity ("I know it when I see it") in the case of *Jacobellis v. Ohio* (1964).

22. Burrus and Moore, "Unsafe Sex," 36.

In the more specialized arena of feminist biblical interpretation, the issue has not been so highly contested, rendering a virtually unanimous negative verdict on pornography. Feminist analysis of various "texts of terror" has exposed not only narrative accounts of the brutal sexual exploitation of women but also prophetic pronouncements of divine judgment in terms of sexually abusive attacks as unmistakably reprehensible speech acts.[23] Regarding feminist interpretation of the Song in particular, while discussion persists on how liberating the text may or may not be for women, no female scholar I know of has unequivocally promoted the pornographic character of the Song. However they interpret the erotic images or problematic potential of the male gaze, they stop short of pornographic ratings.

Only a few male scholars, as it happens, albeit with feminist sympathies, have ventured into this X-treme territory, none more brazenly than Roland Boer who argues flat out that the Song represents a politically subversive "poetic porn text," an egregious triple X one at that, reeling off one salacious scene after another in disjointed fashion (as porn films do) with no discernible plot (who cares about that?), flashing the gamut of sexual practices in an exhausting surfeit of fleshly indulgence.[24] And presiding over this X-travaganza, Boer proposes tongue-in-cheek, is the mega-porn star and producer Sue Lammith (Shulammite). The final *wasf* now under investigation simply offers another episode in the film, sprinkled with a little difference to keep the lust boiling (the tape has been rolling a while now). You can't keep showing the same characters, so Sue invites in "Beth Rabbim" and "Leb Bannon" (boasting prodigious "wood"), not to mention a couple of actual fawns, for a kinky sexual ménage(rie) romp.[25]

23. The classic text is Phyllis Trible, *Texts of Terror: Literary-Feminist Readings of Biblical Narratives*, OBT (Philadelphia: Fortress, 1984). See also T. Drorah Setel, "Prophets and Pornography: Female Sexual Imagery in Hosea, in *Feminist Interpretation of the Bible*, ed. Letty M. Russell (Philadelphia: Westminster, 1985), 86–95, 157–59.

24. Roland Boer, "The Second Coming: Repetition and Insatiable Desire in the Song of Songs," *BibInt* 8 (2000): 297; and "Night Sprinkle(s)." Cf. the "softer" approach of Clines ("Why Is There a Song?," 100–101): "The material cause of the Song of Songs is . . . the need of a male public for erotic literature. . . . the social context is one that approves the existence and distribution of erotic literature that verges on soft pornography" (113–14, 119).

25. Boer, "Night Sprinkle(s)," 64–70.

Perhaps the less said about all this the better. However "radical" many of us may claim to be in our assessments of religion and the Bible, we/I would draw the line well before the "radical, revolutionary dimension of Christianity" espoused by Boer,[26] if his approach to the Song is typical of this perspective. Apart from any "Christian" interests, Boer's pornographic take on the Song seems miles beyond other creative sexual readings: "high" erotica, "low" parody, even fringe grotesquerie.[27] Nonetheless, for all that, pornography remains *serious* business—ethically, judicially, economically—demanding critical assessment, however uncomfortable we might feel in the process. But yet again, it comes down to the more pointed matter of interpreting *this stanza* within *this Song*. Key textual and contextual elements of the Poem, while allowing for considerable interpretive latitude, still provide hermeneutical guardrails preventing readers from careening off track into the gutter.[28] The rails I've been working within in this commentary include:

26. UON, "Left of His Field," University of Newcastle: School of Humanities and Social Science, https://www.newcastle.edu.au/highlights/our-researchers/education-arts/humanities-social-science/left-of-his-field.

27. Drawing on both feminist and queer theory, especially that of Karmen Mac-Kendrick (*Counterpleasures*, SUNY Series in Postmodern Culture [New York: State University of New York Press, 1999]), Burrus and Moore ("Unsafe Sex," 40–49 ) offer another perspective on the Song's erotic genre, situated in the tensive sexual world of "counter-pleasures." Concerning the pivotal beating episode in 5:6-7, they remark: "A crucial question looms: how to distinguish ultimately between the pain-filled pleasure of a bottom and the pleasureless pain of a battered woman? *Both readings of the scene are valid and, indeed, for feminists, indispensable, we could contend.* . . . An adequately theorized feminist erotics may require that we both continue to denounce, and dare to celebrate, the beating of the woman in the Song . . . that we both remain within, and subversively exceed, the normative enclosure of 'sexuality' " (49, emphasis original). While there is certainly much to negotiate in the complex realm of human sexual experience about what brings pleasure to whom, I see nothing to celebrate in the Song woman's assault by the night watchmen; there I can only bring myself to speak of counter*violence*, that is, opposition to the pain that the men inflict—no doubt to *their* pleasure—upon the woman against her desire.

28. On the importance of textual and contextual "guardrails" (not straitjackets) in biblical interpretation, see Merold Westphal, "The Philosophical/Theological View," in *Biblical Hermeneutics: Five Views*, ed. Stanley E. Porter and Beth M. Stovall (Downers Grove, IL: IVP Academic, 2012), 78–79. Westphal draws his "guardrail" image from Jacques Derrida, *Of Grammatology*, trans. Gayatri Chakravorty Spivak (Baltimore: Johns Hopkins University Press, 1976), 158.

1. A sense of *erotic imagery* that is rich, intimate, provocative, and un-abashedly embodied without, however, being narrowly obsessed with sex organs; the beloved bodies include, but do not reduce to, genitalia, without forcing the point with extreme linguistic license.

2. A sense of *dramatic movement* involving as much going as "coming," as much longing expression of desire as consummation, pleading "not to be disturbed" in love because the couple is all too often thwarted by absence and interference; pornography has no patience with such tension; it must finish the job again and again with numbing redundancy.[29]

3. A sense of *character unity* that focuses on the budding relationship of *one male/female couple* throughout; other figures affect this bond in various ways but never take the spotlight away from the two lovers; and the intense, possessive passion each has for the other ("I am my beloved's and he is mine," 6:3) precludes orgiastic interests.

4. A sense of *plot development*, admittedly loose, episodic, and subject to quick transitions, but in my view still weaving the threads of a love story from scene to scene, stanza to stanza—a story worth trying to follow rather than dismissing from the start; at any rate, this single poem, with its widely acclaimed literary sophistication, even as "folk" literature, resists reduction to a mindless mash-up of pornographic clips.

5. A sense of *virtuous purpose*—not Victorian prudery by any stretch and not glossing over difficult problems, including violence—but an overall sense of the goodness of erotic love and its potential for human flourishing as a force greater than death, a force forging a loving bond between embodied persons in harmony with the whole creation; of course, this ideal vision projects its own fantasy, but it seems a lot closer to the Song's poetic world than the muddy wet dreams of pornographic ilk.

The commentary devil, however, persists in the textual details, to which we now turn more closely.

29. At this point, Burrus and Moore ("Unsafe Sex," 39–40) sharply differ with Boer's pornographic reading: "Presenting a slowly shifting, subtly repetitious series of elaborately described scenes that fire anticipation, the Song . . . frustrates the readerly desire for narrative consummation, saturating the text instead with the perverse pleasure of prolonged suspense."

## Shapely Treasures (7:1-3)

The man begins his final ode to his lover by enthroning her beside him as his "queenly maiden" or, literally, a "noble/princess daughter" (בת־נדיב, *bat-nadib*, Song 7:1), which matches her fancying herself beside him in his chariot as her "noble/prince" (נדיב, *nadib*, 6:12). And so the royal fiction keeps rolling, this "aristocracy of lovers," in Michael V. Fox's terms, graced in the present lines with an abundance of master-crafted jewels and wine bowls.[30] Such regal images characterize the woman's feet, thighs, and navel (7:1-2a). They then give way to pastoral pictures of wheat fields, lilies, and gazelles associated with the woman's belly and breasts (7:2b-3). In short work, the man has envisioned a magnanimous portrait of his lover's body, encompassing court and countryside as well as solid manufactured goods and liquid, wispy, and gentle natural elements.[31]

In all this he places a premium on the woman's pleasing shapely contours: her jewel-like, smoothly "curved" (rather than "rounded") thighs (CEB, NAB, NASB); her "round goblet"–style navel (NJPS, NIV, NASB, KJV); her lily-encircled belly; and her perfectly twinned, faunal breasts. The form is as critical as the substance. Also, except for the woman's breasts, the man notices these other parts for the first time in the Song. Even after multiple close look-overs of his lover's body, he still discovers fresh dimensions of her beauty. She never ceases to surprise him in delightful ways.

So what of these "new" parts? The woman referred earlier to her own bathed, bare feet in the infamous night scene with a different term than the man uses here (Song 5:2-7), but this is the first time the man sees and admires them. And this time, her feet are shod with sandals, setting off their "beautiful" or "lovely" (the familiar Song term, יפה) features typical of a regal, aristocratic figure (7:1). As Dianne Bergant comments, "Rural women and professional dancers normally went barefoot. Sandals were considered a decorative or sophisticated addition, more easily available to women of noble or upper-class status (see Ezek 16:10; Jdt 10:4)."[32]

---

30. Michael V. Fox, *The Song of Songs and the Ancient Egyptian Love Songs* (Madison: University of Wisconsin Press, 1985), 155.

31. On the mixture of hard masculine and soft feminine images in the man's description of the woman, see Carol Meyers, "Gender Imagery in the Song of Songs," in *A Feminist Companion to the Song of Songs*, ed. Athalya Brenner and Carole R. Fontaine, FCB (Sheffield: Sheffield Academic, 1993), 197–212.

32. Bergant, *Song*, 82.

Nevertheless, the Song man's description of his darling's sandaled feet remains simple and rather modest: no toe polish, rings, or ankle bracelets required—and no movement either. The rendering "graceful" (NRSV, CEB) over-interprets in the direction of dancing, for which we have scant textual clues other than the man's preceding query that I have taken as a challenge *not* to look on the woman *as if* she were a common camp dancer (6:13). The portrait of the woman's attractive feet is a still life; there are no dance "steps" (διαβήματα, LXX). The lack of pedal movement sets her apart from the Proverbs prostitute, whose restless feet stray from home into the city center, with "one foot in the street, one foot in the public square" (Prov 7:11-12, CEB). But the "feet" reference also eerily evokes the Song woman's ill-fated roaming the streets, perhaps barefoot, in search of her missing lover (Song 5:3-7). Is the man's present ode to her shod, stationary feet some sort of attempt to compensate for or even repress this perilous peregrination that he caused? Or, is it perhaps to control her more tightly, to keep her in a "safe" place? Only the man's psychiatrist knows for sure, but the Poem at least opens up some space for such modern reflection.

Coming up to the woman's midriff—apparently exposed rather than clothed—we confront the strange (to us) images of a goblet navel and a grain-field stomach. As noted above, these parts have been viewed by some interpreters as genital references. But such shape-shifting is not necessary to maintain an aesthetic erotic focus. Bare bellies and belly buttons have long been regarded as sexy in and of themselves, whether in motion or not (no belly-dancing required here).[33] As the woman praised the man's ivory, hard-polished abs (Song 5:14), the man extols the woman's middle, though in somewhat softer and shapelier terms. He loves her "innie" for its reminder of a wine cup brimming with intoxicating delights. And this concave geometry may carry over to the wider belly, reflecting the woman's taut, in-curved core, more similar to the man's.[34] The "heap of wheat" image may, but need not, imply a thicker, more ample tummy, still less a fat, jiggly, or hairy one. "Wheat" might reflect the color "tawny," as one commentator suggests,[35] but

33. See the iconography in Othmar Keel, *The Song of Songs: A Continental Commentary*, trans. Frederick J. Gaiser (Minneapolis: Fortress, 1994), 232.

34. Or, alternatively, envisioning an appealing contrast, Alter (*Strong as Death*, 42) notes, "Visually, the two lines trace a counterpoint between the navel's concavity and the gentle convex of the belly."

35. Fox, *Song*, 159.

more likely it trades on the sustaining, nurturing, satisfying nature of this basic grain. And "heaps" of it may convey rich abundance as much as chunky, superfluous weight, all the more so in an arid environment where harvests are precarious. The circling lilies only enhance the picture of abounding garden-style beauty and pleasantness. In this milieu, the experience of erotic pleasure also fits nicely, in conjunction with the viticultural and pastoral imagery of the Song and with the passionate threshing-floor scene with Ruth and Boaz, surrounded by a heap of winnowed barley and wheat and loosened up by Boaz's drink-induced "contented mood"—and don't forget the footsie play (Ruth 2:23–3:9).

## Stately Towers (7:4-5)

Proceeding upward to the headshot of the woman's neck, eyes, nose, and hair, architectural images associated with named municipal and natural landmarks come to the fore, supporting a tall, stately, statuesque figuration coordinated with the intricate master-sculpted thighs. The man reinforces his recent comparison of the woman to the magnificent capitals of Tirzah and Jerusalem (Song 6:4) with evocations of Heshbon and Damascus, the Syrian capital, adjacent to the gate of Bath-rabbim and the forest of Lebanon (7:4); and his metaphoric association of the woman's hair with the slopes of Gilead (6:5; also 4:1) easily shifts to Mount Carmel (7:5). The previous vision of his lover's towering neck is now supplemented by a comparable impression of her nose. The "tower of David" neck image (4:4) modulates into an "ivory tower," while her nose is cast "like a tower of Lebanon overlooking Damascus" (7:4). The material move to ivory envisions a smoother and more elegant, but no less solid, structure than the rock-terraced tower of David. It presents a more suitably feminine picture of the skin on the woman's neck, though the only other ivory reference in the Song characterizes the man's belly (Song 5:14), one among many Song examples of metaphors applied to both sexes.

As discussed above concerning Song 4:4, stone towers principally functioned as defense watch-posts for a strategic city like David's Jerusalem. Atop her ivory-tower neck, the woman's nose as a wooded tower or forest of Lebanon may seem less formidable except in its representation of height. But what do tall trees have to do with defense? A great deal, as it happens, when the dense forest "overlooks" the Syrian capital of Damascus, making it difficult for enemies to hack through and mount an assault. The Lebanon woods effectively watch over Damascus as security agents. Fine, but how, then, does a stately tree with overhanging branches reflect a woman's *nose* in any flattering sense? In modern Western culture, the long, crooked, aquiline nose is more a mark of hags and witches than beautiful women. Indeed it would compel corrective plastic surgery ("nose jobs") for many elite women concerned about their appearance.[36] As with big bellies, we have no proof that big noses were any more desired in the ancient world. "Aquiline" (that is, eagle-like) captures the strong, protective, "towering" dimension of the woman's physique, but not in any obvious pleasing way. The aesthetic dimension may relate less to shape here than to smell, playing on the famed fragrance of the Lebanon range, reinforced, as we have seen, by the paronomasia with *lebonah* or "frankincense" and associated with the woman's olfactory organ through "the scent of your breath/nose like apples" (7:8).[37] Perhaps the point is that her sweet aroma engulfs and enhances the entire landscape around her.

But, still, she is not all sweetness and light. As Othmar Keel reminds us, the Hebrew word for "nose" (אַף) is closely associated with the emotion of anger, fueling the image of one's nose becoming inflamed or burning hot with "snorting, animosity, anger" (see Gen 30:2; Num 25:3-4; Deut 13:17). Hence, whatever delightful fragrances the Song woman might emit, her towering nose projects "a symbol of proud military preparedness" ready to erupt with ferocious force, if necessary: "anyone who arouses her displeasure must reckon with insurmountable resistance."[38] Furthermore, as the man has been looking up the woman's body from

36. In modern pop culture, the large, crooked Lebanese nose comes in for particular mockery, as in the case of Corporal Klinger in the popular television series *M\*A\*S\*H*.

37. J. Cheryl Exum, *Song of Songs*, OTL (Louisville: Westminster John Knox, 2005), 236; Fox, *Song*, 160. Bergant (*Song*, 86) recognizes the Lebanon-frankincense connection but prefers here a color rather than fragrance association: "the cliffs of the anti-Lebanon mountain range are chalk-colored and frankincense is white."

38. Keel, *Song*, 236; on the Hebrew metaphor "anger is a nose," see Matthew R. Schlimm, *From Fratricide to Forgiveness: The Language and Ethics of Anger in Genesis*, Siphrut 7 (Winona Lake, IN: Eisenbrauns, 2011), 82–87, 185, 195–97. Schlimm's judicious discussion stresses that this metaphor need not assume any necessary physical sensation (hotness, redness) in the nose when expressing anger. Indeed the metaphor might have become largely insignificant (dead metaphor) in common usage and, in any case, certainly does not demand an angry nuance in every mention of "nose" (אַף). Sometimes a nose is just a nose. Though he does not argue the point, Schlimm includes Song 7:4 in a list of biblical "nose" texts he considers unrelated to anger (185 n. 2; 195 n. 12). I think, however, that the military imagery of the Song lends some support to Keel's point.

bottom to top, he now acknowledges her imposing posture of looking down upon an entire city, making him appear rather small. His intimidated awe of her remains unabated.

The previous descriptions of the woman's eyes as "doves" (Song 4:1) or "overwhelming" in their effect on the man (6:5) give way now to comparisons with "pools of Heshbon" (7:5). Heshbon was a city in the region of Moab, south of the Gilead range and east of the Jordan River. The breadth of geographical scope in the imagery of the Song continues to impress. Heshbon was particularly known for its abundant water supply captured in a capacious reservoir holding up to two million liters.[39] The man may thus be suggesting the great depth of the woman's eyes as conduits to her vibrant, life-giving inner being. Of course, the shape of eyes readily compares to pools, and the water element flows nicely with the irrigated garden scenes of lovemaking (4:12–5:1; 6:2-3). But the security factor may also persist, as access to water played a key role in the ability of ancient cities to sustain their people and hold out against sieges. I see water as a consistently pure, prized, and protected element in the Song, unmixed with dirty laundry, soiled bodies, and dumped waste products suggested by Brenner in her parody reading.[40]

Security issues are further reinforced by locating the woman's eye pools near "the gate of Bath-rabbim" (Song 7:4). No such gate is known in the historical record at Heshbon or anywhere else. But city gates were obvious focal points of access, both granted when open and denied when shut. The woman remains in control of her body, particularly who gets to enter it and make close contact, except in tragic cases where her defenses are down or overpowered by watchmen who betray their protective duty and attack the guard "tower" rather than defend it. Gates were also, however, principal spots for civic assemblies and judicial settlements. The literal meaning of Bath-rabbim, "daughter of multitudes," may suggest this communal dimension in a populous city like Heshbon. Applied to the woman's eyes, it may intimate their magnanimous and magnetic capacity to draw not just the male lover but the masses to her commanding visage.

At last, the man scales to the woman's summit, to her crowning head and cascading hair. Her majestic head is compared to yet another famous mountain peak or range (Song 7:5). Carmel is set on a promontory jutting out into the Mediterranean Sea in northern Israel. Like Lebanon,

39. See Lawrence T. Geraty, "Heshbon," *ABD* III (1992): 182.
40. See above, p. 173.

this range is fertile rather than rocky; indeed the very name (כרמל) means "orchard" or "garden" and is often translated in the NRSV as "fruitful field." Directly to the south stretches the verdant Plain of Sharon. Carmel continues to be known not only for its imposing height but also for its rich production of olives, grain, and wine.[41] As in the Song, it is frequently associated elsewhere in the Bible with the territories of Lebanon (2 Kgs 19:23; Isa 33:9; 37:24; Nah 1:4), Sharon (Isa 33:9; 35:2), Gilead (Jer 50:19; Mic 7:14), and Heshbon (Isa 16:10). The Song's man has previously envisioned his darling's hair as beautiful flowing tresses like the stream of dark-hide goats down the slopes of Gilead (Song 4:1; 6:5). Now he leaves out the animal imagery and shifts the topographical focus to the more majestic Carmel range and the color palette to "purple" or deep red, perhaps associated with some floral or vegetative hues (grape purple or red?) prominent in the region, but certainly evocative of royalty.[42] She is, after all, his princess/queen and he her prince/king.

In fact, for the only time in the Song, the man now refers to himself as "king," as she has repeatedly imagined him. But notably, far from projecting a domineering posture, he regards himself as a "captive" king trapped in his beloved's locks (Song 7:5). Of course, he's quite happy to surrender, but this scenario still maintains the man's vulnerable position before his strong princess. His defenses are utterly broken down by her entangling allure. While the experience of "capture" or "binding" (אסר) is clear, however, the instrument of conquest is not. The term rendered "tresses" (רהט) in most versions is ambiguous. It appears only three other times in the Hebrew Bible, denoting "watering troughs" for animals on each occasion, a meaning that seems ill-suited, if not absurd, as imagery for a woman's captivating long hair. Nevertheless, on closer examination, we see that each case happens to be a part of some kind of mating ritual associated with the troughs: the first two involving Jacob's strange breeding scheme for Laban's flocks and the other featuring Moses' first encounter with his soon-to-be wife in Midian.

> [Jacob] set the rods that he had peeled in front of the flocks in the *troughs* [רהטים], that is, the watering places, where the flocks came to drink. And

41. Henry O. Thompson, "Carmel, Mount," *ABD* I (1992): 874–75.
42. The Hebrew term for "purple" in Song 7:5 is ארגמן (*ʾargaman*). But the word "Carmel" itself evokes a similar term, *karmil* (כרמיל) for the reddish-purple or crimson cloth used in furnishing Solomon's Temple (listed with *ʾargaman* in 2 Chron 2:13; 3:14); see Fox, *Song*, 160; Michael Fishbane, *Song of Songs*, JPS Bible Commentary (Lincoln: University of Nebraska Press, 2015), 186.

since they *bred* when they came to drink, the flocks *bred* in front of the rods. (Gen 30:38-39; see v. 41 for the other "trough" reference)

But Moses . . . settled in the land of Midian, and sat down by a well. The priest of Midian had seven daughters. They came to draw water, and filled the *troughs* [רהטים] to water their father's flock. But some shepherds came and drove them away. Moses got up and came to their defense and watered their flock. When they returned to their father Reuel, he said, "How is it that you have come back so soon today?" They said, "An Egyptian [Moses] helped us against the shepherds; he even drew water for us and watered the flock." . . . [Moses] agreed to stay with [Reuel], and he gave his daughter Zipporah in *marriage*. (Exod 2:15-20)

As noted above in our discussion of Song 4:12-15, watering holes, including wells, were cultural type-sites for mating or striking marriage deals (see also Gen 24:10-67; 29:1-14).[43] Hence, these "troughs" are not so alien to love liaisons after all, and related elements of flock-tending and water-coursing have already staked their places in the Song's erotic repertoire.

But we still haven't made the hair connection yet. It might have some loose link with the wet head of the pining man who came calling that fateful night (Song 5:2). A better line of thought, however, recalls those previous pictures of the woman's hair "moving down" the Gilead slopes "like a flock of goats" (4:1; 6:5). These elements of flock and flowing or moving down bear some affinity with the other trough references cited above. Moreover, the particular hair word in 7:5 (דלה), rendered "flowing locks" in the NRSV and NAB, refers to the "thrum" or "warp-threads remaining on the loom after woven material is removed" (see Isa 38:12).[44] Correlating these dangling threads with a woman's hair is not that far-fetched, though perhaps not as flattering as it could be (stringy, ratty hair?). But the image strengthens with the wordplay of the same root (דלה) in its verb form, meaning "to draw water" in conjunction with "watering troughs" in the Moses scene just cited (Exod 2:16, 19). Taken together then, though not without some linguistic effort, the threads and troughs may coalesce into a coherent picture of the woman's flowing locks and cascading tresses drawing the man into a luscious love hold or lock.

The man has begun to move from a static, statuesque portrait of the woman's beauty to a more dynamic one in which he's becoming more

---

43. See pp. 110–11.

44. William J. Holladay, *A Concise Hebrew and Aramaic Lexicon of the Old Testament* (Grand Rapids: Eerdmans, 1971), 71; see Fishbane, *Song*, 186.

intimately involved. In other words, we're beginning to see more of a motion picture's familiar love scene of a passionate woman's long, unbound hair draping around her lover. Familiar, yes, but feminist? On one level, sure: there's nothing unfeminist about a woman using her alluring hair, if she so chooses, to express her sexual passion. But on another level, some concerns surface, particularly related to the entrapment issue. Yes, by all accounts as we've already mentioned, the king-man happily submits to his "capture." But is this not a risky surrender of his authority in its wider cultural context? Is there not a perilous downside for men when women let down their serpentine hair? Isn't this just how women use their wiles to overwhelm a man?

Such links between a loose woman and her loose locks of unpinned hair may underlie the strange trial procedure for a wife suspected of sexual infidelity, including, among other rituals, the "disheveling" of her hair by the priest (Num 5:18).[45] The infamous Delilah (דלילה), whose very name resonates with the term for "thrum/tresses" used in the Song (*dallah*, דלה), used her sexuality on behalf of Philistine interests to emasculate Israel's Super-Judge Samson by snipping off his flowing locks and thus sapping him of his extraordinary strength guaranteed by a lifelong Nazirite vow. Just before divulging the "no razor" secret of Samson's power, he teased Delilah into thinking falsely that he would be rendered impotent by weaving his hair into a tight top-knot secured by a pin; it's all about his hair (Judg 16)![46]

Flipping international politics and preserving feminine chastity amid a bold display of sexuality, the Israelite heroine Judith beguiled the Assyrian tyrant Holofernes in his bedchamber, right up to the point where she grabbed the sword hanging over his bedpost, "took hold of the *hair of his head . . .* struck his neck twice with all her might, and *cut off his head*" (Jdt 13:6-8). Amazingly, she did all of this without actually having intercourse with the wicked general. In her own autobiographical ode—referring to herself in third person—she exclaims, "She anointed her face

---

45. See Alice Bach, "Introduction to a Case History," 461; and "Good to the Last Drop: Viewing the *Sotah* (Numbers 5.11-31) as the Glass Half Empty and Wondering How to View It Half Full," 505–12—both in *Women and the Hebrew Bible: A Reader*, ed. Alice Bach (New York: Routledge, 1999).

46. In commenting on the thread/thrum (*dallah*)-like locks of the woman in Song 7:5, Fishbane (*Song*, 186) adds this delicious parenthetical comment without elaboration: "Thus in Judges 16, there may be more to the Philistine name Delilah than the modern eye tends to perceive."

with perfume; she *fastened her hair with a tiara* and put on a linen gown to beguile him. Her sandal ravished his eyes, her beauty *captivated his mind*, and the sword severed his neck!" (16:7-9). Like the Song's woman, she captures her male target with her regal, beautiful, and fragrant charms, right down to her sandals; but unlike the Songstress, Judith keeps her hair decorously pinned up as she beheads her lusty prey. And the only way that the man in the Song "loses his head" to the woman he desires is figuratively. But we're on the razor's edge here of propriety, authority, and feminist sensibility: while the Song's sexy woman disentangles some of the knotty stereotypes of loose-haired, man-trapping women, there remain nagging loose threads of kingly discomfiture and capture hanging over her—and his!—head.

Surprisingly perhaps for many Christian readers, the closest canonical parallel to the present Song scene may be found in the New Testament banquet episode where a woman repeatedly douses Jesus' feet with a wet mixture of her kisses, tears, and perfume and then dries them with her loosened hair as an expression of lavish love (Luke 7:36-38; cf. John 12:1-3). Jesus wholly accepts, even commends (Luke 7:44-47), this captivating erotic display with no hint of threat or discomfort, unlike that felt by his Pharisee host Simon (7:39), and no doubt the other table guests. Modern Western Christians can approximate the power of this scene by imagining a woman coming off the streets into a mid-week church fellowship dinner, a staple of many American parish programs, and promptly heading to the pastor's table and attending to his feet—or any other body part—with the same passion the woman enacted toward Jesus. It takes no great cultural insight to conclude that the pastor himself and his parishioners would side with Simon the Pharisee's position, not Jesus', in this case.[47]

## Stately Trees (7:6-9a)

After his vertical itemization of the woman's various attractive body parts, the man steps back momentarily and admires her entire portrait and person: "How fair and pleasant you are, O loved one, delectable

47. See the fuller discussion of this passage in F. Scott Spencer, *Dancing Girls, "Loose" Ladies, and Women of "the Cloth": The Women in Jesus' Life* (New York: Continuum, 2004), 108–43; and *What Did Jesus Do? Gospel Profiles of Jesus' Personal Conduct* (Harrisburg, PA: Trinity Press International, 2003), 107–10; for a brief connection of Luke 7:36-50 with the Song of Songs, see Barbara E. Reid, *Choosing the Better Part? Women in the Gospel of Luke* (Collegeville, MN: Liturgical, 1996), 119.

maiden" (Song 7:6). This NSRV rendering fleshes out two Hebrew words at the end of the statement that simply, yet profoundly, convey "O-Love [אהבה] with-delights [בתענוגים, 'luxuries, charms, pleasures']." In the man's eyes, his darling is not simply the object of love but its very personification, brimming with a rich trove of royal treasures. She embodies the panoply of "delights" pursued by another Solomonic persona, Qoheleth: "I also gathered for myself silver and gold and the treasure of kings and of the province; I got singers, both men and women, and delights [תענוגת] of the flesh, and many concubines" (Eccl 2:8). But whereas Qoheleth sought for life's meaning in accumulating as many pleasures as possible, including multiple women, and frankly admits that these amounted to nothing but empty vanity (Eccl 2:1-11), the man in the Song finds all the wealth and satisfaction he can imagine in the one woman who captures him in the very fullness of Love.

### *Illumination 3 Commentary*
*(The depicted Hebrew text is Song 1:1-2)*

A breeze sweeps through a young woman's garden, ruffling curtains, upsetting flasks of perfume, and tipping a clay cask that spills jewels across the mosaic pavement below. But, nothing is broken; the wind and fluttering curtains instead only reveal the treasures hidden within the garden's confines.

The illumination conveys not only the sensuality of the literal poetry but also, through the use of imagery drawn from the midrash and biblical text, an allegory of the relationship between God and the human soul, of the role of the Song of Songs in the greater body of the Hebrew Bible. The white and colored curtains blowing draw upon an image in *Song Rabbah* that describes the human soul. Following Yom Kippur repentance, the soul is likened to a flawless white curtain; while daily activities might sully it—here perhaps adding color—because the soul is always capable of repenting and returning to Torah, it always remains a thing of beauty to God. The wind (*ruaḥ*) is the Divine Spirit that initiated Creation, here acting upon the human soul. The cask spilling jewels and the mosaic fruit basket relate to midrash describing the importance of understanding the love between God and Israel hidden in the Song of Songs, while the perfume dripping from the stone table (in the first-century Burnt House in Jerusalem) relate to a midrash about how Abraham spread knowledge of the One God as he traveled toward Israel from Haran. The palm, drawing on Ps 92:12-13, suggests the righteous person, while flowing water symbolizes Torah throughout Jewish text and lore.[48]

Jewish approaches to plumbing the full value of biblical texts tread paths far steeper and more complex than literal and midrashic exploration. In his Aristotelian commentary on the Song, the Provençal rabbi and philosopher Gersonides (1288–1344) considers the attribution to Solomon to be an indication that the Song will explore the perfection of the material intellect.[49] The Kabbalistic commentary on the Song composed by the slightly earlier Castilian mystic Rabbi Ezra of Gerona sees it as an allegory of the search for reunification among the ten *Sefirot* or emanations of the Godhead. The wise King Solomon is compared to the attribute of Divine Wisdom, the kisses to the "joy attained by the soul in its adhesion to the source of life."[50]

*Debra Band*

From this grand panoramic vision, the man returns for another quick survey of her body, refocusing on her stately height, satisfying breasts, notable nose, and now adding a fresh concentration on her delectable mouth. He extols the woman's towering magnificence with another arboreal image, this time the fruitful palm tree, especially well known in the city of Jericho northeast of Jerusalem, rather than the pines and cedars of Lebanon. As the Psalmist notes, however, these different trees serve together as dramatic symbols of human flourishing in the royal

48. For a full discussion of the midrashic symbolism in this painting, see Debra Band, *The Song of Songs: The Honeybee in the Garden* (Philadelphia: JPS, 2005), 4–8.

49. Levi ben Gershom (Gersonides), *Commentary on the Song of Songs*, trans. and ed. Menachem Kellner, YJS 28 (New Haven: Yale University Press, 1998), 18.

50. Ezra ben Solomon of Gerona, *Commentary on the Song of Songs and Other Kabbalistic Commentaries* (Kalamazoo, MI: Western Michigan University Press, 1999), 39.

realm of creation: "The righteous flourish like the *palm tree*, and grow like a *cedar in Lebanon*. They are planted in the house of the LORD; they flourish in the courts of our God. In old age they still produce fruit; they are always green and full of sap" (Ps 92:12-14). Debra Band exquisitely interprets this and other flourishing natural images in the Song, in dialogue with midrashic insights, in her third illumination and commentary.

Given the Song's penchant for wordplay, it's hard not to detect some allusive link between the term for palm tree, *tamar* (תמר), and two biblical women in Israel's history by that very name who experience some form of sexual abuse. The story of Tamar in Gen 38 has a better ending, as father-in-law Judah eventually acknowledges her "righteous" character (38:26), but only after he had expelled her from the family twice-widowed (by Judah's two eldest sons) and childless, and then impregnated her while unwittingly taking her for a harlot. The second Tamar, the princess daughter of King David featured in 2 Sam 13, has a closer connection to the Song with its royal, fictive ambience. But that link is soon shattered with the heinous rape of this Tamar by her half brother, prince Amnon. Though the family's shame is brutally avenged by brother Absalom's murder of Amnon, Tamar remains forever ostracized. Nothing good comes from this horrible chain of events.[51] But following in the vein of possible "redemptive" strains in the Song, as in restoring some of the garden paradise lost to the first couple, maybe in some way this stanza—with the man's respectful, even awe-full, view of his "Tamar" or palm tree princess amid his passionate desire for her and her for him, as will become clear in Song 7:9b-10—"redeems" or at least offers a healthy, joyous alternative to the unspeakable horror endured by David's daughter.

From the animal comparison of the woman's breasts with two fawns, the man turns to a botanical image of her breasts as luscious fruit "clusters" (אשכול), first of dates on the palm tree and then of grapes on the vine (Song 7:7-8). Earlier the woman described her "kingly" lover lying between her breasts as a "bag of myrrh" and a "cluster [אשכול] of henna blossoms in the vineyards of En-gedi" (1:12-14). Now, however, as he praises her clustered breasts, the man can scarcely contain himself; not content simply to look upon his darling or lie upon her bosom, he aims to "climb" or mount her stately palm tree frame and "lay hold of" (אחז,

---

51. See the chapter on "Tamar: The Royal Rape of Wisdom" in Trible, *Texts of Terror*, 36–63.

"grasp," "seize") her "branches" or "stalks" (arms?) surrounding her succulent date-like breasts. Again the man's love language echoes the woman's as she had previously "held [אחז] him and would not let him go" after her nighttime search for him in the city streets (3:4).[52] The couple's desire for intimate contact remains intense, even desperate.

Continuing to scale up his lover's body, the man finally longs for the intoxicating scent of her nose and the taste of her mouth. Her intimidating tower-nose of Song 7:4 has become the invigorating breath-nose (אף) in 7:8. The NRSV's simple "breath" reading, while getting at the idea, obscures the nasal dimension. The man desires to get close enough to smell the woman's fragrant natural breath emanating from her nose and mouth—an amorous scent "like apples," yet again redolent of the woman's description of the man's delights (2:3-5) and commonly clustered with the joyous passion fruits of grapes, pomegranates, and dates (cf. Joel 1:12, though in a negative context). While pressed up against her, face-to-face, the man also naturally aches to engage her piquant vintage mouth, no doubt including her "kisses" (7:9a). But the term is actually more internal and intimate, targeting the woman's "palate" (חך), the same part on him that she excitedly tasted earlier with her tongue (Song 2:3; 5:16). Such completes a run of corresponding erotic imagery, stressing the couple's mutual delight in each other's bodies and, in the present simile, reinforcing the intense oral component of their sexual experience.

In the heat of the man's mounting passion where we expect him to continue panting forth specific desires for his beloved's body, suddenly, though not all that surprisingly, the woman breaks into his litany and takes over the love scene (Song 7:10). Though statuesque, she is not a cold slab of marble. She lives, loves, and breathes with her own fiery passion, which she expresses in the next several lines. Though we treat her ensuing words as a separate stanza for the sake of analysis, they in fact extend the present scene from her perspective.

---

52. This same "grasping" verb applies to fox "catching" in 2:15 and sword "grabbing" in 3:8.

# Song of Songs 7:9b–8:4

# *Desiring Old and New, Open and Safe Spaces for Love*

After a hiatus since Song 6:3 in vocalizing her feelings, except for a brief interlude in 6:11-12, the woman breaks out again in poignant song. Or more correctly, to repeat our transition into this stanza, she breaks *into* the man's speech, responding to him and taking over the passionate action he has initiated. While she does not mind his adoring gaze and amorous move to "lay hold" of her body (7:8), she will not simply be taken in passive submission. She leans into his pressing embrace and probing tongue and takes charge of matters from there. Or at least she strongly expresses what she would like to have happen. Her use of contingent verbal constructions (imperatives, cohortatives) continues a common pattern in the Song of expressing love's desired outcomes or intense longings as much as, if not more than, its consummation.[1]

---

1. J. Cheryl Exum, "In the Eye of the Beholder: Wishing, Dreaming, and Double Entendre in the Song of Songs," in *The Labour of Reading: Desire, Alienation, and Biblical Interpretation*, ed. Fiona C. Black, Roland Boer, and Erin Runions (Atlanta: SBL, 1999), 73. Exum highlights the use throughout the Song of what she calls the "erotic imperative, the call to love by means of imperatives, jussives, and cohortatives that lend urgency to longing." See also Exum, "How Does the Song of Songs Mean? On Reading the Poetry of Desire," *SEÅ* 64 (1999): 50, 63. Carey Ellen Walsh, *Exquisite*

*Song of Songs 7:9b–8:4*

**[W → M]**
⁹. . . that goes down smoothly,
　　gliding over lips and teeth.
¹⁰I am my beloved's,
　　and his desire is for me.
¹¹Come, my beloved,
　　let us go forth into the fields,
　　and lodge in the villages;
¹²let us go out early to the vine-
　　　yards,
　　and see whether the vines
　　　have budded,

whether the grape blossoms have
　　opened
and the pomegranates are in
　　bloom.
There I will give you my love.
¹³The mandrakes give forth fra-
　　grance,
and over our doors are all
　　choice fruits,
new as well as old,
　　Which I have laid up for you, O
　　　my beloved.

Come, my beloved,
Let us go forth . . .
[Let us] lodge . . .
Let us go out . . .
[Let us] see whether . . .
Oh that you were like a brother to me . . .
If I met you outside, I would kiss you . . .
I would lead you and bring you . . .
I would give you . . .
O that his left hand were under my head . . .

This wistful mode of passion reflects a highly charged space where joyous anticipation and ominous anxiety pulse in tension. The excitement of love-talk and foreplay is obvious enough; wanting and expecting sex is, by many accounts, more stimulating than having and completing it. But desire must also reckon with the painful prospect of foreclosure and frustration—*coitus interruptus* by no choice of the lovers themselves. Underlying the major strain of beautiful budding love in the Song are minor notes—"minor" in amount and tone, not significance—that

---

*Desire: Religion, the Erotic, and the Song of Songs* (Minneapolis: Fortress, 2000). Exemplary of Walsh's impressive, sophisticated treatment of desire in relation to the Song throughout her book: "Desires have never been ours to control. We erect conventions, custom, laws, and morality to corral desire, but it runs free. Like the Song's gazelle, seen running, prancing on spices, slowing to enjoy lilies and a peek through our window, desire stays free in the Song, roaming at will, an undomesticated presence in life" (77).

8:1O that you were like a brother
to me,
who nursed at my mother's
breast!
If I met you outside, I would kiss
you,
and no one would despise me.
2I would lead you and bring you
into the house of my mother,
and into the chamber of the
one who bore me.

I would give you spiced wine to drink,
the juice of my pomegranates.
**[W → D]**
3O that his left hand were under
my head,
and that his right hand embraced me!
4I adjure you, O daughters of Jerusalem,
do not stir up or awaken love
until it is ready.

squelch love's fruition. The woman, in particular, chafes against coun-
termovements launched by callous brothers and watchmen and even at
times her intrusive girlfriends and inattentive lover. The bold woman
will not back down from pursuing love; she will have it if at all possible. But she's been burned before and knows there are no guarantees.
In the present stanza brimming with passionate longing, she lets slip
her desire to display public affection for her lover with no worry that
anyone "would despise me" for doing so (Song 8:1). Clearly, she remains
concerned that she would receive precisely such scorn from some folk.
Moreover, the woman caps off the stanza with another nervous charge
to her daughter-companions: if her dreams come true, she must again
"adjure" them not to wake her until love has been fully satisfied (8:4;
as also 2:7; 3:5).

The woman envisions a flourishing environment of spatial openness
(פתח) and temporal breadth merging the "new as well as old," past,
present, and future in a holistic horizon. She anticipates love bursting forth in harmony with the "opened" (פתח) grape blossoms and the
ripening of "all choice fruits" around "our doors" or "openings" (פתח)
(7:12-13). But she knows all too well that such border spaces remain vulnerable to transgression and obstruction, as on that fateful night in the
not-too-distant past, when her lover pleaded for her to "open" herself to
him (5:2) and plunged his hand into the/her "opening" (5:4). Yet when
she "arose to open" (5:6) to him, he was gone, leaving her precariously
open to assault in the city streets (three uses of the same "open" verb,
פתח, in 5:2-6). With remarkable resilience and courage, she aims to stay
open to love, despite understandable anxieties about how easily—and
tragically—the doors can slam shut in her face.

The woman seeks to position love primarily within spatial coordinates, modulating among three loci: her lover's body, especially his mouth and lips (Song 7:9b-10); the verdant countryside where love has previously bloomed (7:11-13); and her mother's house in the city (8:1-4). The boundaries between rural and urban, rustic and domestic, and field and house that tend to be discrete, even oppositional, in conventional society remain highly permeable in the Song's panoramic vision of the harmonious world, even as it acknowledges the challenges that persist in realizing this idyllic state. We now proceed to track how the woman negotiates these spatial tensions in the present stanza.

## Gliding Over Lover's Lips (7:9b-10)

The woman immediately, even impulsively, reciprocates the man's expressed yearning to taste her intoxicating palate with the supplication that her delicious oral wine juices indeed "smoothly glide over [the] lips" of her lover (Song 7:9b). The abrupt switch to the woman speaker is signaled by the referent "to/for/over my love" (לדודי), which is omitted in the NRSV and which features *dodi* (דודי), the woman's favorite pet name for the man. It is also signaled by the implied directional shift from him licking her palate to her wine-laced saliva flowing back over his lips into his mouth. An emphasis upon the smooth, silky nature of the oral intercourse is reflected in the verb "glide" (דבב), used only here in the Hebrew Bible (7:9). The smoothness is also present in the characterization of the man's lips in a tranquil sleeping pose. A number of modern versions follow the LXX and NRSV in modifying the Hebrew text *yeshenim* (ישנים), designating "sleeping ones," to the similar sounding *shinayim* (שנים), meaning "teeth" (NIV, CEB, NAB).[2] But while "teeth" may appear to be a more suitable concomitant for "lips," the MT reading of "sleepers" still makes good sense. Sleeping lips are pleasantly relaxed in a half-smile and loosely pursed, if not slightly opened, to receive the gentle stream of a lover's sweet wine, perhaps in the afterglow of more intense lovemaking. In light of the woman's prior disturbed sleep and nocturnal struggles to find her lover (Song 3:1-5; 5:2-8), it's nice to

---

2. More specifically, as a dual form, "*two rows* of teeth"; also, the initial *yod* of the MT is read as a consecutive *waw* ("and"); see J. Cheryl Exum, *Song of Songs*, OTL (Louisville: Westminster John Knox, 2005), 214. Michael V. Fox, *The Song of Songs and the Ancient Egyptian Love Songs* (Madison: University of Wisconsin Press, 1985), 163, opts for another slight emendation, *shanim* (שנים), the plural form of "scarlet" (see Prov 31:21; Isa 1:18), hence, "scarlet lips" in Song 7:9.

imagine a more restful and blissful scenario. The general association of lips with speech and with sleepy speech in this particular case may also evoke the man's dazed murmurings of satisfaction. As Michael Fishbane puts it, "The maiden's kisses will glide into her beloved's mouth like an elixir of love—and (by double entendre) even cause him to 'babble' in his love-besotted stupor."[3]

In this vision of calm closeness, the woman reiterates in the most succinct terms (befitting the tight bond she feels) her sense of mutual union with her beloved (דודי, Song 7:10). Although one in thought and close in wording, the examples are slightly different:

My-beloved/for-me/and-I for-him (2:16)
I/for-my-beloved/and-my-beloved/for-me (6:3)
I/for-my-beloved/and-upon-me/his-desire (7:10)

The present case is the most distinct, breaking the "for-me/my" (לי) pattern with "*upon/over-me his-desire*" (עלי תשוקתו). The term for "desire" (תשוקה) appears only three times in the Hebrew Bible, but the two other occurrences, which are related to the postlapsarian experience of Adam and Eve and their eldest son Cain, are suggestive. The predicted consequence of taking the forbidden fruit targets the tragic disruption of the first couple's egalitarian "one flesh" partnership (Gen 1:27-28; 2:23-25). Henceforth, the more physically powerful man, though incredibly weak and passive in taking the fruit from his wife's hand, will "rule over" the woman, and "[her] desire" (תשוקה) will be "toward/for (אל) him" (Gen 3:16). Thus women's submission to patriarchy is born against the ideal order of creation.

But this does not represent a final biblical death sentence to women's freedom and gender equality. In a terse turn of phrase, the Song woman stunningly turns the Genesis "curse" on its head.[4] She happily gives herself to her man and doesn't seek overthrow and counter-rule, but she does not give up her autonomy and agency in the process. She will not

---

3. Michael Fishbane, *Song of Songs*, JPS Bible Commentary (Lincoln: University of Nebraska Press, 2015), 192.

4. Othmar Keel, *The Song of Songs: A Continental Commentary*, trans. Frederick J. Gaiser (Minneapolis: Fortress, 1994), 251–52. Keel entitles the brief section he devotes to Song 7:10, "Lifting the Curse," and concludes: "Thus the curse-like situation is lifted, and the brotherly/sisterly equality given in creation is restored. Love is experienced as a return to paradise." To be more precise about Gen 3:16, patriarchy is presented less as an imposed divine "curse" (or even "curse-like"), as traditionally thought, than as a tragic human consequence of alienation and competition between the sexes.

be subject to his every whim and fancy. Indeed, his desires will bend toward hers as much as the other way around. It's no coincidence, then, that she immediately implores the man to return with her to the fruitful fields and budding vines they have enjoyed—in other words, to their love garden blooming with henna, pomegranates, and "all choice fruits" (Song 7:11-13; also 4:13-15).[5] She longs to go back to Eden to keep open these paradisiacal paths against all threats of closure and obstruction.[6]

Perversion of loving desire is not so easily overcome, however. The tenacious rootedness of oppressive desire in flawed human experience is legendary, the very essence of personified Sin that gripped Cain (the Bible's first mention of this notion; Gen 4:7). In Cain's desire to gain acceptance from God, who had spurned his offering and preferred his brother Abel's instead, Cain murders Abel, only to find he's made matters worse and opened himself and the world to a downward spiral of violence. And so God warns Cain: "If you do well, will you not be accepted? And if you do not do well, sin is lurking at the door [פתח, "opening"]; its *desire* [תשוקה] *is for you*, but you must master it" (4:7). The Song's woman has had enough of violence to last a lifetime, at least partly caused, as I have argued, by her lover's flighty neglect. But at some risk to herself (who's to say he won't bail out on her again?) she eschews revenge and seeks to nurture a deeper connection with her lover, though *not* at the expense of her dignity and safety. She insists that he attend to her desires as she gives herself to him. But in the process she bets on the indomitable power of loving desire to conquer the strong undertow of lethal desire. As she opens the door wide to the full pleasures of love, she still stands guard against all perversions of such desire that crouch at the door, threatening to creep inside.

## Going Out to Fruitful Fields (7:11-13)

We now observe more carefully the country love nest the woman envisions, filled with similar fruits and flowers that both lovers have previously imagined enhancing their romantic trysts (Song 1:13-14; 4:13-15; 6:11; 7:6-9a). In these lush, verdant springtime scenes, no animals appear;

5. On these botanical garden connections in the Song, see Fox, *Song*, 164–65.

6. Phyllis Trible, "Love's Lyrics Redeemed," in *A Feminist Companion to the Song of Songs*, ed. Athalya Brenner, FCB (Sheffield: Sheffield Academic, 1993), 100–120. Though challenged and reformulated in various respects by numerous critics, including myself in this commentary, Trible's pioneering "Love's Lyrics" remains pivotal in unfolding the "redemptive" vision of the Song vis-à-vis Gen 2–3.

the woman and man are the only creatures in sight. In the present case, the woman takes the lead, answering the man's preceding "vineyard" portrait (7:8, 12), though substituting "pomegranates" and "mandrakes" (7:12-13) for his "dates" and "apples" (7:7-8). She also takes a more shared or tandem approach, though still assertive in her own way. Whereas the man planned a more cat-like pounce upon the woman's "fruit," particularly her breast clusters (7:7-8), the woman invites, well, more like beckons, in a brisk triad of first-person plural invitations that they go together to their love garden: "*Let us go forth* to the fields . . . *[let us] lodge* in the villages; *let us go out* early into the vineyards" (7:11-12). Fishbane aptly captures both the insistent and inclusive nuances of the woman's speech as a "charged evocation that initiates a series of verbs denoting shared activity," a "rapid-fire series of invitations for shared behavior."[7]

Though the term for "field" (שדה) appears only two other times in the Song, both times as the habitat of "wild does" or, literally, "does of the field," in the adjuration texts (Song 2:7; 3:5), the idyllic countryside setting for love is common in the Poem. According to Othmar Keel, "field" is a broad designation for "the open country outside the settlements, whether cultivated land (gardens, vineyards) or wilderness." Moreover, in biblical experience, "one goes into the fields to be alone with someone else, unobserved by others," like the rendezvous of Cain and Abel (though for nefarious intent on Cain's part), David and Jonathan, and Ruth and Boaz, the latter two examples in the interest of love (Gen 4:8; 1 Sam 20:5-11; Ruth 3:1-18).[8]

Longing for more than a quick day visit to the country, the Songstress wants to "lodge" there, that is, "pass the night" or "lie through the night" together (לין, Song 7:11; see 1:13; Ruth 3:13). She particularly targets the "villages" (NRSV, NIV, NASB, LXX) or "henna shrubs" (NJPS, CEB, NAB) as their lodging site—the Hebrew כפר can mean either. Perhaps a double meaning is in view: "villages" or small hamlets still suggest a rural, sparsely settled environment, but "henna" better fits the flowering bed of lovemaking with budding vines and blooming pomegranates envisioned here and elsewhere in the Song (1:14; 4:13). Calling this place "There" (שם) in an emphatic position, spotlighting the location,[9] she maintains the ambience of a private safe zone for the couple away from human interference.

7. Fishbane, *Song*, 195.
8. Keel, *Song*, 254.
9. Fox, *Song*, 164.

Removing any doubt of what the woman herself intends for their camping excursion, she shifts from first-person plural to singular mode: "There *I* will give you my love[s]" (Song 7:12, plural *doday*, דדי). This resonates with her autonomous giving of herself to "my beloved" (דודי *dodi*) in 7:10 and with her desire for *his* love-makings and caresses (*dodeka*, דדיך, "your [masc.] loves") from the very outset of the Song in 1:2, 4 . But now she adds a notable twist: it is *her* love-makings, *her* love caresses, that *she* will give to her beloved. This is her love scheme that she orchestrates from start to finish, her very selective and even secretive plan that she has devised. At the end of the next verse, when she speaks of what she has "laid up" (7:13) for the couple's love nest, the verb (צפן) evokes the notion of hiding something or someone.[10] The present love plot is hatched deeply and solely in the woman's heart.

### The Song and Ecology

The Song of Songs is largely an agrarian text. Its imagery is replete with vineyards (Song 1:6, 14; 2:15; 7:12; 8:11, 12), fields (2:7; 3:5; 7:11), wheat (7:2), fruiting trees (2:3; 4:13; 7:11-12; 8:2), and shepherding (1:7-8; 4:1-2; 6:5-6), all of which were staples of ancient Israel's agricultural economy. The Song's ecological sensibility, therefore, is not strictly interested in "nature" (as opposed to "culture"). Instead, it is a considered reflection on the fructifying possibilities of human intervention in the landscape.

In Song 7:11-13, the woman imagines going out into the fields. This itself is an agricultural vision, since "fields" in biblical usage evokes the cultivated space between the city and the wilderness. So it is fitting that the plants mentioned are regional crops: henna, grape vines, pomegranates. When the lovers go out into these fields, then, they are taking a familiar journey common to young and old alike in the ancient world: out into the fields, to see how the crops are growing. This agrarian vision builds on an underlying resemblance between the human cultivators and their crops. The budding fields signal the erotic maturation of the couple: "There, I will give you my love" (7:12). In this way, the lovers are nested in a larger productive landscape in which culture and agriculture, human and nature, are inextricable.

This resemblance is fully realized in the promise of food that the successful crops will

---

10. For example, baby Moses in the basket in Exod 2:2, 3 or the Jericho spies under the flax stalks in Josh 2:4.

supply: "over our doors are all choice fruit . . . which I have laid up for you" (Song 7:13). This theme is echoed throughout the Song. In an early passage, the girl imagines enjoying love like wine (1:2). The poem quickly turns to a consideration of wine's source: the woman's vineyard (1:5-8), where she labors under the sun. The vineyard is multiply significant, as it is a symbol for the woman herself. Throughout the Song, attentive labor and patient waiting will be rewarded with abundance—for the crops and metaphorically for the lovers. This trope is a key to the Song's ecology, which links the cultivation of food to human flourishing. Food constitutes the visible connection between human labor and the continuity and vitality of life; accordingly, eating functions as a kind of agricultural consummation, potently symbolic of sexual consummation. Ultimately, the ecological vision of the Song presses the reader to acknowledge the interdependence of humans in the natural world, who as cultivators are at once distinct from and endlessly embedded in the fecund earth.

*Elaine T. James*

But she continues to enlist the aid of natural forces, including "all [the] choice fruits" she can muster—"new as well as old" (Song 7:13) or "freshly picked and long-stored"[11]—manifesting an integral "congruence between the processes of nature and the events of love."[12] Her bond with her lover best flourishes in harmony with the bountiful earth when she says, "Let us go forth into the fields . . . lodge in the villages [or henna shrubs] . . . [and] to the vineyards" (7:11-12). As Elaine James so aptly comments, "The budding fields signal the erotic maturation of the couple. . . . The lovers are nested in a larger productive landscape, in which culture and agriculture, human and nature, are inextricable."[13] Thus, erotology and ecology again coalesce, but with a "new as well as old" component: fragrant mandrakes, which are "new" in their one and only appearance in the Song, yet "old" in their amorous associations.

11. Fishbane, *Song*, 197.

12. Fox, *Song*, 164; see Jill M. Munro, *Spikenard and Saffron: A Study in the Poetic Language of the Song of Songs,* JSOTSup 203 (Sheffield: Sheffield Academic, 1995), 81; and Fishbane (*Song*, 198), who writes, "The renewal of nature and the arousal of human love are correlated."

13. See James' essay "The Song and Ecology," above, p. 200.

This botanical species (*Mandragora officinarum*), popularly called "love apples," thrived in ancient Israel and surrounding regions and produced a beautiful palette of foliage and colors. As Harold and Alma Moldenke describe the mandrake, it features a "rosette of leaves [from which] arise the flower-stalks, each bearing a single purple, bluish, or greenish-white flower . . . followed in due time by a . . . yellowish berry about the size of a large plum." Put another way, "when perfectly developed the fruits lie in the center of the rosette of leaves like yellow bird eggs in a nest."[14] The fruit has a mild narcotic effect and became legendary for its aphrodisiacal and procreative potency. As one ancient Egyptian poet crooned to his lover, "Your skin is the skin of the mandrake, which induces loving."[15]

In the biblical patriarchal narrative, mandrakes figure prominently in a deal struck between Jacob's rival co-wives, Leah and Rachel. The younger woman, Rachel, the more desired yet still barren wife, covets the mandrakes Leah has obtained from her son Reuben for their supposed fertility powers. Leah exchanges the mandrakes for a night of long overdue lovemaking with husband Jacob (Gen 30:14-22). Again, familial conflict in Genesis serves as a foil for the lovers' relationship in the Song. Unlike Rachel, the Songstress does not festoon the "doors" or openings to the love bower with mandrakes and other fruits in order to boost her chances to conceive a child. The budding love she has for and with her beloved is all that matters now. Further playing on double-*d* sounds discussed above, the mandrakes or love apples (*dudaʾim*, דודאים) help stimulate the intimate love-makings (דדי, *doday*) between the woman and her beloved (דודי, *dodi*) (7:13; see also vv. 10, 12).[16] Moreover, in this cozy country setting, the woman is far away from any potential rivals for her beloved's affection; she has him all to herself, as he is completely devoted to her. Nevertheless, though never rising to the level of competitive strife experienced by co-wives and sisters Leah and Rachel, the relationship between the Song's protagonist and the daughters of Jerusalem remains tinged with some disruptive tension in the city, as the next segment intimates (8:1-4). Indeed, the lovers' getaways to the country may be viewed in part as flights from this fraught urban environment.

14. Harold N. Moldenke and Alma L. Moldenke, *Plants of the Bible* (Mineola, NY: Dover, 1952), 137.

15. Keel, *Song*, 257–60.

16. Munro, *Spikenard*, 81; Robert Alter, *Strong as Death Is Love: The Song of Songs, Ruth, Esther, Jonah, and Daniel: A Translation with Commentary* (New York: Norton, 2015), 46.

## Guiding Home to Mama's House (8:1-4)

From her flight of imagination to a blissful garden love retreat, the woman comes back down to earth or, rather, a different kind of earth that is in fact less earthy, less intimately linked with the land. She comes back to the city, specifically "outside" on its streets and inside the "house" where she dwells (Song 8:1-2).[17] And she does not plan to be alone; rather, she hopes to find her lover in the street and bring him home (as in 3:4). As much as the woman took the lead in compelling the man to "go out" into the fruitful fields, she now aims to guide him "into the house" (8:2). She continues, as Robert Alter remarks, "play[ing] an unabashedly active role."[18] But she's under no illusions that this dual-site (street/house) urban venture will go as smoothly as the private country excursion, given the complicating presence of other parties, particularly three close relations: "brother," "mother," and "daughters of Jerusalem" or girlfriends (8:1-4).

First, the woman mentions her brother in an unexpected context involving her lover on the city streets. She wishes that he, her beloved, "were *like a brother* to me" (Song 8:1). The last thing a modern guy wants to hear from the girl he loves is that she thinks of him as a "brother"; little brother or big brother makes no difference. They are equally deflating. For the Songstress, however, this reflects no diminution of their romantic relationship, still less an indication of some latent incest desire. Like him calling her "my sister, my bride" (4:9-10, 11; 5:1-2), her imagining him as a "brother" speaks of conventional closeness and familiarity. But in the present case it also evokes a sense of propriety in that no one would give a second thought to a sister giving her natural brother a kiss of greeting. The Song woman, however, remains worried that any public affection she might show her beloved would draw not merely second glances but sharp looks of opprobrium, like those directed toward a prostitute who "now in the street, now in the squares . . . seizes [the man] and kisses him" (Prov 7:12-13).[19] She would be "despised" (בוז) or held in contempt, especially by the neighbors, friends, and family who know who her real brothers are (Song 8:1).[20] In truth, it might be her real brothers she is most

---

17. While חוץ can have the more general meaning of "outside" (NRSV, NIV), it also denotes the more particular location of "street," which is preferable in Song 8:1 (NJPS, CEB); see Exum, *Song*, 242, 246–47; Falk, *Song*, poem 25 (no pagination); Fishbane, *Song*, 199.

18. Alter, *Strong as Death*, 48.

19. See Bloch and Bloch, *Song*, 209; Bergant, *Song*, 92.

20. See Prov 11:12; 14:21; 23:22; 30:17 on neighbor and family "despising."

concerned about, these "angry" sons of her mother who have mistreated her and sought to thwart the thriving of "her own vineyard" (1:6). As they affected the woman's life and her pursuit of love at the beginning of the Song, these brothers will have more to say about the love life of their "little sister" in the final stanza (8:8-9). But for now, the woman seems aware of their continuing contempt, perhaps wishing for their replacement by a true brother who will love and protect her. Along this line, she may also imply a subtle challenge to her lover to play his brother role more effectively. Recall the precariousness of the city streets for the woman when searching for her absent lover who abandoned her (5:6-7).

Second, the woman invokes her mother in relation, first, to her brother-lover and, then, to "the house of my mother" (Song 8:1-2). She enhances the close fraternal bond she wishes others would accept for her lover by picturing him as an infant who "nursed at [her] mother's breast"—perhaps even nursing with him herself like a twin (8:1).[21] This image is of a baby boy in a happy and contented state, blissfully innocent and secure, far from angry and contemptible, violent and flighty. Not that the woman wants to infantilize or dominate her brother-lover, but she does envision a warm, gentle, nurturing connection amid the heat of passion.[22] She may also imagine her lover's erstwhile feeding at her mother's breast "as a kind of prolepsis of kissing or sucking the breast of his beloved," that is, of the woman herself.[23] She indeed anticipates offering the man her "spiced wine to drink, the juice of my pomegranates" (8:2), which may allude in part to her delectable breasts. Moreover, the words "I would kiss you" (אשקך, *ʾeshaqeka*, 8:1) and "I would give you to drink" (אשקך, *ʾashqeka*, 8:2) are suggestively homophonic, furthering the gustatory intimacy of their lovemaking.[24]

21. Chana Bloch and Ariel Bloch write, "the Shulamite wants to be as close to her lover as if they were nursing together at their mother's breasts" (*The Song of Songs: The World's First Great Love Poem* [New York: Modern Library, 1995], 209).

22. See Brett Beavers, Kimberly Perry, Neil Perry, and Reid Perry, "Hip to My Heart," The Band Perry, Republic Nashville, 2009. A surprising, unwitting, yet delightful, parallel to the Songstress' reference to her lover as "brother" comes in this song from the popular contemporary country group The Band Perry: "can't even fall for some other man, 'cause brother-man, you know how to get hip to my heart." As it happens, this band is comprised of a sibling trio, who wrote the song together with Brett Beavers and recorded it with sister Kimberly as lead vocalist. Other lyrics in this jaunty tune suggest further resonances with the biblical Song.

23. Alter, *Strong as Death*, 47.

24. Dianne Bergant, *The Song of Songs*, Berit Olam (Collegeville, MN: Liturgical Press, 2001), 93; Roland E. Murphy, *The Song of Songs*, Hermeneia (Minneapolis: Fortress, 1990), 184; Bloch and Bloch, *Song*, 210–11.

While the woman would like the freedom to kiss her lover in public, she's no exhibitionist. As in Song 3:4, she aims to enjoy the most intimate pleasures of love in her mother's house to which she would bring her lover. This arrangement reverses the more typical cultural process where the man brings his lover/bride to *his* mother's residence, as when Isaac brought Rebekah "into his mother Sarah's tent" (Gen 24:67).[25] The present setting is as much about safety as intimacy, since the home of the Song woman's mother is "the place of security *par excellence* . . . in contrast to the city streets."[26] In distinction from Song 3:4, the focus on the mother's house does *not* reach further into the bed "chamber of the one who bore [or conceived] me," though some Hebrew manuscripts and the LXX, which is followed by the NRSV, incorporate this phrase in 8:2 to harmonize with 3:4. But the MT reading, "[where] she/you would *teach* [למד] me," makes good sense as it stands, though the subject can either be the mother ("she") or the lover ("you") the woman addresses. Most likely, the woman refers to maternal instruction, though not necessarily focused, as many commentators assume, on the fine arts of lovemaking.[27] However typical such mother-daughter tutelage might be in preparation for a young woman's wedding night, the passionate female protagonist of the Song already appears well versed in amorous activity in advance of any marriage plans. In her commanding mode, she needs no additional advice from mother or lover. More generally, however, beyond the narrow curriculum of "sex education," the woman longs for the comprehensive nurture of her mother's haven home, refreshing and sustaining her amid the challenges of a precarious outside world. Psalm 25, focusing on the Lord's covenantal care and "steadfast love" for Israel, demonstrates the broad formative, palliative, and protective nature of sage teaching (למד).

> Make me to know your ways, O Lord;
>> teach [למד] me your paths.
> Lead me in your truth, and teach [למד] me.
>> for you are the God of my salvation;
>> for you I wait all day long. . . .

25. Bloch and Bloch, *Song*, 210.
26. Munro, *Spikenard*, 70.
27. Alter, *Strong as Death*, 48; Bergant, *Song*, 93; Bloch and Bloch, *Song*, 210; Francis Landy, *Paradoxes of Paradise: Identity and Difference in the Song of Songs*, 2nd ed. (Sheffield: Sheffield Phoenix, 2011), 94, 246. Naomi's preparation of Ruth for her amorous visit to Boaz at the threshing floor provides something of a model (Ruth 3:1-5).

He leads the humble in what is right,
   and teaches [למד] the humble his way.
All the paths of the LORD are steadfast love and faithfulness (Ps 25: 4-5, 9-10).

Third, the woman issues her final adjuration to her friends, the "daughters of Jerusalem," not to disturb the lovemaking that she envisions, as in 2:6-7, in tight embrace in her lover's hands and arms. Both scenes are set in a "house," though the former was a "house of wine" (2:5), closely associated with the outdoor love nest to which the man had brought the woman,[28] while the present locale is the "house of my mother" (8:2) to which the woman brings the man. Together, however, the scenes reinforce the reciprocal balance of the couple's love and the bridge between countryside and city they seek to forge. Other distinctions in 8:4 from the prior adjurations in 2:7 and 3:5 involve the omission of the animal witnesses "by the gazelles and wild does" and a tilt to a more interrogative form of a negation with the use of "why" (מה), suggesting: "Why would you disturb love before it pleases? Of course, you wouldn't!"

The absence of animals suits the exclusively botanical imagery of the present stanza and hints at a more personal, informal plea to the woman's girlfriends.[29] At this latter stage of the Song, there's no need to stand on legal ceremony; she can speak from the heart directly to her female friends without invoking external witnesses. Similarly, the shift to "why" may strike a more positive and playful tone, on the order of: "Why in the world would you come into my mother's home and disrupt my lover and me, when you've seen how much I love him, even though he's not been perfect, and how much he loves me? Of course, you'll leave us be—and I'll tell you all about it later!" Still, the woman has not become so secure in her relationship with her city friends as to simply assume they would let her be without her swearing reminder. She continues to sense some hesitancy in their support of her love life, whether out of concern for her well-being or twinges of jealousy or even disapprobation. In any case, some tension among the women still percolates beneath the surface.

28. See discussion on 1:12–2:7, pp. 26–27, 31–39.
29. Interestingly, the only "animal" in the scene may be the man! In the woman's statement, "I will lead (נהג) you to my mother's house," the verb carries the force of "drive," as with cattle or other herd animals (see Gen 31:18; 1 Sam 23:5; 2 Kgs 4:24); hence, she may be suggesting to her lover: "I will drive/herd you like a bull to my mother's house."

# Song of Songs 8:5-14

## *The Love Song That Never Ends*

The jarring transition from the adjuration "Do not disturb us in my mother's house" (Song 8:3-4) to the observation that someone is "coming up from the wilderness" (8:5) is just as awkward as the almost identical move from 3:4-5 to 3:6. In both cases, the sense of narrative progression in the Song that I have tried to develop admittedly breaks down. The principal differences between the two sections concern who is speaking and "who" (מי) is "coming" (3:6; 8:5). Earlier the woman alerted her friends to the approach of Solomon's wedding carriage on the horizon (3:6-7); now the friends report about the couple's romantic journey home from the wilderness with the woman "leaning upon her beloved" (8:5a). Whom the friends are addressing is not clear, but the woman hears their question and takes it as her cue to speak directly to her lover (8:5b-7).

The lyrics that ensue through the end of the Song, while resonant with what has come before, are no bland recapitulation. With the woman singing the lead part as she did in the Song's opening stanza, the paean to love soars to a swelling crescendo befitting a grand climactic finale.

- The highest note extols *the creational cosmic force of love*, "strong as death" and hotter than any fire known to nature; in its purest, most passionate form that the woman desires, love *cannot be extinguished* (8:5b-7a).

*Song of Songs 8:5-14*

**[D → W (?)]**

⁵Who is that coming up from the
  wilderness,
    leaning on her beloved?

**[W → M]**

Under the apple tree I awakened
  you.
There your mother was in labor
  with you;
    there she who bore you was in
    labor.
⁶Set me as a seal upon your
  heart,
    as a seal upon your arm;
for love is strong as death
  passion fierce as the grave.

Its flashes are flashes of fire,
  a raging flame.
⁷Many waters cannot quench love,
  neither can floods drown it.
If one offered for love
  all the wealth of one's house
  it would be utterly scorned.

**[W → D (?)]**

⁸We have a little sister,
  and she has no breasts.
What shall we do for our sister,
  on the day when she is spoken
    for?
⁹If she is a wall,
  we will build upon her a battle-
    ment of silver;

- In a similar, though slightly less elevated fashion, the woman also praises *the social and economic price of love* or rather its priceless value, beyond "all the wealth of one's house," even if that house belongs to the renowned Solomon (8:7b-12)! In a world where almost everything is for barter or sale, love stands apart: it *cannot be exchanged*.

- Finally, after a philosophical as well as emotional (the two can go together) assessment of the surpassing power and worth of love,[1] a closing couplet softens the tone with a plea for more intimate connection between the two lovers, *the personal and romantic pleasure of love* (8:13-14). But the outcome is left teasingly and frustratingly open, with signs of anxiety and tension still evident, not so much between the couple as from outside interferers. In any event, it

---

1. Concerning the unique philosophical and pedagogical thrust of Song 8:6-7, J. Cheryl Exum assesses these verses as "the Song's only didactic pronouncement" or "succinct credo on the subject of love" (*Song of Songs*, OTL [Louisville: Westminster John Knox, 2005], 249); similarly, Michael V. Fox regards this text as "the highpoint of the poem, its moment of greatest generality, where it draws a conclusion from the particular experience it has been portraying. Only here does the poet draw an explicit lesson or make an abstract pronouncement" (*The Song of Songs and the Ancient Egyptian Love Songs* [Madison: University of Wisconsin Press, 1985], 168).

But if she is a door,
we will enclose her with boards
of cedar.
<sup>10</sup>I was a wall,
and my breasts were like towers;
then I was in his eyes
as one who brings peace.
<sup>11</sup>Solomon had a vineyard at Baal-
hamon;
he entrusted the vineyard to
keepers;
each one was to bring for its
fruit a thousand pieces
of silver.
<sup>12</sup>My vineyard, my very own, is for

myself
you, O Solomon, may have the
thousand,
and the keepers of the fruit two
hundred!
**[M → W]**
<sup>13</sup>O you who dwell in the gardens,
my companions are listening
for your voice;
let me hear it.
**[W → M]**
<sup>14</sup>Make haste, my beloved,
and be like a gazelle
or a young stag
upon the mountains of spices!

remains painfully clear that love *cannot be expedited*. It will run its own course, exert its own will, carry its own tune. What else should we expect from such a powerful force?

While the woman dominates this final scene, with her lover (on whom she is "leaning") playing a strong supporting part, other figures fill out the picture.

- The woman's girlfriend chorus, the daughters of Jerusalem (8:5a)
- The woman's brothers (8:8-9)
- The man's mother (8:5b)
- The man's companions (possibly) (8:13)
- Solomon in historical rather than fictional guise (8:11-12)
- Solomon's vineyard workers (8:11-12)

The stage is rather crowded, appropriate to a closing curtain call, before ultimately ceding the spotlight to the focal couple. But, as noted above, as much as the lovers desire to be alone to enjoy the fruit of their love in undisturbed peace, and as much as the natural world supports their passionate pursuits, the human environment is not always so hospitable.

## Love That Cannot Be Extinguished (8:5-7a)

The women of Jerusalem, while perhaps focusing most intently on their companion who immediately answers them, in fact address a general audience of hearers and readers, drawing our special attention a final time to the processing couple.[2] Though no ceremony is in view here, the picture may evoke a type of wedding march, where all eyes turn to the approaching bride and/or groom. The present scene envisions the couple walking together in close embrace, with the woman leaning[3] on her beloved—his arm around her?—or, alternatively but less likely, lying on him in a recumbent posture, say, in a palanquin like that featured in Song 3:6-11 when the groom comes in his carriage to collect his bride.[4] In any event, we see the couple coming together now, as if in a final movie clip, from the "wilderness" or "desert" (מדבר), which includes the fertile countryside but pushes farther outside the city limits into more remote and barren terrain. A notable distance from and dissonance with conventional, settled society continues to mark our lovers' situation. They're never completely at ease, fully at home, in the capital city. Associations with Solomon's carriage and court remain figments of their imagination, acts of audacious, even subtly contemptuous, role-playing in full awareness of how far removed they are from the real thing.[5]

Awkwardly, as noted above, but not altogether irrelevantly, the woman breaks in with impassioned speech to the man. If we stay with the motion picture idea, it's as if the director makes a swift cut from the chorus' query—"Who is that coming?" (Song 8:5)—to the couple's trek from the wilderness; or, better perhaps, the question is heard in the background as a voice-over calling attention to the approaching travelers. Along the

---

2. Exum (*Song*, 248–49) observes, "By having the women of Jerusalem speak at this point, the poet once again reminds us of the presence of an audience, onlookers who participate in the unfolding of the lovers' relationship, and so encourages the readers' involvement. We not only look, with them, to see the lovers approaching from the steppe, we also listen."

3. Von Hans Ausloos and Bénédicte Lemmelijn ("Eine neue interpretation des Hoheliedes 8,5ab," *ZAW* 119 [2007]: 556–63) propose emending the verb רפק ("lean") used only here in the Hebrew Bible, inverting the first two letters (metathesis) to the more common פרק ("tear away, tear off"). The resulting meaning in Song 8:5 would be: "Who is she, coming up out of the desert, *breaking free* (*losreißend*) after her lover?" Emendations, of course, remain speculative, and the picture of the woman walking together and "leaning on" her beloved makes adequate sense in the present context without adjustment.

4. Exum, *Song*, 248.

5. See below on 8:11-12, pp. 222–25.

way, the lovers come to a fruitful patch that the woman recognizes as one of their favorite trysting sites, a monumental apple tree (had they carved their names on its trunk or left a makeshift "banner"? see 2:3-5). The memory of love is strong, and the woman can't help but prompt the man: "Remember how I aroused you right here, under this very tree!" (my paraphrase, 8:5).[6] But not only that. She also reminds her lover that this is the same place where his mother "conceived" him. The NRSV reads "there she who bore you was in labor" (8:5 so also LXX, Vg., NIV, NASB, KJV, CEB), but the act of sex and conception suits the text and context better than labor/birth. The verb (חבל) can mean "conceive" or "get pregnant" as well as "travail in labor" or "give birth," and the ground under an apple tree, while apt for al fresco lovemaking, was hardly an ideal birthing place. Hence the NAB rendering is preferable: "Beneath the apple tree I awakened you; there your mother conceived you; there she who bore you conceived" (also NJPS).[7]

Now for many men, thoughts of their mother's sex life, particularly in conceiving them, would seriously dampen the amorous mood! But the point here is more broadly reflective and connective than immediately active and consummative. The woman is not proposing that they stop and have sex again under this love tree here and now; still less does she want to conceive a child. Rather, she takes delightful notice of this sweet and safe spot where, first, her lover's mother and, more recently, she herself have freely expressed their sexuality in relation to the beloved male. She takes pleasure in the bond she has with this maternal figure who,

---

6. In Song 8:5, the woman employs the same verb (עור) positively to describe the "arousing" of her lover that she uses negatively in pleading with the Jerusalem daughters ("Do not arouse/disturb [our] love," 2:7; 3:5; 8:4).

7. See Exum, *Song*, 243, 249; Fox, *Song*, 167–68; Robert Alter, *Strong as Death Is Love: The Song of Songs, Ruth, Esther, Jonah, and Daniel: A Translation with Commentary* (New York: Norton, 2015), 49; Michael Fishbane, *Song of Songs*, JPS Bible Commentary (Lincoln: University of Nebraska Press, 2015), 206. However, while Marvin H. Pope grants that חבל can mean "conceive" apart from the birthing process (as Ps 7:14 clearly indicates), he also notes the prevailing myths of divine/heroic births under trees, like Apollo and Artemis under palm trees and Romulus and Remus under a fig tree. He thus leaves open various options in Song 8:5: "The repetition of the verb [חבל] could refer to the same phase of the generative process, or to different phases, i.e., to conception in both instances, or travail in both, or to conception in the former instance and travail in the latter. Without knowledge of the affair in question, one can only speculate" (*Song of Songs: A New Translation with Introduction and Commentary*, AB 7C [Garden City, NY: Doubleday, 1977], 663-64). Nevertheless, though the Songstress can think of the man as her "hero," she is more concerned with making love with him than giving birth to his child.

like her, "spent time dallying in the countryside."[8] Though obviously involved in the conceiving act, once again the man's father receives no mention (see also 3:11). Instead, she celebrates such open space where *women* choose to "conceive" and "arouse" as *they* desire.

Though not desiring sex at this moment, the woman does urge her man to "seal" his love for her with a most engaging and enduring commitment: "Set me as a seal upon your heart; as a seal upon your arm" (Song 8:6a). The wording here is important. A seal was a personal insignia typically engraved on a small cylinder strung on a necklace hanging next to the heart or a ring or bracelet worn on the arm or finger, and it represented the principal form of ID in the ancient world. Among other things, it would be used as a security stamp to authenticate legal documents detailing one's possessions. The seal or signet ring constituted a virtual extension of the *self* in society. The woman in the Song does not ask the man, however, to set *his* seal on *her*, as if marking her as his own, his commodity to do with as he pleases. She envisions *herself as the seal* she wants him to impress on his heart and arm—not a tattoo of her name or a picture of her, which is but another mark of presumed ownership, but her whole identity, her very self (she *is* the seal, remember) merging with his.[9] She's not losing or surrendering her identity or self to his; neither is she asking him to deny himself. This is a win-win proposition, the two becoming a stronger *one* together.

Once again, the Tamar scene in Gen 38 provides a suggestive intertext. While on a business trip, the patriarch Judah hands over his "signet and cord" (38:18), his official seal functioning like a credit card in this case, as surety to his childless, twice-widowed daughter-in-law Tamar, whom he doesn't recognize but rather takes to be a prostitute. Wisely, she keeps Judah's ID after he propositions and sleeps with her, which she later uses to prove that he is the father of the twins she's carrying. Though the story ends as well as can be expected, with Judah acknowledging Tamar's "righteous" action and his abusive behavior toward her (Gen 38:26), first, by not providing his third son to marry her and, then, by impregnating her, it hardly constitutes an ideal love story. The Song woman also watches out for herself and protects herself against identity theft through male possessiveness. But from her strong, stately palm tree (*tamar*) position (Song 7:7-8), she aims for more proactive than reactive control of her life. The Genesis Tamar had no choice but to make

---

8. Exum, *Song*, 249.

9. Exum (*Song*, 250) writes, "she longs to be as close to him, as intimately bound up with his identity, as his seal might be."

the best of a bad situation, and she did so admirably. But our woman stakes her identity claim up front. She's happy, even hungry, to entwine her life with her lover's, but she insists on doing it on her own terms, on sealing her own deal.

From the wellspring of this longing for mutual self-sharing, the woman draws her most profound analysis of love in relation to death and fire, the most powerful forces of nature: love is "strong as death" and fierce as "a raging flame" (Song 8:6). Her fiery language appears to mount in intensity toward a conflagration. The last four words of 8:6 may be tracked: (1) its [love's]-fire-bolt → (2) fire-bolts (3) of-fire → (4) raging-inferno.[10] The rendering "fire-bolt" for רֶשֶׁף captures the devastating, bellicose associations of the term with lightning bolts, like those that strike down Egypt's cattle in the Exodus plagues (Ps 78:48) and flaming arrows as "weapons of war" (Ps 76:3).[11] Martial imagery is nothing new in the Song, but heretofore it has been used to typify the man's secure position (3:6-11) and, more often, the woman's stalwart character and defensive prowess, standing proud and firm against unwanted advances (4:4; 6:4, 10; 7:4), though she can also hold her lover "captive" when she desires (7:5). Now, however, the woman expresses her embroilment in a pitched battle where she, together with all humanity, finds herself at once both vigorous and vulnerable.

In the face of mortality that defeats all sooner or later and threatens to cast its dark shadow of vanity on all of life's pursuits, as Qoheleth voices so poignantly (see Eccl 3:19-22; 6:1-11; 9:10 ), love proves to be the most worthy match for death, thereby redeeming our fragile existence with meaning, fulfillment, rapture, and transcendence. Yet, as Cheryl Exum rightly insists, the woman makes no comparative claim that love is stronger than death and will inevitably win out in the end.[12] The battlefield may be littered with casualties from both sides. Love, remember, has its

---

10. Noting this intensifying progression, see Fishbane, *Song*, 207; Alter, *Strong as Death*, 50. Alter ends the sequence with "fearsome flame," KJV renders it "most vehement flame," and it is "blazing flame" in NRSV, NJPS.

11. Francis Brown, S.R. Driver, and Charles A. Briggs, *The New Brown, Driver, Briggs, Gesenius Hebrew and English Lexicon: With an Appendix Containing the Biblical Aramaic* (Peabody, MA: Hendrickson, 1979), 958.

12. Exum, *Song*, 251; also Carey Ellen Walsh (*Exquisite Desire: Religion, the Erotic, and the Song of Songs* [Minneapolis: Fortress, 2000], 165) asserts, "But in this comparison, love does not conquer death. It is a worthy contender, to be sure, but not victor. Hence, the verse [Song 8:6] is not simply a celebration of the power of love, for this would privilege the love of the comparison, while ignoring, for the moment, its paired complement, death."

own formidable arsenal of fire bolts and arrows. Indeed, the comparison of love with ("as/like") death attests to the former's potential for lethal action, that is, to love's explosive, death-dealing force that refuses to surrender to mortal control. The melding of the lovers' bodies, hearts, minds, and identities, for all its potential joys, also threatens the "dissolution of the self,"[13] the "loss of autonomy or control, and annihilation or loss of self,"[14] a total surrender of personal agency. But what a way to go, eh? Maybe, but by no means a cheap way. It might well cost you everything you have and are!

The woman stokes the death-like strength of love's firepower with reference to waterworks (Song 8:7a). Again, hydraulic imagery has been frequently employed in the Song, but usually to enhance the lush, paradisiacal flow of lovemaking. Now, however, she conjures the surging energy of "many waters" and great "rivers" flooding in against love's fiery blaze, and in this case, love does win! Love's incredible power for life and death cannot be drowned or diluted. It will burn eternally, one way or another, along its volatile continuum, in turns igniting, energizing, inflaming, and incinerating everything and everyone in its path.

This perpetual contest of life and death, love and dissolution, marks the way not only of the Song couple and all human beings but also of the entire world in which fire and water comprise such vital and volatile elements. The springtime budding of fruits and flowers celebrated throughout the Song evidences the cyclical sprouting of fresh life from winter's burial ground. The woman's awareness of this natural environment overarching and intersecting the couple's personal worlds extends into transcendent cosmic horizons through multiple allusions to multicultural mythological figures.[15]

---

13. Exum (*Song*, 251) glosses the idea of dissolution in positive terms: "Losing oneself in another in the act of love can seem like a transcending of mortality." Francis Landy (*Paradoxes of Paradise: Identity and Difference in the Song of Songs*, 2nd ed. [Sheffield: Sheffield Phoenix, 2011], 118, 123) adds, "Love threatens dissolution in the other—who represents all others—Death is the dissolution of consciousness. . . . The divine flame burns in the dissolution of Sheol; it alone authenticates existence as YHWH, the inexhaustible spark of life. The love of the lovers thus returns us to the beginning of creation."

14. Walsh, *Exquisite Desire*, 167.

15. See Aren M. Wilson-Wright, "Love Conquers All: Song of Songs 8:6b-7a as a Reflex of the Northwest Semitic Combat Myth," *JBL* 134 (2015): 333–45.

| Term | Basic Meaning | Mythological Figure | Cultural Context |
|------|---------------|---------------------|------------------|
| מות | Death | Mot | Canaanite |
| שאול | Grave, Pit, Underworld | Sheol | Hebrew |
| רשף | Fire, Fire-bolt, Flame | Resheph | Ugaritic, Syrian, Egyptian |
| שלהבתיה | Raging Fire/Flame or Flame of Yah | Yah(weh) | Hebrew |
| מים | Sea(s), Waters | Yam(m) | Canaanite, Phoenician |

The personification of Death, the Underworld (place of the dead), and the Sea were commonplace in antiquity—all representing ominous primordial realms of deep, dark chaos pitted against the salutary forces of life, light, and love. These are the cosmic enemies of Love, which takes on its own virtual mythological identity in the present text. Love is more than a feeling or even a passion, more than a concept or even a noble idea. Love is more like a formidable force of nature with immense potential for positive as well as negative energy. Love is more like Fire!

Here, too, emerges a mythological link between the Hebrew term for "fire-bolt" and the ancient Near Eastern war deity Resheph, commonly depicted with weaponry (firepower) in both hands and sometimes with headgear of a gazelle or other staglike figure.[16] His flaming spears or darts have none of the cute features of Eros or Cupid's love arrows, though these can also severely wound. This gazelle is charging ahead in determined battle, not flitting about the countryside and peeping into girls' windows (Song 2:8-9, 17; 8:14). Recall, however, from our discussion of the adjuration formula in 2:7 (also 3:5) that the Hebrew term for female "gazelles" (צבאות, *ṣebᵓaoth*) may evoke the Lord God Almighty or Lord God of Hosts—attended, that is, by angelic, militant "hosts" (צבאות, *ṣebᵓaoth*). Generally in the Hebrew Bible, the *resheph* figure or idea represents one

16. On the ancient Resheph deity, see John H. Choi, "Resheph and YHWH Sebaᵓot," *VT* 54 (2004): 17–28; P. Xella, "Resheph," in *Dictionary of Deities and Demons in the Bible*, 2nd ed., ed. Karel van der Toorn, Bob Becking, and Pieter van der Horst (Leiden: Brill, 1999), 700–703; Lowell K. Handy, "Resheph," *ABD* V: 678–79.

of the "personifications of the scourges" or "malevolent spirits, which accompany God in his destructive action" (see Deut 32:24; Job 5:7; Ps 78:8).[17] And, of course, the biblical God may be manifest in fearsome displays of fiery power for purposes of both revelation and judgment, as events at Mount Sinai and Mount Carmel vividly attest (Exod 3:1-6; 19:16-25; Deut 4:11-15, 24; 5:22-25; 1 Kgs 18:2-40; Heb 12:18-20, 29).

The special divine name YHWH disclosed to Moses via the burning bush also carries inflammatory nuances and infernal sparks in the Song's unique term שלהבתיה, *shalhebetya*, which modifies *resheph* at the end of Song 8:6. The יה suffix attached to שלהבת, denoting a life-consuming "flame," such as the Lord God's "blazing flame" of judgment (Job 15:30; Ezek 20:47), may represent a theological descriptor, "the Flame of Yah[weh]," or a theophoric intensifier, "raging flame." The latter seems more strictly correct, since the Song never invokes Israel's God in any direct sense. But the overall cosmic mythological picture the woman paints in 8:6-7 alludes to Resheph and Yah(weh) as titanic partners with Love enmeshed in universal conflict with forces of Death, the Underworld, and the Deep. In the New Testament, the supreme essence of the deity is Love: "God *is* love [ἀγάπη]" (1 John 4:16). In the Hebrew Bible, God is also characterized by love (אהבה, *'ahabah*). But such love is by no means a meek, mushy quality. Note especially the pronouncement of the prophet Zephaniah, paralleling the Lord's combatant and compassionate sides: "The LORD, your God, is in your midst, a warrior who gives victory; he will rejoice over you with gladness, he will renew you in his love [אהבה]" (Zeph 3:17; see Jer 31:3; Hos 11:4).[18]

As the woman compares love with death and fire in military and cosmic senses, she also forges an intense emotional connection between these elements and passion (note the parallel similes: "love is as strong as death, passion fierce as the grave"; Song 8:6). The "passion" term (קנאה) is unique in the Song and more typically refers in the Bible to "zeal" or, more specifically, to "jealousy" (ζῆλος, LXX), both of people and of God: "I the LORD your God am a jealous [קנא] God" (Exod 20:5). Jealousy

---

17. Xella, "Resheph," 703; Choi, "Resheph," 20.

18. Wilson-Wright ("Love Conquers All," 343, 345) concludes, "Through the use of an inherited Northwest Semitic formula and [combat] mythic language, Song 8:6b-7a identifies love with the victorious divine warrior. Like YHWH and Baal, love tangles with Death and Sea and proves an equal match for both opponents. . . . the Song identifies love with the most powerful force in the Israelite imagination—YHWH, the divine warrior."

closely aligns with fiery passion: "For the LORD your God is a devouring fire, a jealous God" (Deut 4:24). It teeters on the sharp edge of a positive possessiveness or unreserved loyalty to a loved one and a negative peevishness or outright hostility to anything or anyone perceived as threatening the exclusive love bond. In Wisdom thought, jealousy is typically indicted for its destructive wrath-inducing, "bone-rotting" effect on human relations (Prov 6:34; 14:30; 27:4). Although not using the "jealousy" term, the story of Cain and Abel represents the primordial case of jealousy: Cain explodes in murderous rage because Abel has garnered the Lord's prime approval that Cain jealously thought was his exclusive right. As noted above, in contrast to the Song woman and man's mutually submissive "desire" (תשׁוקה, Song 7:10), Cain's "desire" (Gen 4:6) reflects its most selfish, sinful, obsessive, and destructive tendencies.

So why does the woman now invoke jealousy as a partner with both love and the grave? Is it simply to reinforce the ferocity of love's hold on one's life, for good and ill? Or does it speak to a more particular and more targeted experience typical of this emotion? Jealousy does not usually manifest as some vague sense of insecurity but rather as a sharp feeling *against* someone or something that jeopardizes the tight bond between someone and his or her beloved. So who or what triggers the woman's jealousy? Michael V. Fox focuses on social context: "The interfering and threatening party presupposed by her warning must be society conceived generally, including any outside party who might try to interfere, as have her brothers and the watchmen."[19] Detecting less social tension here and across the Song, Exum sticks with a more existential reading befitting the comparison with death/grave: "Nothing in the poem has suggested that these things [brothers, watchmen, society] pose a real threat to love. There is no sense of insecurity about love in the Song. . . . For the Song of Songs, love's ultimate rival is mortality . . . death's ineluctable claim on the loved one."[20]

I prefer to amalgamate (with qualifications) rather than adjudicate these interpretive options. Throughout this commentary, while not denying elements of playful teasing between the couple, on the one hand, and between the woman and her girlfriends, on the other hand, I have taken seriously various threats to the lovers' relationship mounted by the woman's brothers and the city's guards and even occasionally hinted at

19. Fox, *Song*, 170.
20. Exum, *Song*, 253.

by the Jerusalem daughters and the beloved man himself. The woman's mention of "one's house" at the end of Song 8:7, together with her reflection on her brothers' attitudes in 8:8-9, maintains some sense of extended family tension surrounding the couple. The lovers' bond may be strong, but it isn't entirely secure and it certainly isn't invincible. The specter of death looms over everyone's love life ('til death do us part); even if both lovers die simultaneously or virtually so, like Romeo and Juliet, there will be no continuity of love in Sheol. If one lover predeceases the other, the survivor is left bereft in the present life and hopeless in the shadowy postmortem realm.

Higher mortality rates in antiquity only exacerbate this angst. In the Song the social and existential spurs of the woman's jealousy converge with particular force on the brothers and watchmen. She shows no real signs of classic jealousy toward other women, including her girlfriends, though they seem to show some jealousy of her! She may well be jealous, however, of these *men's* power over her life and not least her love life. This is a power granted by a patriarchal society that can include a malevolent power to take her life and/or the life of her beloved. In exposing her brothers' anger toward her (Song 1:6), the woman does not specify how they expressed it; but given the all-too-common patterns of family abuse, then and now, we may reasonably infer some violent action as well as vituperative speech. Of course, the Songstress does report the watchmen's stripping, beating, and wounding her, perhaps within an inch of her life, as she was searching for her lover (5:6-7). For all its idyllic beauty and ecstasy, the world of the Poem retains a shadowy remnant of the rough and perilous real world women must negotiate.[21]

Remarkably, however, these vestiges of jealous insecurity, including prospects of violence and death, do not dampen the woman's enthusiasm for love; she is no cynical pessimist on the order of Qoheleth. But neither is she a naïve optimist. She knows what and whom she's up against in her struggle for love, and she's knows Love's—like Death's—potential to swallow her whole. And yet she makes the choice to dive in anyway. At this point, a critical feminist hermeneutic asks the hard question: Can, to say nothing yet of should, a woman freely choose to surrender herself wholly to a beloved person or cause, to consent to the "dissolution" of her very self to another power? Does such "choice" not inher-

---

21. Though some hint of nature's threat may attend the reference to mountain lions and leopards in Song 4:8, overall in the Song the natural world is in harmony with the lovers. The disharmony and dysfunction come from the human—primarily masculine—environment.

ently prove to be self-defeating, a choosing to give up choice, autonomy, and agency? Is such "choice" not necessarily coerced by some external force, rather than truly chosen? And accordingly, ought not—here the "should" issue inevitably presses in—such coercion be resisted as much as possible? Surely we must question Dido's choice of suicide as the only or best response to her beloved Aeneas' journey to Carthage.[22] But we keep being pulled back to the crux of the matter: Is it in fact possible for anyone—female or male—ultimately to resist the cosmic colossi of Love and Death? Is resistance futile, a mere myth in the popular sense of the term? Such philosophical, metaphysical queries defy precise resolution, even as they merit serious reflection. To the credit of the Song, especially in its female voice, it prefers complex analysis over cheap answers.

## Love That Cannot Be Exchanged (8:7b-12)

Although continuing in the same vein of touting love's preeminence, the woman shifts from comparative images of firepower and death to those of financial value, from matters of strength to those of worth. In this case, however, it's not a fair fight. While Love and Death may be evenly matched powers, Love is unequivocally superior in value to Mammon, to borrow the semi-divine Aramaic term for Wealth/Money used by Jesus (Matt 6:24; Luke 16:13). Indeed, anybody who tries to purchase love, even if he were to offer "all the wealth of his house" is destined to be "utterly scorned" (Song 8:7b). Love is not for sale to the highest bidder; it is not a commodity or a medium of exchange on any level. Like Wisdom, Love, which is a feminine noun in Hebrew, is "better than silver . . . better than gold . . . more precious than jewels, and nothing you can desire can compare with her" (Prov 3:14-15). The word for "scorn," applied to the fool who dares to think he can buy love with his estate in Song 8:7b, is the same Hebrew term rendered "despise" in 8:1 (בוז), reflecting critical public opinion concerning the couple's more-than-brotherly love. While, on the one hand, the woman seeks refuge in her mother's house (8:1) and spurns the scorn of a disapproving society including that of her biological brothers who want to control her life and keep unapproved brothers-in-law out of their house, on the other hand, she heaps scorn on any who aim to use their household prosperity and authority to manage her life, especially her love life (8:7b). She and the Love she both serves

---

22. I owe the Dido reference to Walsh (*Exquisite Desire*, 166). Her entire chapter on "Passion Fierce as the Grave: Death and Desire" (159–84) brims with stimulating insight.

and gives will not be owned by anyone. We may add to the love banner spanning the couple in bold print: NOT FOR SALE!

It doesn't matter how tightly the kinship ties bind, as with the brothers, or how abundantly the riches overflow, as with the historical Solomon, the woman in the Song resolutely refuses to be bound or bought. In general oration, somewhat like a soliloquy spoken to a wide audience (virtually all hearers/readers), probably including the beloved man and the "daughters of Jerusalem" companions within the Poem's world, the woman addresses in turn the power dynamics related first to her brothers (Song 8:8-10) and second to Solomon (8:11-12).

First, she channels her brothers' earlier deliberations about her future, specifically, how they fretted over their "little sister's" prospects for marriage in her prepubescent state, before her breasts had developed. While the emotional tenor of the brothers' concern in this case appears gentler than their anger toward the girl reported in Song 1:6, their demeanor is no less controlling and domineering. They assume patriarchal authority on behalf of their (deceased?) father to arrange "*our* sister's" marriage for the social and economic benefit of the household more than for her personal fulfillment (8:8). Just as they put her to work in their vineyards to the neglect of her "own vineyard" (1:6), representing both, literally, her employment in the sunbaked field and, figuratively, her identity as a female sexual being, so they also schemed to set to work *on her* to maximize her "value" for their purposes. They proposed two plans of action for their sister, depending on her compliance. If, ideally, she remained a *wall*, with her virginity safeguarded, the brothers would "build *upon her* a battlement of silver"— both reinforcing her sexual virtue and enhancing her economic worth to make her more attractive to a worthy suitor in the brothers' estimation. If, however, she became a *door*, slipping out of the brothers' control, since they can't watch her every step, and opening herself to some premarital fling, then they must promptly step in to control the damage by "enclosing her with boards of cedar" (8:9).[23] The term rendered "enclose" (צוּר) in the NRSV carries the much stronger sense of "lay siege to" or "besiege," extending the military image of "battlement" in the first plan.[24] Here they aim to "barricade"[25] or "board her up with cedar planks" (NAB, NASB, CEB), their version of a chastity belt to protect their investment.

---

23. Treating the *waw* before "if she is a door" (וְאִם־דֶּלֶת) as adversative rather than conjunctive: hence, "*but* if she is a door" (NRSV, NAB, NASB).

24. Alter (*Strong as Death*, 51) writes, "we will besiege her with cedar boards."

25. William J. Holladay, *A Concise Hebrew and Aramaic Lexicon of the Old Testament* (Grand Rapids: Eerdmans, 1971), 305.

The brothers clearly regarded their sister as an economic commodity to manipulate and exchange as they willed. Suggestively, the word for "wall" (חומה, *ḥomah*) resonates with "wealth" (הון, *hon*)[26] in Song 8:7 and "seal" (חתם, *ḥotam*) in 8:6. The brothers resist having their little sister *choose* to whom she will give herself as "seal" or, in other words, whom *she* will own.[27] She has already asserted that she and her love are not for sale or exchange. This rebellious attitude, from the perspective of the brothers, would have only stirred them to redouble their efforts to wall their sister in and impose their martial law on her body. The cluster of military (battlements; siege works), economic (silver), and natural (cedar) images used to express the brothers' oppressive designs on their sister perverts images used elsewhere in the Song to extol the woman's strength and independence as well as the "rich" bond between her and her lover.[28] Moreover, the brothers' corruption of the security "wall" around their sister into a means of abusive control and confinement rather than protective freedom and nurture eerily recalls the violent treatment by "those sentinels of the walls" of the woman as she searched for her beloved (5:7-8).

So what does the sister-woman have to say about all of this now? By this point, we have a pretty good idea of how she feels, and she doesn't disappoint here. She boldly asserts in mock answer to her brothers, "Oh I am a wall all right, and my breasts have become towers!" (Song 8:10a, my paraphrase). Her opening words are emphatic: "I—a wall!" (אני חומה). In the absence of a verb in the original Hebrew, she speaks of her abiding nature up to the present (the NRSV's "I *was* a wall" is too limited to the past; most other versions opt for the present tense). To paraphrase further:

> Though it's not been easy and there have been setbacks, I have taken ownership of my life, watched out for my own security, and asserted my own sexuality as I desired. And I've done this despite your attempts, big brothers, to lock me in and shut me down. Though my quests to find my beloved have been frustrating and even dangerous at times, ultimately I have found peace in the depths of my beloved's adoring and caring eyes, where others have tended to look down on me.[29]

---

26. See also Baal-*hamon*, המן, "lord of riches" in 8:11.

27. See above on 8:6 at p. 212.

28. See military images as battlements and siege works in Song 3:7-8; 4:4; 6:4, 10; 7:4-5; silver images in 1:11; 3:10; and cedar images in 1:17; 5:15.

29. Song 8:10 is better rendered, "*finds* (מצא) peace," rather than the NRSV's "*brings* peace," though see the NRSV's textual footnote; the same verb applies elsewhere in the Song to the woman's quest to "find" her lover (3:1-4; 5:6-8; 8:1).

In light of the "wall" scenario, there may also be an allusion to a "town that finds peace"[30] or, more militantly, a "city suing for peace."[31] In this picture, the woman casts herself in the role of the city, which was typically referred to as "feminine," letting down her guard and surrendering herself to her lover's advances. A problem with this martial viewpoint, however, is that it places the woman in a position of being attacked and defeated by her lover—close to being *forced* to open her gates to him. Of course, this pushes (forces) the metaphor to the limit, and there are historical examples of powerful city populations welcoming conquerors as liberators, as some in Babylon received Cyrus.[32] But even in a figurative mode, the image of the "wall" retains shades of conquest and subjugation potentially at odds with the woman's insistence on her independence in the present stanza. Yet she gives in willingly, with her eyes wide open, and even reasserts her power in the love battle through "a rather nice irony," as Exum propounds. Taking the man's eyes in Song 8:10 not only as the desired object in which the woman finds peace but also as the subject—constructed by the woman—from which he views her (as Exum asserts, "she describes how she thinks he perceives her"), the woman grants him his little conquest fantasy with tongue in cheek. But, of course, the record already shows, certified by the man's affidavit, that in fact *he is the "ravished" and "captive" party* (4:9; 7:5). She has conquered him![33]

The woman's reflections move from her possessive brothers and talk of the love and "peace" (שלום, *shalom*, Song 8:10) she found for herself to the renowned possessions of Solomon (שלמה, *shlomoh*), including myriad vineyards and, by implication, women in his harem (8:11-12). Despite the *sh-l-m* linkage, many commentators detect a speaker shift in these lines, with the man now voicing his feelings about Love's surpassing worth in comparison with the historical Solomon with whom he has been likened in the Song.[34] But in the absence of a grammatical marker signaling the speaker's gender, it is logical to assume that the woman continues her comments, all the more since the other two Solomon references in the

30. Alter, *Strong as Death*, 52.

31. Exum, *Song*, 258–59.

32. I owe this insight to Lauress Wilkins Lawrence via email.

33. Exum, *Song*, 259.

34. E.g., Marcia Falk, *The Song of Songs: A New Translation and Interpretation* (New York: HarperCollins, 1990), 195–96; Othmar Keel, *The Song of Songs: A Continental Commentary*, trans. Frederick J. Gaiser (Minneapolis: Fortress, 1994), 282–83; Chana Bloch and Ariel Bloch, *The Song of Songs: The World's First Great Love Poem* (New York: Modern Library, 1995), 218; Exum, *Song*, 259–61; Fox, *Song*, 174–75.

Poem come from her (1:5; 3:7) and the emphatic comment about "my own vineyard" (8:12) echoes the woman's self-expression in 1:6.[35]

Notably, the woman now breaks off the fictive royal drama featuring the starring role of Solomon she assigns to her beloved. That has been a delightful imaginative exercise, playacting king and queen, prince and princess, in a kind of Camelot paradise. What fun for a country girl and her beau, who may be from the country or city, but it's still a fiction; no real chariots or palanquins, gold or silver surplus, appear in their common lives. And now, at the end, the woman opts to lift the curtain and expose the real Solomon, but not so much as a paragon of love, which comes as no surprise to anyone who knows Solomon's history, but instead as a parody of it. Turns out, she's been poking a bit of fun at the great king of Israel all along, effectively subverting his reputation for gross accumulation of wealth and women by the thousands. As Jill M. Munro puts it, "Solomon is integrated into this [Song's] metaphorical system only to denounce it at the last minute and thereby lay bare the limits of language to speak about love."[36]

The Songstress continues to trade on the *vineyard* image, representing both fruitful property and womanhood. With banal matter-of-factness, she reports that "Solomon had a vineyard at Baal-hamon" (Song 8:11). Well, yes, he had extensive vineyards and landholdings to go along with his harem of wives and concubines. This vineyard at "Baal-hamon" denotes no historical place we know of but aptly reinforces Solomon's standing as "Lord of Possessions," "Possessor of Wealth,"[37] or "Owner of Great Wealth."[38] It may also allude to his control over female property as " 'lord of a bevy (*hamon*)' of women (2 Chron 11:23)."[39] Solomon demanded that this "vineyard" turn a substantial profit under the management of hired "keepers" or tenant laborers.

Primarily, the business model assigned each worker a sales quota of one thousand silver shekels per share of the vineyard (Song 8:11), of which the laborer could retain two hundred for personal maintenance (8:12).

---

35. See the persuasive discussion in Jill M. Munro, *Spikenard and Saffron: A Study in the Poetic Language of the Song of Songs*, JSOTSup 203 (Sheffield: Sheffield Academic, 1995), 41–42. Alter (*Strong as Death*, 53) and Walsh (*Exquisite Desire*, 130–31) both regard the woman as the speaker in 8:12, without commenting on who's speaking in 8:11.

36. Munro, *Spikenard*, 42.

37. Fox, *Song*, 174.

38. Bloch and Bloch, *Song*, 219; cf. Exum, *Song*, 260.

39. Fishbane, *Song*, 221.

How generous of Solomon to take a mere 80 percent cut! We may also assume that any shortfall from the thousand-unit goal was counted as rollover debt, perpetuating an oppressive system of indentured servitude. The Deuteronomic History exposes Solomon's penchant for slave labor, including of his own people (see 1 Kgs 9:15; 11:26-28; 12:1-11).[40] Secondarily, the vineyard "keepers" might suggest protectors, typically eunuchs, of Solomon's thousand-women harem. While these women would have been valuable commodities enhancing Solomon's power, we have no evidence, however, that he bought and sold them for a profit, still less that he ran a high-end "bordello,"[41] pimping out these women to foreign dignitaries—at a thousand shekels a night? a year's retainer? In any case, the Song woman's emphasis is on Solomon's immense economic power, far beyond any amount of "silver" her brothers claimed (Song 8:9). But unlike the queen of Sheba, our woman is not impressed. Solomon "may have the thousand" (8:12) pieces of silver shares from his vineyard estate and myriad women to boot, but the woman in the Poem has what really matters, which she wouldn't trade for all the grapes in Israel.

What she possesses of superlative worth is "my vineyard, my very own . . . for myself" (Song 8:12a). This triple use of the personal pronoun is emphatically asserted in three consecutive Hebrew words: "my-vineyard [כרמי] that-is-to/for-me [שלי] to/for-my-face/self [לפני]." Her singular self, her entire embodied being, under her personal "keeping" is of greater value than all the assets of King Solomon, of her brothers, or of anyone else. She will be no kept woman by anyone but herself and in mutual partnership with anyone to whom she chooses to give herself. By no means, however, can she or will she be bought or bound anymore. At the outset of the Poem, she lamented the days of being forced to be the keeper of her brothers' vineyards at the expense of her own: "but my own vineyard [כרמי שלי] I have not kept" (1:6). But across the Song she has broken free of such entanglements toward safekeeping and self-possession, not without pain and frustration, to be sure, but with resolve and resilience all the same and a remarkable openness to love on her own terms. Though no stranger to tragic setbacks, the Songstress maintains—and magnifies—a sharp-eyed, confident "comic vision" of

40. Isa 7:23 refers to "a thousand vines, worth a thousand shekels of silver" (individually or collectively?). The Song does not specify how many workers or vineyards Solomon had. But given Solomon's opulent and tyrannical reputation, perhaps we should imagine his demanding a thousandfold yield each from a thousand vineyard managers.

41. Suggested in Keel, *Song*, 283.

life and love, as Melissa Jackson argues in her Contributing Voice essay. From 1:6 to 8:12 we may track an arcing "radical reversal of women's fortunes,"[42] epitomized as the female protagonist conclusively "asserts her autonomous sexuality."[43] Though wrongly, in my judgment, attributing the speech in 8:11-12 to the man, Marcia Falk nicely makes the right feminist point, and if she's right about the male speaker, it's all to the good that he gets the point!

> Woman as sexual other may be treated as a beloved (the speaker's relationship to his "own" vineyard) or as a sexual object (Solomon's vineyard is a harem which must be kept under constant guard). Using the motif of regality as a foil, the Poem advocates the one-to-one I-Thou relationship and rejects the debasement of sexuality inherent in treating others as sexual objects or property.[44]

### The Song's Comic Vision

To describe comedy as "an experience" and to define it, in part, as "perception" of incongruity is to acknowledge the inherent subjectivity of the comic. With this understanding, someone with a "good sense of humor" is not simply one who usually "gets the joke" but is rather one who engages the world expecting to experience and perceive the comic— especially over against the tragic. Possessing this humor-based "sense" of the world is to have a *comic vision* of life.[45]

When it comes to material reality, what distinguishes this comic vision is its celebration of the physical, biological, carnal world, its enjoyment of life's pleasure without becoming bogged down in society's "rules" that seek to constrain those pleasures. A tragic hero is at war with his desires; a comic anti-hero seeks the ways she might express and indulge hers. While tragedy marches to the inevitable ending of death, the trajectory of comedy moves ever onward in life, to life. The Song reflects a comic vision such as this, a worldview that is persistently celebratory, playful, fun, impulsive, adventurous, and relentlessly life-affirming, its trajectory ever-bending in the direction of love and the life it gives.

---

42. Munro, *Spikenard*, 42.
43. Walsh, *Exquisite Desire*, 131.
44. Falk, *Song*, 133; also cited by Fox, *Song*, 175.
45. For detailed exposition of this "comic vision," see Melissa A. Jackson, *Comedy and Feminist Interpretation of the Hebrew Bible: A Subversive Collaboration*, OTM (Oxford: Oxford University Press, 2012); and William J. Whedbee, *The Bible and the Comic Vision* (Cambridge: Cambridge University Press, 1988).

The comic vision does not, however, promise that this trajectory is to be a smooth and straight line or that it will eventuate in a perfectly "happy ending." This worldview does not ignore life's injuries or the marks they leave; it just refuses to allow those injuries or the ones who inflict them ultimately to prevail. The woman of the Song, despite injurious actions and words devised to subdue and control her, remains standing, confident, arms akimbo (at least in my imagining of the scene), and asserts, "my vineyard, the one that is mine, for myself" (8:12). Knowing the subjectivity of comedy, rooted in experience and perception, we would not expect any smiles of assent from her brothers, but this woman's defiant, subversive speech is in the same moment deadly serious and delightfully comic.

The comic vision's affirmation of life over death often leads to a lack of closure. Because life will continue even beyond what is currently visible, the experience of *an ending* is never *the end*. The Song lacks closure: the book's "ending" verses seem instead to be the beginning of yet another chapter; more life awaits "upon the mountain of spices" (8:14), life for the woman, for her lover, and for any who share the comic vision.

*Melissa A. Jackson*

## Love That Cannot Be Expedited (8:13-14)

Though more freely chosen and mutually shared than the bond between the woman and her brothers and between Solomon and his harem members, just how close and secure is this one-to-one I-Thou relationship between the Song's focal couple at the last notes' soundings? Each lover gets a final say in the closing couplet, but with what finality do they speak? As it happens, for all the woman's bold assertions in Song 8:10-12, all is not perfectly settled in her mind; and the man senses her unsettledness. The narrative arc of the Song, while suggestive, is not definitive. It remains open at the end, daring to shoot out in new vectors. Inexorable, omnipotent Love cannot be micromanaged or expedited even by our ideal lovers.

First, the man gets in a last word edgewise, his first words in our scheme since the woman's interruption in Song 7:9a—it's been a while. He addresses the woman using a feminine participle, referring to her as "one dwelling in the gardens" (8:13), recalling the lush verdant image of her embodied person bursting with love: she both *is* and *has* a love garden (4:12–5:1; 6:2-3). Unlike in her brothers' vineyard, however, in her garden she controls the flow of experience. She remains securely "locked" and "sealed" (4:12) until she chooses to open her garden's delights to her beloved (4:16). He must wait for her vocal summons: "Let my beloved come to his garden" (4:16); only then may he enter and enjoy his share of her paradise. And notably, prior permission does not grant permanent access. The man has no master passkey; he must continue to respect the woman's personal, spatial, and sexual boundaries. So he pleads here at the end when he is "listening to your voice" (feminine singular), hoping to "hear it" beckoning him to her garden once again (8:13). His ongoing "listening" responds to her abiding "dwell[ing]"—both participial forms suggest iterative activity. But he's not listening alone. As in 1:7, he's joined here by male "companions" (חברים) who attend with him to the woman's voice. By this stage, it's hard to view the man's friends or any other males as serious competitors for the woman's affection. She has made her choice for him quite clear. But still he has no right to take her or her love for granted. It's as if he returns after each "garden" encounter to a pool of potential suitors, back to the skulk of foxes (2:15), awaiting the woman's next call. While the image should not be pressed too far (the woman is scarcely playing the field), it retains a healthy sense of insecurity about the man's position. Love must repeatedly be nurtured, even to some degree earned, to continue the economic thrust of the stanza, and in all matters be considerate of each lover's interests and sensibilities.

So the man waits for the woman's call, reversing the modern scenario of the girl languishing by the phone in hopes of the post-first-date call. Does she deliver? Well, yes and no. She does answer his longing, but not exactly in the way he (or we) might presuppose or prefer. As in Song 2:17, she commands "my beloved" to move "like a gazelle or a young stag" upon some kind of hills or mountains (8:14). But she uses a different verb of motion. Previously, in 2:17, she had summoned her gazelle-like lover to "turn" (סבב), a verb that can mean "turn away," though the context more readily suggests the direction of "turning around" or "turning toward," that is, back *to* the woman, as Debra Band depicts the gazelle with his neck swiveled back almost a full 180 degrees, straining with anticipation atop his taut and erect body.[46]

---

46. See Band's fourth illumination and commentary on pp. 228–29.

### Illumination 4 Commentary

As dawn glimmers above, the door of the walled garden opens, and a gazelle representing the male lover peers over his shoulder for a last glimpse at the garden's beauties before leaping away. With the last verse of the poems, we see a reflection of the lovers' good-bye; in the absence of angst or pain, they reveal their confidence that they will meet again. Chana Bloch and Ariel Bloch suggest that the final verse of the Song can only mean that the girl "is urging her lover to run away before sunrise so that he will not be caught. . . . The song thus ends with the motif of the lovers parting at dawn, as in the aubade of later traditions— an ending that looks forward in anticipation to another meeting."[47] In the illumination, the gazelle to which the woman has so often compared her love casts one last look over his shoulder as he leaves her alone in the garden, but alone only until their next meeting.

As the caper branches suggest, just as the woman looks forward to next embracing her love, Israel perseveres and dreams of the day when she will be reunited with her God. The Targum of the Song of Songs, or early Aramaic paraphrase of the poetry probably dating from the Second Temple period, suggests that in this last verse Israel and God part at the end of the age of prophecy, looking forward to redemption at the coming of the Messiah. Gersonides completes his telling of the soul's search for philosophical enlightenment by suggesting that the man departs from the woman's garden, symbolizing the world of the senses, for the mountains of spice, indicating the world of metaphysics.[48]

In Kabbalah, the lovers—both Israel and God and the ten *Sefirot*—part yet look forward to eternal union at the time of the Messiah, culminating on

47. Bloch and Bloch, *Song*, 221.

48. Levi ben Gershom (Gersonides), *Commentary on the Song of Songs,* trans. and ed. Menachem Kellner, YJS 28 (New Haven: Yale University Press, 1998), 94.

the day [in the seventh millennium] that is entirely Sabbath and rest, for life eternal. Souls will be bound up in the body of life and they will be a throne for the Lord. Then the river which is the life and existence of the world, flowing forth from the Eden of Wisdom, will cease its flow. This is the meaning of *Flee, my beloved*: pointing to the rising of the Glory, its ascent into the upper light.[49]

*Debra Band*

But now, however, the woman's language urges dismissal rather than invitation. Despite a number of modern versions' attempts to finesse the meaning of the verb ברח (Song 8:14) with primary stress on velocity as in "make haste" (NRSV, KJV) or "hurry" (NASB, NJPS), it fundamentally denotes "take off in flight" (CEB) or, more simply, "flee" as a fugitive (φύγη, LXX; *fuge*, 8:14, Vg.). It is routinely used in situations of desperate escape from perilous situations, such as:

- Hagar running away from an abusive Sarah (Gen 16:6, 8)
- Moses' flight from Pharaoh (Exod 2:15)
- The Israelites' exodus from Egypt (Exod 14:5)
- David outrunning Saul's wrath (1 Sam 19:18; 20:1; 21:10)
- Jeroboam escaping Solomon's forced labor (1 Kgs 11:40)
- Zedekiah's and his warriors' retreat from Babylonian invaders (Jer 39:4; 52:7)
- Jonah's mad dash from the Lord's onerous (as the prophet perceived it) assignment (Jonah 1:3, 10; 4:3)

So what dire threat is the Song woman imploring her beloved to flee in her last words—*the* last words—of the Poem? Though she has suffered at the hands of brothers and watchmen and in the eyes of suspicious onlookers, he has gone unscathed, except for his deep longing for her, which has not always been fully satisfied. But overall he has moved as

49. Ezra ben Solomon of Gerona, *Commentary on the Song of Songs and Other Kabbalistic Commentaries* (Kalamazoo, MI: Western Michigan University Press, 1999), 145.

he pleased, flitting and bounding about when it suited him with unfettered liberty accorded a free man in this society. Yet, as I argued above, though suffering no personal harm, the man's flightiness triggered the woman's ill-fated search for him on the city streets, leading to her brutal attack by the night watchmen. Maybe, then, even after finding her lover again and rekindling her deep desire for him since 5:6-8, she's finally had enough. No more waiting around for him when he decides to call; no more risky searching for him when he drifts away. She's taken full charge of her "very own vineyard" (8:12) or self now apart from any man, including this one she has loved so much. She loves herself more. Her freedom matters most, including a freedom at last to tell him to "flee," to skedaddle, to buzz off. And yes, he should take that as a threat—from *her!*—from her formidable self-position, which he must genuinely respect in all respects.

Carey Ellen Walsh discerns in the woman's closing words the crystallization of a bold "transformation" in her sexual identity, "where she dispenses with the lover who is absent anyway, and proclaims instead her own sexuality. While she has pined for him with ardent love throughout these eight chapters, by the final chapter her desire changes in tone." Oddly, Walsh does not reinforce her point by appealing to the woman's dismissal of the man in Song 8:14. Instead, Walsh accepts the NRSV's "make haste" rendering (rather than "flee") as a token of the woman "inviting him one last time to hurry up and join her." Yet Walsh still argues for a marked tonal adjustment:

> But somehow the desperation is gone. By this point she is no longer expecting a response, and so the book ends without one. What she does do is reclaim her sexuality and her passion for herself: "My vineyard, my very own is before me" (8:12). She is now sole owner, the brothers no longer having the land rights they presumed to have with her in 1:6. . . .
>
> What had been controlled by her brothers she wrested from them and claimed for her own, and even had the gumption to compare to Solomon's vineyard. There is pure joy in her celebration of self here, for she rests content with her sexuality, not even needing Israel's wisest king. . . .
>
> This is one of the paradoxes of the Song; it has been about the intense sensual yearning between two lovers and has ended with the woman alone, yet resolved and strengthened.[50]

50. Walsh, *Exquisite Desire*, 167–68.

I agree that the Song ends with a strong assertive, self-assured woman who does not *need* a man or anyone else to complete her. She is a marvelous, integral being in and of herself, as the man has frankly recognized in his various encomia to her embodied self.

And I also agree with Walsh's related observation that the book does not come to a surging *climax*, literarily or sexually, a viewpoint that she regards as "androcentric" and "undoubtedly gender-influenced," as evidenced by its preference among male commentators.[51] Nevertheless, while I get the point about male tendencies to rush to orgasmic climax or premature interpretation, if I may call it that, toward a more consummative concluding experience of the couple's love, this "let's finish this already" propensity is not exclusive to male readers and might even be resisted by some men. A lot of factors—including textual and sexual factors, but not only those—go into interpreting endings. It seems clear to me, at least, that the Song's closing couplet ends on an open note, an extended fermata left to the reader's imagination when or if to cut off.

Yet openness does not necessitate aloneness, as Walsh avers: "yearning between two lovers . . . has ended with the woman alone." The man calls, hoping to hear his darling's voice but not quite sure if or when it will come. She answers him as "my beloved," but with a tantalizing order to go away and frolic "upon the mountains of spices" (Song 8:14). So her attitude is not adamantly dismissive, as if to say unequivocally: "Get lost, bub. Get out of my sight. I don't care where you go—just do it and let me be!" She in fact does care where he goes, specifically, to these spicy slopes that evoke, along with deer imagery, erotic encounters between the man and woman, especially involving her breasts and *mons pubis* (see 1:12-14; 2:7-9, 17; 3:5; 4:5-8, 13-15; 5:1, 13; 6:2). But why, then, urge him to flee to the "mountains" rather than join her in her "garden"—unless she really wants to go away *with him* ("Come away, my beloved," NIV) or play a giggly game of chase and see if he can catch her and successfully "mount" her, as she really desires? This reading appreciates the open ending while extending the lovers' pursuit of each other consistent throughout the Song. Though changing the game, Munro nicely captures

51. Walsh (*Exquisite Desire*, 175–77) particularly implicates the following for their use of "climax" or "climactic point" language: Pope, *Song*, 675; Roland E. Murphy, *The Song of Songs*, Hermeneia (Minneapolis: Fortress, 1990), 196; André LaCocque, *Romance, She Wrote: A Hermeneutical Essay on Song of Songs* (Harrisburg, PA: Trinity Press International, 1998), 160, 171.

the final theme: "The effect is to assure us that love will never end. The lovers will evermore be engaged in love's game of hide and seek."[52]

Such a concluding viewpoint may seem more apt for a light romantic comedy than a serious feminist commentary. But the persisting quest for love is no trivial pursuit, however many games we might play in trying to win love. Love beats loneliness every time. Love marks the highest, worthiest experience of life, bordering on the divine. Yet it also lays claim to being the scariest, riskiest experience we can have, bordering on the deadly. Love is worth it all—and might well take it all from us! A certain gamesmanship is inevitable in the pursuit of love, a certain risk of loss in the sense of not finding love (hide and seek) and, perhaps, not surviving it (life and death). But on the flip side, the incomparable joy of finding the love pearl of highest price and flourishing in its presence is worth the risk, if anything is. In her stimulating analysis of *A Feminist Ethic of Risk*, Sharon Welch, keenly aware of the oppressive challenges historically and currently facing women, nonetheless resists caving into a paralyzing cynicism and bitterness. Informed by African American (Toni Morrison), Caribbean American (Audre Lorde), Algerian French (Hélène Cixous), and Belgian French (Luce Irigaray) feminist writers, Welch raises a banner extolling the *jouissance* of love over the risk of loss. Toward the end of her work, Welch inscribes on that banner poignant words generously laced with Irigaray's insights.

> Irigaray writes of a love that does not require sacrifice of "one" to "another." She speaks of a love that emerges from plenitude, not from lack. "We are not lacks, voids, awaiting sustenance, plenitude, fulfillment from the other." The love that emerges from plentitude enlarges the world, and the joy that is achieved in such love is not static: its movement is the product of pleasure. "When you kiss me, the world grows so large that the horizon itself disappears. Are we unsatisfied? Yes, if that means we are never finished. If our pleasure consists in moving, being moved, endlessly. Always in motion: openness is never spent nor sated."[53]

And so the Love Song of Songs keeps playing, keeps moving—and moving all who hear and read it with open heart and mind.

---

52. Munro, *Spikenard*, 89.

53. Sharon D. Welch, *A Feminist Ethic of Risk* (Minneapolis: Fortress, 1990), 171; citing Luce Irigaray, *This Sex Which Is Not One*, trans. Catherine Parker (Ithaca, NY: Cornell University Press, 1985), 209–10.

# Works Cited

Abu-Lughod, Lila. *Veiled Sentiments: Honor and Poetry in a Bedouin Society*. 2nd ed. Berkeley: University of California Press, 1999.

Adichie, Chimamanda Ngozi. *We Should All Be Feminists*. New York: Anchor, 2015.

Ahmed, Sara. *The Cultural Politics of Emotion*. New York: Routledge, 2004.

Allen, William Loyd. "Bernard of Clairvaux's *Sermons on the Songs*: Why They Matter." *RevExp* 105 (2008): 403–16.

Almog, Yael. " 'Flowing Myrrh upon the Handles of the Bolt': Bodily Border, Social Norms and Their Transgression in the Song of Songs." *BibInt* 18 (2010): 251–63.

Alter, Robert. *Strong as Death Is Love: The Song of Songs, Ruth, Esther, Jonah, and Daniel; A Translation with Commentary*. New York: Norton, 2015.

Ausloos, Von Hans, and Bénédicte Lemmelijn. "Eine neue Interpretation des Hoheliedes 8,5ab." *ZAW* 119 (2007): 556–63.

Bach, Alice. "Good to the Last Drop: Viewing the *Sotah* (Numbers 5.11-31) as the Glass Half Empty and Wondering How to View It Half Full." In *Women and the Hebrew Bible: A Reader*, edited by Alice Bach, 503–22. New York: Routledge, 1999.

———. "Introduction to a Case History." In *Women and the Hebrew Bible: A Reader*, edited by Alice Bach, 461–62. New York: Routledge, 1999.

Band, Debra. *The Song of Songs: The Honeybee in the Garden*. Philadelphia: JPS, 2005.

Barthes, Roland. *A Lover's Discourse: Fragments*. Translated by Richard Howard. New York: Hill and Wang, 1978.

Baumgardner, Jennifer, and Amy Richards. *Manifesta: Young Women, Feminism, and the Future*. 2nd ed. New York: Farrar, Straus, and Giroux, 2010.

ben Gershom (Gersonides), Levi. *Commentary on the Song of Songs*. Translated and edited by Menachem Kellner. YJS 28. New Haven: Yale University Press, 1998.

ben Solomon of Gerona, Ezra. *Commentary on the Song of Songs and Other Kabbalistic Commentaries*. Kalamazoo: Western Michigan University Press, 1999.

Ben-Ze'ev, Aaron, and Rouhama Goussinsky. *In the Name of Love: Romantic Ideology and Its Victims*. Oxford: Oxford University Press, 2006.

Bergant, Dianne. *The Song of Songs*. Berit Olam. Collegeville, MN: Liturgical Press, 2001.

Bishop, E. F. F. "Palestiniana in Canticulus." *CBQ* 29 (1967): 20–30.

Black, Fiona C. *Artifice of Love: Grotesque Bodies in the Song of Songs*. LHBOTS 392. London: T & T Clark, 2009.

———. "Beauty or the Beast? The Grotesque Body in the Song of Songs." *BibInt* 8 (2000): 302–23.

———. "Nocturnal Egression: Exploring Some Margins of the Song of Songs." In *Postmodern Interpretations of the Bible: A Reader*, edited by A. K. M. Adam, 93–104. St. Louis: Chalice, 2001.

———. "Unlikely Bedfellows: Allegorical and Feminist Readings of Song of Songs 7:1-8." In *The Song of Songs*, edited by Athalya Brenner and Carole R. Fontaine, 104–29. FCB, 2nd ser. Sheffield: Sheffield Academic, 2000.

———. "What Is My Beloved? On Erotic Reading and the Song of Songs." In *The Labour of Reading: Desire, Alienation, and Biblical Interpretation*, edited by Fiona C. Black, Roland Boer, and Erin Runions, 35–52. Atlanta: SBL, 1999.

Bloch, Chana, and Ariel Bloch. *The Song of Songs: The World's First Great Love Poem*. New York: Modern Library, 1995.

Blue, Debbie. *Consider the Birds: A Provocative Guide to Birds of the Bible*. Nashville: Abingdon, 2013.

Boer, Roland. "Night Sprinkle(s): Pornography and the Song of Songs." In *Knockin' on Heaven's Door: The Bible and Popular Culture*, 53–70. Biblical Limits. London: Routledge, 1999.

———. "The Second Coming: Repetition and Insatiable Desire in the Song of Songs." *BibInt* 8 (2000): 276–301.

Brenner, Athalya. "An Afterword." In *A Feminist Companion to the Song of Songs*, edited by Athalya Brenner, 279–80. FCB. Sheffield: JSOT, 1993.

———. "'Come Back, Come Back, the Shulammite' (Song of Songs 7.1-10)." In *A Feminist Companion to the Song of Songs*, edited by Athalya Brenner, 234–57. FCB. Sheffield: Sheffield Academic, 1993. Reprinted from *On Humour and Comic in the Hebrew Bible*, edited by Athalya Brenner and Yehuda T. Radday, 251–76. Sheffield: Almond Press, 1990.

———. "To See Is to Assume: Whose Love Is Celebrated in the Song of Songs?" *BibInt* 1 (1993): 266–84.

———. "Women Poets and Authors." In *A Feminist Companion to the Song of Songs*, edited by Athalya Brenner, 86–97. FCB. Sheffield: Sheffield Academic, 1993. Reprinted from Brenner, *The Israelite Woman: Social Role and Literary Type in Biblical Narrative*, 46–56, 138. Sheffield: JSOT, 1986.

Brown, Francis, S. R. Driver, and Charles A. Briggs. *The New Brown, Driver, Briggs, Gesenius Hebrew and English Lexicon: With an Appendix Containing the Biblical Aramaic*. Peabody, MA: Hendrickson, 1979.

Burke, Edmund. *A Philosophical Enquiry into the Origin of Our Ideas of the Sublime and Beautiful and Other Pre-Revolutionary Writings*. Edited by David Womersley. London: Penguin, 1998 (orig. 1757–1759).

Burrus, Virginia, and Stephen D. Moore. "Unsafe Sex: Feminism, Pornography, and the Song of Songs." *BibInt* 11 (2003): 24–52. Reprinted in Moore, *The Bible in Theory: Critical and Postcritical Essays*, 247–72. Resources for Biblical Study 57. Atlanta: SBL, 2010.

Carr, David M. *The Erotic Word: Sexuality, Spirituality, and the Bible*. New York: Oxford University Press, 2005.

Carson, Anne. *Eros the Bittersweet*. Princeton: Princeton University Press, 1986.

Chesler, Phyllis. *Women's Inhumanity to Woman*. 2nd ed. Chicago: Lawrence Hill, 2009.

Choi, John H. "Resheph and YHWH Sebaʾot." *VT* 54 (2004): 17–28.

Clines, David J. A. "Why Is There a Song of Songs and What Does It Do to You If You Read It?" In *Interested Parties: The Ideology of Writers and Readers of the Hebrew Bible*, 94–121. JSOTSup 205. Gender, Culture, Theory 1. Sheffield: Sheffield Academic, 1995.

Cox, Harvey, and Stephanie Paulsell. *Lamentations and the Song of Songs*. Belief: A Theological Commentary on the Bible. Louisville: Westminster John Knox, 2012.

Darwin, Charles. *The Expression of the Emotions in Man and Animals*. 4th ed. Oxford: Oxford University Press, 2009 (orig. 1872).

Davis, Ellen F. *Proverbs, Ecclesiastes and the Song of Songs*. Westminster Bible Companion. Louisville: Westminster John Knox, 2000.

Dobbs-Allsopp, F. W. "The Delight of Beauty and Song of Songs 4:1-7." *Int* 59 (2005): 260–77.

———. "'I Am Black *and* Beautiful': The Song, Cixous, and *'Ecriture Féminine*.'" In *Engaging the Bible in a Gendered World: An Introduction to Feminist Biblical Interpretation in Honor of Katharine Doob Sakenfeld*, edited by Linda Day and Carolyn Pressler, 128–40. Louisville: Westminster John Knox, 2006.

Douglas, Mary. *Purity and Danger: An Analysis of the Concepts of Pollution and Taboo*. London: Routledge, 1966.

Douglas, Susan J. *Enlightened Sexism: The Seductive Message That Feminism's Work Is Done*. New York: Times Books, 2010.

Duguid, Iain M. *The Song of Songs: An Introduction and Commentary*. TOTC. Downers Grove, IL: IVP Academic, 2015.

Earth Bible Team. "The Voice of Earth: More than Metaphor?" In *The Earth Story in the Psalms and the Prophets*, edited by Norman C. Habel and Shirley Wurst, 23–28. Sheffield: Sheffield Academic, 2001.

Ekman, Paul. *Emotions Revealed: Recognizing Faces and Feelings to Improve Communication and Emotional Life*. 2nd ed. New York: St. Martin's, 2007.

Etcoff, Nancy. *Survival of the Prettiest: The Science of Beauty*. New York: Anchor, 1999.

Exum, J. Cheryl. "How Does the Song of Songs Mean? On Reading the Poetry of Desire." *SEÅ* 64 (1999): 33–49.

———. "In the Eye of the Beholder: Wishing, Dreaming, and *Double Entendre* in the Song of Songs." In *The Labour of Reading: Desire, Alienation, and Biblical Interpretation*, edited by Fiona C. Black, Roland Boer, and Erin Runions, 71–86. Atlanta: SBL, 1999.

———. "Seeing Solomon's Palanquin (Song of Songs 3:6-11)." *BibInt* 11 (2003): 301–16.

———. *Song of Songs*. OTL. Louisville: Westminster John Knox, 2005.

———. "Ten Things Every Feminist Should Know about the Song of Songs." In *The Song of Songs*, edited by Athalya Brenner and Carole R. Fontaine, 24–35. FCB, 2nd ser. Sheffield: Sheffield Academic, 2000.

Falk, Marcia. *The Song of Songs: A New Translation and Interpretation*. New York: HarperCollins, 1990.

———. "The *Waṣf*." In *A Feminist Companion to the Song of Songs*, edited by Athalya Brenner, 225–33. FCB. Sheffield: Sheffield Academic, 1993. Reprinted from Falk, *Love Lyrics from the Hebrew Bible: A Translation and Literary Study of the Song of Songs*, 80–87. Sheffield: Almond Press, 1983.

Fewell, Danna Nolan. "Reading the Bible Ideologically: Feminist Criticism." In *To Each Its Own Meaning: An Introduction to Biblical Criticisms and Their Application*, edited by Steven L. McKenzie and Stephen R. Haynes, 266–82. 2nd ed. Louisville: Westminster John Knox, 1999.

Fish, Stanley E. "Literature in the Reader: Affective Stylistics." In *Reader-Response Criticism: From Formalism to Post-Structuralism*, edited by Jane P. Tompkins, 70–100. Baltimore: Johns Hopkins University Press, 1980.

Fishbane, Michael. *Song of Songs*. JPS Bible Commentary. Lincoln: University of Nebraska Press, 2015.

Fisher, Helen. *Why We Love: The Nature and Chemistry of Romantic Love*. New York: Henry Holt, 2004.

Fowler, Robert M. *Let the Reader Understand: Reader-Response Criticism and the Gospel of Mark*. Minneapolis: Fortress, 1991.

Fox, Michael V. "The Song of Solomon." In *The HarperCollins Study Bible*, edited by Harold W. Attridge, 903–11. Rev. ed. New York: HarperCollins, 2006.

———. *The Song of Songs and the Ancient Egyptian Love Songs*. Madison: University of Wisconsin Press, 1985.

Frijda, Nico H. *The Emotions: Studies in Emotion and Social Interaction*. Cambridge: Cambridge University Press, 1986.

———. "The Laws of Emotion." *American Psychologist* 43 (1988): 349–58.

Fuchs, Esther. "Structure and Patriarchal Functions in the Biblical Betrothal Type-Scene: Some Preliminary Notes." In *Women in the Hebrew Bible: A Reader*, edited by Alice Bach, 45–51. New York: Routledge, 1999. Reprinted from *JFSR* 4 (1988): 7–13.

Garrett, Duane. "Song of Songs." In Garrett and Paul R. House, *Song of Songs/ Lamentations*, 1–265. WBC 23b. Nashville: Thomas Nelson, 2004.

Gault, Brian P. "A 'Do Not Disturb' Sign: Reexamining the Adjuration Refrain in Song of Songs." *JSOT* 36 (2011): 93–104.

———. "An Admonition against 'Rousing Love': The Meaning of the Enigmatic Refrain in Song of Songs." *BBR* 20 (2010): 161–84.

Geraty, Lawrence T. "Heshbon." *ABD* III (1992): 181–84.

Gilligan, Carol. *Joining the Resistance*. Cambridge: Polity, 2011.

Goldie, Peter. *The Emotions: A Philosophical Exploration*. Oxford: Oxford University Press, 2009.

Goulder, Michael D. *The Song of Fourteen Songs*. JSOTSup 36. Sheffield: JSOT, 1986.

Habel, Norman C. "Six Ecojustice Principles." In *Readings from the Perspective of Earth*, edited by Norman C. Habel, 24. Earth Bible 1. Cleveland: Pilgrim, 2000.

Habel, Norman C., and the Earth Bible Team. "Where Is the Voice of Earth in Wisdom Literature?" In *The Earth Story in Wisdom Traditions*, edited by Norman C. Habel and Shirley Wurst, 23–34. Earth Bible 3. Sheffield: Sheffield Academic, 2001.

Hagedorn, Anselm C. "Of Foxes and Vineyards: Greek Perspectives on the Song of Songs." *VT* 53 (2003): 337–52.

Handy, Lowell K. "Resheph." *ABD* V (1992): 678–79.

Harding, Kathryn. "'I Sought Him but I Did Not Find Him': The Elusive Lover in the Song of Songs." *BibInt* 16 (2008): 43–59.

Hardy, Thomas. *Far From the Madding Crowd*. London: Penguin, 2000 (orig. 1874).

Held, Virginia. *The Ethics of Care: Personal, Political, and Global*. Oxford: Oxford University Press, 2006.

Holladay, William J. *A Concise Hebrew and Aramaic Lexicon of the Old Testament*. Grand Rapids: Eerdmans, 1971.

hooks, bell. *Feminism Is for Everybody: Passionate Politics*. Cambridge, MA: South End, 2000.

Hrdy, Sarah Blaffer. *Mothers and Others: The Evolutionary Origins of Mutual Understanding*. Cambridge, MA: Harvard University Press, 2009.

Hunter, Maxine L. "Colorstruck: Skin Color Stratification in the Lives of African American Women." *Sociological Inquiry* 68 (1998): 517–35.

Hunter, Richard. "'Sweet Talk': *Song of Songs* and the Traditions of Greek Poetry." In *Perspectives on the Song of Songs*, edited by Anselm C. Hagedorn, 228–44. BZAW 346. Berlin: Walter de Gruyter, 2005.

Irigaray, Luce. *This Sex Which Is Not One*. Translated by Catherine Parker. Ithaca, NY: Cornell University Press, 1985.

Iser, Wolfgang. "The Reading Process: A Phenomenological Approach." In *Reader-Response Criticism: From Formalism to Post-Structuralism*, edited by Jane P. Tompkins, 50–69. Baltimore: Johns Hopkins University Press, 1980.

Jackson, Melissa A. *Comedy and Feminist Interpretation of the Hebrew Bible: A Subversive Collaboration*. OTM. Oxford: Oxford University Press, 2012.

Jenson, Robert W. *Song of Songs*. Interpretation. Louisville: Westminster, 2005.

Johnson, Elizabeth A. *Ask the Beasts: Darwin and the God of Love*. London: Bloomsbury, 2014.

Jones, Serene. *Feminist Theory and Christian Theology: Cartographies of Grace*. Guides to Theological Inquiry. Minneapolis: Augsburg Fortress, 2000.

Kant, Immanuel. *Observations on the Feeling of the Beautiful and Sublime and Other Writings*. Translated and edited by Patrick Frierson and Paul Guyer. Cambridge: Cambridge University Press, 2011 (orig. 1764–1765).

Keel, Othmar. *The Song of Songs: A Continental Commentary*. Translated by Frederick J. Gaiser. Minneapolis: Fortress, 1994.

Knust, Jennifer. *Unprotected Texts: The Bible's Surprising Contradictions about Sex and Desire*. New York: HarperOne, 2011.

LaCocque, André. *Romance, She Wrote: A Hermeneutical Essay on Song of Songs*. Harrisonburg, PA: Trinity Press International, 1998.

Lambert, Ellen Zetzel. *The Face of Love: Feminism and the Beauty Question*. Boston: Beacon, 1995.

Landy, Francis. *Paradoxes of Paradise, Identity and Difference in the Song of Songs*. BLS 7. Sheffield: Almond Press, 1983.

———. *Paradoxes of Paradise: Identity and Difference in the Song of Songs*. 2nd ed. Sheffield: Sheffield Phoenix, 2011.

———. "Two Versions of Paradise." In *A Feminist Companion to the Song of Songs*, edited by Athalya Brenner, 129–42. FCB. Sheffield: Sheffield Academic, 1993. Reprinted from Landy, *Paradoxes of Paradise: Identity and Difference in the Song of Songs*, 183–89, 269–70. Sheffield: Almond Press, 1983.

Landy, Francis, and Fiona Black. *Song of Songs through the Centuries*. Blackwell Bible Commentaries. Malden, MA: Wiley-Blackwell, 2017.

Largen, Kristin Johnston. "The Erotic Passion of God." *Dialog* 49 (2010): 7–8.

Lazarus, Richard S. *Emotion and Adaptation*. New York: Oxford University Press, 1991.

Levine, Amy-Jill. "Introduction." In *A Feminist Companion to Matthew*, edited by Amy-Jill Levine with Marianne Blickenstaff, 13–23. Sheffield: Sheffield Academic, 2001.

Linafelt, Tod. "The Arithmetic of Eros." *Int* 50 (2005): 244–58.

———. "Lyrical Theology: The Song of Songs and the Advantage of Poetry." In *Toward a Theology of Eros: Transfiguring Passion at the Limits of Discipline*, edited by Virginia Burrus and Catherine Keller, 291–305. New York: Fordham University Press, 2006.

Long, Gary Allan. "A Lover, Cities, and Heavenly Bodies: Co-Text and the Translation of Two Similes in Canticles (6:4c; 6:10d)." *JBL* 115 (1996): 703–9.

Longman, Tremper, III. *Song of Songs*. NICOT. Grand Rapids: Eerdmans, 2001.

Lord, M. G. *Forever Barbie: The Unauthorized Biography of a Real Doll*. New York: Avon, 1995.

Lucretius, *The Nature of Things (De Rerum Natura)*. Translated by A. E. Stallings. London: Penguin, 2007.

Mariaselvam, Abraham. *The Song of Songs and Ancient Tamil Love Poems: Poetry and Symbolism*. AnBib 118. Rome: Pontifical Biblical Institute, 1988.

Merkin, Daphne. "The Women in the Balcony: On Rereading the Song of Songs." In *Out of the Garden: Women Writers on the Bible*, edited by Christina Büchmann and Celina Spiegel, 238–51. New York: Fawcett Columbine, 1994.

Mernissi, Fatima. *Dreams of Trespass: Tales of a Harem Girlhood*. Cambridge, MA: Perseus Books, 1994.

Meyers, Carol. "Gender Imagery in the Song of Songs." In *A Feminist Companion to the Song of Songs*, edited by Athalya Brenner, 197–212. FCB. Sheffield: Sheffield Academic, 1993. Reprinted from *Hebrew Annual Review* 10 (1986): 209–23.

Moldenke, Harold N., and Alma L. Moldenke. *Plants of the Bible*. Mineola, NY: Dover, 1952.

Moore, Stephen D. *The Bible in Theory: Critical and Postcritical Essays*. Resources for Biblical Study 57. Atlanta: SBL, 2010.

———. "More Than a Feeling: Affect Theory and Biblical Studies." Paper delivered at annual SBL meeting, San Diego, CA, 2014.

———. "The Song of Songs in the History of Sexuality." *Church History* 69 (2000): 328–49. Reprinted in Moore, *Bible in Theory*, 225–45.

Morrison, Toni. *Song of Solomon*. New York: New American Library, 1977.

Mulvey, Laura. "Visual Pleasure and Narrative Cinema." *Screen* 16 (1975): 6–18. Reprinted in Mulvey, *Visual and Other Pleasures*, 14–27. 2nd ed. Houndsmill Basingstoke: Palgrave Macmillan, 2009.

Munro, Jill M. *Spikenard and Saffron: A Study in the Poetic Language of the Song of Songs*. JSOTSup 203. Sheffield: Sheffield Academic, 1995.

Murphy, Roland E. *The Song of Songs*. Hermeneia. Minneapolis: Augsburg Fortress, 1990.

Newman, Karen. "'And Wash the Ethiop White': Femininity and the Monstrous in Othello." In Newman, *Fashioning Femininity and English Renaissance Drama*, 71–93. Chicago: University of Chicago Press, 1991.

Noddings, Nel. *Caring: A Feminine Approach to Ethics and Moral Education*. 2nd ed. Berkeley: University of California Press, 2003.

Norris, Richard A. *The Song of Songs: Interpreted by Early Christian and Medieval Commentators*. The Church's Bible. Grand Rapids: Eerdmans, 2003.

Nussbaum, Martha. *From Disgust to Humanity: Sexual Orientation and Constitutional Law*. Inalienable Rights. New York: Oxford University Press, 2010.

———. *Hiding from Humanity: Disgust, Shame, and the Law*. Princeton: Princeton University Press, 2004.

Oatley, Keith. *The Passionate Muse: Exploring Emotion in Stories*. Oxford: Oxford University Press, 2012.

Ostriker, Alicia. "A Holy of Holies: The Song of Songs as Countertext." In *The Song of Songs*, edited by Athalya Brenner and Carole R. Fontaine, 36–54. FCB, 2nd ser. Sheffield: Sheffield Academic, 2000.

Pardes, Ilana. *Countertraditions in the Bible: A Feminist Approach*. Cambridge, MA: Harvard University Press, 1992.

Parmelee, Alice. *All the Birds of the Bible: Their Stories, Identification, and Meaning.* New York: Harper, 1959.

Patton, Tracey Owen. "Hey Girl, Am I More Than My Hair? African American Women and Their Struggles with Beauty, Body Image, and Hair," *NWSA Journal* 18 (2006): 24–51.

Paul, Shalom M. "An Unrecognized Medical Idiom in Canticles 6,12 and Job 9,21." *Bib* 58 (1978): 545–47.

Polaski, Donald C. "What Will Ye See in the Shulammite? Women, Power and Panopticism in the Song of Songs." *BibInt* 5 (1997): 64–81.

Pope, Marvin H. *Song of Songs: A New Translation with Introduction and Commentary.* AB 7C. Garden City, NY: Doubleday, 1977.

———. "The Song of Songs and Women's Liberation: An Outsider's Critique." In *A Feminist Companion to the Song of Songs*, edited by Athalya Brenner, 121–28. FCB. Sheffield: Sheffield Academic, 1993. Reprinted from Pope, *Song*, 205–10.

Rabin, Chaim. "Song of Songs and Tamil Poetry." *SR* 3 (1973–1974): 205–19.

Reid, Barbara E. *Choosing the Better Part? Women in the Gospel of Luke.* Collegeville, MN: Liturgical Press, 1996.

Rogers, Mary. *Barbie Culture.* Cultural Icons Series. Thousand Oaks, CA: Sage, 1999.

Sasson, Victor. "King Solomon and the Dark Lady of the Song of Songs." *VT* 39 (1989): 407–14.

Scarry, Elaine. *On Beauty and Being Just.* Princeton: Princeton University Press, 1999.

Schlimm, Matthew R. *From Fratricide to Forgiveness: The Language and Ethics of Anger in Genesis.* Siphrut 7. Winona Lake, IN.: Eisenbrauns, 2011.

Schüssler Fiorenza, Elisabeth. *Wisdom Ways: Introducing Feminist Biblical Interpretation.* Maryknoll, NY: Orbis Books, 2001.

Scott, Mark S. M. "Shades of Grace: Origen and Gregory of Nyssa's Soteriological Exegesis of the 'Black and Beautiful' Bride in Song of Songs 1:5." *HTR* 99 (2006): 65–83.

Scruton, Roger. *Beauty: A Very Short Introduction.* Oxford: Oxford University Press, 2011.

———. *The Soul of the World.* Princeton: Princeton University Press, 2014.

Setel, T. Drorah. "Prophets and Pornography: Female Sexual Imagery in Hosea." In *Feminist Interpretation of the Bible*, edited by Letty M. Russell, 86–85, 157–59. Philadelphia: Westminster, 1985. Reprinted in *A Feminist Companion to the Song of Songs*, edited by Athalya Brenner, 143–55. FCB. Sheffield: Sheffield Academic, 1993.

Siegel, Daniel J. *Mindsight: The New Science of Personal Transformation.* New York: Bantam Books, 2010.

Snaith, John G. *The Song of Songs.* New Century Bible Commentary. London: Marshall Pickering, 1993.

Solomon, Robert C. *About Love: Reinventing Romance for Our Times.* Indianapolis: Hackett, 2006.

———. *Love: Emotion, Myth, and Metaphor.* Garden City, NY: Anchor/Doubleday, 1981.

Spencer, F. Scott. *Dancing Girls, "Loose" Ladies, and Women of "the Cloth": The Women in Jesus' Life.* New York: Continuum, 2004.

———. "Feminist Criticism." In *Hearing the New Testament: Strategies for Interpretation,* edited by Joel B. Green, 289–325. 2nd ed. Grand Rapids: Eerdmans, 2010.

———. *Salty Wives, Spirited Mothers, and Savvy Widows: Capable Women of Purpose and Persistence in Luke's Gospel.* Grand Rapids: Eerdmans, 2012.

———. "Those Riotous—yet Righteous—Foremothers of Jesus: Exploring Women in Matthew's Comic Genealogy." In *Are We Amused? Humour in the Biblical World,* edited by Athalya Brenner, 7–30. LHBOTS 383. London: T & T Clark, 2003.

———. *What Did Jesus Do? Gospel Profiles of Jesus' Personal Conduct.* Harrisburg, PA: Trinity Press International, 2003.

Stanko, Elizabeth. *Everyday Violence: How Women and Men Experience Sexual and Physical Danger.* London: Pandora, 1990.

Sumi, Akiko Motoyoshi. *Description in Classical Arabic Poetry Waṣf, Ekphrasis, and Interarts Theory.* Leiden: Brill, 2004.

Tallis, *The Hand: A Philosophical Inquiry into Human Being.* Edinburgh: Edinburgh University Press, 2003.

Tannen, Deborah. *Gender and Discourse.* New York: Oxford University Press, 1996.

———. "The Relativity of Linguistic Strategies: Rethinking Power and Solidarity in Gender and Dominance." In *Gender and Conversational Interaction,* edited by Deborah Tannen, 165–88. Oxford Studies in Sociolinguistics. New York: Oxford University Press, 1993.

———. *You Just Don't Understand: Women and Men in Conversation.* New York: William Morrow, 1990.

Tawil, Hayim. "Paved with Love (Cant 3,10d): A New Interpretation." *ZAW* 115 (2003): 266–71.

Thompson, Henry O. "Carmel, Mount." *ABD* I (1992): 874–75.

Trible, Phyllis. "Depatriarchalizing in Biblical Interpretation." *JAAR* 41 (1973): 42–48.

———. "Love's Lyrics Redeemed." In *A Feminist Companion to the Song of Songs,* edited by Athalya Brenner, 100–120. FCB. Sheffield: Sheffield Academic, 1993. Reprinted from Trible, *God and the Rhetoric of Sexuality,* 144–65. OBT. Philadelphia: Fortress, 1978.

———. *Texts of Terror: Literary-Feminist Readings of Biblical Narratives.* OBT. Philadelphia: Fortress, 1984.

Van de Sande, Axel. "Le souffle du jour et la fuite des hombres en Ct 2:17 (4:6): matin ou soir?" *VT* 62 (2012): 276–83.

Viviers, Hendrik. "Eco-Delight in the Song of Songs." In *The Earth Story in Wisdom Traditions*, edited by Norman C. Habel and Shirley Wurst, 143–54. The Earth Bible 3. Sheffield: Sheffield Academic, 2001.

Wallace, Michele. *Black Macho and the Myth of the Superwoman*. New York: Dial, 1979.

Walsh, Carey Ellen. *Exquisite Desire: Religion, the Erotic, and the Song of Songs*. Minneapolis: Fortress, 2000.

Weems, Renita J. "The Song of Songs: Introduction, Commentary, and Reflections." In *Introduction to Wisdom Literature, the Book of Proverbs, the Book of Ecclesiastes, the Song of Songs, the Book of Wisdom, the Book of Sirach*. Vol. 5 of *New Interpreter's Bible*, edited by Leander E. Keck, 361–434. Nashville: Abingdon, 1997.

Welch, Sharon D. *A Feminist Ethic of Risk*. Minneapolis: Fortress, 1990.

West, Christopher. *Heaven's Song: Sexual Love as It Was Meant to Be*. West Chester, PA: Ascension, 2008.

Westphal, Merold. "The Philosophical/Theological View." In *Biblical Hermeneutics: Five Views*, edited by Stanley E. Porter and Beth M. Stovall, 70–88. Downers Grove, IL: IVP Academic, 2012.

Whedbee, William J. *The Bible and the Comic Vision*. Cambridge: Cambridge University Press, 1988.

Wilson-Wright, Aren M. "Love Conquers All: Song of Songs 8:6b-7a as a Reflex of the Northwest Semitic Combat Myth." *JBL* 134 (2015): 333–45.

Wolde, Ellen van. "Sentiments as Culturally Constructed Emotions: Anger and Love in the Hebrew Bible." *BibInt* 16 (2008): 1–24.

Wolf, Naomi. *The Beauty Myth: How Images of Beauty Are Used Against Women*. 2nd ed. New York: Harper Perennial, 2002.

Xella, P. "Resheph." In *Dictionary of Deities and Demons in the Bible*, edited by Karel van der Toorn, Bob Becking, and Pieter van der Horst, 700–703. 2nd ed. Leiden: Brill, 1999.

Yee, Gale A. " 'I Have Perfumed My Bed with Myrrh': The Foreign Woman (ʾiššâ zārâ) in Proverbs 1–9." *JSOT* 43 (1989): 53–68.

———. *Poor Banished Children of Eve: Woman as Evil in the Hebrew Bible*. Minneapolis: Fortress, 2003.

Yoder, Christine Roy. "The Women of Substance (אשת־חיל): A Socioeconomic Reading of Proverbs 31:10-31." *JBL* 122 (2003): 427–47.

Zack, Naomi. *Inclusive Feminism: A Third Wave Theory of Women's Commonality*. Lanham, MD: Rowman & Littlefield, 2005.

Zhang, Sarah. "The Canvas of Emotion." Paper delivered at annual SBL meeting, San Diego, CA, 2014.

# Index of Scripture References
## and Other Ancient Writings

# Index of Subjects

## General Editor

Barbara E. Reid, OP, is a Dominican Sister of Grand Rapids, Michigan. She holds a PhD in biblical studies from The Catholic University of America and is vice president and academic dean and professor of New Testament studies at Catholic Theological Union, Chicago. Her most recent publications are *Wisdom's Feast: An Invitation to Feminist Interpretation of the Scriptures* (2016) and *Abiding Word: Sunday Reflections on Year A, B, C* (3 vols.; 2011, 2012, 2013). She served as president of the Catholic Biblical Association in 2014–2015.

## Volume Editor

Dr. Lauress Wilkins Lawrence is an African American Hebrew Bible scholar. Previously on the religious studies faculty at Regis College in Weston, MA, she now balances her scholarship with work in philanthropy in Maine.

## Author

F. Scott Spencer is professor of New Testament and biblical interpretation at the Baptist Theological Seminary in Richmond, Virginia. He has also served as past president of the Southeastern Commission for the Study of Religion and current co-chair of the Bible and Emotion group for the Society of Biblical Literature. Spencer's longtime interest in feminist biblical interpretation is evident in the monographs *Dancing Girls, "Loose" Ladies, and Women of "the Cloth": The Women in Jesus' Life*; and *Salty Wives, Spirited Mothers, and Savvy Widows: Capable Women of Purpose and Persistence in Luke's Gospel*.